Becoming a
SECONDARY SCHOOL TEACHER

Alison Scott Baumann,
Alan Bloomfield
& Linda Roughton

D1347948

Hodder Arnold

A MEMBER OF THE HODDER HEADLINE GROUP

British Library Cataloguing in Publication Data

A catalogue entry for this title is available from The British Library

Scott-Baumann, Alison
    Becoming a secondary school teacher
    1. High school teaching - Great Britain 2. High school
    teaching - Vocational guidance - Great Britain
    I. Title   II. Bloomfield, Alan   III. Roughton, Linda
    373.1´1´00941

    ISBN - 10: 0 340 68371 6
    ISBN - 13: 978 0 340 68371 2

First published 1997
Impression number 10
Year   2006, 2005

Hodder Headline's policy is to use papers that are natural, renewable and recyclable products
and made from wood grown in sustainable forests. The logging and manufacturing
processes are expected to conform to the environmental regulations of the country of origin.

Illustrations by Harry Venning

Typeset by Wearset, Bolden, Tyne and Wear
Printed in Great Britain for Hodder Arnold, an imprint of Hodder education, a member of the Hodder
Headline Group, 338 Euston Road, London NW1 3BH by Martins the Printers, Berwick upon Tweed

Contents

PART 3: THE LEARNING SCHOOL

Chapter 13 was written by Michael Scott Baumann; Chapters 18, 30 and 40 by Jane Salway; Chapter 29 by Steve Thompson; Chapter 34 by Jan Urban-Smith and Chapter 35 by Richard Giddy.

Acknowledgements

We are acutely aware that it is an impossible task to acknowledge all the individual contributions that have made this book possible. Throughout the years that the Gloucestershire PGCE has been in operation, developments have always been the result of discussion and co-operative work between trainees, teachers and college tutors. The real sense of ownership of the course by all those involved has meant that good ideas are sometimes untraceable back to their original source; they have become modified by groups of people often on several occasions. So our first acknowledgement is to everyone who has contributed by being a trainee, a subject mentor, a subject co-ordinator, a teacher in the department taking a trainee, the training managers and the headteachers. They have all made their special mark on this book, even if the fingerprints are not identified. To all these people we dedicate this book.

Lynda Taylor was her usual wonderful self in coping with the difficult task of getting the manuscript into a form that could be used by the publishers. That she managed to do so with her normal good humour and endless patience confirms what we knew about her all along.

The Information Services staff helped to make the original idea come true: thank you therefore to Lynnette Bailey, Keith Brooke, Dick Hanson and Lyn Oates.

Our thanks are also due to everyone at Hodder and Stoughton who nursed this book into the light of day. They managed to cope with our requests for changes and were always prepared to discuss our plans. So many thanks to Lisa Hyde, Anna Clark and Alison Bond.

The prime movers behind the original partnership scheme were Mick Abrahams (Head of Professional Education), Barry Howells (Headteacher Dene Magna School Mitcheldean) and Larry Montagu (Headteacher St Peter's High School Gloucester). Their support in the planning stage and throughout the years that the PGCE has been in operation has been vital. The involvement of headteachers through the Gloucestershire Association of Headteachers (GASH) has been a real strength of the course and an indication of the depth of partnership.

In working with schools we have been able to call on experienced colleagues with the support of Chris Arnold who has represented GASH and been an invaluable source of advice and guidance. The list of teachers that follows is therefore only an attempt to list those people whose words, beliefs and ideas appear in the book. We apologise profusely to those who have been omitted. Our only defence is that we have been working as hard as they have.

Main contributors

Acknowledgement for Mike Francis and Susan Goble's material on School Improvement, based on work done with Jeff Hale at the Professional Development Consultancy, Gloucester.

Christine Counsell, History Co-ordinator for the Gloucestershire ITE scheme, Chairman of the Secondary Committee of the Historical Association, working on a PhD about the Character of Professional Knowledge of the History Teacher.

Mike Francis, Deputy Headteacher at Farmor's School, Fairford and Staff Development Tutor. Recently he has led the school to achievement of the Investors in People standard.

Irene Hunt, Acting Deputy Headteacher (Pastoral) at The Headlands School, Swindon with 18 years teaching experience in Special Educational Needs (Primary and Secondary). Her current special interest is the more able child.

John Matthews, Deputy Headteacher at Heywood Community School, Cinderford, currently working with Bath University on a three-year School Impovement Programme. John is particularly interested in mentoring as an aspect of school improvement and has recently completed an MA in Educational Management with the Open University.

Jill Rundle, Head of Modern Languages at Brockworth School, Brockworth and doing an MEd on Mentoring, which enables her to contextualise the Gloucestershire model within the international scene.

Michael Scott-Baumann, Director of Studies at Wycliffe College, Stonehouse and author of several history textbooks at both GCSE and A level. He is an Ofsted inspector and is currently working with staff on appraisal by pupils of staff.

Steve Thompson, Senior Careers Adviser at CGCHE. He offers advice to undergraduates and has 15 years experience as a careers adviser including 7 years in higher education. Steve's particular interest is in equal opportunities.

Richard Giddy, Co-ordinator for Personal, Social and Careers Education at Brockworth School, Brockworth. His particular interests in school are learning and motivation, personal development and records of achievement.

Jan Levenson, Deputy Headteacher at Cheltenham Kingsmead School, Cheltenham, responsible for pastoral guidance systems, staff development and appraisal. Jan is looking at value added issues. She also works with the Cheltenham & Gloucester Education Business Partnership organisation, bringing pupils, industry and schools together.

Sylvia Odell, Senior Manager at Severn Vale School, Quedgeley, responsible for staff development. At present she is revising appraisal policy to link with the School Development Plan, incorporating the proposed plans from the Teacher Training Agency (TTA). Sylvia is also doing research with King's College, London (Association for Science Education) on the use of Science Investigation at Key Stage Three.

Jane Salway, Deputy Head at Berkeley Vale Community School, Berkeley. Her professional interests include staff development, initial teacher training and special needs.

Jan Urban-Smith, Head of Sixth Form at Chosen Hill School, Churchdown. She is developing strategies for effective academic monitoring, to improve student learning.

Ray Keeley, Head of Special Needs at Cotswold School, Bourton-on-the Water.

Sue Goble, Deputy Headteacher at St Peter's High School and Sixth Form Centre, Gloucester who is also writing a PhD on ritual and symbol in Catholic schooling.

Dr Virginia Webb, archaeologist and academic, teaching Latin and Greek in Canterbury, at Simon Langton School for Girls.

Contributors

Rachel O'Sullivan, Rachael Jelfs, Maria Foster, Christopher Morgans, Andrew Mills, Adrian Barsby, Pooneh Roney, Russell Crew, Peter Callaghan, Sarah Masey, Manrouf Mohamed, Darren Leatherbarrow, Anne Guest, Elaine Lansdell, Catherine, Anna, Deepinder, Jo Pavey, Helen Dennis, Derek Plumb, Laurence Aubry, Steve Longton.

Advisors and critical readers

Peter Callaghan, Gareth Nutt, Jill Rundle, Les Southam.

Chapter 2: Barbara Baumann, Support Teacher, Marissa Davis, Headteacher, Janet Forde, Headteacher, Dr Laura Huxford, CGCHE, Dr Keith Ross, CGCHE, Pamela Swain, Deputy Headteacher.

Chapter 12: Professor Howard Glennerster, LSE, Harjit Khaira, The Trinity School, Dr Anne West, LSE.

Chapter 15: Daphne Philpot, CGCHE.

Chapter 27: Carmel Hand, Senior Educational Psychologist, Bristol, Anne Bush, Director of Children's Services, South Gloucestershire.

Chapter 29: Andy Roughton.

Photographs

John Ryan worked creatively to interpret picture requests, and we thank the following schools for making the photographs possible: Balcarras, Barnwood Park, Central Technology College and Cleeve School. Gareth Nutt provided the photograph at the end of the Code of Practice chapter.

Foreword

by Professor John Furlong

Learning how to teach can be a painful and challenging experience for student teachers. This is probably because it involves learning of a very different sort from that which most students have been used to. Firstly, it involves learning at a personal level: learning to be *the sort of person*, for example, who can command the respect and interest of children and facilitate their learning. Secondly, what has to be learned is profoundly practical. To make the age old distinction, it involves learning *to* rather than learning *about*. Finally, although teaching may be a practical skill, it is at one and the same time also deeply theoretical and moral. Helping pupils to express in writing what they have just observed in a scientific experiment may demand practical skills, but it also involves theoretically based judgements about how children learn best and the value of asking them to transform their learning from a practical to a written form; helping pupils to appreciate symbolism in literature involves theoretical assumptions about the nature of literary texts; dealing effectively with a case of bullying involves moral assumptions about the values that are appropriate and necessary within a learning community such as a school. Theoretical and moral assumptions at all of these different levels are inevitably built into the practice that trainee teachers will see around them and which will also become part of their own practice.

And this brings us to the value of this particular book. The team who have written it are all deeply committed to the importance of practical training. They have themselves been involved in developing one of the most distinctively 'school-based' teacher training courses currently offered in England and Wales; it is a course where partner schools have been given far greater responsibility for the training programme than is currently the norm. And their commitment to practical training is demonstrated throughout the text both by the examples they give and by their emphasis on reflection, case studies and action as key strategies to help trainee teachers learn. These strategies also recognise that the learning which trainees must do is personal learning because the text encourages trainees to learn for and about themselves through engaging in the practical business of teaching and through school-based enquiry.

But what makes this book distinctive and particularly useful is that it is also explicitly theoretical. The three sections of the book on how children learn, on the process of teaching and on whole school issues are designed to help trainees explore these critical issues as personal, practical and theoretical issues at the same time.

For almost all of us learning to teach is a difficult and demanding process. However, a well structured programme with appropriate forms of practical and theoretical support can make a huge difference to the quality and efficiency of the learning that has to go on. In my view this book provides a valuable resource that can be used by both trainees and their teacher educators in the development of such effective programmes – in making sure that trainees deal equally with the personal and the practical as well as the theoretical ways of learning that are inextricably linked in the process of learning to teach.

John Furlong
University of Bristol
April 1997

How to Use This Book

Gaining Qualified Teacher Status

Teaching in a secondary school is a demanding yet immensely rewarding profession. Teachers and schools are often the focus of public attention; sometimes this results in ill-informed criticism of the profession. However, this merely reflects the importance of the role that teachers play in shaping the future. If you are training to be a teacher, you have already embarked upon a career which will provide you with challenge and reward. It may seem impossible at times for you to become as effective as the experienced teachers you observe. This book will help you on that journey from novice to expert, which we all continue to travel.

This book is designed to help you obtain Qualified Teacher Status. The Government Circular of 1992 ensured that all secondary trainees would be assessed against a profile of competences. Recent developments have included a 'career entry profile' and within a National Curriculum for Initial Teacher Training there are new Standards for the award of QTS.

Within the consultation documents for these new generic standards, there are four main themes: Subject Knowledge and Understanding (**SKU**), Planning, Teaching and Class Management (**PTCM**), Monitoring, Assessment, Recording, Reporting and Accountability (**MARRA**) and Professional Requirements (**PR**). This pattern is already typical of PGCE Secondary programmes, although each course may structure these slightly differently. These themes can be described in fairly simple terms, since as teachers we need to know our subject (**SKU**), we have to explain it to children and we have to manage a class so that effective learning can happen (**PTCM**). We have to find out what children know and can do (**MARRA**) and we need to place our teaching in a wider context (**PR**).

The National Curriculum (England and Wales)

It will be helpful to readers outside England and Wales to understand the terminology used to describe ages and assessment stages.

Key Stage 1	Ages 4/5 to 7 years	called Reception, Years 1 and 2
Key Stage 2	Ages 7 to 11 years	called Years 3, 4, 5 and 6
Key Stage 3	Ages 11 to 14 years	called Years 7, 8 and 9
Key Stage 4	Ages 14 to 16 years	called Years 10 and 11

A spiral curriculum

This book is based on material which has been developed and evaluated within a highly successful school-based initial teacher training partnership in Gloucestershire over a period of years (McKay, Strutt and Bloomfield, 1994; Nutt and Abrahams, 1994; Nutt *et al*, 1997) and contains many teachers' and pupils' voices. During the course of this collaboration between schools and colleges of higher education a spiral curriculum for initial teacher training has evolved. This textbook will provide a 'spiral' structure for your personal and professional development as a teacher during your year of training. It will give you the opportunity to consider the major themes two or three times within your training at increasing levels of sophistication and challenge.

Within these themes we provide you with ideas, examples and tasks. These will enable you to compare your implicit theories and beliefs about education with some of the big ideas about teaching and learning and develop a critical understanding of your knowledge and that of others (Bloomfield and Scott Baumann, 1997).

Our experience has shown that you will need to work at these themes throughout the programme and that the order we have suggested has much to commend it in practice (Arnold and Bloomfield, 1997). The sequence is also intended to be flexible depending on individuals' needs. You will need to use the reference list of activities in Appendix 4 in order to check that you are aware of all the items which may be relevant to you at your personal stage of development. They are arranged under the four Standards.

Developing a Professional Development Portfolio

In this book you will find generic guidance on creating a Professional Development Portfolio, which you will need to complete as evidence of your meeting the Standards required of a teacher. Appendix 1 contains documentation from the Gloucestershire course, which gives you exemplars of how this model of training can be implemented. There are instances of trainees' reflective writing and advice as to how the Standards can be interpreted in a subject-specific context. The exemplars are intended to give you a possible way of interpreting and writing about your own experience. Recording is an essential aspect of reflecting on experience. It is likely that the act of recording will in itself help to clarify your own understanding of what has happened and will act as a catalyst to planning your future development. You can use the activities in this book to chart your progress and your needs, during training and your NQT year.

Activities

The activities are arranged in three categories each with its own icon: **Reflection**, **Case Study** and **Action**. We believe that reflection upon your beliefs and your professional practice forms a central part of your development. The Case Studies provide real examples of problems, choices and solutions. The Action sections will give you a carefully sequenced progression of school-based tasks. Each activity can be used as the basis for work in your PDP. All three types of activity can be used to support your developing expertise in the four competence areas meeting the Standards for QTS and can be used to provide evidence and material for your Portfolio.

Practitioner research

In order to help you implement these activities we provide you with guidance on practitioner research. Practitioner research, as its name implies, provides the means by which you can analyse your own teaching and that of others in order to understand the essential factors underlying a lesson sequence or key elements in the success of a department or a whole school. You will use two main types of research strategy: case study and action research. Some methods are common to both but the outcome will be different. The case study approach is designed to enable you to analyse the learning styles and educational experiences of individual pupils (Part 1) and to look productively and critically at whole school issues (Part 3). In both these areas you will be functioning as commentator and analyst, able to develop understanding of what is happening now and to make suggestion about future developments and improvements for a child, a department or for a whole school. You should not act as a change agent, since the implementation of change is inappropriate to someone who is not directly involved as part of the long-term solution to the problem. However, Part 2 provides you with the opportunity to use action research techniques to improve your own teaching of individuals, groups and whole classes. Within this personal context you will be a change agent since you are central to the intended transformation. Action research strategies will enable you to improve your own teaching through personal change, as a result of reflection and analysis. You and your mentors will find it valuable to work together on this vital aspect of continuing professional development. This will prove to be invaluable throughout training and indeed throughout your career.

Professional relationships

You are entering a community which is committed to the education, inspiration and welfare of children. It is important that you develop good professional relationships with your mentor and other colleagues. School-based initial teacher education is of value to the whole school and community: 'My own teaching has sharpened in focus from watching trainee teachers teaching and from engaging in professional dialogue with them' (training manager).

Using this text to guide you through your training you will be able to work with your general mentor and with your subject mentor. It will provide you with opportunities to enhance your professional development as a teacher. The whole of this book will be of interest to your mentors, but the sections with the mentor symbol will be of particular value. Each will provide a possible focus for discussion between you and your mentor.

Symbols used in this book

  The ACTION activities

  The CASE STUDIES

  The REFLECTION activities

  The MENTOR sections, of particular value in this professional relationship.

References

Arnold, C. and Bloomfield, A. (1977) in Fuller, M. and Rosie, A. (eds) **Teacher Education and School Partnership.** Edwin Mellen Press.

Bloomfield, A., McKay, C. and Strutt, D. (1994) 'Secondary Partnership in Practice', *Mathematics Education Review*, No. 4. Association of Education Teachers.

Bloomfield, A. and Scott Baumann, A. (1997) **First Steps in Initial Teacher Training.** Mathematics Education Review 9.

Nutt, G. and Abrahams, M. (1994) 'Physical Education in Teacher Education: The Gloucestershire Partnership', in *British Journal of Physical Education*, Vol. 25, No. 4.

Nutt, G., Longton, J., Hollingsworth, C. and McNee, J. (1997) **Gloucestershire Tales: A Teacher Education Partnership Four Years On.** In Press, BJPE.

PART

Teaching and Learning

1

Introduction

I arrived on the course very enthusiastic but very naive. Now I've learnt what children and schools are really like and I'm even more enthusiastic. Now I know I want to be a teacher. (Robert, trainee 1994–95)

In Part 1 the major focus will be on the pupil. In order to develop an understanding of how pupils learn we will look initially at learning in the primary school. This is followed by a review of the work of five major writers, each with very different views about the learning process (Piaget, Skinner, Donaldson, Bruner and Vygotsky). We will consider the implications their views have for classroom practice, using a number of activities. This material will enable you to decide what your own beliefs are. For example, do you believe that children are the solitary constructors of their own reality, following predetermined developmental pathways, as Piaget did? Do you believe that children are social and learn better in group situations, as Vygotsky did? Or do you believe that both these ideas are useful in certain situations?

These materials and procedures are designed to provide you also with a basis for further development during your teaching career. You will learn simple research methods which will enable you to reflect upon your development, evaluate your progress and, vitally, come to an understanding of pupils' learning and the relationship between teaching and learning. Early success in lesson observation leads to later success in lesson management.

It was really important to focus on pupil learning at the very beginning: it made me think much more clearly about teaching and learning than if we'd gone into being a teacher immediately. That came soon enough. (Elaine, PGCE trainee 1994–95)

In order to improve the effectiveness of pupils as learners you will also be considering issues such as motivation, personality, the self-fulfilling prophecy and adolescence. Chapters on other issues of fundamental importance for you are also included, covering pupil management, differentiation, assessment and the National Curriculum.

You will also begin to develop methodology approaches which will be useful to you throughout your professional career. These include classroom observation, interview techniques and other methods of collecting information.

In conclusion, Part 1 has been written with the joint aim of introducing you to:

● a wide variety of ways in which children think and learn
● a variety of methods of collecting and interpreting information

You will learn to understand and record what you see taking place in lessons. We hope that this process will help you to develop your own beliefs about how you want to teach and your own methods for putting these beliefs into practice.

THE CASE STUDY APPROACH

Teacher as Researcher and Writer

1

A theory that fits all the facts is bound to be wrong, because some of the facts will be wrong. (Crick, cited by Lewis Wolpert in a lecture 'The Unnatural Nature of Science')

As a teacher researcher you will be looking at theories and facts and how they fit the real world.

Educational research is designed to improve the education of pupils. In order to improve your teaching you need to be informed and critical about your own teaching and about the ideas and beliefs of expert teachers.

LEARNING OUTCOMES

When you have read this chapter you should be able to consider the three main research areas – looking at what people do, talking to them about what they do and studying documentation which they produce or use in their work in school.

You should understand a variety of techniques of data collection, and be able to use simple triangulation. You should know how to use the data collection techniques made accessible to you in this chapter (in other words, the structured data collection pages, classroom observation forms and a variety of systematic observation techniques). If you have a research background you will be able to introduce other methodologies.

You should understand how to use ideas and theories from the chapters in this book, to help you explain what goes on in lessons. You will be able to use these approaches as a teacher–researcher, to analyse the contrasting learning experiences of several pupils.

You will have the opportunity to become sensitive to the issues relating to learning support, and read a case study about special educational needs provision: this is important as you will come into contact with special needs issues during these early observations, as well as throughout your teaching career.

Introduction

The aim of this material is to introduce you to the first steps towards becoming a competent teacher: you will focus on learning and teaching and you will use your research findings to develop your own professional practice. Research involves asking yourself a question to which you do not know the answer, planning how you will find out and then reporting what you've discovered. The process is just as important as the product. One way of bringing together your work at this stage, is by undertaking the first task as set on page 13.

Although you may be able to make recommendations about how a pupil's learning could be improved, your main interest will lie in working out why some pupils fail and some succeed. To do this you should consider questions from the following areas:

1 Thinking and learning

(See Donaldson, Vygotsky, Bruner and Domains of Thinking in Chapters 5, 6, 7 and 26)

- Do pupils find the work easy? Is it at the right level for them? (Refer to the relevant National Curriculum Programme of Study.)
- Do they need concrete examples (see Chapter 5 on human sense) or have they developed the underlying concepts (see Chapter 5 on disembedded thinking)?
- Do they need much consolidation and repetition?
- Do they prefer to learn alone or do they enjoy and benefit from group work? (See Chapter 6 on Vygotsky.)
- Do they apply knowledge to new areas?
- Do they seem to have learning difficulties or to need more difficult work?
- Do they make good use of differentiated learning materials?

2 Organisational/study skills

(See Chapter 5 on Donaldson)

- Do they have and use reference skills (library, computer, for example)?
- Can they read, write and spell to an adequate level for the task?
- Do they do their homework?
- Do they ask the teacher when they don't understand?

3 Motivation

(See Chapter 8 on Motivation)

- Do they respond to extrinsic motivation (school rewards, long-term goals, for example)?
- Do they lack intrinsic motivation (lack of interest, refusal to use potential)?
- How do they respond to competitive learning situations?
- Do they perceive themselves as successful or failing?
- Are they accurate in their self-perceptions? (See Chapter 12 on Self-fulfilling Prophecy.)

4 Personality

(See Chapters 9, 11 and 12 on Adolescence, Personality and Self-fulfilling Prophecy)

- Are they seen as conformist or non-conformist?
- Are they sociable or solitary?
- Have they got the confidence to develop their ideas verbally or in written form?

Lesson observations: how to be professional

Being a non-participant observer

The fly on the wall is a hard act to follow. You may wish to observe and not participate, in order to be able to concentrate fully on the teacher and pupils: if this is so, you must explain it to the teacher beforehand, so that you are not given any tasks.

Here are some guidelines:

- Ask the teacher where you should place yourself in order to be unobtrusive.
- Discuss how you wish to be introduced and how your presence can be explained.
- Develop a body posture which is calm and still and do not make eye contact with pupils.
- Focus your attention on the teacher.
- Systematic observation schedules can be used, supplemented by ethnographic data collection.

Being a participant observer

If you have decided to take part in the lesson as well as recording observations, you need to consider the following:

- Arrange with the teacher beforehand what the nature of your task in class should be and combine it with ethnographic data collection.
- When this involves working with a pupil or small group, position yourself so that you can see the teacher and look up at regular intervals to see what is going on in the lesson.
- When the teacher calls for the attention of the class, you should tell your pupil/group to focus on the teacher rather than on you. Clearly when the teacher is addressing the whole class, you and the class are listening.
- Finish writing your field notes/observation proforma as soon as possible after the lesson: you will be busy for much of the lesson and cannot keep your notes up to date as you go along.
- Do not mark books or work: establish with the teacher whether you may correct spellings or give specific advice.

If disorder occurs and the teacher does not notice it, you need to decide whether you can take action unobtrusively or move away or ignore completely – with all these you also need to decide whether to discuss it with the teacher or not.

Looking at what people do: systematic observation

This is a method of recording information by noting how often certain pre-selected events take place. How do you decide how often to record and which events to record?

The systematic observation chart on page 7 is an example of how to record lesson events once a minute in order to look at the sequence of the lesson. If you look carefully at it you will see that there is a pattern. Here is one possible interpretation: the teacher started the lesson with a whole class discussion, used a question and answer session and then set up some group work. During group work some inappropriate behaviour took place and the teacher addressed the class as a whole group again. The lesson finished with pupils working on their own instead of in groups. There are other ways of interpreting this information: it could be that the pupils themselves found group work to be unsuitable and that they asked to work on their own.

You can see that systematic observation provides the raw data of sequences and types of events. This should then be analysed in terms of other information, for example what people said at the time (this kind of information will become available to you as a result of ethnographic data collection – see page 8).

Observation schedules

Make a blank observation schedule which is similar to the one opposite, but perhaps with fewer columns. Negotiate with a teacher to observe a lesson and use the blank systematic observation form to tick off the teacher and pupil activities you observe.

SYSTEMATIC OBSERVATION CHART

School:
Teacher:
Observer's name:

Class:
Focus of lesson:
Length of lesson:

Minutes	Teacher talks to class	Teacher questions class	Teacher uses praise	Teacher uses criticism	Teacher uses disci-pline	Teacher–pupil inter-action	Pupils working solo	Pupil–pupil inter-action	Group work or pair-work	Pupils off-task
1	✓									
2	✓									
3	✓									
4		✓	✓			✓				
5	✓									
6		✓	✓			✓				
7										
8			✓							
9			✓							
10	✓									
11	✓									
12					✓			✓	✓	
13					✓	✓		✓	✓	✓
14						✓		✓	✓	✓
15						✓		✓	✓	✓
16					✓			✓		✓
17	✓			✓						
18	✓			✓						
19	✓				✓					
20				✓	✓		✓			
21							✓			
22							✓			
23							✓			
24	✓		✓				✓			
25	✓		✓							
26	✓		✓							
27	✓		✓							
28		✓		✓						
29	✓									
30	✓									

Here is another example of systematic observation, focusing on the individual in the Pupil Behaviour Observation Sheet. This could be used as a comparative measure of how one of the pupils you are focusing on behaves in several different lessons (see the task on page 13).

PUPIL BEHAVIOUR OBSERVATION SHEET

Child's name: Date:

Place/context:

Observe the child for a ten minute period, in different lessons, using a new behaviour observation sheet each day. Once a minute, look at the child and tick the behaviour s/he is showing. Some example behaviours have been entered here, but you should construct your own observation sheet to reflect the particular behaviours that concern you. This example has been designed for a child whose behavioural difficulties are interfering with his/her learning. You could equally well devise a chart for a high achiever, focusing on such categories as reading, writing, speaking to teacher, speaking to peers and groupwork, depending on the nature of the lesson.

Observations										
	1	2	3	4	5	6	7	8	9	10
Daydreaming										
Interfering with others' work/ property										
Out of seat (with no reason)										
Arguing or fighting with others										
Other										

Ethnographic data collection techniques

Ethnography is the study of social interaction in natural settings through observation, informal participation and conversation. In contrast to the non-participatory nature of systematic observation, ethnography lends itself to participant observation techniques, that is finding out about events by taking part, as in working with pupils in class. Ethnographic evidence which you collect should include the following if possible:

● a daily fieldwork diary which contains notes about classroom observation, teacher style and classroom resources

- an informal record of a session spent working with each pupil in class, for example using the classroom observation form; a completed example from a trainee teacher illustrating the learning difficulties of Oliver, a Year 9 pupil aged 13, is given later in this chapter)
- a sample from the pupils' books
- analysis of strengths and needs using, for example, the structured data collection sheets (see the end of this chapter)
- a summary of National Curriculum areas as they apply to each pupil, using departmental records
- notes about conversations or interviews with the teacher and each pupil (plan some questions beforehand)

You can see from the items listed earlier that the ethnographic approach uses words (more qualitative) and is less number-oriented (quantitative) than the systematic observation approach. For example, systematic observation will allow you to record how many times a teacher used open question forms in a lesson; ethnographic data collection will allow you to record which sequence the teacher used in developing a question and answer session, what tone of voice the teacher used, and so on.

Contrast the classroom observation form on page 10 with the block graph (shown on this page) of another of Oliver's lessons: how do we know it's a different lesson from the one recorded on the classroom observation form? Note how much less information we get from the block graph – yet it is still useful to find out this information, which can be collected by using systematic observation techniques.

Block graph of systematic lesson activity, Oliver

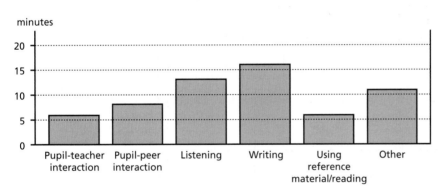

You can also use the ethnographic approach to help you decide which categories to use in your systematic observation form, for example if you make notes about a pupil who is frequently off-task, can you decide upon a set of criteria which allow you to measure what the pupil *does* while off-task – talking to friends, doodling, day-dreaming?

CLASSROOM OBSERVATION FORM FOR OLIVER

Lesson 1 Year 9   Oliver

| **Teacher** | CP | **Day/date** | Wed 12/10 | **Time** | 9:00–10:00 |
| **Subject** | Maths | **Group** | C (bottom) | **Observer** | Matthew |

Room plan

tables in groups
two 2s   12 boys
two 3s   2 girls
one 4

Focus of observation

Pupil pursuit
Oliver

Time	Sequence of events	Observer's comments
9:05	Discuss about prep problems	Not much done! Lots of excuses. (O one of the few to have done it) Detentions given out O given extra work. Complained about having to go for a haircut
9:15	teacher explaining work from book	work about plans and elevations O asked if he understands – Answer = 'sort of'
9:25	teacher hands out square paper (and rulers) then leaves to fetch blocks	
9:35	Individual work begins on drawing plans	I go to work with O. Initial problems – not much understanding; can see it with help, then left alone gets it wrong again. (Wood's 5 levels useful.) Is this task too difficult? (for whole group?)
9:55	O and I finish task about same time as the quicker pupils	V hard work – I needed to suggest virtually every step Having finished we chatted about the new dining block – O doesn't fancy being an architect after this exercise Spatial problems/orientation
10:00	Completed prep collected pupils leave in dribs and drabs	
10:05	Oliver last to leave after a talking to.	

Compare this with an extract from a Case Study on page 11.

Thinking and learning

Does the pupil find the work easy to learn?

For Philip, the answer to this question would seem to be yes. In class, Phillip comes across as a 'low maintenance' pupil, in so much as he rarely 'gets stuck' or requires individual attention.

Using the imagery of Bruner this would translate as a minimal need for 'scaffolding'. However, I would suggest that this is more a reflection on the level of work being set than an indication of Phillip's potential level of ability which is clearly not being tested.

Oliver, on the other hand, sometimes finds his work very difficult. At the beginning of week one for example, I spent two half hour periods working with Oliver on some book work. The topic of this work was 'Plans and elevations', (Maths Attainment Target 4, Level 6: (a) Use 2-D representation of 3-D objects). During the first of these one-to-one sessions I found that I had to use all five of Wood's levels of support. At the time I noted that Oliver had great problems with this task. He could see it with help, but then left to his own devices he invariably got it wrong again. I persevered and spent a part of the next lesson with him doing the next exercise (which was intended as a consolidation section). During this period there were definite signs of improvement. Oliver was able to work his way through the exercise with a decreasing level of support. Interestingly, when 9C were given a pencil and paper test to assess their understanding of recent topics on the Friday before half-term Oliver got full marks on the 3-D section. I am quite sure that without the individual attention Oliver would not have made much progress.

As for Kate, she was the only pupil out of both classes who said that she found the work too easy (Q4 from questionnaire). I would suggest that Kate does find the work easy to learn but is held back by her lack of motivation. On occasions when Kate has had problems with her work and has sought help from the teacher they have usually been cleared up with a minimal increase in support (a few verbal prompts).

Does the pupil prefer to work alone or does (s)he benefit from group work?

I asked this as a straightforward question on the questionnaire and got three different answers! Kate said she preferred to work with a partner, as did all but one of the girls questioned. This preference would seem to support the theories of educational researchers such as Burton (1986) who would say that 'girls are advantaged by a learning environment in which they can talk about their mathematics with others'.

Phillip worked well in a pair (while gathering data for the map project outdoors), but said he preferred to work on his own, which was evident from observing him in the classroom.

Oliver does tend to work on his own but this is probably because he is new to the school and has not yet formed a working relationship with any of his peers. However, as I mentioned, Oliver is a sociable child, his verbal skills are good and I feel he would benefit from group work.

Talking to people about what they do

A central part of looking at the different ways in which pupils learn is actually talking to pupils and their teachers. What are they doing? Why? What do they *feel* about what they are doing?

REFLECTION

2

Read the following passage by Jean Rudduck:

I became interested in the boy behind me. In his vocabulary book he wrote all the French words in the left-hand column and then he proceeded to write all the English translations as a separate list. It seemed that, following this procedure, he was not making a link between the word and its translation. Moreover, he missed out one English word, so that for the rest of the list, the translations were not opposite the word they represented in French! There was no self-monitoring going on in relation to the writing of the words – it merely seemed a task of making a list rather than thinking about and remembering meanings.

One task involved pupils in looking at a series of cartoon pictures with dialogue coming out of mouths in bubbles. Pupils had to answer questions, which were in English, by finding the French phrase in the balloon dialogue and copying it down. I asked the two pupils sitting behind me how they identified the right answer. One boy said that he looked for one of the words that he knew – for instance, when the question referred to 'young men', he said that he looked for the sentence that had the word 'jeune' in it, because he knew that that was the French word for 'young'. It seemed therefore, that he was working on a single-clue procedure rather than working at the level of translating the whole sentence. The other boy had a different strategy – one that was more about logic than language! He told me in relation to a set of three questions, that he knew that he had the right answer to the first one, and knew he had the right answer to the third one, and therefore the answer to the second one – which was one he couldn't do in sequence – must be the only line of dialogue that was left in the cartoon! Again it was noticeable that these two boys were not using any checking device after they had written down their answers. Their motivation was to get the task finished and marked. (Hull et al, 1985, p. 54)

This is only an extract and it is a highly selective look at three boys. We cannot draw completely full and accurate conclusions about lesson events on the basis of incomplete data. The device of triangulation, discussed later, will help us to add more information.

Talking to pupils

During these early stages of your course, you will be spending time with pupils in a variety of settings – some of these will be when you sit in on a lesson to work with one or two pupils, or a group of them. The following points are vital if you are going to derive full benefit from these sessions:

● Remember that you are part of the lesson. Therefore, if the teacher calls for everyone's attention, you need to direct the pupils to focus on the teacher again, and sit back until the opportunity arises for you to resume your work with them.

● When working with pupils, you may realise that you do not understand much of the work they are doing. Fear not. If you ask them to tell you what they are doing, and how and why and by when, they will tell you. Sometimes they will lie to you, but this is rare. They will be interested in your questions and show you their work to illustrate the situation.

Analyse the contrasting learning experiences of several pupils

Task

- 2000 word written assignment
- 15 minute long presentation, which will be videotaped for moderation purposes

For this task you will be a teacher-researcher, looking at different aspects of the learning experience for a variety of pupils. In your department, with your Head of Department, identify several pupils in different age groups who have different learning experiences. You need to see pupils who are very different from each other, for example, one pupil from each of three different age groups, or two pupils from each of two age groups separated by two years (for example Year 7 and Year 9) if the timetable allows. If your observations are of pupils who you will subsequently be teaching, you will need to adopt a different manner as a teacher to that of a teacher-researcher.

You will be using a combination of 'ethnographic' and 'systematic observation' methods, which will complement each other.

You will need to consult Part 1 of this book starting with Chapter 1 in order to shape your work.

Modify for your purposes the sheets on structured data collection, systematic observation and classroom observation.

Remember the following when writing an assignment:

- A clear introduction of about 2 paragraphs, which sets out your intentions and puts your work briefly into the context of the thinkers, ideas and teaching proposals.
- In a short methodology section you will explain how you collected your evidence and how you analysed it.
- In the middle section you will go into these areas in more detail: give practical examples and analysis of the different types of learning and the 'goodness of fit' between the pupils' learning needs and how they have been met. Consider aspects of your subject specialism also.
- Analyse how your findings fit with your beliefs and the ideas and teaching techniques which you have been working on in Part 1.
- *Conclusion and summary:* bring together the 5–10 points which you think are of major importance, in your case study. It is a small study, but you can use it to consider issues which are of major importance to you as a teacher.
  N.B. You need to make use of between 10 and 20 references.

Remember the following for your video presentation:

- Take the 20 main ideas from your assignment to formulate your script for the video presentation. Do not read your assignment out.

Structured Data Collection Sheet

Learning strategies

Which of the following ways of learning do you believe is productive for the pupil?

☐ learning by rote
☐ experiential (through action)
☐ social (through pair or group work)
☐ solitary (e.g. through reading, or through own research)
☐ problem solving
☐ through spoken language
☐ through use of IT
☐ with teacher support — will the pupil ask for help?

Which one of the above could be focused on to help the pupil more in the immediate future?

....

Teaching strategies

● How does the pupil respond to whole class teaching? ....

....

● Is group work successful? ....

● Is pair work successful? ....

● Is solitary work successful? ....

Language of instruction

● How does the pupil respond to a class discussion with open and closed questions? ....

....

● Does the pupil understand spoken/written instructions? ....

....

● Does the pupil respond within a group, e.g. brainstorming in order to start a discussion, working with

others to allocate jobs within the group (note-taker, timekeeper, etc)? ....

....

● Can the pupil explain ideas, beliefs, plans, etc, to you and to peers? ....

....

● Does the pupil have the language and social skills to make good use of group work? ....

....

Differentiation
- Does the teacher use any of the following types of differentiation?
- Does the pupil find any of the following types of differentiation useful?

Differentiation by support	Teacher	Pupil
support from other adults (from the wider community?) and pupils (older pupils?)	☐	☐
individual support from the teacher	☐	☐
support in the form of recording and praising the pupil's successes	☐	☐
co-operative teaching/team teaching	☐	☐
small group tutoring – group members can be disparate in attainment, but friends	☐	☐

Differentiation by response	Teacher	Pupil
regular clarification of work objectives (short term and long term)	☐	☐
making assessment criteria explicit (e.g. making examples of good work available)	☐	☐
work logs (where the pupil keeps a record of work covered, time taken, views of it, etc)	☐	☐
small group tutoring, with individual members close in attainment levels	☐	☐
individual action plans, or individual education plans (under the Code of Practice – see Primary School chapter)	☐	☐
new targets set in the context of what has already been achieved	☐	☐

Differentiation by resource	Teacher	Pupil
appropriate worksheets etc	☐	☐
wide variety of media (audio, visual, tactile, etc)	☐	☐
use of IT	☐	☐
regular rehearsal and discussion of study skills	☐	☐
advice from colleagues at school with special interests in, e.g., concept keyboards	☐	☐

Differentiation by task	Teacher	Pupil
availability of a range of tasks	☐	☐
identification of the long term results of successfully completing certain tasks	☐	☐
the use of learning routes (some tasks common to all, with more open-ended extension work for the more able and less open-ended work for the less able)	☐	☐
making possible a variety of end products (acceptable outcomes might include an audio tape, a comic strip, a written story, or a poster)	☐	☐

Talking to teachers

It is very useful to be able to talk to the teacher about the lesson afterwards. If this is possible follow these golden rules every time:

3 *Before and during the interview*

- Explain what your work is about, i.e. studying the different learning styles and learning experiences of two or three pupils for your assignment.
- Arrange a mutually convenient time, and ask for fifteen minutes. Teachers are very busy people. Keep to fifteen minutes.
- Guarantee confidentiality (see Ethics, later in this chapter). If you want to audio-tape it, ask for permission and check your equipment carefully.
- Plan a small number of questions beforehand, possibly five. The teacher may want to know what they are before the interview. They could be based on the Structured Data Collection Sheets on pages 14 and 15. Discuss your questions beforehand with a colleague or friend to clarify ambiguities.
- Refer to the chapter on Language in the Classroom for a discussion of open and closed questions. Open-ended questions are more useful, for example *Could you tell me something about John's difficulties with his project work?* An example of a closed question with scope for more information to come after a *yes* or *no* response is: *Ann didn't seem to want to work in a group – does that make a difference to the work she produces?*
- Do not use leading questions as they betray bias and may influence the answer, for instance don't say *Why didn't you stop that argument between those two by the door?* More appropriate would be *How do you deal with disagreements among pupils?*
- Don't be afraid to ask for clarification if you don't understand.
- Make notes during the interview if possible and say thank you at the end!

After the interview

1 Use the data for triangulation, a technique where the researcher uses new information to complement a picture already built up by other methods. The teacher will have made comments about the pupil which help to understand:

- something you've already noticed during classroom observation or in discussion with the pupil, for example low motivation
- something new to your investigation which you need to look at in the light of your other evidence, for example, look at the pupil's work again.

2 Be prepared to go back to the teacher at a later date, in the light of new information: *Can I just check up on something . . . ? Did you mean . . . ? What was that you said about . . . ?*

Studying the documentation people produce or use in their work

You will find it necessary to study the work pupils produce in class.

Documentation also includes textbooks, worksheets, programmes of study or National Curriculum documents.

You have already considered an example of how to analyse documents in this chapter: Jean Rudduck's observations of a French class, discussing pupils' work with them. If you wish to make a copy of pupils' work or teachers' work, ask permission. Documentation of all types is valuable as evidence of learning or ignorance, of good or bad practice and can be used as evidence of your learning.

Triangulation

This is a research technique which enables you to use several different types of data to develop a fuller picture: classroom observation (both of the systematic and ethnographic type) will be complemented by finding out about pupils from their teachers (informal discussion and interview) and also by analysis of work produced and material used by teachers and pupils. Cohen and Manion (1985) give a detailed analysis of the different types of triangulation.

Even then you will only have some snapshots of how pupils learn. You will need to make it clear that you can only make tentative conclusions and proposals about the future progress of these pupils.

Everyone is a participant observer, acquiring knowledge about the social world in the course of participating in it. And, in our view, such participant knowledge on the part of people in a setting is an important resource for the ethnographer – though its validity should not be accepted at face value, any more than should that of information from other sources. (Hammersley and Atkinson, 1995, p. 125)

Ethics

1 Obtain permission, through your general mentor and Head of Department, to observe in lessons.
2 Obtain permission to look at pupils' work, school records.
3 Obtain permission to quote people's views and beliefs.
4 Guarantee confidentiality: pupil and staff surnames should be eliminated from your written information. Comments made to you by staff should not be repeated to pupils.
5 You will need to set a certain distance between yourself and pupils because you are now adopting the standards of the teaching profession. You do not wish pupils to make personal comments to you or complain to you about teachers. If in doubt, discuss this with your general mentor.
6 Have humility: you will see a different lesson, in some respects, from that which the teacher sees – you will see events which take place out of the teacher's sight. You are privileged to be invited into that lesson; do not abuse the privilege by being inappropriately critical.
7 Be careful to avoid sweeping generalisations in your research: you can only make tentative conclusions about a pupil's learning from the limited lesson time which you have observed.
8 Be sure to support your conclusions with evidence. Explain how you came to those conclusions.

9 With all case study work there is an ethical issue of 'ownership': who 'owns' the information you have collated and the opinions you have formed? Walker (1993) suggests that all participants in such fieldwork should have equal access to the data collected. There are many problems with this, in terms of practicality and timescale. However, it is a good test of your professionalism: write up your findings in such a way that they can be read by the participants. If you have doubts or criticisms you should present your alternatives in a positive way. You will be able to decide on feedback issues in discussion with your mentor. Consider the extract from trainee Matthew's conclusions about Oliver on page 11.

Learning support issues

Learning support is often provided during lessons by extra staff. You will need to familiarise yourself with the role of support staff for two reasons: first because you need to use similar strategies to those of a support teacher at the beginning of your training, and secondly because you need to learn how to work with support staff when you become a teacher.

Ray Keeley is one of the Training Managers (general mentors) who uses this chapter with his trainees during their first school placement. He perceived the need to strengthen it by giving them an introduction to learning support, as preparation for their early observations. He adds the following:

Learning support

The development of whole school approaches to special educational needs in the late 1980s and the early 1990s radically changed the way children with individual learning needs were taught. No longer were such pupils segregated away from their peers into small remedial classes and taught a mixed diet of basic literacy skills and watered down curriculum content; they were in with everyone else, with equal status and equal entitlement although not necessarily with equal outcome.

Children with special educational needs, including children with statements of special educational needs, should, where appropriate and taking into account the wishes of their parents, be educated alongside their peers in mainstream schools.
(Code of Practice, DFE, 1994, 1.2)

The teaching implications for such a radical shift in educational thinking were enormous. Almost overnight the word differentiation became a key term for educational theorists and practitioners alike. Subject specialist teachers found that they had to teach a common curriculum to the full ability range, and they needed help! Learning support, which had previously at best been a piecemeal operation in some innovative schools, was about to become an integral part of the teaching and learning process.

Special educational needs (SEN)

'**The Code of Practice on the Identification and Assessment of Special Educational Needs**' is a document published by the Department for Education intended to provide guidance for the Special Educational Needs component of the 1993 Education Act. The Act states that children have special educational needs if they have a *learning difficulty* which calls for *special educational provision* to be made

At some time during their school years about 20 per cent of the school population may need special provision. The Government believes that most of this provision can be met by school resources. Only about 2 per cent of pupils will have a statement of special education needs maintained for them by the local education authority (LEA), with extra funding. Over the last thirty years there has been an increasing emphasis on integration into the mainstream for pupils with SEN (Special Educational Needs) and less segregation (in special classes, units or schools). However, this policy shift has not been accompanied by a transfer of funds from special units to mainstream.

It is a complex Code which contains many good ideas and yet is very difficult to implement as required because of resource implications (little money and time) and the changed role of the Special Educational Needs Co-ordinator – SENCO (who should now support staff more than working with pupils).

Within the Code of Practice the SENCO is given an enhanced role, with a preventive and a supportive element. This can and should be seen as a way of building on existing good practice and as a way of strengthening the role of the teacher, as opposed to de-skilling subject specialists by imposing the knowledge of outside experts.

The Code of Practice (2:2) states that nationally about 20 per cent of children may have some form of special educational needs at some time.

These needs include: specific learning difficulties, physical difficulties, behavioural and emotional difficulties, and organisational difficulties. It is important to note that such difficulties occur throughout the ability range but, most particularly, with the least able and the most able.

Who provides learning support?

1 **The classroom teacher,** with the planning, preparation and delivery of differentiated lessons. Differentiation must be implemented within an inclusion model so that a coherent class identity can be established and maintained. Opportunities for collaborative work should be planned, even if some pupils do different work from others.

2 **The special needs teacher.** Possibly the former remedial teacher in a new role, requiring different skills, or a teacher trained in specific learning difficulties, but not necessarily a subject specialist. Now known as the Special Educational Needs Co-ordinator, this teacher's role has been transformed by the Code of Practice into a support role for colleagues more than for pupils (see Chapter 27).

3 **The classroom assistant.** Not a trained teacher, but perhaps a trained educational care specialist, although training in classroom support may have been provided, either within the school or on specific courses.

4 **Parents, governors,** volunteers with an interest in the school and its students. These often include qualified teachers who have been out of the classroom for a while and who may be considering re-entry to full, or part time, teaching.

5 **Older students,** often sixth formers, who wish to gain some experience in working with children, either in a classroom or on a one to one basis, before pursuing a related career.

6 **Trainee teachers,** who recognise that the teaching role can encompass responsibility for the full ability range. An integral part of early teacher training involves the development of planning and preparation of differentiated lessons and materials, and an appreciation of the value of learning support.

The roles and responsibilities of each group vary considerably and need to be clearly defined.

What do Learning Support Staff do?

Before the lesson

- They liaise with the subject teacher.
- Prepare differentiated materials for the most and/or the least able.
- Modify existing teaching materials to allow access for all students.
- Suggest teaching strategies appropriate to the needs of the group.
- They may need to ensure access for any students with physical disabilities. Examples of this are the provision of enlarged materials for the visually handicapped and ensuring appropriate seating positions in the classroom, for the hearing impaired.
- In collaboration with subject teachers they will set learning targets for individual students.
- Set behavioural targets for individual students.
- Set organisational targets for individual students.

During the lesson

- They will work collaboratively with the subject specialist to ensure the lesson develops as planned, and work with a group of students and individual students as and when the need arises
- Support teachers can also lead parts of the lesson so that the subject teacher may work with individuals or small groups
- Help individuals with note taking
- Help individuals with reading difficult texts
- Monitor individual understanding and monitor progress towards agreed targets in literacy, behaviour and organisation
- Help with IT skills
- Help with recording and understanding of homework. Occasionally dictaphones may be used for this purpose

Outside the lesson

Integration into mainstream classrooms means that learning support teachers may have difficulty identifying time during a school day when they can work with students, on an individual or a small group basis, on the development of basic skills. Opportunities are taken whenever possible but they can be counter-productive if the student misses important content in any subject area.

Individual and group sessions can focus on:

- developing reading skills
- spelling skills
- handwriting skills
- numeracy skills
- specific subject areas
- organisational skills
- help with homework
- clarifying and monitoring specific targets

Children with special needs may be entitled to support in external examinations at Key Stage 3 and GCSE level. Support can take the form of reading examination questions and/or acting as a scribe for written responses. These facilities may also be provided for internal tests and examinations.

It is important that learning support is seen as a collaborative process between the subject teacher, the support worker and targeted students. The status of each individual needs to be defined and acknowledged if the process is to be meaningful and successful.

Learning support

Consider the roles and responsibilities of the various people involved in learning support. How do they vary and what are the main issues involved in defining them? Discuss with your mentor which of the above roles you can undertake and monitor your experiences and successes in working collaboratively with pupils and staff. Remember to be clear and brief when talking to very busy teachers.

5

Headlands Learning Support

Irene Hunt's case study provides a picture of how one school provides learning support. She is a General Mentor for ITE, with a specific interest in special educational needs.

6

SEN – The Headlands Way

When a school of 750 pupils has 215 on its Special Needs Register, the response has to be whole-school.

Pupils at Stage 2 on the Special Needs Register are largely identified from a literacy survey at 10 to 11 years, which is monitored annually from 11 to 15. There are some pupils who have specific needs for physical or sensory impairment and others who need behaviour support.

There is a strong team of Educational Support Assistants (ESAs), but no support teachers. Each ESA is linked with a curriculum area and also has responsibility for monitoring a particular year group. This arrangement supports pupils, subject specialist and tutors.

The team works closely with the SENCO (Special Educational Needs Co-ordinator) in implementing the Code of Practice, devising and monitoring IEPs (Individual Education Plans), maintaining the Register, record keeping and reviews (see Chapter 27).

There is also an EBD (Emotional and Behavioural Difficulties) support worker, newly appointed, who is an important link between SEN (Special Educational Needs) provision and mainstream needs.

Weakness in core skills is a real challenge to all staff. With a full curriculum entitlement for all pupils, every teacher must address these issues through the subject base.

Literacy

1   There are small groups of Year 7 pupils who attend fifteen minute sessions before school in the morning and at lunchtime. An ESA has responsibility for organising and running these sessions, supported by Year 10 and Year 11 pupils through peer tutoring schemes. For some, this is also a recognition within the Duke of Edinburgh Award Scheme.
2   Word Walls are a key feature in all classrooms to encourage observation, self-reliance and ultimately spelling and vocabulary development. Improved signs and notices are planned around the school to enhance communication through the written word.
3   The whole-school approach is supplemented by our 'Target' scheme (a derivation of 'Arrow') which uses audio tapes to deliver activities related to comprehension, spelling and dictation. Talking books form an important part of this system and pupils participate at an individual level.

Numeracy

Every classroom displays a Multiplication Square and pupils are challenged to learn tables as a weekly competition, through work done in maths lessons. In addition, all teachers fire quick questions about multiplication tables at the start of each lesson and also 'test' other teachers who have occasion to interrupt their lessons.

Individual Education Plans

Having battled with mountains of paperwork to little effect, the Support Team has refined IEPs (Individual Education Plans) to an A4 sheet and put most of the emphasis into negotiated target-setting with the pupil. Those are renewed every six weeks for Stage 5 (or statemented) pupils and termly for Stage 3 pupils (pupils with some external involvement, usually educational psychologist and an IEP). The form is sent to tutors and fastened into the pupil's Contact Book so that all staff are reminded about the targets. The information builds into a useful record for annual reporting to parents.

More able pupils

Headlands has relatively few pupils who achieve the highest levels in examinations, but the More Able Pupil programme is an important part of school life. Those who excel in sporting achievement are encouraged to participate in teams and represent the school across Wiltshire. Each year a group is identified by teachers from intake scores, who show particular strengths in academic areas. They join the Fast Thinkers Club in

Year 7 to meet weekly after school for a range of challenges. They attend a residential course which begins the process of study skills and target setting. In Year 9 their work is enriched by a further residential course to consider Key Stage 4 demands and beyond to FE and HE. Working with parents to raise their expectations is also important. Business links and monitoring schemes are developed in Key Stage 4. They are encouraged to enter quizzes and competitions. By the time Key Stage 4 study is begun teachers have planned extension work, after school topics, communication and presentation skills courses to encourage high achievement and enhance classroom input.

There is still much to do; to evaluate and refine, so the system is manageable and seems to give results. Review of the SEN policy concentrates on the areas outlined here and is set within the Learning Strategies Policy rather than a discrete document. This reinforces the whole-school approach.

Individual Education Plan

Name .... Teaching Group ....

Tutor .... Date ....:

Stage (CoP) ....

Behaviour/Learning

Where I am now (Pupil/teacher to identify needs)

My Targets

How I will get there

Support needed (outline provision and resources in school)

Help at home

Review date...

Pupil.............................   Teacher ....   Parent ....

Headlands School

REFLECTION

During your observation time in lessons you will also be working with individual pupils and small groups. Use the above case studies to make yourself sensitive to the issues involved in working with pupils with a wide variety of learning needs.

SUMMARY

You will be conducting a case study for a clearly defined purpose: to gain insight into how children learn, and to test theories, ideas and teaching sequences presented in this textbook. To this end you will be collecting and recording data systematically so that it can be looked at by others, if required. You will be critically examining your evidence and your analysis of it, to make sure that you can support your conclusions. You will be writing your case study in a way which will allow others to learn something from your research, and you will relate your findings to the theories and ideas in this textbook, so that your knowledge and understanding can be placed in the wider context of educational thinking. An example of writing from a case study can be found on page 11.

At all times during your development as a teacher researcher you need to remember the strengths and limitations of any approach. We all have a tendency to make sweeping generalisations, illustrate them with individual examples and then imply that there are many other similar examples. Tversky and Kahneman (1971) have shown how cleverly deceptive we can be in moving from particulars to generalities. Ethnography should not be used in this way: you will be writing small-scale case studies, which will teach you a lot about individual pupils' learning and individual teachers' teaching. This process of finding out about teaching and learning will bring you nearer to becoming an expert teacher, yet you need to accept that you will only be able to hypothesise general laws about teaching and learning when you have observed many children and taught many lessons.

Useful references

Bryman, A. (1992) **Quantity and Quality in Social Research.** London: Routledge.

Burgess, R. G. (ed.) (1985) **Strategies of Educational Research: Qualitative Methods.** London: Falmer.

Cohen, L. and Manion, L. (1985) **Research Methods in Education.** London: Croom Helm.

Croll, P. (1986) **Systematic Classroom Observation.** London: Falmer.

Hammersley and Atkinson (1995) **Ethnography.** 2nd edition. London: Routledge.

Hopkins, D. A. (1985) **A Teacher's Guide to Classroom Research.** Milton Keynes: Open University Press.

Hull *et al* (1985) **The Language Gap: How Classroom Dialogue Fails.** London: Methuen.

SCCA (1996) **Supporting Pupils with Special Educational Needs: Consistency in Teacher Assessment Key Stage 3.**

Tversky, A. and Kahneman, D. (1971) **The Belief in the Law of Small Numbers.** *Psychological Bulletin* 76 (2) 105–110.

Walker, R. (1993) **Doing Research: A Handbook for Teachers.** London: Routledge.

Wolpert, L. (1996) **The Unnatural Nature of Science** in Proceedings of the Royal Institution vol. 67, pages 143–155. Oxford: Oxford University Press.

Wragg, E. C. (1994) **An Introduction to Classroom Observation.** London: Routledge.

CHAPTER 2

The Primary School

'They said they'd give me a present.'

'Well, now, I'm sure they didn't.'

'They did! They said: "You're Laurie Lee, ain't you? Well, just you sit there for the present." I sat there all day but I never got it. I ain't going back there again!'

Laurie Lee (1962) **Cider With Rosie**

LEARNING OUTCOMES

You will need to read this chapter before you make your primary school visits. The purpose of these visits is to give you a flavour of the first seven years of formal schooling in terms of social, emotional and educational experiences. You will see Key Stages 1 and 2 of the National Curriculum in operation and should spend two days in both an infant and a junior classroom, if possible. Requirements may be different on different courses.

The Actions in this chapter fall into the following three areas:

Organisational factors:	Actions 9, 21, 24, 25, 26
Social and emotional factors:	Actions 8, 20, 25
Curriculum-related factors:	Actions 10–19, 22, 23, 24

You do not need to attempt all the actions. Choose at least one action from each of these three areas. This will give you a relatively balanced introduction to primary education.

When you have read this chapter you should have an understanding of the major issues relating to the development of social and moral responsibility and language up to the age of eleven.

Introduction

The morning came, without any warning, when my sisters surrounded me, wrapped me in scarves, tied up my boot-laces, thrust a cap on my head, and stuffed a baked potato in my pocket.

'What's this?' I said.

'You're starting school today'.

'I ain't. I'm stopping 'ome'.

'Now, come on, Loll. You're a big boy now.'

'I ain't.'

'You are.'

'Boo-hoo.'

They picked me up bodily, kicking and bawling, and carried me up to the road.

'Boys who don't go to school get put into boxes, and turn into rabbits, and get chopped up Sundays.'

I felt this was overdoing it rather, but I said no more after that. I arrived at school just three feet tall and fatly wrapped in my scarves. The playground roared like a rodeo, and the potato burned through my thigh. Old boots, ragged stockings, torn trousers and skirts, went skating and skidding around me. The rabble closed in; I was encircled; grit flew in my face like shrapnel. Tall girls with frizzled hair, and huge boys with sharp elbows, began to prod me with hideous interest. They plucked at my scarves, spun me round like a top, screwed my nose, and stole my potato.

(Laurie Lee, 1962, **Cider With Rosie**)

Going back is very strange – when I started school at five the classrooms, corridors and dining hall seemed enormous. My memories are therefore very different from my current perceptions of primary school: very small children, small chairs and small lavatories in the infant department; the pupils gradually growing up to secondary transfer 'Top Class' pupils.

REFLECTION

Can you remember the teacher who taught you when you were very young? What do you remember about your friends, lessons, dinner time, the playground?

8

In the English and Welsh school system there are three major transition points: at four or five, seven and eleven years of age. In this chapter we will look at the four to seven and seven to eleven age groups in some detail and then the transition at eleven.

Children are required to attend school from the term which follows their fifth birthday. Flexible intakes are not uncommon however, partly because research suggests that summer born children are disadvantaged by less school. Summer born children will have six or seven terms, whereas the older ones have nine. This can be overlooked when they transfer to junior school. Many children therefore start at four ('rising five') and the end of their infant career is marked by National Curriculum Key Stage 1 testing at the age of seven.

Most seven to eight year-olds start their 1st year of junior school at Year 3. In a first school system they move to middle school at Year 5. The end of the junior curriculum phase is marked by National Curriculum Key Stage 2 testing at age eleven, in Year 6. (For a more detailed look at National Curriculum Key Stages see Chapter 15 on the National Curriculum.)

Key Stage One – four to seven years of age

Social and moral aspects of infant school life

Starting school is demanding. Let us pause for a moment to consider a four year-old. This year (Reception) is a quarter of the child's life so far. Development between the ages of 4 and 7 is greater than any other span in school. To make sense of a new cultural environment the four or five year-old needs to get to grips with three different types of 'social competence':

Procedural routines (for example 'lining up') and **organisational routines** (for example 'You're in the Red Raiders group')
Interpersonal relationships: responding appropriately to teachers and getting on with peers
Learning 'how to be taught': listening carefully and following instructions

As teachers, we expect children to make major adjustments at this point. Instead of having their parent or substitute parent most of the time, they now share a teacher and teaching resources with up to thirty-five others.

When they start school some children may appear over-boisterous, while others may appear withdrawn. Judgements about their behaviour need to be based on the 'goodness of fit' model; that is different children have different temperaments and may have variable success in how they fit into the social context of the classroom.

Teachers have firm expectations about how they want to organise their classrooms. This has implications for the way they want children to behave. In order to facilitate the smooth running of a classroom, pupils need to learn to accept classroom routines. Therefore the 'ideal' pupil is often seen as quiet and responsive to routine and to the teacher's voice.

Moral development is often considered to be relatively basic at this point, that is a child seeks to do 'right' more because this is what the teacher wants rather than because of any beliefs in right and wrong. Recent research suggests that issues such as gender and ethnicity can and should be discussed in simple terms at this stage, in order to give children insight into decisions teachers make (see Chapter 12 on Self-fulfilling Prophecy).

The infant school child may come to see the playground as a place where right and wrong battle it out without adult intervention. There is widespread concern now about apparent increases in bullying and disruptive behaviour in the playground and the related belief that traditional play-ground games are in decline. You should consider the role of emotive press coverage. You also need to look at the complex web of interrelated factors which may make life difficult for some families: unemployment, working Mums, attitude to authority, parenting. Even more important is the power which schools have to engender positive attitudes within their pupils, in the knowledge that long-term psychological damage can be caused by bullying.

Classroom organisation

Make a note of classroom organisation features and say if you think they encourage responsible behaviour, for instance monitors, classroom rules and independent work habits.

9

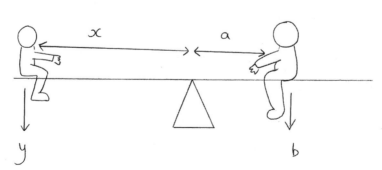

For the seesaw to remain level the force exerted by the person x the distance from the person to the pivot must be equal on both sides.

ie $xy = ab$

Educational development of infant school children

In the 1960s and 1970s much of Piaget's work was influential in the primary school, based on his view of children as the solitary constructors of their own reality who must be allowed to discover phenomena for themselves (see Chapter 3). This led to the use of 'discovery learning', where learning could be facilitated by the teacher but teaching was a less important issue.

The index to the Plowden Report of 1967 (on primary education) has thirty-four entries on 'learning' but none on 'teaching'. This 'child-centred' approach led to some disillusionment, partly because it is very difficult for the teacher to establish what each child has learnt if the environment is geared towards open-ended discovery. Vygotsky's belief (see Chapter 6) that the teacher is of prime importance seems more useful in the applied setting of the classroom. It should be made clear at this point that Piaget did not intend his theories to be used as a basis for educational practice.

Bruner's writings have influenced and captured accurately the child-centred yet also teacher-led learning of the present day infant classroom (for a more detailed look at these theories see Chapter 7 on Bruner).

Example from Bruner

Reception (4 to 5 year-old) pupils will not be able to understand the mathematical equation that describes 'moments about the fulcrum'. However, Bruner's three types of learning (**enactive**, **iconic** and **symbolic**) can be used as illustrated opposite:

Enactive (doing) Children can be presented with the problem of making a seesaw work – a piece of equipment familiar from most playgrounds (see the 'human sense' concept from Chapter 5 on Donaldson). This can be translated into working with weighing apparatus.
Iconic (recording) Making pictures and diagrammatic representations of what they find out is the next step.
Symbolic (analysing) This should take the form of some kind of equation and would probably not be achieved at infant level.

National Curriculum Key Stage 1 Science, at its best, combines guided discovery with learning. Bruner's 'spiral curriculum' is appropriate here – teaching the same concepts at increasingly difficult levels.

Infants and Juniors

During your primary school visit see if the infant class is working on topics relevant to your main subject. Compare their work with that of a junior class. How is the work assessed?

Metacognition

Metacognition means thinking about thought. Between the ages of four and seven years many children develop new strategies with regard to thinking about their own thoughts and thinking about how to learn. A four or five year-old may be naturally good at Kim's game (remembering objects that are laid out on a tray and then concealed). By the age of seven or eight many children will be able to use those memory skills in applied settings, for example learning tables or spellings.

Moreover, children may be able to tell you a little about how they do it. They may learn tables by repeating over to themselves, learn spellings by remembering the shape of the word, remember the difficult letter combinations and practise writing them.

These improvements in metacognitive skills are probably a combination of several factors:

● Maturational processes (for example more long-term memory storage)
● Learning how to learn (for example teacher-taught techniques for memorising)
● Improved use of language to talk about what they do
● Motivational issues, for example intrinsic motivation (where an activity is pursued purely for pleasure) is still powerful, as is the desire to please teacher (see Chapter 8 on Motivation)
● More all-round experience of using thinking for classroom learning (in other words the more you practise something, the better you become)
● Increased collection of concepts, for example chair as part of furniture. Concept formation is highly complex, yet we know that infants categorise and sort new experiences according to existing concept knowledge. We categorise phenomena together when we find them to have similar properties and to be different from other phenomena, in other words chairs are recognisable, and also recognisably different from other furniture. Rosch and Lloyd (1978) called this the 'basic level' concept category because it is fundamental. Concepts are not necessarily stable (Meadows, 1994) and infants certainly need to be given time to experiment with concept formation.

Infant language

Donaldson, from her research, points out that many infants use language differently from adults. For example, they believe that 'more' simply means 'some', and would appear therefore not to understand the difference between 'more' and 'less'.

David Crystal (1976) has evidence to show that most language structures are known by the age of five, and simply need a lot more practice. Infant age pupils usually have a better *receptive* understanding than *expressive*, which means that they understand to a higher level than is reflected in their spoken language. Therefore they may benefit if stories being read to them are expressed in slightly more sophisticated language than they themselves would use.

Spoken language

Can you record any interesting examples of spoken language that you witnessed during your primary school visit? Examples might include teacher/pupil talk, peer group talk and word games.

11

Learning to read

Donaldson believes that learning to read is one of the major factors which will facilitate 'disembedded thought' (abstract thought). Whether this is true or not, it is certainly the key to most curricular activities. The greater part of the National Curriculum is locked up within the written word – if you can't read you are profoundly disadvantaged. Unfortunately it is still true that each class, from the ages of five to sixteen, contains at least one pupil who cannot read up to the level of their understanding. There are also those who read well but do not understand the content: they will score well on a reading test which involves reading individual words, but will not perform well when reading for meaning. There are many children whose reading age is significantly below their chronological age.

Over the past thirty years, there have been heated debates on this topic which are still raging. One is about dyslexia, the other is about methods of teaching reading. Some experts and the press have polarised this into the 'Phonics versus Real Books' debate. This is an unfair simplification of the situation. Most teachers use many different reading techniques to meet the needs of each child, including:

● **phonics** – making clear the sound/symbol connection, that is a letter makes a sound, and letters build words
● **look and say** – sensitising pupils to the shape of a whole word so that they can build a visual memory; flash cards are a common technique.
● **real books** – encouraging children to enjoy books even if they cannot read them; many children describe the pictures or memorise the text when it is read to them, and can repeat it later.
● Highly structured reading schemes (such as the Oxford Reading Tree scheme) integrate many different approaches, for example frequent repetition of new words in narrative, with other context cues such as illustrations and teaching which is based on research about sequences of sounds and complexity of syntax.

A thread which runs through this debate is that of dyslexia, which is also known as a specific learning difficulty. Both terms are used in different ways by different people, to describe literacy difficulties which are unexpected in relation to a child's age and other cognitive and academic abilities. These difficulties are not the result of generalised developmental disability or sensory impairment. Emotional factors can be of major importance. There is a great deal of research, controversy and conflicting evidence in this area.

You should consider two important implications of this: first, you should not feel intimidated by complex diagnostic theories, which are often based on syndrome models and deficit models. In medical terms a syndrome is a combination of a set of symptoms. Such knowledge can be useful for diagnosis and for treatment. In educational terms, this approach is not always useful and can lead to the use of a deficit model, in which the child's thinking and perceptual functioning are defined by what he cannot do, instead of what he can do. It is better to build on a child's strengths. Secondly, each child's strengths and needs are unique and may vary in different learning situations. You therefore need to develop knowledge about literacy and accumulate experience of working with pupils so that you can combine the two and assess through teaching. Informal diagnostic work in context will be of inestimable value to you.

Assessment strategies

Use this opportunity to identify strategies for assessment through teaching: can you see some of the following activities taking place in an infant classroom?

12
- teacher and class sharing a book 'on the carpet'
- a non-reader 'reading' a book from the pictures
- a beginning reader picking out some known words
- paired reading (experienced and inexperienced reader working on a book together)
- child reading to a teacher
- child reading to a teacher's assistant
- child finishing a book from a reading scheme and choosing a harder one
- literacy skills used for reference work – looking in books for project information
- child reading classroom labels out loud, for example names on trays
- use of reading skills for carrying out a piece of work, for example science experiment or maths worksheet
- flash cards being used for learning words
- phonic rules being discussed and learnt
- spelling being learnt for a test
- differentiation of the various spelling lists

Key Stage 1 Checklist

At the end of their infant school education all children in England and Wales are supposed to sit the Key Stage 1 Standard Attainment Tasks (SATs). In addition, teachers review the pupils' progress because they are finishing one stage of education to move on to junior school. Some schools devise a checklist like the KS1 checklist in Appendix 2. With the teacher's consent, choose one

13

Year 2 pupil to observe; see how many of the items you can find out about. (Mark your answers on the KS1 checklist)

Looking at Key Stage 1 and Key Stage 2

Before we leave the infant school to visit the junior school, it is worth looking at the three National Curriculum core subjects: English, Mathematics and Science. You can undertake the following investigations at Key Stage 1 and Key Stage 2 levels and develop an impression of continuity and progression.

Mathematics

You will realise that much of the learning which takes place in an infant classroom arises naturally in the course of activities which come to serve many purposes. You will hear questioning by the teacher to establish understanding levels of, for example, sorting, classifying and measuring. Broadly speaking, two of the many situations in which these mathematical events can occur are:

procedural events: such as counting hot dinners, lining up, counting in pairs

topic work: number occurring and being worked with in specific curriculum contexts (music, dance and games, for example)

Mathematics

Spend an hour in an infant classroom and make notes on all the mathematical activities of which you see evidence within Using and Applying Mathematics and all the number activities of which you see evidence within Number.

Mathematics

In order to look at the section of the Programme of Study 'Number', you should attend a mathematics lesson. Here you may well see mathematics which may seem more like the mathematics you were taught at school. Collect some written and documentary evidence, such as evidence of computational skills, recording difficulties and why it should be that particular apparatus is being used. The attainment target for Space, Shape and Measure will probably be less in evidence, partly because numeracy is a Core Skill and tends to dominate.

For all these areas you need to familiarise yourself with the views of the thinkers (Piaget *et al*) about how understanding develops.

Science

In National Curriculum Science, the attainment target called 'Experimental and Investigative Science' functions as a sort of umbrella structure, indicating the scientific approaches which need to be developed. It is often topic-based. For example, pupils might be investigating which balls bounce the best. They will be encouraged to change only one characteristic at a time to make the test fair – the same ball, dropped from the same height, on to different materials. When the children are invited to predict likely outcomes, these thought processes should function as precursors of hypothesis testing. Science progresses through the creation of ideas (hypotheses) which then have to be tested against reality. School science has tended to emphasise the testing aspect, but the current National Curriculum does encourage teachers to develop the creative side of science: playing with ideas. Consider for instance the size and direction of shadows. Children's ideas about how shadows form can be tested in bright sunlight in the playground. Those who realise that shadows are caused by the absence of light will predict correctly that shadows are on the opposite side of the object relative to the sun. Other children may draw detached or coloured shadows. When you see science in the primary school you need to look for the children's emerging ideas as well as their ability to carry out fair testing.

Science

Observe some science happening. Look for evidence of investigative science being used within the other three ATs. This overlap could happen in investigation of materials, sorting, feeling or categorising.

English

There are three headings at all four key stages: speaking and listening, reading, and writing. Speaking and listening is an attainment target which covers many complex thinking skills as well as language skills. You will find that Vygotsky's beliefs about language are illuminating (that language enables us to develop thought, and does not merely reflect existing ideas). Speaking and listening covers the variety of purposes which language can fulfil: telling stories, discussing ideas, describing events (and giving reasons for actions). It also covers 'talking to different audiences': it is difficult for the infant age group to come to a conscious understanding of this. However, they have a lot of experience in talking to small groups, which helps to develop the sense of 'different audiences'. You also need to look for levels of listening, being able to show understanding in their response, and participation in drama (including improvisation and role play).

Writing, especially at KS2, looks at different 'genres'. This word seems to be used to imply both 'form' and 'purpose'. In the older pupil you can look for variety within the following non-fiction (re-telling, reporting and persuasion) and fiction (poetry, description and narrative).

Writing

Talk to children about their views on writing. Do they enjoy it? What mechanisms do you see teachers using for improving vocabulary and descriptions?

Spelling

Look at the teaching of spelling. How is it taught? Observe and discuss with staff if possible.

18

Reading

Reading includes a wide range of poetry, prose and drama. Observe a teacher or trained helper while they hear a child read. Now try it yourself (with permission) using the following guidelines:

19

- Use a book/text which the teacher tells you is appropriate: perhaps the child's current reading book.
- Try some techniques to 'warm up the text', such as talking about the cover, the title, the story so far if the child has started, and the child's relevant personal experience.
- Develop a sense of timing: if the child sticks on a word, do not jump in too quickly: attempt the sequence 'Pause, prompt, praise'. You may decide to tell the child the word quite quickly anyway, to maintain momentum.
- Prompts can include: 'What do you think the word starts with?', 'What do you think is going to happen?', 'Is there a word inside that word that you know?', 'Try re-reading the beginning of the sentence'.
- If a child reads a word wrongly, but uses a word with similar meaning (for example 'home' for 'house') let it pass and correct it after the reading, especially if, as in this example, the initial letter is correct.
- If these don't work, sound the beginning of the word out or tell the child the word.
- Pick out several correct features in the child's reading, at the end, and draw attention to similarities between words.

Junior school – seven to eleven years of age

Transfer from infant to junior school may or may not involve going to a completely new school. In many cases both schools are in the same premises with varying degrees of liaison.

Social and moral aspects of junior school life

These are the progressions from social patterns already laid down in the infant school and include a new sense of self. The ability to see oneself as others do, to see the difference between the 'me' (controlling) and the 'I' (impulsive) (see Chapter 8 on Motivation), and to go into a new phase of friendships, are all part of this.

Rubin (1980) summarises these complex developments as becoming able to:

- take someone else's point of view
- see people in psychological as well as physical terms
- see social relationships as long term and based on trust

A project on bullying

Between the ages of seven and eleven many pupils cover considerable ground in terms of social and moral development.

20 This is epitomised by a research project run by a deputy head, Marissa Davis, in which Year 6 pupils (11 to 12 year-olds) were invited to work with 'naughty' Year 3 pupils (7 to 8 year-olds) to improve their behaviour in the playground. Pupils . . . 'have a uniquely informed view of what goes on and their "evidence" is therefore crucial' (Blatchford 1990). Garth the beetle boy was a seven year-old child who had no friends except the beetles and other insects with which he played. 'These are my best friends', he said. The older pupils were concerned about his isolated state, but the project did not go on long enough to enable them to do anything for Garth.

At the beginning, three major areas of concern in the playground were highlighted by the children:

- other children bumping into them
- name calling
- accidents with the ball

As 'peer educators', the Year 6 pupils decided for themselves that low self-esteem was a major factor in causing bad behaviour and that it would be valuable to support Year 3 pupils in various practical ways (such as role play).

The deputy head witnessed frequent use of both Bruner's scaffolding (a technique where support is removed a step at a time until a task can be performed unaided; see Chapter 7) and Vygotsky's zones of proximal development (a method of learning by progression from existing knowledge; see Chapter 6). These techniques were used by the more able Year 3 peers as well as by the teacher and the Year 6 pupils. The Year 3 teacher reported clearer thinking from the pupils after Year 6 had worked with them. Particularly successful were the role plays, which highlights again the growing ability to see yourselves as others see you.

A Year 3 child noted:

It was fun. I liked the bit where I played the part of the boy being left out. I know what that feels like.

A Year 6 child stated:

I definitely think you should carry on with this, Miss. Let the children in Year 3 make up their own plays next time, showing good and bad characters. I'll tell Year 5 about it so they can do it for you next year.

According to Kohlberg these Year 6 pupils are making high level moral judgements based on concern for the values of the school community and deep personal principle. At least one of these pupils was a partially reformed bully who made considerable efforts to work constructively. At junior age most pupils recognise the importance of the separate and overlapping social worlds of children and adults, each with a distinctive set of rules (Davies, 1990).

School rules

Try to find out whether the school staff have any worries about the children's behaviour and what the school policies and rules are on good behaviour and/or bullying. Be careful not to ask negative questions and remember the professional points about talking to teachers on page 16.

Educational and language development of junior school children

Many changes occur between the ages of seven and eleven years, ranging from mastery of joined-up handwriting, through the loss of milk teeth to the visible and invisible manifestations of puberty.

In cognitive terms – how they think and what they think about – junior pupils acquire new skills and knowledge and develop new behaviours, attitudes and ways of learning. Progress is made in reading levels, number work and increased scientific information. One of the major developments in all curriculum areas is the children's ability to be constructively self-critical and explain their own thought.

This is stated clearly in the proposed summary of the Key Stage Two physical education Programme of Study:

In the six areas of study at KS2 (competitive team games, gym, swimming, dance, athletics, outdoor and adventurous activities) pupils should learn to make appropriate decisions quickly, measure and compare results of their own performance and suggest how to improve it, in simple technical language.

Another major development is the increased use of iconic and symbolic representation as described by Bruner (see Chapter 7 on Bruner). For example, discussing the concept of negative numbers: a six year-old might be able to understand the example of a temperature gauge; for a nine year-old the example of borrowing money from a bank might be comprehensible; and a secondary-aged pupil might be able to move from these context-embedded examples to the symbolic representation of multiplying two negative numbers, for example $-1 \times -2 = +2$. Yet the above sequence from iconic to symbolic will probably need to be structured by the teacher, even for a highly competent Year 6 pupil (see Scaffolding in Chapter 7).

The teacher's responsibilities towards the increasingly sophisticated learner can be summarised as follows. The teacher should:

● provide a bridge between familiar skills or information and those needed to solve a new problem
● arrange and structure the problem-solving
● gradually transfer the responsibility for managing the problem-solving to the child
● provide a variety of activities for consolidation

One way of achieving this is to develop pair and group work within a class. In the 1992 Department of Education and Science report **'Curriculum Organisation and Classroom Practice in Primary Schools'** a consensus among head-teachers and teachers was reported:

> . . . the primary classroom should provide 'active learning experiences' and teaching should have a 'practical bias' . . . *Moreover* . . . learning by doing rather than teaching by telling . . . *was held to be the preferred methodology.* [our emphasis]

Many teachers would prefer to teach in this way, but there are constraints on time and practicality: learning by doing takes longer than teaching by telling when it involves the whole class. Group work is often the best solution to this problem, although it needs to be carefully set up and monitored (see Chapter 6).

Pupil talk

22

Observe a group of two to five pupils working together. Develop a set of categories for describing what goes on. The following list is one way of doing it:

Initiating – dialogue which moves discussion in a new direction irrespective of its suitability and which is not dependent upon previous lines of thought

Eliciting – dialogue aimed at further clarification of a point of view

Supporting – dialogue which establishes clear agreement about the formulation/direction of a proposal

Positive extension – dialogue which clearly assists in the development of a line of thought via additional qualification

Negative extension – dialogue which challenges the development of a line of thought via contradiction or by not taking up an idea

Do you see evidence of significant learning taking place? Is there opportunity for moral development? Are the social aspects beneficial to learning? Can you see the benefits of solitary learning?

Comparison between primary and secondary teaching situations

In infant, junior and secondary teaching you will see the following:

- exposition by the teacher (teaching, explaining, etc)
- discussion between teacher and pupil, and between pupils themselves
- appropriate practical work
- consolidation and practice of fundamental skills and routines
- problem-solving, including the application of new knowledge to everyday situations
- investigational work

The foregoing is a list of good teaching and learning opportunities, modified from the Cockcroft Report on mathematics (Cockcroft Report, 1982).

One major difference between primary and secondary is that the primary pupils are with the same teacher most of the day for a whole year. At secondary level we are dealing with blocks of twenty to seventy minutes, once or more in the week.

Key Stage 2 Checklist

23

At the end of their junior school education all children in England and Wales are supposed to sit the Key Stage 2 Standard Attainment Tasks (SATs). In addition, teachers review the pupils' progress because they are moving on to Secondary school. Some schools devise a checklist like the Key Stage 2 checklist in Appendix 2 on page 380. With the teacher's consent, choose one Year 6 pupil to observe; see how many of the items you can find out about. (Mark your answers on the Key Stage 2 checklist.)

The Code of Practice

The Code of Practice is one of the most important areas of primary and secondary differentiation and support. Discuss the SEN area with the member of staff designated as SEN Co-ordinator (this may or may not be the Head Teacher).

If possible ask the following questions:

● What do you find difficult about being a SENCO?
● Which aspects of the work do you enjoy?
● How do you see SEN at this school over the next year?

Primary and Secondary

Consider these aspects of primary education and compare them with what you know and remember about the secondary situation. When you begin observations in your parent school, consider how they influence teaching.

Aspects of primary education	How do they compare with the secondary situation?
Learning environment, for example use of wall displays, noise levels	
Furniture, for example tables, rows, different functions for different parts of the room	
Pupil management, for example independent learning, class rules, monitors	
Relationship between teacher and pupil	
Differentiation, special educational needs support (SEN)	
Teaching styles	
Learning styles	
Assessment techniques	

Secondary transfer liaison

If possible, discuss secondary transfer liaison with the SENCO, ascertaining the relationship between the primary school and the local comprehensives.

SUMMARY

In this chapter we have explored the three major transition points: at four or five, seven and eleven years of age. The rate of change at these ages is dramatic, in terms of both social and moral development as well as educational progress. It is also a time of great change in a child's life: starting school and, later, changing from infant to junior, and from junior to secondary. Year 6 children take on major responsibilities as the oldest in the school. How do they cope with being so new and vulnerable when they start at secondary school? It is important that teachers – regardless of the age group they intend to teach – have a broad understanding of primary education.

Useful references

Alexander, R. (1984) **Primary Teaching.** London: Holt, Reinhart and Winston.

Blatchford (1990) in Woodhead, M. (ed.) **Growing Up in a Changing Society: Child Development in a Social Context: 3.** London: Routledge in association with the Open University.

Bruner, J. S. (1986) **Actual Minds, Possible Worlds.** Cambridge, Mass: Harvard University Press.

Committee of Inquiry into the Teaching of Mathematics in Schools (1982) **Mathematics Counts: Reports of the Committee of Inquiry into the Teaching of Mathematics in Schools under the Chairmanship of W. H. Cockcroft.** London: HMSO.

Crystal, D. (1976) **Child Language, Learning and Linguistics.** London: Edward Arnold.

Davies, B. (1990) in Woodhead, M. (ed.) **Growing Up in a Changing Society: Child Development in a Social Context: 3.** London: Routledge in association with the Open University.

Department for Education (1994) **The Code of Practice on the Identification and Assessment of Special Educational Needs.** London: HMSO.

Department of Education and Science (1992) **Curriculum Organisation and Classroom Practice in Primary Schools.** London: HMSO.

Galton, M. (1989) **Teaching in the Primary School.** London: Fulton.

Grieve, R. and Hughes, M. (eds) (1990) **Understanding Children.** Oxford: Basil Blackwell.

Hinson, M. (ed.) (1991) **Teachers and Special Educational Needs: Coping With Change.** 2nd edition Harlow: Longman.

Hopkins, D. (1986) **A Teacher's Guide to Action Research.** Milton Keynes: Open University Press.

Huxford, L. (1994) **The Spelling Book.** Cheltenham: Stanley Thornes.

Kohlberg, L. (1976) in Lickona, T. (ed.) **Moral Development and Behaviour.** New York: Holt, Rinehart and Winston.

Lee, L. (1962) **Cider With Rosie.** Harmondsworth: Penguin.

Meadows, S. (1994) **The Child As Thinker.** London: Routledge.

Pollard, A. (ed.) reprinted 1992 **Children in the Primary Schools.** Basingstoke: Falmer Press.

Pollard, A. and Tann, S. (1987) **Reflective Teaching in the Primary School.** London: Cassell.

Pumfrey, P. D. (1995) The Management of Specific Learning Difficulties (Dyslexia): Challenges and Responses in I. Lunt, B. Norwich and V. Varma (eds) **Psychology and Education for Special Needs: Recent Developments and Future Directions.** London: Ashgate.

Rosch, E. and Lloyd, B. (1978) **Cognition and Categorisation.** Hillsdale New Jersey: Erlbaum.

Rubin, Z. (1980) **Children's Friendship.** London: Fontana.

Webb, R. (ed.) (1990) **Practitioner Research in the Primary School.** Basingstoke: Falmer Press.

Wragg, E. C. (1994) **An Introduction to Classroom Observation.** London: Routledge.

Jean Piaget 1896–1980

3

We learn more from experience than from mere observation. (Millar, 1968)

LEARNING OUTCOMES

When you have read this chapter you should have an understanding of Piaget's beliefs about the following: the development of knowledge, the role of the teacher, the importance of making mistakes and the importance of learning by personal experience.

Introduction

Piaget's constructivist theory of cognitive development has been a major influence on British educational policy and practice over the last thirty years. He believed that children construct their own reality by means of experimenting on their environment and that this process follows a biologically predetermined sequence.

Piaget's is not a theory of child development and still less is it a theory of education. It concerns cognitive development processes in the abstract. Sometimes Piaget looked at specific issues, but always as a theorist reflecting on practice. He emphasised self-activity as the source of knowledge. This belief was interpreted by educationists in terms of **discovery learning**, where teachers set up situations in which pupils could find out things for themselves.

Piaget's constructivist ideas have been consistently misunderstood and misapplied, yet their influence has only recently begun to diminish. It is important to consider his beliefs, their strengths and weaknesses and the effect they have had on the British educational scene.

Piaget's theories

Piaget was interested in intelligence as the means whereby children, adolescents and adults develop knowledge and alter their environment. He developed a theoretical framework, broadly based on the concept of **ages and stages**:

0–2 years – the sensory-motor period
Action is crucial at this stage. The infant combines sensation and movement to construct a permanent picture of the world. A mental structure (schema) develops for understanding basic actions which assimilates new objects and adapts to new situations.

2–7 years – the pre-operational period
The development of language enables mental structures to be transformed into symbolic ones, and discussion of past and future as well as consideration of the present. Animism (attributing life to inanimate objects) and egocentrism are both evident.

7–adulthood – the operational period, sub-divided into:
a) 7–11 years The period of concrete operations. Children can now perform the mental operation of reversibility (for example ability to reason about plasticine which changes shape while remaining the same in volume). They also overcome egocentrism by attending to several aspects of a situation at once.
b) 11–adulthood The period of formal operations. Development and maturation of logical reasoning, that is the ability to plan hypothetically a series of experimental transformations. This will enable complex causal relationships to be deduced even when conflicting observable phenomena emerge. Abstract concepts such as energy can be managed without reference to concrete examples.

A typical example of Piaget's theories is where he asked children to reproduce a certain chemical change (Piaget's 'chemical combinations problem'). This task was tackled in different ways according to age:

Stage 1 Pre-operational level (5–6 years)
Piaget allowed children of this age to mix two chemicals at random. The children made no attempt to explain the results.

Stage 2 Early concrete operational level (7–8 years)
Children combined each of the chemicals separately with liquid in a bottle. There was no spontaneous mixing of chemicals.

Stage 2B Late concrete operational level (9–11 years)
There was still no system to the children's experimentation, but they began to try adding drops of one chemical to another.

Stage 3A Early formal operational level (12–13 years)
At this stage there was the first sign of a systematic approach to the mixing of the chemicals and the recording of results.

Stage 3B Late formal operational level (14 years onwards)
Children employed a systematic series of tests to prove or disprove their conclusions – *the experiment is organised with an eye to proof.*

REFLECTION

Look at the chemistry worksheet which follows (designed and produced by Dr Anne Guest). Decide which of Piaget's stages is represented here.

27

Chemistry worksheet

An experiment to investigate acids, alkalis and indicators

In this activity you are going to use chemical indicators to investigate a number of solutions.

The aim is to introduce you to some new indicators and to allow you to discover the different pH ranges over which they change colour.

You are going to use universal indicator together with two other indicators.

Data table

Indicator	Low pH colour	pH range for colour change	High pH colour
Universal Indicator			
Methyl orange	red	3.2–4.4	yellow
Bromothymol blue	yellow	6.0–7.6	blue
Litmus	red	5.0–8.0	blue
Phenolphthalein	colourless	8.2–10.0	red

Method
1) Stand 3 test tubes in a rack.
2) To each tube add about 2 cm depth of the solution you are going to test.
3) Test the contents of the first tube by adding 2–3 drops of universal indicator. Note the colour and read off the pH from the colour chart.
4) Now use the data table to predict the colours you expect to see when you add the other indicators to this solution.
5) Test your prediction by adding 2–3 drops of one indicator to the second tube and the other indicator to the third tube.
6) Empty and rinse out the tubes. Repeat steps 1–6 with other solutions.

Record your observations and predictions in a copy of the table on the board. Put a tick by the correct predictions and correct the predictions that were wrong.

In his scientific model (of which the worksheet is probably level 3A) Piaget analysed the development of thinking in terms of action: by acting on my environment, I, the child, discover how to understand it. I 'assimilate' understanding of my surroundings and develop mental structures as a result of a complex interplay between looking, listening, touching and experimenting. When a new experience provides information which is not consistent with my already existing beliefs, this causes conflict and may lead to heated debate. I may reject the new idea, or transform it or the existing structure in order to 'accommodate' it. This interplay between 'assimilation' and 'accommodation' provides the means by which I 'adapt' to my environment. When learning about integers (whole numbers) for the first time young children are able to assimilate additional facts and skills without destroying their concept of number, for example they may have an image of the number line as a model for whole numbers, which allows for subtraction as well as addition to be visualised. This model has to be adjusted to deal with the concept of fractions. Fractions can appear as unrelated to the number line. The images of cakes being carved up to give a picture of fractional parts, do not fit easily with their earlier visual image of the line. A similar, uncomfortable accommodation occurs in older students when they meet complex numbers for the first time. Having often been told 'you cannot get the square root of a negative number', suddenly they are expected not only to accept what was previously impossible – that is that the square root of -1 exists, but also that their previously familiar real numbers have to be reconceptualised in order to accommodate these strange new entities. To create a more complex system, the older one has to be discarded. Such accommodation can often be uncomfortable for the learner and presents challenges for the teacher.

Piaget also developed the notion of 'equilibration' and he worked on this idea for many years. It seems to be analogous to the biological concept of equilibrium in bodily functioning, for example our body temperature is controlled by a system of physiological checks and balances. Piaget seems to have developed this idea within cognitive development: that our thinking is ultimately consistent and based on reliable knowledge bases, even if we experience conflict and misunderstanding while moving towards full understanding. For Piaget, 'proper thinking' must follow predictable patterns and must be consistent with logico-mathematical thought patterns. His ideas therefore fit well within the scientific tradition of which he himself was a product. We know, however, that our own thinking is often characterised by inconsistencies. As a researcher he observed children's actions in order to find evidence for his beliefs about children's thinking: although this approach was limited by being based on a logico-mathematical structure, he did give us the confidence to look at what children do and to learn from them by the mistakes they make and the way they talk about their knowledge.

Areas not covered by Piaget

- Piaget had no intention of introducing his ideas to the classroom or any other applied setting. Earlier than Piaget, educators like Montessori and Froebel initiated ideas of 'discovery learning' and Piaget's ideas were later used in that context also.
- He deliberately took no account of the role of teaching, yet many would assert that teaching is a key in much learning (Vygotsky and Bruner among them).
- He had little interest in the consequences for learners and teachers of

the social organisation of the pedagogic and educational settings, nor in the most effective ways of providing them (Donaldson and Light criticise this omission). However, contrary to popular belief, he was sensitive to the social components integral to learning, especially in peer group learning settings.

Areas in which Piaget has been misunderstood

Despite these deliberately self-imposed limitations to his theory of genetic epistemology (growth of knowledge), Piaget's ideas have had a profound influence on British educational policy and practice.

In 1967 the Plowden Report reflected many aspects of Piaget's theories which resembled those of Rousseau, that is a child-centred concept, in which the child was seen as the 'prime mover' in the educational setting instead of the teacher. As we see in Chapter 2, the Report's index contains thirty-four entries on 'learning' and none on 'teaching'.

In the 1960s and 1970s many teachers came to see themselves as providers of an appropriate context in which the child would develop when ready. This assumption was based partly on a mis-application of Piagetian sequential developmentism (commonly and simplistically referred to as 'ages and stages') and the associated notion of 'readiness'. It is a true but only partially adequate representation of the role of teachers, who see themselves now, in the 1990s, as the active transmitters of knowledge.

In modern psychology there is great interest in Vygotsky, who maintained that all learning is social and that both the teacher and the peer group are vital to the learner. These two great thinkers are often played off against each other in the literature. Piaget's child is seen as a solitary explorer, discovering knowledge alone at a predetermined rate. Vygotsky's child is seen as a sociable communicator, needing structure and support from others.

This polarisation has some truth to it, and the contrast will help you to interrogate your own implicit assumptions about how children learn. However, it is necessary to be wary of putting Piaget and Vygotsky on opposing teams, as they have much in common.

Areas in which Piaget's theories are frequently criticised

- The chemical operations test, and the rest of Piaget's theory may not be such accurate measures of universally applicable logical reasoning as Piaget believed. Martorano (1977) showed considerable intertask and intra-individual variability in ten formal operation tasks, when attempted by girls ranging from eleven to seventeen years of age. Intra-individual variability means that an individual pupil may function better on some tasks than on others. This is contrary to Piaget's prediction that a pupil should develop at the same rate of competence across all of these tasks.
- Piaget assumed the biological inevitability of stages of development, yet King (1985) showed that a sizeable proportion of the normal adult population does not reason at formal levels when tested on tasks involving formal operations.

- Piaget assumed that development of thought follows the same pattern in all, with no real consideration of factors such as individual differences, motivation, personality, the differing information loads of different tasks, familiarity with materials, and the possibilities of teaching or possibly a partnership with peers. We will consider these in later chapters.
- The possible flaw within the logic model:

Logic – 'Incorrect conclusions can be reached through logical means if the original assumptions are faulty.'

(Reber, 1985)

SUMMARY

Piaget was interested more in the structure of knowledge than in the social or cultural factors involved in learning. He believed that children construct their own view of reality by trying out their ideas. The sequence of these ideas is predetermined by the age of the child – it is certainly true that a 12 year-old can achieve more than a 3 year-old. However it is also true that Piaget's theory links ages and stages in a way which is probably too prescriptive.

Despite the limitations and poor application of his theories, it is still true that Piaget has made a major contribution to twentieth-century psychology. He underestimated young children's potential and overestimated that of teenagers. Nor did he have much faith in the role of teachers. Yet, consider the following he has given us:

- a fascinating stage theory for understanding the child's mind
- an enduring belief that children actively construct their own learning experiences (a good contrast with behaviourism or the *tabula rasa* of Locke)
- a strong desire to see whether real understanding has taken place, rather than merely actions which may give a false impression of knowledge
- a wonderful insight into the child's and adolescent's worlds
- a belief that a child's mistakes can usefully reveal thought processes which are developing rather than dismissing them as 'wrong'.

Useful references

Boden, M. A. (1979) **Piaget.** London: Fontana Paperbacks.

Donaldson, M. (1978) **Children's Minds.** London: Fontana (especially Donaldson's appendix, *Piaget's Theory of Intellectual Development*).

King, P. M. (1985) *Formal Reasoning in Adults: A Review and Critique* in Mines, R. A. and Kitchener, K. S. (eds) **Adult Cognitive Development.** New York: Praeger Press.

King, R. (1978) **All Things Bright and Beautiful? A Sociological Study of Infants' Classrooms.** Chichester: Wiley.

Martorano, S. C. (1977) *A Developmental Analysis of Performance on Piaget's Formal Operations Task* in **Developmental Psychology.** 13, pp. 666–672.

Meadows, S. (1993) **The Child As Thinker.** New York and London: Routledge.

Millar, S. (1968) **The Psychology of Play.** Harmondsworth: Penguin.

Reber, A. S. (1985) **The Penguin Dictionary of Psychology.** Harmondsworth: Penguin.

Richardson, K. and Sheldon, S. (eds) (1988) **Cognitive Development to Adolescence.** London: Lawrence Erlbaum Associates in association with the Open University (especially Chapter 1 by Piaget and Chapter 2 by Sara Meadows).

Burrhus Frederic Skinner 1904–1990

4

LEARNING OUTCOMES

When you have read this chapter you should be able to define the following concepts: associationism, the law of positive reinforcement, observable behaviour, task analysis.

You should be able to devise five rules for running a class, and be able to consider the importance of devising effective rewards and punishments.

Introduction

Skinner is famous, perhaps even notorious, for having taught rats to press levers and pigeons to play ping-pong for rewards such as food. He extrapolated from rats and pigeons to human beings, arguing that learning is achieved by association between stimuli, or between stimuli and responses.

For Skinner, learning is the formation of habits under the influence of stimuli which are kept constant. He developed **operant conditioning** whereby a reward such as food or praise (reinforcement) is given for any response which is at all similar to the ultimately desired response. Gradually the behaviour can be brought closer and closer to the desired response by controlled use of stimulus-response associations.

His work has now lost the hold which it had in the 1960s over areas such as perception, cognition, psycho-linguistics and developmental psychology. This is largely because most cognitive processes are now recognised as being too complex to be broken down into simple stimulus-response mechanisms, and also because it would be impossible to control the environment so that it only consisted of the desired associations.

Yet Skinner's legacy remains useful in two specific areas: teaching programmes for children with learning difficulties, and behaviour management in the classroom. These are areas of great significance.

Skinner's theories

Skinner's ideas are founded on three basic principles:

- **Associationism** originated in Aristotle's beliefs about the way we use associations to incorporate new elements into our learning; for example we remember things if they are similar to, or different from, something we already know, or if they occur close to something we know in terms of time. Skinner believed that all learning is based on such associations, and that rewards are the most powerful way of causing learning to happen. Every learning theory contains elements of associationism, to a greater or lesser extent.
- Skinner's associationist ideas are also strongly flavoured by **positivism**, a form of social science which maintains that explanatory laws should make possible the development of more rational and effective social policies and practice.
- Closely allied to positivism is **operationalism**, the supposition that scientific concepts should ultimately be defined in terms of the directly observable properties of things. Skinner's approach is based on the belief that observable behaviour is the only measurable feature, as opposed to unobservable mental acts, such as thoughts, learning processes or motivation. Ideas such as 'freedom', 'will' and 'dignity' are considered to be useless as explanatory mechanisms. He therefore saw observable behaviour as the evidence of learning: if you can see it happening, then you can measure it and that proves that it exists. Skinner drew an analogy between the way we learn language and the way we interpret situations. We point at an object when young and are taught its name. Similarly, he would argue, when a child who knocks its knee is comforted by an adult with the words, *There, there, you're crying because your knee hurts*, the adult is explaining to the child the appropriate behaviour for that situation. In future the child will cry when it knocks itself, whether in pain or not, and expect adult attention as a consequence. Skinner believed that such explanations of behaviour are mis-used by both teachers and pupils in the school setting. He believed that teachers ensure the repetition of unacceptable behaviour by expending a good deal of time, energy and attention on punishment.

Skinner developed an educational theory based on Thorndike's Law of Effect. He called this the **law of positive reinforcement**, that is he believed that a stimulus-response sequence which leads to pleasing consequences for the pupil is more likely to be repeated (as that stimulus-response sequence has been reinforced).

This means that pupils working quietly at their desks will be more likely to repeat the behaviour if they have received a response which indicates the teacher's satisfaction.

Similarly, attention-seeking pupils who flick paper at their neighbours will be more likely to repeat the behaviour if they receive some response from the teacher even if it indicates strong disapproval of the act. Such negative reinforcement can be just as powerful as praise. Both good and bad behaviour can be rewarded by teacher attention.

In terms of teaching materials, Skinner developed schedules of reinforcement with very small steps of learning, a high probability of error-free learning and a built-in verbal praise sequence for the teacher. Language laboratories are an example of this.

Skinner's contribution to the classroom – educational material

- He insisted on careful preparation and pre-testing of teaching materials.
- The learner would (he maintained) achieve a high level of success by a high level of reinforcement and highly structured materials.
- The teacher follows a script, word for word, with, usually, one sentence of instruction followed by pupil response.
- He suggested that the pupil's existing knowledge be established to give a baseline.
- There should be small steps of learning to ensure a high level of success or 'mastery'. This is sometimes called 'errorless learning'.

In order to integrate the above points into a learning programme, Skinner believed that we should use rigorous **task analysis**.

'Apostrophes' Task Analysis

28

An example of this is teaching the use of the apostrophe. The task is broken down into a series of steps: its use in the singular of possession (for example *the pupil's bag*), its use in the plural of possession (for example *the pupils' bags*), its use in contraction (for example *it's cold today, she's gone home*) and exceptions (for example not used with 'its' and for possession – *its label was torn*).

The task analysis should include the following:

- establish a way of finding out what the group knows before you start teaching, for example a short diagnostic test to see how well they know these four rules or use existing assessment records in school if they exist on this topic
- choose one of the above uses (for example singular possession, or contraction) to teach initially, based on the 'test' results and other data if you have it
- develop examples to prove the rule and exceptions, using a reliable resource book
- give exercises to practise specific uses of the apostrophe
- decide on method of presentation, method of pupil feedback and method of checking understanding

You can apply the above task analysis to your own assignment writing. Moreover, from a Professional Development point of view this is a valuable tool in identifying the critical steps which the pupils need to follow in order to reach better understanding.

Task Analysis

Think of a specific area of your subject specialism, *or* a skill you have recently learned or taught to someone. Carry out a task analysis of part of it.

29

An example of a different type is the application of BODMAS in mathematics (priority of operations: Brackets Of Division, Multiplication and Subtraction). If you are not familiar with BODMAS find someone who is and ask them to explain it to you.

Weaknesses of Skinner's approaches to educational material

- The 'scripts' customarily produced for teaching programmes based on Skinner's methods can be boring and restrictive to administer, for example DISTAR. Teachers often deviate from the text, which may weaken the impact.
- These scripts are also boring and restrictive to write; programme designers find it uninspiring work.
- Skinner's views of learning as habit formation mean that complicated mental procedures such as 'concept development' are often not accounted for.
- Skinner's emphasis on observable behaviour and small steps of learning may make it possible for pupils to give the right answer without understanding the question.

Skinner's contribution to the classroom – behaviour management

Packages have been developed with training material, videos and practical advice for teachers, for example **Assertive Discipline**. These are often based on the belief that behaviour must be tackled at a whole school level and consistently, with support from senior staff. Moreover, it is worth mentioning here that, although they are not 'objectively measurable quantities', group 'ethos' and the individual attitudes of staff and pupils are powerful factors.

These programmes are based on the following Skinnerian assumptions:

- A class needs to be told by the teacher what behaviour is expected. Such observable behaviour should be described whenever possible in positives, for example *Listen and look at me in silence when I clap my hands (click my fingers, etc)* instead of *Don't talk when I start talking.* A class can be run well on between three and five such instructions.
- Praise and reward are the major factors.
- Verbal praise and reward systems should be used to shape up the behaviours you want repeated in your class, and rewards already given should not be taken away as punishment.
- The individual members of the class need to take an active part in behaving. They must know what will happen if individuals or groups disobey the instructions. Small sanctions/punishments should be available and agreed with an established senior member of staff. The sanctions should be morally and practically acceptable to you and disliked by the pupils.
- More serious punishments need to be planned and explained to the class, especially a 'severe clause' for potentially dangerous behaviour.
- Significant, rarely given rewards, for both individuals and the whole class, should be planned and explained to pupils.
- There should be insistence on objective clarity of expression, for example if you analyse the statement *Boys are more disruptive than girls in assembly*, what does 'disruptive' mean? Specific instances of observable behaviour need to be described before action can be taken (is it foot-shuffling or elbowing?) Why has such an emotive word as 'disruptive' been used?
- Analyse the context; there will usually be **antecedents** and **consequences** of the inappropriate behaviour (is there a specific trigger which sets the pupil off, and/or a specific reinforcing consequence?) How can these be changed?

Positive rules

Write five rules for running a class. Try to phrase the rules in positive terms when possible, for instance 'stay in your seat' rather than 'don't move around', and make them 'observable' (can you see their effect?)

Subject-specific issues

Now consider any special factors which may influence the teaching of your subject area. In Art, Science, Physical Education and Design and Technology there are safety factors which must become automatic responses. Are there habits for your subject which can be encoded in simple, yet effective, rules?

Weaknesses in Skinner's approach to behaviour management

- No account is taken of individual differences, such as different cultural expectations, family difficulties and so on.
- It presupposes that adults are prepared to change their own behaviour.
- There will often be one pupil who is ultimately resistant.
- Skinner failed to take into account the complexity of motivation: secondary-aged pupils may need to feel that they have some independent control over their own learning, before they will accept adult praise. Deci (in Biggs and Telfer, 1987) carried out research on rewards. He and his co-workers concluded that every reward has two aspects, a controlling aspect and an informational aspect. Therefore, when a learner receives a reward, he or she gains information about who is in control of the situation as well as finding out how well the task was completed. Teenagers can be made to feel that they are in control of the situation if they can earn rewards which they find acceptable (probably *not* gushing praise in front of the whole class). Pupils need to take responsibility for their own learning before they will respond to praise and reward systems. Yet reward systems can also be very useful if a task is difficult or uninteresting.
- Finally, Skinner can be attacked for being reductionist, because of his emphasis on stimulus-response associations, and his apparent lack of interest in such vital, yet invisible, features of social learning such as individual differences in motivation.

SUMMARY

Skinner has made a substantial contribution to education in the areas of highly structured teaching materials and behaviour management. He presents a refreshing invitation to move away from value judgements about 'bad' pupils towards a consideration of practical solutions for helping pupils learn better. His faith in learning machines and programmed learning led him to believe, as long ago as the 1950s, that teachers are out of date as reinforcers. Yet he has given us a great deal of useful guidance for good teaching, such as the need for clear task analysis and the importance of responding more to appropriate behaviour than to inappropriate behaviour. Possibly his major contribution has been the belief that, in order to change a *pupil's* behaviour, teachers must be committed to changing *their own* behaviour.

Useful references

Biggs, J. B. and Telfer, R. (1987) **The Process of Learning.** 2nd edn Tasmania: Prentice Hall (see discussion of Deci).

Richardson, K. (1988) **Understanding Psychology.** Milton Keynes: Open University Press.

Stones, E. (1979) **Psychopedagogy.** London: Methuen.

Wheldall, K. and Merrett, F. (1990) *What is the behavioural approach to teaching?* in Lee, V. (ed.) (1990) **Children's Learning in School.** London: Hodder and Stoughton in association with the Open University.

Margaret Donaldson

5

These pictures are so delicious my brain could eat them up. (a five year-old)

LEARNING OUTCOMES

When you have read this chapter you should have a general understanding of Donaldson's beliefs about children and how they learn. Specifically, you should be familiar with her theories of **human sense** and **disembedded thinking**.

In terms of subject specialism you should be developing the ability to think about an area of your subject and introduce 'human sense' to it, in order to make it more accessible to pupils.

Introduction

Children's Minds was first published in 1978 and is still recommended reading on many courses relating to education, schooling and philosophy. In it, Margaret Donaldson works within a broadly Piagetian framework, yet she is highly critical of some of Piaget's assertions and offers alternative explanations for many of his findings. She believes that he underestimated the thinking powers of children, partly because he believed that abstract thinking is superior and that it is only attained in late adolescence. Her work concentrates on 2 to 7 year-olds, yet her ideas about child development, language and education have practical implications for all age groups.

Donaldson's work considers the social context in which the child learns and the child's understanding of that context. In a formalised setting, such as the conservation experiment described below, children are actively working out what the experimenter wants and may well misjudge the situation through no fault of their own. This is a viewpoint in which Skinner the behaviourist, Chomsky the rationalist and even Piaget the constructivist had no interest.

Donaldson believes that context and social interaction should be emphasised as key features of pupil functioning.

Number conservation

Donaldson re-interpreted Piaget's work by looking, with McGarrigle and others, at how to understand children's thinking better. Her criticism, analysis and change of the Piagetian experiment about number conservation can be used as a typical example of her child-centred views.

According to Piaget, a child needs to be at least 7 years old to fully understand and correctly explain the following event, that is to realise that numbers are invariant despite change of array:

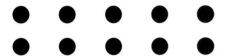

A) *Do you see these Smarties in two rows? Is there the same amount of Smarties in each row? Now watch carefully.*

Experimenter lengthens one row:

B) *Is there still the same amount of Smarties in each row or does one of the rows have more?*

McGarrigle (1974, in Donaldson 1978) showed that children made fewer errors of conservation (that is they recognised that the numbers of Smarties had not changed) when the intervention was apparently accidental. When a 'naughty teddy' 'barged in' and 'messed up', changing the A configuration to B as above, 4 to 6 year-olds seemed to find it easier to state that the number of Smarties had not changed. In the traditional Piagetian framework of experimenter questions, many 4 to 6 year-olds fail to conserve. With McGarrigle 70 per cent of a sample of 80 conserved.

Why is this? Is it easier to tell a teddy that he's done it wrong and it's all still really the same, than it is to tell an adult?

Let us now consider the repetition of the experimental question. Susan Rose and Marion Blank (referred to in Donaldson, 1978) wondered whether children felt uneasy about the repetition of the question. They found that more children could conserve if the initial question was omitted. One of their main hypotheses was that if a question is repeated a child may assume that the first answer was wrong – this device is often used in classrooms. This example shows how Donaldson believes that children tend to respond more to the context in which language is used, than to the language itself in any purely linguistic way. This can cause confusion because the teacher may not realise precisely which context cues the child is responding to.

Rochel Gelman's work on **phenomenism** is also used by Donaldson. Gelman's research established that children and adults will respond immediately to a change in a situation, for example the rearrangement of furniture or an alteration to a display, only later disregarding the change if it is unimportant. Phenomenism is about our response to visible changes in our environment. Donaldson and her co-workers suggest that

Piagetian questioning catches the children at that initial point of noticing change before they've had a chance to decide whether or not it's an important change.

Some critics (Light and Gilmour, 1983) would argue that Donaldson and her team of researchers actually change the task so that it tests different ways of thinking from those of the Piagetian task. This may well be true, yet Donaldson has made a valuable contribution in focusing on the child's interpretation of events.

Human sense

Donaldson has also made interesting assertions about two areas which are of vital importance to all teachers. She calls the first of these **human sense**.

Human sense refers to a context which is fully understood by a child, that is a situation which makes 'human sense' to the child. The 'Naughty Teddy' experiment seems to make better sense to children than the Piagetian situation.

Human sense and disembedded thinking

Maria, a Biology teacher, used human sense and disembedded thinking in a series of Science lessons for 13 year-olds on investigations into pulse rates.

32 Human sense

Examples include:

- measuring pulse rate as an indication of heart rate changes
- explaining the concept of a 'fair test' by use of examples, such as removing shoes before weighing yourself, or having the same partner doing all the exercises

Disembedded thinking

- understanding concepts such as variables, reliability and validity, hypothesis testing (that is making predictions which pupils can then test), the fair test (and how to implement this), the general application of experimental methods and findings to other areas of biology
- the ability to analyse examples in order to recognise their common features, such as having been given two examples of a fair test, pupils should be able to think of and recognise further examples.

More recent work is critical of Donaldson (for example Light, 1988, in Richardson and Sheldon, 1988) and suggests that the level of understanding between the experimenter and the child (or teacher and pupil) is the key, rather than the introduction of a teddy. This 'level of understanding' is so powerful that Paul Light has shown how children will agree with an experimenter if the impression is given that the transformation is unimportant, as in the following 'field experiment'.

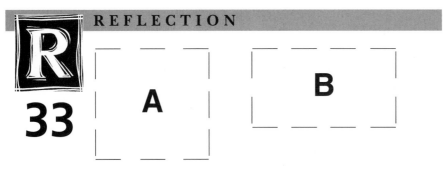

R **REFLECTION**

33

When an experimenter moves the 'fencing', as represented in A and B above, children accept the statement that the enclosed area remains the same, perhaps in order to help the experimenter fit a model farmhouse into B.

Are the children right when they accept this statement? What does this say about the teacher–pupil relationship? In fact the areas of A and B are different. Light is making the point that we can deceive children by making a problem seem more straightforward than it actually is.

Disembedded thinking

Donaldson calls the second of her central theories **disembedded thinking**. This refers to her approach to Piaget's formal logical operations. Disembedded thought refers to the ability to see the general truth which makes similar things become united as a concept, for example if asked why a cat and a mouse are similar it should be possible for a child of junior school age to explain that they are both animals, even that they are both mammals. She quotes Wason (1966 and 1983) and the 'selection problem', which takes two forms.

Wason's selection problem

1 You are presented with four cards, each with a letter on one side and a number on the other. The cards should conform to the rule:

If there is a vowel on one side of the card, then there is an even number on the other side.

Which of the following cards will you have to turn over to decide whether this rule is true?

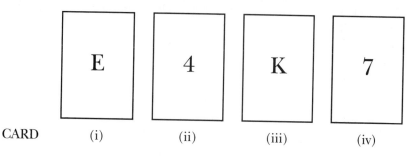

CARD   (i)   (ii)   (iii)   (iv)

2 Each of the four cards below has information about a person sitting at a table. One side of a card shows a person's age and the other side of the card shows what the person is drinking. Here is a rule:

If a person is drinking beer, the person must be over 21.

Which card or cards will you have to turn over to decide whether or not the rule is being broken?

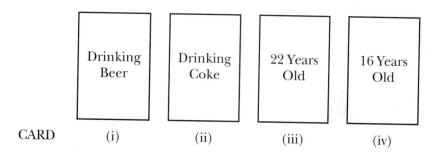

CARD   (i)   (ii)   (iii)   (iv)

Problem 1

In order to establish whether the rule is true, you need to turn over cards (i) and (iv). If the rule is true, card (i) will have an even number on the other side. Also card (iv) will not have a vowel on the other side, as it has an odd number on the side you can see.

Problem 2

This problem has exactly the same solution as Problem 1. You need to turn over cards (i) and (iv), card (iv) being the most important one. A 16 year-old should not be drinking beer ... if card (iv) says 'drinking beer' on the other side, then the rule is not true.

Research has shown repeatedly that adolescents and adults find Problem 2 much easier than the disembedded thinking required for Problem 1. Why is this? It seems likely that our motivation level can affect how clearly we think. Motivation often reflects our familiarity with the subject matter.

Donaldson believes that the formal education system should necessitate the ability to solve Problem 1. She sees many problems in this and her concerns should not be disregarded. However, there is more recent psychological research which suggests that many of us simply build up more and more examples like Problem 2, the beer drinking problem, and use them in the appropriate situations. This is discussed in Chapter 26 on Domains of Thinking.

The mass media

C

35

Melanie is starting a six month Programme of Study on mass media with Year 12 students (16–17 year-olds).

Establish to your own satisfaction her use of human sense and disembedded thinking, and explain it to a friend.

We are starting with TV advertising as the way in to mass media. Advertising comes in bite sizes and it's very accessible in that they can readily bring the resources to class themselves and they know what an advert is. That's where we start. Also, encapsulated within TV advertising are many of the concepts and issues we'll be wanting to raise as the thread running through the mass media. The Year 12 students won't be aware of that at this stage, that's something that will develop. TV adverts convey values, attitudes and beliefs. We're going to take some adverts apart and see how that is achieved.

Human sense and common sense

In her more recent book, *Human Minds*, Donaldson discusses the difference between human sense and common sense and cites Geertz' example about rain.

Clifford Geertz gives an apt illustration of the sort of distinction I have in mind. He considers the 'common-sense opinion' that one ought to take shelter from rain if one can, and he divides this opinion into two constituent parts: the knowledge that rain will make us wet and the belief that this outcome is to be avoided. Then he points out that the knowledge part is universal: we all know that rain wets us. On the other hand, judgements about the desirability of taking shelter can be variable. It might be held that braving the elements, scorning the rain, is a good and proper kind of thing to do. Geertz might have added that, in parts of the world where rain is very scarce, one may rejoice in the feel of it when it comes.

Now knowing that rain makes us wet is part of human sense. However, judging what behaviour is appropriate in regard to that fact is part of common sense; and I agree with Geertz when he says this is socially constructed. At the same time it is experienced as so basic that it tends to assume for itself universality. As Geertz puts it: 'What simple wisdom has everywhere is the maddening air of simple wisdom with which it is uttered.'

Human Sense

36

Find someone who shares your main subject. Discuss briefly with that person a concept in your subject which you can make easier to understand by giving a 'human sense' example. For example, in mathematics one way of helping a pupil to understand the concept of negative numbers is to think of temperatures below zero or to think of a bank balance which has gone into the red. Make notes on a proforma such as this one. Add to it through the year.

KS	Level	Human sense	Disembedded thinking

SUMMARY

In conclusion, Donaldson has given modern education a great deal. She:

● emphasises the need to consider the whole child: *Are you teaching the subject or the child?* Donaldson clearly believes that you cannot teach the subject (however well you may know it) unless you know the child and the child's level of understanding

● stresses the need to consider the situation from the child's point of view

● points out the necessity for, and problems of, formal education for the child

- bases her views on naturalistic observations of children and uses these to make specific curriculum-related recommendations about teaching, such as the value of teaching reading – a) because it is symbolic representation and enables the child to become familiar with an abstract recording system and b) because it opens up a new world for the child of knowledge, information, imaginings and possibilities
- believes that Piaget's psychological theory has underestimated the reasoning powers of children
- believes that children, especially junior aged pupils, use language differently from adults and often in a more context-bound way
- emphasises that children are sensitive to context cues which adults may give unintentionally and which may confuse the child as often as not

Donaldson also enabled many educationists to begin to push back the limitations of some of Piaget's beliefs, by proposing that it is necessary to consider the problems of schoolwork. Many children flourish at primary school and become disaffected at secondary school. For Donaldson, one of the major factors contributing to this disaffection is the move away from 'human sense' to 'disembedded thought', which she perceives as essential. However, as we have already seen, it may often be more productive to consider teaching pupils to build up many different examples of 'human sense' for different situations. (See Chapter 26 on Domains of Thinking for more examples of the different ways of thinking which we use in different contexts.)

Useful references

Donaldson, M. (1978) **Children's Minds.** London: Fontana.

Donaldson, M. (1992) **Human Minds: An Exploration.** London: Penguin Books.

Geertz, C. (1983) **Local Knowledge.** New York: Basic Books.

Light, P. and Gilmour, A. (1983) *Conservation or Conversation? Contextual Facilitation of Inappropriate Conservation Judgements.* **Journal of Experimental Child Psychology**, 36, pages 356–63.

Richards, M. and Light, P. (eds) (1986) **Children of Social Worlds.** Cambridge: Polity Press, pages 170–190.

Richardson, K. and Sheldon S. (eds) (1988) **Cognitive Development to Adolescence.** London: Lawrence Erlbaum Associates in association with the Open University.

Wason, P. C. (1966) *Reasoning* in Foss, B. (ed.) **New Horizons in Psychology.** Harmondsworth: Penguin, pages 135–155.

Wason, P. C. (1983) *Realism and Rationality in the Selection Task* in Evans, J. (ed.) **Thinking and Reasoning: Psychological Approaches.** London: Routledge and Kegan Paul.

CHAPTER

Lev Semonovich Vygotsky 1896–1934

6

Vygotsky was plainly a genius. Yet it was an elusive form of genius. In contrast to say, Piaget, there was nothing massive or glacial about the flow of his thought or about his development. Rather, it was like the later Wittgenstein: at times aphoristic, often sketchy, vivid in its illuminations. (Bruner, 1986)

LEARNING OUTCOMES

When you have read this chapter you should be able to describe Vygotsky's zone of proximal development, understand the importance of social factors and peer interaction, and appreciate the strengths and weaknesses of pair and group work.

Introduction

During Vygotsky's short life he developed a powerful and radical alternative to the ideas of Jean Piaget, whose work he knew.

Vygotsky believed that even the youngest infant is a social being and that all learning is social. Gradually, through interaction with others, the child develops an awareness and understanding of self, and a capacity for thinking about self and others. For Vygotsky, development proceeds from the social level to the individual level. He believed that *We become ourselves through others*, not only in how we learn but also in what we learn; our culture determines our beliefs and our knowledge.

Broadly speaking it is a stage theory. When contrasted with Piaget, Vygotsky offers a substantially different emphasis. Vygotsky described three stages of development:

● instinct
● training (or conditioning of reflexes)
● intellectual functions

The earlier stages eventually become incorporated into the later ones.

Vygotsky's emphasis on social interaction can partly be explained by looking at his background. He was a Russian, deeply committed to Communism and working within the collectivist ideology of the Soviet Union. It is perhaps not surprising that, for Vygotsky, the individual exists first and foremost in connection with others. His psychology stands on its own however, as a convincing theory of growth and change, regardless of political beliefs. In fact his work was banned by his own Communist Party, partly because he looked too closely at the need for good education, instead of following the accepted party line that the mind will rise above its circumstances (Bruner, 1986).

The teacher–learner relationship

Vygotsky emphasised the child's need for interaction with those who have more knowledge and experience (generally speaking, older children and adults).

He argued that by deliberately eliminating the teaching element in his experiments Piaget elicited artificially strange responses from children. For Vygotsky, the relationship between teacher and learner was the key to development. He called this the **zone of proximal development**, that is the zone of overlap and creative tension between what the learner knows and what the teacher is teaching.

Vygotsky believed that children would be able to solve problems with assistance from an adult or more capable peer before they could solve them alone. He developed three ideas out of this:

1) that the zone of proximal development can be used to identify which skills can most effectively be taught
2) that learning consists of the internalisation of social interactional processes (Peterson *et al*, 1981)
3) that social problem solving will be more effective than solitary problem solving – two heads are better than one! (Slavin *et al*, 1984)

At one level this appears obvious: children benefit from teaching. However, when attempting to teach you will find that it is not always easy to achieve. We often give children examples, support them by working through the examples and then set them a series of similar tasks. Often we withdraw support too soon and they are unable to generalise. This weakens the support which children need.

Appropriate support

37

Consider the following example of appropriate support: a pupil might ask a teacher what 7 times 8 is. The teacher, knowing that certain number facts seem to be easier to remember, asks 'Can you tell me what eight times eight is?' The pupil is able to recall 64 and teacher and pupil can then use this fact and the relational understanding that links this to the required answer. 7 times 8 is one lot of 8 less than 64; hence the answer is 56. Here the teacher is building upon existing knowledge, modelling a problem solving strategy to determine what is required. The teacher is offering support which enables the child to function better than would be possible alone.

The support has two characteristics: it builds on the pupil's previous knowledge and it provides strategies which will enable the pupil to think better now and more independently in the future.

Going independent

38

Choose an example from your subject area that shows highly structured support, and also facilitates gradual withdrawal of support so that the pupil can work independently. Make a written or diagrammatic record of this sequence.

Vygotsky believed that the zone of proximal development can be assessed by using a testing procedure which he developed and which he called 'dynamic testing'. He first tested children on psychometric measures and then worked with them in a structured way (on comparable problems to the ones assessed psychometrically). Mediation of the task was provided by discussion between the tester and the children about possible strategies, and the children worked through problems in this way until they could not benefit any further even with support. Vygotsky found that this structured, supported thinking was a good predictor of the next two years of schooling.

How does this fit in with National Curriculum? It is considered that a pupil will progress, on average, through one National Curriculum level every two years – you may find it useful to assess a pupil's potential by working in a higher National Curriculum level together, although sequences are not very reliable and do not take individual differences into account.

Beasley and Shayer (1990) found a similar predictive power, that is they believe that the ZPD (Zone of Proximal Development – see page 64)

extends forward about two mental age years. In other words, with support from a more experienced person a pupil can function up to two years ahead of the levels they can achieve when they are working unaided. Clearly the language which a teacher uses while supporting must be effective in mediating meaning.

The importance of language

Discussion in a group does for thinking what testing on real objects does for seeing (M. L. Johnson-Abercrombie, 1960)

One of the major differences between individual and group work is the use of spoken language. Vygotsky believed that language is a vital instrument for the development of thought, not merely a reflection of thought processes (as Piaget believed). Vygotsky maintained that ideas develop in the child at an **intermental** level, (talk *between* individuals) and then become internalised at an **intramental** level, (*within* the individual). Thus, for Vygotsky, all learning is social. Language is the prime example of this and also the vehicle for it. Research indicates (Peterson *et al*, 1981) that two types of pupil benefit most from group work: pupils who give explanations and help others, and pupils who seek this help and ask for explanations. Within a group it is therefore recommended that there should be a mixture of high attainers with middle attainers, or middle attainers with low attainers – if there is a completely mixed group the middle attainers may miss out. It is true to say that a group of pupils with very similar attainment levels should also be able to teach each other and learn from each other if there is an atmosphere of trust and open discussion. Each pupil will have a unique approach to problem solving.

It is reasonable to assume that the sharing of ideas is a valuable learning technique. Forman and Cazden (1985) did indeed find an association between high levels of social collaboration (co-operative procedural interactions) and the use of certain experimentation strategies (combinatorial strategies). However, it would be like the worst kind of 'discovery learning' situation simply to put groups to work on a task and expect them to do the rest.

It is clear that precise procedural habits must be developed so that pupils know how to work together productively, for example choose a note-taker, take timed turns at the keyboard and so on. Moreover, the teacher must have a clear idea of what the end product should be, and confirm by subsequent class discussion and demonstration that the result has been achieved and understood.

The importance of peer interaction

Vygotsky's work has inspired much practical and useful research on peer interaction, the value of which can be summarised in the words of Forman and Cazden:

Although such peer interactions take place in home and community as well as at school, they may be especially important in school because of limitations and rigidities characteristic of adult–child interactions in that institutional setting. The contrast between [home] learning environments and the classroom is striking. In school lessons, teachers give directions and children non-verbally carry them out; teachers ask questions and children answer them, frequently with only a word or a phrase. Most importantly, these roles are not reversible, at least not within the context of teacher–child interactions. Children never give directions to teachers, and questions addressed to teachers are rare except for asking permission. The only context in which children can reverse interactional roles with the same intellectual content, giving directions as well as following them, asking questions as well as answering them, is with their peers. (Wertsch, 1985)

Weaknesses in Vygotsky's work

1) Before his untimely death, Vygotsky worked in psychology for only about ten years and wrote relatively little. His writings are not easy to read in translation.
2) The zone of proximal development is difficult to implement on a one-to-one basis with a class of twenty to thirty pupils.
3) Increasingly, doubt is being cast on the value of stage theories – although Vygotsky's stage theory is more flexible than Piaget's, it nevertheless assumes that adults are generally more sophisticated thinkers than children. This is undoubtedly true but there is more to it than that. (See Domains of Thinking, Chapter 26).

Group work

Use the following Summary to plan, implement and evaluate a small group session or several small group sessions. Be realistic and choose a small task, in discussion with your Subject Mentor.

39

SUMMARY

Vygotsky's contribution to the classroom

1) He offers a different story about learning to that of Piaget.
2) His views embody 'social constructivism' and encourage us to look at the social aspects of teaching and learning. For a social constructivist analysis of learning to take place it is essential to analyse the whole context in which learning takes place: for group work this context includes:

- the group's experiences of group work: train them in group processes
- the task: make it clear to the pupils
- the way the pupils are organised for the completion of the task: ensure that they understand the group's goals
- the group construction: ensure that pupils at similar 'zones of proximal development' work together (high with middle attainers, or middle with low attainers)
- ability levels, age, gender and ethnicity must be seen as opportunities for choices in teaching materials (Shan and Bailey, 1991, in Chapter 12 on Self-Fulfilling Prophecy)
- gender: if the school is mixed, a balance of girls and boys is recommended

3) the prime importance of the teacher as facilitator, catalyst, guide and communicator
4) the value of peer interaction, for cognitive/social cognitive reasons
5) the power of language as a tool for communicating, socialising and learning to think
6) the picture of the child as a social communicator, needing structure and support from others
7) the importance of good organisation by the teacher: few teachers choose to organise collaborative learning in small groups, because the more groups are running concurrently, the more organisation is necessary and the less teaching is possible.

Useful references

Beasley, F. and Shayer, M. (1990) **Learning Potential Assessment through Feuerstein's LPAD: Can Quantitative Results be Achieved?** International Journal of Dynamic Assessment and Instruction, 1, 2, 37–48.

Bruner, J. (1986) **Actual Minds, Possible Worlds.** Harvard University Press, Cambridge Massachusetts and London, England.

Edwards, D. and Mercer, N. (1987) **Common Knowledge: The Development of Understanding in the Classroom.** London: Methuen.

Forman and Cazden (1985) 'Exploring Vygotskian Perspectives in Education' in Wertsch, J. V. (ed.) (1985) **Culture, Communication and Cognition: Vygotskian Perspectives.** Cambridge: Cambridge University Press.

Johnson-Abercrombie, M. L. (1960) **The Anatomy of Judgement.** London: Hutchinson.

Peterson, P. L., Janicki T. C. and Swing, S. R. (1981) **Ability/Treatment Interaction Effects on Children's Learning in Large Group or Small Group Approaches.** American Educational Research Journal 18, 452–474.

Slavin, R. E., Madden, N. A. and Leavey, M. (1984) **Effects of Co-operative Learning and Individualised Learning on Mainstreamed Students.** *Exceptional Children*, 50 (5) 434–448.

Vygotsky, L. S. (1978) ed. M. Cole **Mind in Society: The Development of Higher Psychological Process.** Cambridge: Harvard University Press.

Jerome S. Bruner 1915–

If I had to choose a motto for what I have to say, it would be one from Francis Bacon, used by Vygotsky, proclaiming that neither mind alone nor hand alone can accomplish much without the aids and tools which perfect them. And principal among those aids and tools are language and the canons of its use. (Bruner, 1986)

LEARNING OUTCOMES

When you have read this chapter you should be familiar with Bruner's three stage theory of learning (**enactive**, **iconic** and **symbolic**), his concepts of scaffolding and contingency. You will also have worked with Wood's ideas: Wood's five levels and their implications for teaching are a further development of Bruner's 'scaffolding' and his proposals for a spiral curriculum.

Introduction

Over the past forty years Bruner has developed a view of the growing individual which, in certain important respects, combines the best of Piaget and Vygotsky.

Like Vygotsky, he supports a broad stage theory concept. With Piaget he shares the belief that the 'mistakes' children make can provide us with valuable insights into the way they think. Bruner's response to mistakes is to use the power of language to help children develop their ideas – an area of interest he shares with Vygotsky. He does not accept Piaget's belief that development follows tightly pre-determined sequences. Nor does he accept Piagetian formal logic as the most appropriate device for representing cognitive structures. For Bruner, logic need not always be the basis for mature, adaptive thinking. It can however, be one of several 'special' ways of thinking.

Bruner believes that we use different types of thinking strategies according to our knowledge, the situation and the materials available. Creative problem solving may make use of different processes, according to the individual and the subject matter. This contrasts with Piaget for whom the adolescent attains logico-mathematical, hypothetico-deductive thinking and can henceforth apply it to any subject and any situation. For Bruner, thinking is greatly enriched and facilitated by language. Language (as for Vygotsky) is used for communicating the processes by which we learn to think.

Although not as radical, Bruner also shares Vygotsky's interest in the cultural knowledge and social processes which underlie development.

Bruner's three stages

Bruner has defined three stages by which we 'represent' the environment to ourselves when we are learning:

Enactive representation

consists of **actions** or the memory traces of actions.

Such segments of our environment – bicycle riding, tying knots, aspects of driving – get represented in our muscles, so to speak (Bruner, 1966)

In other words, certain commonly performed actions become automatic, forming items in a 'muscle memory bank'. This is called kinaesthetic feedback. For example, we can hold a conversation whilst climbing stairs because, for most of us, the action of climbing stairs takes little or no conscious thought. Learning and teaching are closely involved here. We often use enactive techniques (learning through doing) to master new areas, for example you learn how to teach by going into a classroom and teaching.

Science and mathematics teaching involves a considerable amount of 'doing'. The Cockcroft Report (1982) proposed that all levels of mathematics teaching should include opportunities for the following:

- exposition by the teacher
- discussion between teacher and pupil and between pupils themselves
- appropriate practical work
- consolidation and practice of fundamental skills and routines
- problem solving, including the application of maths to everyday situations
- investigational work

Which of these areas could include practical 'doing' activities?

Language is a major factor at all levels of internalising knowledge. It is important to consider the difficult position in which the teacher is placed when attempting to teach a skill which, for the teacher, has become completely internalised.

REFLECTION

40

Imagine you are teaching someone a skill which has become automatic to you such as driving or riding a bicycle. Focus on one specific subskill, e.g. changing gear, and make notes on your approach to its teaching. You will probably find that you need to think about your actions quite carefully in the light of breaking down automatic actions and thought processes. Try this out with a friend.

Iconic representation

relies on **connected images**; the environment is thought to be represented internally in a 'concrete' way, *a match by direct correspondence* as Bruner calls it. We use spatial arrangements, colour patterns, movement, for instance, to help us remember things we have experienced. Drawings and diagrams can be used to explain what we mean.

Iconic representation

41

Postgraduate Laurence Aubry discusses a French lesson with her Subject Mentor Steve Longton:

Read this passage and consider the solution offered by Steve.

L: The questions they ask – on this map there is a little icon of a church – 'Miss, what's that?' They are confused by anything which is not familiar to them. I need to anticipate that more.

S: Yes it's very difficult – were the symbols on the map, the same as the icon they'd seen in the book before?

L: No, but they are on any map. It can't be anything other than a church.

S: It's probably to do with age; when you're 20 you've got that background of experience. You're introducing it with flashcards and those icons are followed up in the book. Maybe you could have used the same symbols that are in the book – that would have triggered off 'église' in their mind.

Iconic representation can be useful for adult learning, for example in the area of pupil management. It is much easier to recall the names of pupils in a new class if they sit in the same seats for the first few lessons, therefore we use spatial features and patterns of desk and room arrangements to remember names and faces. It is likely that we will be unable to explain how we use these techniques; we are often unaware of them until some of the cues are missing and then we wonder what has gone wrong.

Symbolic representation

is the most sophisticated level, in which the connection between object and representation is arbitrary yet accepted by those with whom we are communicating. Language is the most powerful example. The word 'table' does not look like a table, it merely stands for it, and it stands for any sort of table. Mathematical and chemical formulae are other examples of symbolic representation.

Bruner's three stages

The following is an example of Bruner's three stages (enactive, iconic, symbolic), relating to reception pupils (4 to 5 year-olds) looking at how see-saws work. The three stages are presented here in the wrong order. Identify and put them in the correct order.

1) **'Recording'**: making pictures and diagrammatic representations of what they find out about how see-saws work
2) **'Doing'**: pupils can be presented with the problem of making a see-saw work by using their body weight; this can be translated into working with weighing apparatus
3) **'Analysing'**: this should take the form of some kind of equation describing the motion of a see-saw and would probably not be achieved at infant level

Enactive:	
Iconic:	
Symbolic:	

Many theorists argue that the psychological factor which transforms human learning is the ability to let one thing stand for another. This is seen in the development of symbol systems and especially in the use of language, for example in learning to read. For Bruner, as for Vygotsky, all three levels of representation interact with each other, although there must be a broad element of ages and stages. In other words, you adapt your teaching technique to the age and experience of your pupil. As adult learners we often use a combination of all three in order to master a new area.

Collecting Stages

During your early lesson observations, pupil pursuits and small group work, you will see examples of Bruner's enactive, iconic and symbolic stages. They will not always be in the same lesson, not necessarily in that order and possibly only with some members of a group. You need to make full use of these early opportunities to collect brief descriptions of how experienced teachers do it. These will then form the basis for your own development as a teacher.

Scaffolding and Contingency

Bruner sees the infant as an active and intelligent problem solver from birth, with intellectual abilities basically similar to those of the mature adult. For instance, 3 year-olds can learn to read, which suggests that they can operate at a level of symbolic representation. He is also aware of the differences between children's and adults' intellectual abilities. While acknowledging broad age limits, he emphasises the power of the teacher – algebra can be taught to primary school children if sufficient connections are made between concrete examples and abstract formulae.

Thus there is a well-defined educational component built into Bruner's theory, and although he has concentrated on younger children, he has given us two teaching concepts which have a major impact on the classroom, **scaffolding** and **contingency**.

These are based on Vygotsky's idea of the zone of proximal development:

. . . the gap that exists for a given child at a particular time between his level of performance on a given task or activity and his potential level of ability following instruction
(Wood, 1991)

Bruner offers his own imagery for this, calling it scaffolding, thus:

One sets the game, provides a scaffold to ensure that the child's ineptitude can be rescued by appropriate intervention, and then removes the scaffold part by part as the reciprocal structure can stand on its own (Bruner, 1983)

'Contingent' means 'next to' and refers to the nearest level of knowledge.

David Wood (1988) looks more closely at these concepts, establishing **five levels of support**: general verbal encouragement, specific verbal instruction, assisting pupil in choice of material, preparing material for pupil to assemble and demonstrating an operation.

These levels become increasingly specific and supportive, and, correspondingly, expect less and less pupil responsibility for what happens next. Level 1 is least controlling, level 5 most controlling. Wood's levels can be demonstrated in terms of, in this case, hurdling skills:

Level	Example
1) General verbal prompts	Make your way over the line of hurdles to finish at the end
2) Specific verbal instructions	Try to move quickly and get to the end first without hitting a hurdle or slowing down
3) Identifies material and/or key subskills	Practise specific ways of getting the lead leg and the trailing leg over the hurdle
4) Prepares for assembly or breakdown of whole sequence into separate steps	Static positioning of body for position in flight, landing and instruction on striding in between hurdles
5) Demonstration	Teacher demonstrates parts of the skill and the whole of the skill

REFLECTION

Consider how you would teach a 12 year-old to walk in a 'figure of eight'. How would this differ from teaching a 3 year-old? Can you use Wood's five levels?

44

These techniques are valuable in supporting group work as well as in teaching a whole class and working with individuals. If, in a lesson about conditions in the Arctic, the teacher realised that one group was stuck on its collection of ideas about clothing and temperature (working at level 3 or 4) it would be advisable to give support at level 2 (for example *Think about living in a deep freeze cabinet – that's what it would be like*).

Wood's 5 Levels

1 Collect some examples of this type of sequencing which you have observed in lessons.
2 Select a specific area of work which you have encountered in early lesson preparation for group work, and break it down into five levels of control – (1) least controlling to (5) most controlling. Incorporate the levels 1 to 5 into a lesson plan and try it out. Plan and discuss it with your mentor.

45

The hierarchy

Wood's hierarchy of increasing control should be operated by use of his **two rules of contingency:**

1 Any failure by a child to succeed in an action after a given level of help should be met by an immediate increase in help or control. For example, if the teacher provided the child with a specific verbal instruction and then found that the child did not succeed in the task, the teacher should give more help by either indicating the materials implicated in the previous instruction or by preparing materials for assembly.
2 Success by a child then indicates that any subsequent instruction should offer less help than that which preceded the success, to allow the child to develop independence.

With hurdling, Rule 1 of contingency could work in the following way:

A pupil repeatedly knocks into the hurdle, despite good strides and despite snapping back his lead leg very quickly and controlling the trailing leg – the teacher would, after observation, be able to recommend that the pupil counts the number of strides between hurdles. This pupil is generally at level 1, that is *general verbal prompts* because of high competence at the component skills, but needs level 2, that is *specific verbal instructions* to clarify one particular factor.

In the example of hurdling it is necessary to use Wood's hierarchy critically. A combination of all five would be necessary in order to teach a whole class. After the initial introduction, emphasising 2, 4 and 5, the class would be able to attempt the task – at this point levels 1 to 5 come into play for monitoring individual pupils.

REFLECTION

What would you conclude about the introductory session if more than a third of the class needed 4? What would you do?

46

Lesson Structure

47

With a colleague, work through the lesson structure on this page for a lesson about conditions in the Arctic. The structure of the lesson represents a form of scaffolding, as the task is sequenced carefully. As you work through the exercise try to relate your activities to the theories of Bruner and Wood.

	Jan	Feb	Mar	Apr	May	Jun	Jul	Aug	Sep	Oct	Nov	Dec
Britain												
Greenland												

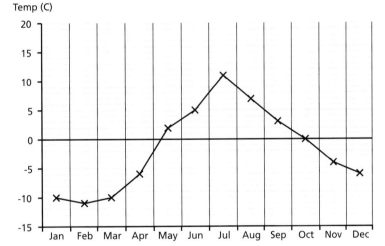

Monthly temperatures, Augmagssalic, Greenland

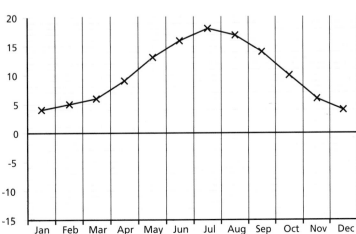

Monthly temperatures, Britain

Lesson plan for Action 47

Step 1 Solitary action. Choose the temperature graph of Britain or the Arctic above (your partner should choose the one you don't choose). Transcribe the temperatures from the graph to the boxes above it.

Step 2 Read your temperatures to your partner and vice versa, so that both of you have completed both rows.

Step 3 Discuss, compare and contrast the two rows of temperatures.

Step 4 Join with another pair of students to discuss the implications which these temperature changes have for the inhabitants of Britain and the Arctic. Consider clothing, food supplies, leisure activities, and so on. Decide which of you will take notes for the group.

Subject specific issues

Develop a (summary) lesson plan which uses these two main structures: a) giving pupils information/data to work on, and b) developing work from the individual, to the pair, to group work.

48

The spiral curriculum

Bruner has made popular the idea that subjects can be taught with increasing complexity as the child grows older and becomes a more experienced learner. An integral part of this idea is the belief that we should teach accurately and honestly; this enables a pupil to build on existing knowledge without having to 'unlearn' something which was simple yet distorted. This is extremely difficult to achieve: one reason being that we make use of devices such as analogy, simile and modelling. These may be misunderstood by children, because each child brings different belief systems to the learning process.

In his book *Actual Minds, Possible Worlds*, Bruner recounts a discussion which he had with university students about education:

Halfway through, a young woman said she wanted to ask me a question. She said she had just read my Process of Education, *in which I had said that any subject could be taught to any child at any age in some form that was honest. I thought, 'Here comes the question about calculus in the first grade.' But not at all. No, her question was, 'How do you know what's honest?' It stunned me. She had something in mind all right. Was I prepared to be honestly open in treating a child's ideas about a subject, was our transaction going to be honest? Was I going to be myself and let the child be himself or herself?*

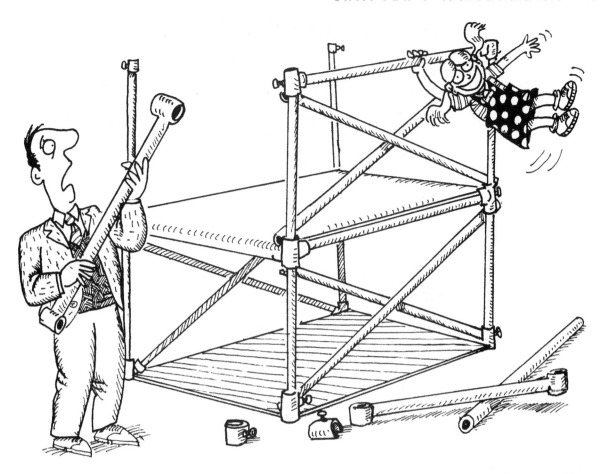

The strengths of Bruner's theories

1 Bruner has given us an opportunity to combine some of the best of Piaget and Vygotsky, in addition to contributing his own original thinking.
2 He has developed Vygotsky's ideas to a stage where David Wood and others can look at 'scaffolding' and 'contingency' in specific learning contexts. For example, Janet Maybin and co-workers are looking at a definition of 'scaffolding' which includes the intention on the part of the teacher to improve the learner's competence through specific techniques.
3 Bruner has contributed greatly to the view of the child as an active and sociable re-inventor of cultural reality. He believes that we use different kinds of thinking strategies according to our knowledge, the situation and the materials.

The limitations of Bruner's theories

Bruner focused on young children, the function of play, concept formation in junior-aged children and the value of pre-school enrichment. Yet the possibilities for application of these theories in secondary education are endless. Through such work he has enriched the general educational field enormously.

SUMMARY

Bruner's view of the learning process combines many of the best features of the theories of Piaget and Vygotsky with his own original thinking.

Bruner's three stages by which we represent the environment to ourselves are: **enactive representation** (automatic actions which have become items in a 'muscle memory bank'), **iconic representation** (representing by connected imagery) and **symbolic representation** (where the connection between object and representation is arbitrary yet accepted by those with whom we are communicating).

Scaffolding and contingency refer to a process whereby the teacher removes levels of support for a specific task a step at a time, until the pupil is able to perform the task independently. Wood takes this further, describing five levels of support and two rules of contingency (describing the process of moving between adjacent levels of support, depending on the child's performance at the task).

Useful references

Bruner, J. S. (1960) **The Process of Education.** Cambridge, Mass: Harvard University Press.

Bruner, J. S. (1966) **A Study of Thinking.** Chichester: Wiley.

Bruner, J. S. (1966) **Towards a Theory of Instruction.** New York: Norton.

Light, P. *et al* (eds) (1991) **Child Development in a Social Context – Vol. 2 Learning to Think: A Reader.** London: Routledge in association with the Open University.

Maybin, J. *et al* (1992) 'Scaffolding Learning in the Classroom' in Norman, K. (ed.) (1992) **Thinking Voices: The Work of the National Oracy Project.** London: Hodder and Stoughton.

Wood, D. (1988) **How Children Think and Learn.** Oxford: Basil Blackwell.

Motivation

8

'When you wake up in the morning, Pooh,' said Piglet at last, 'What's the first thing you say to yourself?'

'What's for breakfast?' said Pooh. 'What do you say Piglet?'

'I say, I wonder what's going to happen exciting today?' said Piglet. Pooh nodded thoughtfully.

'It's the same thing!' he said.

'What's that?' the Unbeliever asked.

'Wisdom from a western Taoist!' I said. (Hoff in **The Tao of Pooh**)

LEARNING OUTCOMES

When you have read this chapter you should be familiar with the four main types of motivation, attribution theory in terms of gender differences and the teaching implications of differences of motivation.

Introduction

Why do people do the things they do? Why does the human race contain people who do bungee jumping and people who shriek at the sight of a spider? Is it possible to work out the feelings connected to these actions?

REFLECTION

Think of a person you know who is highly motivated and then of one who is apparently lacking in motivation. Consider some possible reasons for this difference, and explain them to a friend.

49

Types of motivation

Motivation is a vast topic, covering many varied attempts to explain behaviour. Inevitably it relates closely to personality, and both are areas in which research should be regarded with deep suspicion if it comes up with clear answers. There are no clear answers, but it is useful to differentiate between **intrinsic motivation** (wanting to learn because the task is of interest), and **extrinsic motivation** (where factors outside the task play a major role).

Broadly speaking, there are four types of motivation (which often occur in a variety of combinations). We will take music as a curriculum area, and you can then see parallels in your own subject.

1 **Intrinsic motivation**, which arises from interest in the activity itself. Think of something from your own life that you do purely for pleasure, such as the personal enjoyment of listening to music.
2 **Social motivation**, where the task or activity is valued, but valued in the context of pleasing other people; for example activities characteristic of many infant or junior-aged pupils. In music it can be the social satisfaction of performing for or with others by playing an instrument.
3 **Achievement motivation**, in which the person wishes to do well at the task in order to compete with others; for instance examinations are usually taken for achievement motivation, not for the sheer joy of taking them. In music, the achievement of grades for good work, given by the subject teacher.
4 **Instrumental motivation**, where motivation is brought about by rewards and punishments which are extrinsic to the task. The task is completed to either obtain a reward or avoid punishment. Good grades in music can lead to the attainment of 'merits' which count towards the school's acknowledgement of excellence or effort, or both.

Types of motivation

50

Read the passage on this page and pick out the different types of motivation to which Katie refers. Then write down three techniques you would use in question and answer sessions in your subject to avoid the situations Katie describes. (You may be interested to know that Katie valued highly the invitation to write a case study for initial teacher education. She consciously adopted a more formal style than she usually uses.)

It is undeniable that most pupils in Mr M's Year 10, set 1 French group are usually very reluctant to volunteer answers in French to questions asked. Mr M puts this down to 'embarrassment of speaking in front of friends'. I think this is a fundamental misunderstanding on his behalf.

Although a genuine lack of understanding, shyness and self-consciousness probably account partly for this state of affairs, as might the potential embarrassment of speaking out in front of friends; I believe that these are not the principal reasons. In my opinion, and from what I have gathered from others in the class, the reason why people are unwilling to offer answers is because they fear being humiliated and patronised by Mr M. Maybe he is not aware of this aspect of his teaching method, and thus does not understand why answers are not freely volunteered.

Language lessons should not be uncomfortable experiences. Yet sometimes I for one am certainly ill at ease (and even nervous) during my French classes. Surely when learning and practising a foreign language, confidence is essential to progression. Mr M insists (rightly) that speaking practice is the best way to improve our French and our French accents. However, I personally am disinclined to proffer answers, knowing from experience that any even minor errors are picked out and scrutinised at length, leaving me feeling stupid and useless! I am not usually a shy or withdrawn person, but find myself increasingly becoming so in French lessons. Any confidence or self-assurance seems to leave me; consequently my French suffers, becoming broken and often incorrect.

I believe the situation could be improved if Mr M appreciated that we are not all naturally brilliant at French, and also if he was more generous in his praise of the (sometimes) good French we produce and most importantly, by offering more encouragement to us.

By complimenting us on our good French he will increase our confidence. This boosted confidence will greatly aid our work, especially oral work. Our French lessons would be much more productive if Mr M were to concentrate on encouragement and helpful criticism, rather than indulging in what seems to give him malicious delight, that is, patronising (and humiliating) his pupils. (Katie, Year 10, aged 14)

The teacher thinks it is a problem of social motivation, that the pupils are socially motivated *not* to contribute. In fact it is instrumental motivation, that is they are avoiding the punishment of humiliation. Mr M uses no rewards or instrumental motivation – Katie suggests that he should.

The following techniques may be useful in question and answer sessions in all subjects:

- encourage fluency over accuracy in order not to inhibit responses, although accuracy must be the major ultimate goal
- offer help if pupils make mistakes, for example repeat phrases correctly in a matter of fact way. In some circumstances pupils need to be 'allowed' to make mistakes – as part of their conceptual development
- comment on errors in the broad context of common mistakes and how to remember the correct versions – avoid making personal comments which pick out individual pupils' specific errors
- carefully monitor question and answer sessions and provide feedback about common errors to the whole class
- try to reduce pressure on individuals by putting pupils in pairs, giving examples of what is expected, getting them to develop conversational exercises
- vary the format, by using alternatives to whole class question and answer sessions, for example ask for written answers, work on partially complete sentences, use free discussion

Subject-specific issues

Consider your subject area in terms of motivation. Take music, for example: most pupils wish to make music and the tasks which are set should aim to satisfy this desire. Can you give an example from your own subject?

Mr M seems to have forgotten that there is a natural curiosity within most children which drives them on to discover, explore and experiment. This intrinsic motivation is believed by many to characterise the young child, particularly at infant and junior school level (see Wood, Bruner). Adult support for the child's thirst for novelty and knowledge can add extrinsic motivation, producing great activity and confidence. Adults can also be disapproving and cause the child to become frustrated.

Both the behaviourist theories (of Skinner) and social constructivist theories (of Vygotsky) assert that the social relationship between adult and child, or expert and novice, can be the major determinant of a child's motivational patterns, in a positive or a negative sense.

I and me

In order to understand recent work on motivation in social constructivist psychology it is necessary to look briefly at the work of a sociologist, G. H. Mead. Although he wrote at the start of this century, his work on the 'self' has become influential again because of his 'symbolic interactionist' theory about the complex interactions between individuals and the society in which they live.

Mead believed that the 'self' is made up of two collaborating parts, the 'I' (spontaneous, impulsive) and the 'me' (which acts as a check and controller). The 'me' acts according to imagined responses of other people to a completed or contemplated act. As I think about what I'm doing, I imagine what others will think of my actions. I internalise my ideas about what they think of me and that motivates me to act in certain ways in the future and affects the 'I'. The 'I' responds to the 'me' and they collaborate with each other. Mead's model cannot be proved – yet you may find it useful for explaining some relationships: consider for example pupils who are being reprimanded about good behaviour. You would be wise to consider whether they have, perhaps, simply taken the line of least resistance in going along with the reprimand.

You need to consider their role as a pupil and the implications of that. They have decided that you will respond even more harshly if they protest. Keeping quiet is the best way to avoid further conflict. They have responded to the imagined attitudes of the teacher towards their own imagined response. They have, briefly, taken account of the role of the teacher and become a 'me', to control their impetuous 'I'.

Remember that, for G. H. Mead, pupils' behaviour can change – they may have been good last week. Thus, the I/me relationship is fluid.

Motivation and self-esteem

The I/me concept can also be useful when looking at self-esteem. Cooley used the image of a looking glass – we see ourselves reflected in others and feel influenced by the reflection, whether we perceive it accurately or not.

. . . people develop images of one another . . . As these images are established – of bravery, refinement, tact, competence, kindness, cruelty and the like – people imagine their own appearance to others in terms of them. That is, the person forms an image of the other, then imagines their appearance to the other from the standpoint of that image, and feels good or bad accordingly. (J. P. Hewitt, 1979)

This process leads to cumulative self-esteem built up in a variety of settings. As such it is a motivational state, it affects how sensitive the person is to others and the judgements they are imagined to make. Sometimes it can elicit complex emotions.

Similarly, it seems likely that the transition from primary to secondary education can provide negative or threatening experiences for many pupils. Their intrinsic motivation may suffer (Donaldson) as a result of inappropriate or inadequate extrinsic motivation.

Motivation and achievement

Motivation is related to choice and our motivation is an aspect of choice. We often choose to do the things we do, even if it sometimes appears to be a forced choice (filling in a tax form has little intrinsic motivation for some of us). Often we are motivated to do something because it gives us a sense of **achievement**. McClelland and Atkinson argued that we have a need for achievement as part of our personalities.

Atkinson used a test of personality called the **Thematic Apperception Test** to look at these achievement needs, particularly with regard to the achievement motivation of people in countries with successful economies. This test consists of a series of pictures, each of which could have a number of interpretations (perhaps a picture of an adult looking over the shoulder of a child who appears to be writing). If these pictures are interpreted in terms of opportunities for achievement (in the example above, this could be seen as an opportunity for the child to achieve something, or improve their performance) the viewer is considered to be high in achievement motivation. Although this is regarded as an important piece of research it is open to the criticism that a person who is *aware* of opportunities for achievement will not necessarily *use* them.

Competitive situations arise at school because of a large number of pupils being gathered together. The teacher may choose to build on this and develop a competitive atmosphere, or develop teaching and learning situations in which each pupil endeavours to improve their own performance (to compete against themselves). However, even the latter situation can be intimidating for some pupils.

Atkinson realised that fear of failure is also a major issue in motivational terms.

REFLECTION

Can you think of a situation in your life where you were motivated *not* to do something and used delaying tactics to avoid it? What made you feel this way?

52

Attribution theory

One of the factors which motivates or demotivates us is the way we feel about our situation. There are many pupils who appear demotivated by school, but put a great deal of energy into non-school activities. Such pupils may believe that they stand more chance of success outside school. Attribution theorists, such as Weiner and Bar-Tal, believe that pupils attribute causality to school events (*If I muck about at school, it's because I'm not clever enough to do the work*). This can lead to the self-fulfilling prophecy (see Chapter 12).

Implications within the learning situation

Arriving at lessons without sufficient equipment, spending a lot of energy misbehaving, writing very little in class, leaving work until the last minute so that it can't be done properly, disturbing other pupils who are trying to work ... all these behaviours can be seen as characteristics of 'bad kids' and they can be resolved partially by using the school's reward and punishment systems. However, it is one thing to increase the likelihood of a particular pupil coming to a lesson with a pen and quite another to motivate them to put pen to paper constructively.

Classroom motivation: effort and ability

Young children (four to six years) tend to regard ability as a changeable feature. Nicholls claims that at five years of age the child fails to distinguish between ability and effort. A child who does well is thought by his peers to be clever and also hardworking. A child who fails at school is considered to be lacking in ability and effort. The effect of this seems to be that the young child is still prepared to respond to teacher encouragement by making an effort even if they are not succeeding. In other words, the pupil of infant school age is still prepared to believe that making an effort will produce the right results.

In pupils of junior and secondary school age there are two factors of which many become conscious – gender differences in the classroom and the possibility of repeated failure.

Gender: classroom motivation of boys and girls

Teachers tend to pay more attention to boys than girls in the following ways:

- Teachers often make complaints about boys' inappropriate behaviour and praise boys' work.
- Teachers give the opposite types of attention to girls – they praise girls' appropriate behaviour and complain about their work standards.
- Teachers tend to attribute the poor work of a boy to lack of motivation rather than lack of ability. For a girl it is the opposite – poor work is perceived as resulting from lack of ability rather than poor motivation (Dweck and Bush, 1978).
- Girls increasingly find themselves attributing their failure to lack of ability, and tend to lose sight of the fact that there may be several factors involved in success or failure, such as the nature of the task and the clarity of explanation.

The implications of these differences in attitude to boys and girls are profound, gender taking on educational meanings which are too simplistic.

REFLECTION

53

You are teaching a subject with a major oral component. On the third lesson with a new Year 11 class, you notice a pupil whom you haven't seen before. She is sitting by the wall, eyes down, hunched over, very still. She nods at your enquiry as to whether she has been in your class before. The others tell you that she's very quiet and wants to be left alone. A quick glance at her work shows you that she has been following the lessons well, but she seems to tense up even more when you are by her desk. What can you do?

This girl's quietness may not be a problem in lessons if, as seems to be the case, she is following the work well. However, there may be cause for concern if there is a major oral component in your subject at GCSE.

Talking to her friends may be informative, as will talking to her Form Tutor and/or Head of Year. You need to differentiate between the professional (and personal) worries which she may evoke in you and the possible practical implications, if any, of her silences.

The pupil's self-perception

Teachers' behaviour can have a major influence on pupils' motivation in the classroom. Pupils' assessment of their own ability or lack of ability is usually closer to the teachers' views than to their parents' views (Bar-Tal 1984). This suggests that teachers often have more influence on pupils' self-perceptions than parents do.

Pupils have other sources of information, for instance their own performance. When a pupil succeeds, this success is often attributed to internal causes, such as one's own intellectual brilliance, perceptiveness and so on. When a pupil fails, this failure is often attributed to external causes, like bad luck or a badly set piece of work.

The pupil can compare present and past achievements, thereby establishing whether the outcome of a particular piece of work was consistent with usual performance.

Another source of information about performance is the nature of the task that is set. Pupils measure their own ability, luck and effort in terms of how they perform and in terms of what they think of the task.

Practical approaches

It should be possible to work within the reward system of the school as a whole – marks, reports, grading systems, tests and examinations. Every aspect of a reward system contains the potential to become too pressurising, which will lead to cheating and absenteeism. However, many pupils respond and even the weakest and the strongest students should be able to feel motivated by appropriate reward. There should be the possibilities within any reward system for praising even the smallest achievement if that is appropriate for a particular pupil.

For you, as the teacher, it is necessary to know your subject specialism very well. Once that is achieved you will be able to structure the lesson so that the pupils can think their way through it with you and achieve success. Success is motivating, even in small steps. Differentiation of the task is vital. It is also necessary to believe in what you are doing, so that you can present a calm, secure environment and be respected. You represent value systems which can offer safety to most of the difficult teenagers you meet, and give them someone with whom they can identify. Showing respect and showing that you care about their learning are valuable strengths.

Motivation of staff and pupils

Build up an informal log for your PDP of the many different motivating events which you will witness in class. Here are some examples:

54
- Pupils' decisions about the learning situation being encouraged
- Teacher emphasis on control of your own actions
- Fast learning pace, with lots of activities
- Getting pupils to do demonstrations
- The teacher being self-critical
- Appropriate use of praise
- Giving pupils choices

Some general rules

The teacher should be able to give direct feedback about effort, for example praising pupils after extra effort has led to success on a difficult task. Keys and Fernandes (1994) carried out research on a sample of 2000 pupils aged 11 to 15. Forty per cent of their sample claimed that they had not had individual discussions with their teachers about their work during that school year.

Comments from the teacher about lack of effort can also be used to indicate the teacher's standards and expectations. Both the above strategies (praise and criticism) should be used appropriately – if negative and positive comments are used randomly, they are assumed by pupils to be a characteristic of the teacher's attitude and not directly related to their own work.

It is necessary to know the pupils well in order to be able to judge whether they are making the effort required of them. Keys and Fernandes (1994) found that a quarter of pupils thought their teachers were 'fairly easily satisfied' with their work.

Teachers often doubt their ability to influence pupils' attitudes, especially when adolescents can appear to resent guidance. We can motivate in several ways: by example, by enthusiasm, by self respect and respect for others and by knowing what we want and being clear about it!

SUMMARY

It is important that teachers are aware of the different types of motivation (intrinsic, social, achievement and instrumental) and how these can be used to inspire pupils to think clearly about the tasks they have been set and to take responsibility for their own learning. Reward systems should cater for the needs of pupils throughout the ability range, without becoming so pressurising that they become counter-productive (which can lead to increased absenteeism or cheating). Teachers should never forget their importance as role models – enthusiasm and a respect for pupils are vital.

Useful references

Bar-Tal, D. (1984) in Barnes, P. (ed.) **Personality, Development and Learning.** London: Hodder and Stoughton.

Biggs, J. B. and Telfer, R. (1987) **The Process of Learning.** 2nd edition. Tasmania: Prentice-Hall.

Dweck, C. S. and Bush, E. S. (1978) *Sex Differences in Learned Helplessness: Differential Debilitation with Peer and Adult Evaluators* in **Developmental Psychology** 12, pp. 147–156.

Fontana, D. (1981) **Psychology for Teachers.** London: Macmillan.

Hewitt, J. P. (1979) **Self and Society.** Needham Heights USA: Allyn and Bacon Inc.

Hoff, B. (1989) **The Tao of Pooh.** London: Mandarin.

Keys and Fernandes in Moon, B. and Shelton Mayes, A. (eds) (1994) **Teaching and Learning in the Secondary School.** London: Routledge.

McClelland, D. C. *et al* (1953) **The Achievement Motive.** New York: Appleton-Century-Crofts.

Mead, G. H. (1934) **Mind, Self and Society.** Chicago: University of Chicago Free Press.

Stones, E. (1979) **Psychopedagogy.** London: Methuen.

Weiner, B. (1984) in Ames and Ames (eds) **Research on Motivation in Education** vol. 1 *Student Motivation.* London: Academic Press.

CHAPTER

Adolescence

9

In our health book there's a chapter on teenage emotions. According to this book, I'm supposed to be caught in a whirlwind of teenage emotions.

(from Margaret Atwood's *Cat's Eye*)

> ### LEARNING OUTCOMES
>
> When you have read this chapter you should be able to be critical of the view that adolescence is an illness, yet also aware of the pressures which teenagers can bring to bear on the adults close to them.
>
> You should make yourself familiar with the six characteristics of adolescence summarised at the end of this chapter, and their implications for us as teachers and ex-teenagers.

Introduction

Adolescence is a word we all use, yet few of us can define it with any accuracy. The Shorter Oxford English Dictionary defines it as the growing up period between childhood and maturity, said to extend over a period of some ten years. But where is the cut-off point between childhood and adolescence? When does an individual leave adolescence to become regarded as a fully mature adult? To answer these questions we must look at adolescence from physiological, emotional and cognitive viewpoints.

There are three areas of adolescence which reflect extreme manifestations of alienation from the parent culture: activists, drop-outs and delinquents. They are, by definition, no longer in school and will not be dealt with here. Adolescents are best discussed here in the context of the school and the culture around the school.

REFLECTION

Consider your teenage years. Can you recall the beliefs you held about the big ideas of life, about your teachers, about yourself? Have you changed much since then?

Physiological definitions of adolescence

The period of development marked at the beginning by the onset of puberty and at the end by the attainment of physiological maturity. It should be noted that the term is much less precise than it appears since both the onset of puberty and the attainment of maturity are effectively impossible to define or specify. (Reber, 1985)

The physiological changes during adolescence are complex. The production of oestrogen (a female sex hormone) gradually rises in both sexes from about seven years of age, with a second very large and rapid rise in girls at puberty.

The production of androgens (the male sex hormones) also increases in both sexes at about eight to ten years of age. A few years later there is a further much sharper rise, an event much more marked in boys than girls. In both sexes the androgens are the hormones which have the most effect on sexual energy and drive and adolescence is a period of greatly increased sexual desire. 'Growth spurts' are a feature of adolescence and can cause poor co-ordination and clumsiness.

In girls puberty begins about two years earlier than in boys and extends over a slightly shorter period, three to four years rather than four to five. For girls puberty may commence at any time between ten to sixteen years of age, while for boys the commencement may be at some point between eleven and seventeen years of age.

The implications of this great variety in growth and definition are many and varied in the classroom, and it is necessary to contend with many facets of the adolescent's personality and position in life.

Emotional development in adolescence

The concept of adolescence seems to belong to advanced technological societies. Children are kept dependent at home until they begin an adulthood full of difficult choices. In more 'primitive' societies, they are often apprenticed to work or marry at puberty (see Margaret Mead). Adolescence is often depicted as a period in an individual's life which is fraught with acne, emotional crises, psychiatric illness and the ruination of relationships with parents.

Longitudinal research by Michael Rutter in Britain and Thomas and Chess in America suggests that many of the problems which surface in adolescence have their roots in pre-pubertal relationships between parent and child.

Alienation and rejection may take on a more public form in the teenage years, but are often simply a manifestation of deeply-rooted problems which have existed within the family for years. This places adolescence on a continuum of development. Family-based explanations are not adequate, however. There is some evidence that secondary schools with similar catchment areas (implying a similar range of family backgrounds) can have marked differences in such areas as examination results or deviant behaviour (Rutter). More recently (1993) The National Commission on Education commented on socio-economic factors and education.

It is estimated that just under a third of under-5s – a higher proportion than of all children – live in households with less than 50% of the national income. Poverty and the associated problems of ill-health create stressful conditions for parents raising families and can jeopardise children's success in school. Over 20% of young people in some poor urban areas of England leave school without qualifications, compared with about 9% in the country as a whole.

Educational achievement is strongly associated with family background. Parental education, particularly the level of education achieved by the mother, has a powerful influence on children's educational progress. When the mother herself has not had the benefit of a good education or learned to recognise its value, there is a risk that her child's early learning experience will be impoverished and certain groups exhibit a strong resistance to education because they perceive it as reflecting the values and aspirations of other social classes.

It is certainly true that adolescents often develop strong sub-cultural bonds with their peers at school. These seem to adults to represent codes of value and of behaviour which are deliberately chosen to be the opposite of those codes presented by the school, such as respect for the weaker members of society.

Such sub-cultures can lead to friction with authority figures at school. It is usually true to say that these groupings are intended to make adults feel excluded. They usually succeed.

It is, however, often the case that these groups operate strict, highly moral codes of conduct. Coffield (with Borrill, 1983) found this to his cost. He worked as a youth leader in a youth club, and was perceived by them to be a bully: he inadvertently violated one of the gang's unwritten rules by trying to be strict with one of their weaker characters. It is more productive to assume that a level of basic trust can be achieved, rather than deciding that there will be fundamental misunderstandings. Coffield realised, too late, that he had failed to achieve a level of basic trust which could have been achieved if he had understood their moral code.

The 'selective amnesia' of adults is an interesting phenomenon in this respect. Many adults have been evasive and secretive and even rebellious as teenagers, yet this is too easily forgotten (see MacFarlane and McPherson, 1987).

Cognitive definitions of adolescence

In Piagetian terms, adolescence is the period which marks the attainment of the capacity for formal operations and to think in a hypothetico-deductive way. In fact, this view has been shown to be false. Martorano (1977) found individual students able to solve some formal operational tasks but not others. However, many adolescents do develop complex thinking. It may be more useful to look at other writers on the subject.

Keating believes that we all possess a strong biological predisposition to impose structure on the world about us, and that this is present soon after birth. By adolescence, there is a great deal more experience and motivation at our disposal.

He proposes that this advanced thinking seems to be developing in adolescence and gives the following five types:

1 **Thinking about possibilities**   Here the teenager is able to look at the real *versus* the possible (or concrete *versus* abstract). There is consideration and examination of possibilities that are not immediately present, for example *Would it be possible to bring about peace in the Middle East?*
2 **Thinking through hypotheses**   Adolescents often play this game, for example *Peace in the Middle East will only be possible if the PLO acknowledges Israel*, versus *Peace in the Middle East will not be possible.*
3 **Thinking ahead**   Planning activities become more common in problem-solving situations. This seems more likely to be carried out competitively by older adolescents, for example *If I want a comprehensive collection of newspaper articles on the Middle East, representing different British views, how can I set about it?*
4 **Thinking about thoughts**   Awareness of one's ability to think about the way we think is called metacognition, for example *What is the nature of racial prejudice?* Sometimes the action itself takes over from the subject matter (*Why am I thinking this?*). Introspection about oneself develops, as does second order thinking. This involves thinking about rules for thinking, for example *Can I use rules of ethics to work out the Middle East problem or are the practical rules of politics the only workable ones?*
5 **Thinking beyond old limits**   This is the area where topics such as identity, society or religion are explored, for example *If there is a God, how can he let wars happen?*

Keating also maintains that much younger children use rules to organise their behaviour and asserts that we should never underestimate the abilities of pre-pubertal children to think in these ways.

Driver looks at the implications which these thought processes can have for the teenager in the classroom:

Secondary school pupils are quick to recognise the rules of the game when they ask, 'Is this what was supposed to happen?' or, 'Have I got the right answer?' The intellectual dishonesty of the approach derives from expecting two outcomes from pupils' laboratory activities which are possibly incompatible. On the one hand pupils are expected to explore a phenomenon for themselves, collect data and make inferences based upon that work; on the other hand, this process is intended to lead to the currently accepted law or principle. (Driver, 1983)

Rosalind Driver, as a scientist, locates her analysis within the laboratory. Edwards and Mercer look at this problem more generally in terms of the teacher's language:

The teacher's dilemma is having to inculcate knowledge while apparently eliciting it. This gives rise to a general ground-rule of classroom discourse in which the pupil's task is to come up with the correct solution to problems seemingly spontaneously while all the time trying to discern in the teacher's clues, cues, questions and presumptions what that required solution actually is. Ritual knowledge is a measure of both the success and the failure of this ground-rule; pupils succeed in the sense that they can say or do the right things, but fail in the manner so insightfully analysed by John Holt (1969), in having acquired a procedural, 'right-answer' – oriented competence instead of a principled, explanation-oriented one. (Edwards and Mercer, 1987)

Given the pressures of covering material necessary for the National Curriculum, these dangers are something the teacher often has to accept, while attempting to acknowledge them by taking certain measures. These can include:

● introduction of a topic at a whole class level, to ensure initial sharing of common knowledge
● carefully structured group work, in which the pupils are clearly aware of the task limits
● intervention by the teacher at regular intervals, when needed, using Wood's five levels of control and his 'two rules' (see Chapter 6 on Vygotsky)
● class discussion at the end of the session for further clarification and individual as well as group contributions

Subject-specific issues

Consider a practical problem for adolescents within your subject: in music, for example, singing is an important activity. There are implications for music lessons when boys' voices start to break. In modern languages, the mismatch between mother tongue communication and the restricted level of the target language can cause frustration. What about your subject?

SUMMARY

Six characteristics of adolescence

To a greater or lesser extent, many writers have agreed on the following characteristics of adolescence. Some implications within the classroom and school are considered.

1 Role identity and individual identity come into conflict (Erikson), that is, the importance of the peer group may increase, but so will the desire to be a unique person with an identifiable style. Much experimentation may take place.

Implications It is necessary to be sensitive to peer group pressures; some individuals need to be disciplined quietly, away from the group (Coffield).

2 Acceptance by the opposite sex may become an important factor (MacFarlane and McPherson).

Implications Both sexes need to be treated with the same respect and dignity. Unexplained emotional undercurrents may emerge in class which should be noted but not allowed to interfere with teaching. You need to be sensitive to the possibility of 'teenage crushes', and be firm about keeping your distance. Consult a senior colleague if in doubt.

3 Predictions about status and worries about adult life can begin to dominate the thoughts of the sixteen to eighteen year-old.

Implications Subject teachers need to be aware of support systems available within the school for training and further education.

4 Major idealistic dissatisfactions may emerge often focusing on the injustices and violence of the adult world. Ideological discussions may erupt (Piaget).

Implications Classroom management needs to embody discipline techniques which are as fair and consistent as possible. Willingness to set up debates is useful, as is the sensitivity to stop them happening if they detract from subject teaching.

5 Adults are watched very carefully – partly as role models, partly as emotional supporters and comforters, and third to be criticised because they inevitably fail to do things 'properly'.

Implications It is essential to maintain clear expectations of reasonable conduct and reasonable work standards and not to be negotiated downwards into lowering of standards (Rutter), or into loss of self esteem. 'Going native' would make it impossible to teach effectively.

6 Relationships with adults become problematic, characterised by misunderstandings which arise because of the three different – yet in practice not easily differentiated – tasks described in point 5 above (role model, supporter, scapegoat).

Implications Many of us may find that unfinished business surfaces from our own adolescence, perhaps a feeling that we were not properly listened to by our own parents, feelings about unjust discipline, missed opportunities and so on. These should be acknowledged within ourselves and taken into account when dealing with confrontations. It is too easy to fight our own old battles when we should be looking closely at specific situations as they present themselves in class.

Useful references

Adelson, J. (ed.) (1980) **Handbook of Adolescent Psychology.** New York: Wiley.

Atwood, M. (1992) **Cat's Eye.** London: Virago.

Coffield, F. and Borrill, C. (1983) *Entrée and Exit* in **The Sociological Review** 31.

Driver, R. (1983) **The Pupil as Scientist?** Milton Keynes: Open University Press, p. 3.

Edwards, D. and Mercer, N. (1987) **Common Knowledge: The Development of Understanding in the Classroom.** London: Methuen.

Edwards, D. and Mercer, N. (1989) *Reconstructing Context: The Conventionalising of Classroom Knowledge* in **Discourse Processes** 12, pp. 91–104.

MacFarlane, A. and McPherson, A. (1987)**The Diary of a Teenage Health Freak.** Oxford: Oxford University Press.

Martorano, S. C. (1977) *A Developmental Analysis of Performance on Piaget's Formal Operations Tasks* in **Developmental Psychology** 13, pp. 666–672.

Mead, G. H. (1934) **Mind, Self and Society.** Chicago: University of Chicago Free Press.

National Commission in Education (1993) **Learning to Succeed.** London: Heinemann.

Reber, A. S. (1985) **Penguin Dictionary of Psychology.** Harmondsworth: Penguin.

Rutter, M. (1979) **Fifteen Thousand Hours: Secondary Schools and their Effects on Children.** London: Open Books.

Townsend, S. (1982) **The Secret Diary of Adrian Mole aged Thirteen and Three Quarters.** London: Mandarin.

Language Awareness (1)

10

Language is a city to the building of which every human being brought a stone.

(Emerson)

LEARNING OUTCOMES

When you have read this chapter, you will be more aware of the complex relationship between language and identity. You will also recognise that language diversity has implications for teaching and learning.

Introduction

Our language is an important part of our identity and many of our judgements, about ourselves and about others are to do with language. It is difficult, at times, to see language as acquired, or culturally transmitted. We often feel that how people speak and how they write is purely an expression of their personality or intelligence. Their language may inspire us, or it may irritate us. We find some accents more pleasing than others. We may be annoyed by other people's verbosity or by their reticence, while for many, swearing is a moral, rather than a linguistic, issue. All these are judgements about people's language.

REFLECTION

R

57

Have any judgements ever been made about you, do you think, because of your language? Do you write particularly fluently? Do people say that you tell jokes well? Or have you ever been humiliated by poor spelling; teased because of your accent; accused of being boring? Or bossy?

Can you see any links between the qualities you warm to, or dislike, and your own language history? A preference for a particular accent would be a simple example. When we are aware of our own feelings about language, we can have more confidence in our professional judgements about the children we teach. We can become more effective communicators by examining how we use language ourselves.

Language skills audit

58

Complete a language skills audit on yourself, which may be used in your Profile of Competence. What language skills do you feel are your strengths? Be generous. Don't forget good listening skills or dramatic performance or the ability to efficiently chair meetings. All these skills can help you communicate in the classroom. Any gaps or areas you feel need development? How could you begin, *through your teaching*, to address them?

Extracts from Language Skills Audits completed by trainee teachers:

Language strengths	Gaps in weaker areas	Action for development
I can explain things clearly. I was a demonstrator in a University laboratory for a year while doing my Master's Degree.	I tend to interrupt others. I jump in too quickly.	While demonstrating the burning fuels experiment I'll ask the pupils to describe what is happening, and give them time to answer, rather than tell them first. I am confident that I can then weave some of their words and ideas into my follow-up explanation.
Good listener. Remember people's names easily.	Soft voice that may not be heard at the back of the class.	Insist on a routine at the beginning of lesson. Year 7 are particularly chatty. Have a signal for them to be quiet. Raise my hand? Make lots of eye contact when talking. Speak to individuals who are difficult – let them know I am interested in them.
I am assertive. Good at encouraging people, getting them to do what I want and I can lead teams. I've led several outward bound expeditions and been on many field trips.	My handwriting is untidy and I am still told that my spelling is weak.	I am now word processing my work sheets and handouts. Before the lesson I work out what I will have to write on the board and I make sure I spell all the terminology correctly. I have found that it's best to admit to mistakes rather than try to cover them up.
I have written and edited articles for magazines. I worked for a publishing house for a year. I had to be very organised and efficient to get on with my boss.	My mentor told me that I sound very formal and strict and that the pupils are reacting to the way I say things. I am really very anxious and worried about losing control.	I have decided to set a greater variety of written tasks. I have written a guide to their next assignment which gives more individual choice to the children. I think giving the children more choice will relax them (and hopefully me).

Standard English in schools

There is a high probability that, however varied the speech of the readers of this book, most of the *formal* speaking you do and almost all the writing will be Standard English. SE is the language of Government, Law and Education. This is an accident of geography. The South East of England was the seat of power and learning when the language was standardised by Caxton's printing press and encoded in Johnson's dictionary. It was, and is, a dialect like any other. There is an idea, widespread in our society, that SE is *correct* English and other variations are *wrong*. This is not so. All dialects geographical, social, or temporal, have grammatical rules which linguists can describe in the same way as they can explain the rules of SE.

However, matched guise tests in which people are rated for qualities such as intelligence, honesty and friendliness, show that we tend to stereotype people according to their accent or dialect. In these tests, people listen to recordings of speakers with different accents or dialects. Unknown to the listeners, the different accents or dialects are spoken by the *same* speaker, that is in a different guise. These tests clearly reveal specific widespread attitudes to ethnic and regional variations.

These are stereotypes, which we need to be aware of in a classroom. They may affect us and the children we teach.

I hated it when I first came. The first time I spoke to the class some of them looked at each other and I saw them raise their eyebrows and smirk. I got sick of the jokes about sheep and leeks. (A newly qualified teacher)

We moved from Bath to the Midlands and I cried every day. Not just because I missed my friends but because they keep on at me about my accent. They'd say, 'Say we walked to Bath, along the path to the castle.' And then they'd laugh at me.

(A Year 12 girl)

Some people try, not always consciously, to lose the accent they had when growing up. Others are proud of their origins and keep their accents and dialect throughout life, however far from home they move. Research by Labov, Milroy, Cheshire and others show that some people's identity with their origins, or with their peer group, and their alienation from the prestige culture, is so keenly perceived that certain features are exaggerated in the language they use. This may be especially so during adolescence when membership of the peer group is an important part of their identity.

Vicky

Over the last ten years I have taught three children from one family, Surinder, Harvinder and Vicky. The eldest, Surinder, told me that his parents spoke Punjabi at home and that he dealt with most of the correspondence that came into the house. I also taught his brother, Havinder, who was keen to do well and was very conscientious. He said he found English difficult but liked it and he drafted and redrafted work until he got it right. I was delighted with his GCSE B Grade.

A few years later I had a girl in my new Year 8 class who was not working and who was avoiding putting pen to paper. Trying to start a conversation, so that I could find out what the problem was, I asked if she was bilingual. Her reaction was a frosty, 'What?'

'I just wondered if you speak another language at home?' By this time I knew I'd over-stepped the mark.

'What do you think I am? I'm British,' she said with such anger that I never dared mention it again, even though I soon realised that she was from the same family who I knew spoke Punjabi at home. I understood why she was called Vicky. It was the Anglicised name she had chosen for herself. At 14 she truanted excessively and soon dropped out of school altogether.

REFLECTION

Is there any mention of bilingualism in your subject's National Curriculum? Can you find any examples of how your school acknowledges the cultural backgrounds of pupils? Do the teachers use analogies or examples in their teaching from these cultures?

Language stereotyping

There are stereotypes, other than those associated with regional or ethnic variation, that are just as deserving of a teacher's sensitivity. Research shows that men and women tend to use language differently and we know that there are complex relationships between language and social class. One experiment, cited by Coates, neatly illustrates the interrelationship of language and gender, language and social class.

The ambiguity of the position of middle-class male speakers and working class female speakers is nicely pinpointed by the results of the following experiment (Edwards, 1979)

Adult judges were presented with tape recordings of twenty middle class and twenty working class children and asked to identify whether children were male or female from their speech. In a minority of cases the judges were not able to do this accurately . . . The judges did not make random mistakes; they made mistakes about two sets of children; middle-class boys and working-class girls. Middle-class boys sounded like girls to the judges, while working-class girls sounded like boys.

(Jennifer Coates, 1992, *Women, Men and Language*)

Concern is presently expressed about the under-achievement of boys despite an HMI/Ofsted report (*Boys and English, 1993*) that concluded there is no evidence of differences between boys' and girls' *innate* linguistic ability. At GCSE in 1995 13 per cent more girls achieved A to C in all subjects, yet girls are still reluctant to opt for Science subjects in equal numbers to boys. Some researchers feel that teachers have a crucial interactional role to play in these issues of Equal Opportunities.

There are other occasions when linguistic expectations can blind us to a child's ability or lead us to misconstrue their behaviour. All these comments were made in a staffroom within a few days of each other.

It went really well, except for Sarah. She only wrote four lines and they were awful. Look at her spelling and all this crossing out. Yet she answered well in the lesson. When they started writing, she just looked out of the window most of the time.

John can't stand criticism. If you go near him to correct his work, he becomes very nervous. He won't work in a group like the others. Do you know, I don't think he's ever looked at me. He was really rude to the visiting speaker. At 5 to 12 he looked at his watch and started to pack away his things. Shall I put him in detention?

I'm amazed. Simon got a Level 5 Science SAT. I know he had an amanuensis but even so, I didn't think it was possible and I'd given him a Level 3. What set are we going to put him in next year?

REFLECTION

61

What is your initial response to these remarks?

Does it make a difference if you are told that Sarah is severely dyslexic, John suffers from Aspergers Syndrome (a variety of autism) and Simon comes from a family with an inherited language impairment which leaves him illiterate but of average intelligence?

It would really have helped me on teaching practice if I'd have had a list of children's reading ages and special needs.

I didn't want to know who was difficult or who had special needs. I didn't want to anticipate problems. I wanted to find out what I thought first.

What are your views? Are labels ever useful?

Are any children in your class noticeable or labelled because of their language? What effect, if any, beneficial or detrimental, does it have on their achievement *across the curriculum*? With the consent of the school, track a child throughout the school day. Be sensitive to the needs of the child. People are often interested in children who seem odd in some way. This was picked up in one school where a pupil remarked that the observer was here to watch 'Psycho'. The tracking may therefore have to be very discreet. How do others react to the child? The teacher responsible for a child's pastoral welfare may find your observations helpful.

SUMMARY

- Language is an important part of a child's identity and self-esteem.
- The child belongs to at least three different speech communities; home, school and peer group.
- Competence in Standard English is desirable as the most universally understood dialect and we need to help children use it to communicate. Rather than thinking of changing language, we should aim to extend the range of styles available to children.
- Teachers should be wary of labelling and stereotyping children.

Useful references

Carter, R. (ed.) (1990) **Knowledge about Language and the Curriculum.** London: Hodder and Stoughton.

Coates, J. (1993) **Women, Men and Language.** 2nd edition. London: Longman.

Cox, B. (1991) **Cox on Cox: An English Curriculum for the 1990s.** London: Hodder and Stoughton.

Crystal, D. (1987) **The Cambridge Encyclopedia of Language.** Cambridge University Press.

Jackendorff, R. (1993) **Patterns in the Mind – Language and Human Nature.** Hemel Hempstead: Harvester/Wheatsheaf.

Langford, D. (1994) **Analysing Talk.** London: Macmillan.

Perera, K. (1984) **Children's Writing and Reading: Analysing Classroom Language.** Oxford: Basil Blackwell (particularly pp. 325–328).

Sutton, C. (1981) **Communicating in the Classroom.** London: Hodder and Stoughton.

Tough, J. (1985) **Listening to Children Talking.** School Curriculum Development Committee.

Trudgill, P. (1975) **Accent, Dialect and the School.** London: Edward Arnold.

Trudgill, P. (1983) **Sociolinguistics: An Introduction to Language and Society.** London: Penguin Books.

Trudgill, P. and Hannah, J. (1985) **International English: A Guide to Varieties of Standard English.** London: Edward Arnold.

Personality

11

He was humming his hum to himself, and walking along gaily, wondering what every-one else was doing, and what it felt like, being somebody else. (from *Winnie the Pooh*)

LEARNING OUTCOMES

When you have read this chapter you should be familiar with the main theories of personality and their usefulness. These are: **psychoanalytic** theory, **trait** theory, **situationist** theory, **interactionist** theory, **phenomenal** theory and **humanistic** theory. Each, in turn, will be examined for its explanations of and solutions to a case study of bullying.

Introduction

There are as many theories of personality as there are weeks in the year. Many contradict each other and it seems extraordinary that psychology cannot present a more coherent picture of human nature. Perhaps this reflects the complexity of the human character and of our beliefs about ourselves and others.

It is important to clarify your views and to consider the opinions of others, because your beliefs about personality will influence two important aspects of your teaching life:

- it affects what you think about pupils' and colleagues' behaviour
- it will affect your approach to sorting out problems

We will look at six theories of personality in turn. Psychoanalytic and trait theories focus on the individual. Situationist theory focuses on the environment. Interactionist, phenomenal and humanistic theories are concerned with individuals' perceptions and the interaction between these individuals and their environments.

Jack

We will consider a case study of bullying, attention-seeking and lack of motivation and then see what different view-points can be brought to bear on it.

Jack is 13. He is causing disruption and producing very little work. He came up from his junior school with a group of friends and perpetuated with them the Cuckoo

Club which they had developed in Year 5. If a child hears a cuckoo call close by in the playground, it means that they are likely to be beaten up or verbally tormented by a member of Jack's gang. His form tutor is very worried.

Jack is heavily built, wears very thick spectacles and is reported by the school to have slight fine-motor co-ordination problems (his hand movements are clumsy). He achieved very high scores on Verbal Reasoning Tests and appears to have no difficulty with reading and writing. He possesses extensive general knowledge and talks to adults with great animation on subjects in which he is interested. His mother and father are very supportive.

Psychoanalytic theories: focus on the individual

Freud is the most famous of the psychoanalytic thinkers. His work can also be called a 'self-theory' of personality because it places more emphasis on the individual (self) than on social factors.

He explained behaviour in terms of the human being as an energy system, driven by sexual and aggressive drives and operating in the pursuit of pleasure (tension reduction). In order to try to understand the unconscious mind he analysed dreams and neuroses, slips of the tongue, works of art and cultural rituals. The unconscious mind can be observed only indirectly and therefore evidence in support of Freud's theories is hard to find and very subjective.

Freud's theory is deterministic, that is experiences in infancy will to a large extent determine your adult personality. The only way to reduce the effect of bad experiences in infancy is to recall them, discuss them and resolve them (psychoanalysis).

Psychoanalytic theory of the bully

Bullies are often bullied themselves by other members of the family or by other children and they 'pass on' the treatment by doing it to others. There is also an assumption that the bully derives pleasure from his bullying.

Solution

Psychoanalysis, which will go on for several years, can be used for the reduction of the aggressive need to bully. Counselling might be provided for Jack within the school. His past may need to be discussed and reworked.

Critique

Is this solution realistic, given the time constraints of the school day? The theory also assumes that the problem will remain unresolved unless treated by psychoanalysis, yet there appears to be little evidence of the success of such treatments.

Trait theory

This presents the belief that there are features within each personality which are stable over time and throughout situations, and allow us to predict consistently how a person will behave. This theory is not easily able to account for inconsistencies in behaviour. Eysenck is the best-known modern trait theorist, using polarities such as introversion–extroversion, and setting individual differences within a context of personality types. If inventories (questionnaires) produce consistency over time, it may be that they reflect one of the ways in which we perceive ourselves, when we sit down to answer a questionnaire about our personalities.

Trait theory of the bully

This would hold that there is an inherent personality trait within Jack which makes him a bully; perhaps he needs to dominate, or inflict pain.

Solution

Jack should be encouraged to own up to this problem trait and use the positive sides of his nature to control his dark side.

Critique

Is this a rather simplistic approach? Suggesting that we can predict personality features may produce a powerful and sometime counter-productive form of the self-fulfilling prophecy (see Chapter 12 on The Self-fulfilling Prophecy). There may even be a similarity here to astrology.

Situationist theory: focus on the environment

This maintains the view that we are all influenced to a major extent by the situations in which we find ourselves. Thus, for behaviourists like Skinner, personality is a bundle of habits learnt from others.

Situationist theory of the bully

Jack has picked up inappropriate habits.

Solution

In order to change his behaviour, the situation needs to be changed. How can this be achieved? First, he needs to replace the inappropriate behaviour with appropriate behaviour, for example we need to get him to work well in class. Secondly, he may need social skills training to develop more peaceful ways of interacting with his peer group in class and in the playground.

Critique

This situationist approach can be quite useful as it implies that there is some mismatch between the child and the environment, but it relies on observable behaviour.

Interactionist theory

This has developed as a combination of some of the most useful ideas from both trait theory and situationist theory. Pervin summed it up in an article, *Am I me or the situation?* Here there is an interaction between the environment and personal characteristics of the individual which determines the individual's behaviour. This can develop over a period of time and may become self-perpetuating. It can be similar to the mechanisms discussed in Chapter 12 on The Self-fulfilling Prophecy.

Example 1

A pupil and a teacher may find a situation developing in which the pupil is labelled as disruptive over a period of time and in which they are competing for the control of the classroom. Can this be the case with Jack?

Interactionist theory of the bully

Jack finds himself – or puts himself – in situations where he can bully and dominate others. He may have certain personality features which encourage this, for instance he may be self-conscious about his thick spectacles.

Solution

Analysis of the situations is essential in order to change them. What is it about lessons and playtime that makes Jack so reactive and disruptive? How can the staff change this? It must be remembered that the adults form an important element in these situations.

Critique

The interactionist approach can also be useful because it suggests that other people, as well as Jack, may need to change in order to help him outgrow his predicament. What it lacks is the means to analyse the environmental characteristics: such methods of analysis need to be developed.

The phenomenal approach to personality

This is based on the attempt to understand personality by looking at how a person sees the world and how that person understands events.

Kelly (1963) has developed a **personal construct theory**. This is based on the belief that we make our own personal construction of reality by seeing recurrent emotional patterns unique to each of us.

Kelly also believes in our power to shape events by thinking creatively and thereby changing our behaviour. He calls this **constructive alternativism**. He explains that *even the most obvious occurrences of daily life might appear utterly transformed if we were inventive enough to construe them differently.*

Example 2

A new teacher entering a classroom may be greeted with giggles or a chair crashing over. These events may be seen by the adult as threatening when in fact they conceal the pupils' fear of an unknown adult.

Solution: the phenomenal theory of control

If teachers can show calm confidence and control of situations, their pupils will feel safe and their behaviour will become appropriate. Teachers' **self-image** (that is the way they see themselves) needs to be positive. Teachers need high **self-esteem** (that is the way they evaluate themselves), and they need to have a realistic mental image of an **ideal self** (that is the way they would like to be). It would be unrealistic to have an ideal self who was either a 'pal' to all the pupils or an autocrat.

Critique

A problem with Kelly's theory is that it is difficult to work out what people really think. It is even harder to develop a link between what people think and what they do, that is between attitudes and actions, or beliefs and behaviour.

Example 3

Many pupils with severe behavioural difficulties have lost sight of how to behave acceptably. If Jack can make a commitment to change, then supportive adults can help, but it is a complex interaction between attitude change and behaviour change. It may be easier to change Jack's behaviour in order to change his attitudes!

Humanistic theories

Humanistic theory comes within the phenomenal approach. Carl Rogers is the major humanistic theorist and he places a great deal of emphasis on freedom of choice and the uniqueness of each individual. Vernon and Maslow are also important.

Here we will concentrate on Rogers. He believes that we can understand others only by letting them be themselves and by respecting their views even if they are different from our own. He would maintain that individuals who are in trouble actually know the answer to their problems, if we give them the chance to express it. Rogers can be seen as the main inspiration behind the counselling movement.

Rogers gives justification for the power of respect. Many behavioural or motivational problems can be helped by what he calls 'unconditional positive regard', or warmth and respect given without strings attached.

As a means of supporting 'good' aspects of a person he also advocates 'conditional positive regard', or warmth and respect given only when the person responds appropriately. Busy teachers often find this is the last solution they would think of, yet it is often highly effective.

Humanistic theory of the bully

Jack underestimates the needs and feelings of others and undervalues himself.

Solution

He needs a greater sense of self-worth, to understand what his victims experience and to be able to offer them something which is more supportive than destructive.

Critique

In the school situation it is not possible to be entirely non-judgemental, as we have to think of the safety and self-respect of others. However, if disciplinary action has to be taken to control anti-social behaviour, Rogerian methods of therapeutic counselling can be used later to resolve the pupil's anger and to plan for the future. (See also the Listening for Answers section in Chapter 38.)

Behaviour

Return to the description of Jack and make notes on these three issues:

● What do you perceive to be the most appropriate theory to explain Jack?
● What would you do to change the story?
● What behaviour policies do you meet in your first few weeks in school?

SUMMARY

The sequence of theories about personality considered in this chapter moves from a focus on the individual to a focus on the environment and finishes with theories which focus on the complex interaction between two. None of these is particularly satisfactory as each overstates its case. Moreover, those theories which favour interactions between the child and its context are bedevilled by the fact that each changes the other continually, and nothing stays still for long enough to be analysed. Analysis of the process of these changes is even harder, although as teacher-researcher you will develop some robust techniques for this purpose. You should familiarise yourself with these theories in this chapter in order to clarify your own beliefs, and read further with a critical eye.

We will need to find out more about Jack and his friends and the situations in which they find or put themselves. This can best be achieved by taking different ideas and solutions from the various personality theories and combining them. Jack's case study will be developed further in Part 3, Chapter 33.

Even more important is the need to use our knowledge of the teaching and learning process and of good teaching skills in order to decide what is appropriate and possible for each pupil. School cannot transform an unhappy child, yet we can strive to develop an individual's sense of purpose, self-esteem and respect for others by careful, firm and sensitive management of difficult situations and appropriate support with schoolwork. Keep an open mind.

Useful references

Barnes, P. *et al* (eds) (1984) **Personality, Development and Learning.** Milton Keynes: Open University Press.

Brown, J. A. C. (1961) **Freud and the Post-Freudians.** London: Penguin.

Colman, A. (ed.) (1995) **The Longman Essential Psychology Series.** Longman.

Cook, M. (1984) **Levels of Personality.** London: Cassell.

Gross, R. D. (1992) **The Science of Mind and Behaviour.** 2nd edition. London: Hodder and Stoughton.

Kelly, G. A. (1963) **A Theory of Personality: The Psychology of Personal Constructs.** London: Norton.

Oden, S. and Asher, S. R. (1977) *Coaching Children in Social Skills for Friendship Making* in **Child Development**, 48.

Rogers, C. R. (1983) **Freedom to Learn for the 80s.** Columbus: Charles E. Merrill.

The Self-fulfilling Prophecy

12

'Boy angels have golden balls'

LEARNING OUTCOMES

When you have read this chapter you should be able to explain Rogers' analysis of the **self-fulfilling prophecy** and be sensitive to its implications with regard to gender, ethnicity and class. A self-fulfilling prophecy is a prediction which is fulfilled simply because it is made. In other words, a definition of a situation evokes a new behaviour, which makes the original concept come true. Whatever your views are about free will, you need to consider the influence which we can and do have on others. This can be used to raise pupils' levels of attainment and self concept – or it can be used to lower them, often unintentionally.

Introduction

Children develop through social relationships. They can assimilate their ideas about themselves by their interactions within these relationships, as well as by the different treatment they receive.

This boy [Muswell] is very poor but a very nice little kid, but he is illiterate, of course, but he's helpful, he'd do anything for you. I got on with him very well, very, very well, different from some of these illiterates – behind your back merchants, aren't they?

Now the girls, I don't know so much about. Sandra, she's a pleasant girl. This one [Dianne] is very pleasant, not much ability but pleasant. Shirley is very difficult to get through to, always reserved, doesn't say much, a bit sullen. (Woods, 1979)

We don't have many of them here.

Ethnic minorities are not my department. See the remedial teachers.

I treat them all the same and you are asking me to treat them as if they are different and calling attention to the problem.

My subject does not lend itself to a multicultural approach. (Batelaan, 1983)

Peter Woods conducted interviews with teachers as part of his research into teachers' expectations of their pupils. He found a strong tendency to look for 'cues' to identify pupils, for example 'illiterate', 'broken home' or 'nice'. This type of shorthand is used by most of us at some time or other and typifies a labelling habit which is particularly noticeable in big institutions such as hospitals, schools and offices. In school staffrooms, conversations can create images of pupils regarding their background, sex and race which reinforce our expectations of their educational potential.

All teachers have expectations of their pupils. These expectations range from hoping that the pupils will stay in the room to hoping that they will learn what they are being taught. It seems to be a human characteristic to have expectations of others. One of the major purposes they serve is to enable us to predict responses and behaviours. Thus the parents who state, within earshot of their child, that she is always carsick, may well be ensuring that they can predict the future . . . but at what a cost!

Teacher expectancy is inevitable. When it occurs, however, there is a danger that patterns of behaviour can be established which *lock the various participants into rather predictable pathways* (Rogers, 1982).

Rogers suggests that there are two kinds of expectancy effects:

1   those resulting from administrative decisions;
2   those resulting from teacher/pupil interactions.

Administrative decisions, such as classroom groupings, subject settings or examination groupings, are more likely to affect secondary-aged pupils. However, the ability to understand the teacher's expectations starts very young. Crocker and Cheeseman (1988) found that five to seven-year-olds can rank themselves for academic ability according to their teachers' view of them, and where teachers grouped children, often children knew the significance of the groupings. It seems clear that even five year-olds are aware of their teachers' expectations of them because there was a high degree of agreement between self, peers and teacher as to the order of children in any particular classroom.

How does the **self-fulfilling prophecy** work? Rogers (1989, in Woodhead, 1991) lists seven steps:

1 The teacher forms an expectation of a child.
2 The teacher behaves differently based on that expectation.
3 The pupil notices the change in the teacher's behaviour.
4 The pupil's self-concept and motivation are influenced (a psychological factor).
5 The pupil behaves differently (more in line with expectations).
6 Effects can be seen in the pupil's conduct and educational performance.
7 Feedback to the teacher finds the teacher's expectations confirmed.

ADHD

65

Read the following case study and number each stage in accordance with Rogers' seven steps. What action would you take to avoid this deterioration of your relationship with a pupil in a similar situation?

Last week – Diary by Elaine (Year 8 form tutor)

I received a letter from Jimmy's GP. The GP wrote about Jimmy's behaviour difficulties. He has told Jimmy's parents that he believes he probably has Attention Deficit Hyperactivity Disorder. I felt rather stunned really, because I was not particularly worried about Jimmy and there are certainly worse behaviour problems in this group. Have I been negligent in failing to notice something?

I suppose I had better re-consider my discipline procedures – I mean, if he can't help it, perhaps I'd better make allowances and ease off a bit. I have been quite strict with him.

A week later. I've been using the ADHD checklist which the GP sent me, and I must say I can tick off most of the items for Jimmy, e.g. 'inattention': often has difficulty sustaining attention in tasks or play activity, or 'hyper activity/impulsivity': often talks excessively and often has difficulty awaiting turn.

Perhaps he has got ADHD. In fact his behaviour seems to have got worse. I don't see how he could have noticed that I have decided to 'ease up' on him, but he is certainly less respectful to me at the moment. I wonder if he has sensed something? He seems more 'jumpy' as well, and I worry about whether this will affect his work.

Two weeks later. Trouble with Jimmy. He seems not to be interested in work at the moment – he also doesn't seem interested in keeping within the rules – poor concentration, impulsive behaviour, lower standards of work. Put him on report? I thought I had a good relationship with him and now I just don't know. [At this point the teacher's expectations seem confirmed. Re-referral to the GP might lead to Jimmy being given Ritalin, a drug associated with ADHD and commonly used in the United States to reduce activity. Jimmy's difficulties may actually have been made worse by this diagnosis and a teacher in this position could decide to take the following action.]

What could the teacher do now?

● Round robin (request information in writing from other staff about Jimmy's progress)
● Ask Jimmy to use a standard school 'on report' form for self-assessment purposes or
● Devise a specific behaviour sheet for him to monitor behaviour and work
● Talk to him about the situation: use structured discipline or 'brief therapy' techniques (see Listening for Answers in Chapter 38).

R **REFLECTION**

66

Please consider the case study on page 113 in the light of the following information.

The DSM-IV (American Psychiatric Association 1994) criteria for making an ADHD diagnosis requires six or more symptoms of inattention, or six or more symptoms of hyperactivity/impulsivity to have persisted for at least six months to a degree that is maladaptive and inconsistent with developmental level. Yet these 'symptoms' are described with the use of terms such as 'often', 'quite' and 'excessively' – which are difficult to measure reliably. The United Nations' International Narcotics Control Board believes (New Scientist March 1996) that between 3–5% of American schoolchildren are being treated for ADHD with methylphenidate (known as Ritalin). Ritalin is a potentially addictive stimulus that boosts norepinephrine levels (Norepinephrine is a neurochemical that, with others, has been implicated in mental illness for decades). ADHD is often presented as a construct which has the explanatory power to tell us that children are suffering from 'it' when their behaviour fits the DSM-IV criteria and is hindering their progress significantly. Whalen and Henker (1996) believe this to be unrealistic.

As children grown and learn, they reach complex understandings about their social and cultural background and they learn to distinguish significant features of that background such as gender, ethnicity and social class. As if by osmosis, they will absorb factors which they believe to be significant within their own personal construction of reality. As with most human events, this developmental interplay between context and the individual is highly complex: research evidence in these three areas is often contradictory and contentious, yet influenced by self-fulfilling prophecies in such powerful ways that we ignore them at our peril.

Gender and the self-fulfilling prophecy

According to Lloyd and Duveen (1986), the biological sex of a baby acts as a **signifier**. This assigns the child to a gender category which is part of a gender system residing in members of society as *a shared set of beliefs about the nature, behaviour and value of females and males.* By six months of age boys are being encouraged to play in different ways from those encouraged for girls. For research purposes Lloyd and Duveen dressed infants as boys or girls regardless of biological sex. They found that all those dressed as boys received from the 'experimental' mothers much more verbal encouragement to gross motor activity. It seems likely that the gender system is expressed very early through linguistic and lucid (play-related) systems.

A four year-old boy returns from acting in a nativity play as an angel and is asked 'Did you wear tinsel?' The withering reply is 'Mummy, girl angels wear tinsel, boy angels have golden balls'.

At even as early an age as three the pupil comes to the teacher at least partly moulded by a socially constructed gender identity. By the age of six to seven many children appear to hold strong opinions about what is appropriate for boys and girls. It seems reasonable that we should want to know what makes a girl different from a boy: the problems arise if we find ourselves believing that it is inappropriate for a girl to be good at science or a boy to be good at languages.

It is worth differentiating, at this point, between the naive beliefs of toddlers (*I am going to be a man when I grow up* say some little girls) and the later sophistication of junior school-aged male/female stereotyping. Clarricoates (1987, in Skelton, 1988) noted that girls are vulnerable to *male definitions of achievement*, and quotes Smith (1984) who states that *girls prefer familiar, straightforward, repetitive work requiring care and accuracy, to new challenging concepts and problems.* Clarricoates recommends that . . . *what researchers must do is to take into account the intuitive grasp that children have of the processes that mould them.* One way of doing this is for the teacher to become a researcher: if pupils are asked for their opinions they will state that, for example, boys are used for moving furniture and girls are used for running errands. Delamont believes that schools 'do not simply reflect the different sex roles and gender differentiation of the wider society but exaggerate and amplify such distinctions' (Delamont and Galton, 1980, p. 272).

Eleven years of gender differentiation will lead to the pupils' secondary school perpetuating or amplifying it in terms of subject-related achievement (girls to modern languages and English, boys to sciences and maths). These tendencies are now less marked at GCSE in Mathematics where the trend narrows the gap annually between boys and girls, although at the highest levels (Level 8 or above at age 14, grades A* at GCSE) there are still only two girls to every three boys.

Gender differences

Consider your own subject area. Are there any instances where gender makes a difference, for example boys opting for German instead of French because of its more 'macho' image. How might you redress any imbalances?

Croll and Moses (1990, in Rogers and Kutnick) point out that teachers often perceive boys as more 'difficult' than girls. Girls are expected to be conformist, boys are seen to be more demanding and to require more teacher time. Croll and Moses conclude that schools differentiate on gender, yet they believe that the opportunities provided for both sexes within schools are greater than they would be out of school.

Some studies have shown that girls may often be thought by teachers to be too limited in ability for A level studies. This may be true in individual cases (undoubtedly A levels are too hard for many girls *and* boys) but such judgements may also be the surface effect of years of gender stereotyping. There are still twice as many boys as girls taking A level mathematics. Moreover there are relatively few young women taking A level courses in physical science and technology.

The evidence would appear to suggest that schools are providing children with the opportunity to re-inforce existing gender beliefs. Schools may be contributing to inequalities seen later in higher education. Schools need to focus more on improving pupils' aspirations and strengthening their life choices and chances (EOC and Ofsted, 1996).

REFLECTION

68

Choose a passage from a popular romance where boy meets girl. Read it aloud changing the boy's name to a girl's and vice versa. Change she to he. With luck his heart will flutter at her approach and her muscles will ripple as she roughly forces her mouth down on his.

Ethnicity and the self-fulfilling prophecy

Millions of the world's children are fluent in two or more languages and have access to two or more cultures. In Britain the children of the dominant culture usually speak only one language and enjoy one culture. There is no assumption being made here that bilingualism leads to racial tolerance – the Indian sub-continent is multi-lingual yet is split by conflict. Nevertheless, our insularity can lead to problems in understanding others.

The Swann Report (DES, 1985) states that:

Britain is a multi-racial and multi-cultural society and all pupils must be enabled to understand what this means ... (and that) ... it is ... necessary to combat racism, to attack inherited myths and stereotypes, and the ways in which they are embodied in institutional practices.

The Swann Report insists that *all* schools, regardless of ethnic composition, must deal with the issue of racism as part of a programme of political education. This point has been emphasised at local and national levels since the beginning of the multi-cultural debate in the 1960s.

The terms **racism**, **culture** and **ethnicity** need brief clarification:

● **Racism** is the belief there is more than one race and that certain races are inherently superior to others.
● **Culture** includes the values, language, habits, foods, customs and artistic conventions which are shared by people from the same race. This is

also an inadequate concept, since cultures are constantly changing, and culture and race are not necessarily synonymous. When filling in a census return, a person is required to classify themselves as Pakistani, or Black or Asian or Muslim, yet may wish to use more than one or none of these terms.

● **Ethnicity** describes a group of people bound together by shared cultural values and social structures. Ethnic groups are described in terms of imprecise national labels. An individual person may use any or all of the following markers: country of origin, language, skin colour, culture or religion.

Ten years after the Swann Report, Gillborn and Gipps argue against complacency despite an increasing commitment by educational policy makers to give value to other cultures. 'Multiculturalism' has become a strong trend in subject teaching. Despite this, circumstances still weigh against success for many ethnic groups in formal education.

Gillborn and Gipps (1996) insist that issues of race and equal opportunity must be put back into policy agendas, so that the following improvements can be consolidated and the deficiencies can be remedied.

There have been widespread improvements in GCSE performance yet in many LEAs the gap between the highest and the lowest achieving groups has increased and the lowest achieving groups include a statistically significant excess of African Caribbeans, especially young black men. Research suggests that they may be subjected to a combination of certain gender and race stereotypes. African Caribbean pupils are between three and six times more likely to be excluded from school than white pupils of the same sex, at both primary and secondary levels. If racial stereotypes are involved here, research must look at ways of decreasing misunderstandings and increasing harmony. (Statistics also indicate that two out of three pupils who are permanently excluded from school never return to full-time education.)

There are other big variations in success as measured by examination performance: for example, Indian pupils achieve high levels of success, but Asian pupils as a group can be subject to stereotypes about their language and their home communities and this can be especially damaging for Asian girls. Asian pupils seem especially likely to be victimised by their white peers. (See the case study of Vicky in Chapter 10 on Language Awareness.)

Gillborn and Gipps have collected, conducted and analysed both quantitative and qualitative research studies on the achievements of ethnic minority students. They distinguish between these two types of research approach and their respective strengths and weaknesses.

Ethnographic qualitative research (on small samples) can look more at the 'how' and the 'why' of situations than the quantitative, number-based research. The latter is useful for showing trends in big samples and looks more at the 'what'. Quantitative research, based on analysis of questionnaires and surveys, shows that many teachers are deeply committed to providing equal opportunities. Yet ethnographic research indicates that there is often conflict between African Caribbean pupils and white teachers.

There are many different reasons offered for this tension between policy and practice; Foster considers the teachers' actions to be reasonable responses to rule-breaking pupils (Foster, 1991: the self-fulfilling prophecy may be seen in action here). Mac an Ghaill's study of the *Young, Gifted and Black* (1988) found a tendency for the Asian male students to be seen as of high ability and conformist, and African Caribbean students to be seen to be of low ability and to present potential discipline problems. If it is true, and this appears likely, that white teachers often perceive black pupils as more threatening than white pupils, and respond to them accordingly, increased conflict will arise and result in further educational failure.

Gillborn and Gipps recommend the following initiatives:

- monitoring the experiences, achievements and needs of ethnic groups, as outlined recently by the DfEE, at school, LEA and national level
- ethnic diversity must be acknowledged
- research can help to reduce racial harassment and improve academic success, by monitoring trends
- teaching and learning in multi-ethnic schools needs to be analysed
- why are some schools better at this than others?
- can we look at success systematically?
- the school-based processes leading up to examinations need to be analysed – how can teachers and pupils be supported?

It is to be hoped that such initiatives will be facilitated by Ofsted inspections, in which, according to the amended Framework for the Inspection of Schools, instructions are given to inspectors to ensure that the full range of age, gender, ability, SEN and ethnic background of all the pupils in a school is taken into account.

There is conflicting evidence about how to proceed. It is clear that teachers are often resistant to the idea of political education as a whole, partly through lack of confidence in their ability or about their right to express strong views on such matters. And yet, there is evidence from as early as 1936 (Horowitz, in Jeffcoate) and supported more recently by Jeffcoate (1979) that racial prejudice can be found even in pre-school children.

One area of concern should be, yet again, the legacy of Piaget. His belief that young children's egocentricity prevents them from taking other people's viewpoints appears in the past to have prevented teachers from intervening with regard to controversial issues such as gender and ethnicity. Towards the end of his life Piaget was modifying some of his beliefs and probably did not intend his view of 'egocentricity' to be understood in this way.

Short (1988, in Carrington and Troyna) shows that primary school teachers have often been reluctant to confront sexism and racism in young children. Robin Alexander (1984) has christened this phenomenon the 'primary ideology', and doubts the value of Piaget's 'sequential developmentalism'. It is indeed true that three to four year-olds can express racist and sexist beliefs, and it would seem more reasonable to look to Bruner and Vygotsky for inspiration and guidance. They place considerable emphasis on the power of the teacher to influence children's cognitive, social and moral development.

Allport (1954) presents a very similar argument to those of Bruner and Vygotsky, and describes how issues such as racism can be tackled:

The age at which these lessons should be taught need not worry us. If taught in a simple fashion all the points can be made intelligible to younger children and, in a more fully developed way, they can be presented to older students . . . In fact . . . through 'graded lessons' the same content can, and should be, offered year after year. (Allport, 1954)

This approach resembles Bruner's 'spiral curriculum'. What are the possible solutions? Bruner's spiral curriculum would need to be backed up by a secondary school ethos which incorporates the following:

● The school deals openly with incidents of racial discrimination.
● Graffiti is removed quickly.
● Racist symbols (for example on clothes or badges) are forbidden.
● An explicit statement on race relations has been made by the school.
● Discussions between staff (including non-teaching staff), pupils, governors and parents' representatives have led to a 'whole school' view.
● There are staff, particularly senior staff, from ethnic minority groups.
● Careful attention has been given to the possibility of bias in curriculum content and materials.
● The general ethos of the school supports the idea of respect for all pupils. (HMI, 1983)

REFLECTION

69

The above list is presented to you as an example of HMI's views on good practice in terms of 'race relations'. It is worth considering whether this sort of approach can work. Any oppression by any group of any other group is unacceptable. Can you re-word this list so that it gives practical guidance to help staff develop an atmosphere of mutual respect and trust for all?

Implementation

Find out whether your school's policy documents take account of gender, race and class issues. Can you find examples of their implementation?

70

Consider also the National Curriculum documentation in your subject area and try to find evidence for implementation of such assertions as those expressed by HMI in 1983.

Example: the PE department's policy. Some secondary schools provide single sex lessons, some provide mixed. Both can be justified. Whichever is implemented, it needs to be monitored and evaluated.

In Part 3 (The Learning School) you will have an opportunity to return to this area if you wish, for comparison, contrast and conflict between policy and practice.

Practical reflections of policy need to become part of the curriculum, not as token gestures but truly integrated.

Example: Year 9 pupils write a story book.
Parents create a dual textbook by translating stories into their home language. Year 9 pupils use this with Year 7 for storytelling and sharing perspectives.

Example: A mathematics class studies the number systems of ancient cultures and considers their contribution to the development of mathematics.

In their book *Multiple Factors: Classroom Mathematics for Equality and Justice*, Sharan-Jeet Shan and Peter Bailey provide real understanding of the need for equality and justice in mathematics, in class and in the school.

Over the last twenty years there has been an increasing tendency to use some primary school techniques (such as developing multi-cultural resources with parents) in the first years of the secondary school (Savva gives examples). This can also be recommended for middle schools. A greater integration of curriculum areas for eleven to twelve year-olds could lead to more emotional stability at secondary transfer. Increasing the likelihood of contact between home and school is also essential. Tizard *et al* (1988) emphasise the importance of this for educational success. Parent-school links can be developed with a good pastoral system, that is a system involving form tutors and year heads which aims to look after the emotional, social and behavioural needs of the child as well as the curriculum-related needs.

Class and the self-fulfilling prophecy

Class is still considered a major determinant of success in all groups, yet there is not much current research available. A useful basis for research related to matters of class is very difficult to find because there is debate about which characteristics make up class distinctions. What is class anyway? There is no nationally representative research on achievement, so the relative achievements between groups cannot be compared.

Research on class often uses two measures: income and perceived differences in status. Manual workers and non-manual workers are sometimes taken to represent the divide between working class and middle class. Such measures seem rather crude yet, whichever way you look at it, social class is strongly associated with achievement regardless of gender and ethnic background. On average, the higher the social class the higher the achievement (Glennerster and Low, 1990). Conversely, the lower the social class the greater the potential gain would be from post-compulsory education (Bennett *et al*, 1990).

Learning to Succeed

71

Read the following extracts from *Learning to Succeed*:

Social class is among the arbitrary factors which most affect the quality of education in the United Kingdom. Children from social classes 1 and 2 of the Registrar-General's classification, on average, do better in examinations at 16, are likely to stay on longer in full-time education and are more likely to go to university than those from classes 3 to 5. There has been little change over the years in the proportion of entrants to higher education that come from working-class families . . .

. . . Not only are [different people] born with different kinds of ability or intelligence, but what they choose to do with them is much influenced by home and the community in which they grow up and mature . . .

. . . It is well established, for example, that the children of parents with post-compulsory schooling are likely to do well at schoolwork. Conversely, poverty is likely to impact on a home in a way that holds a pupil back. Accordingly, it is not surprising if a school which draws many of its pupils from a relatively prosperous neighbourhood figures higher in a league table than one in a deprived working-class area, especially if significant numbers have English as a second language. There is no telling, however, whether it is a better school on that account . . .

. . . In deprived areas, multiple disadvantages combine to make educational success difficult to attain. People living with the effects of poverty, long-term unemployment, poor housing, a lack of good amenities, high levels of crime, vandalism and, increasingly also, drug trafficking are severely disadvantaged. We share the anxiety of many that we may be witnessing the emergence of an underclass: people for whom the problems of unemployment and poverty are so great that they lose a sense of belonging to the mainstream of society and of sharing its aims and aspirations, and instead become increasingly isolated . . .

. . . real difficulties can arise for low-income and single-parent families and those drawing Income Support or Family Credit if their children opt for full-time [post-compulsory] education.

REFLECTION

R

72

Use these extracts to formulate your own assessment of what 'class' is. Then consider how you respond to the following in school: a strong regional accent, poorly spelt absence notes, a pupil's family which has long-term unemployed members. This could be a group activity.

Consider also your own story: why did you embark on higher education? Were there examples among family members? Expectations of parents and friends? An understanding of the sequences which lead to certain qualifications?

SUMMARY

The **self-fulfilling prophecy** and the **teacher expectancy effect** seem powerful, yet hard to pin down. Research shows varying results of the teacher expectancy effect – sometimes it seems to work, sometimes it doesn't. The famous study by Rosenthal and Jacobson, *Pygmalion in the Classroom* (1968), which appeared to show some educational expectancy effects in young children, has proved impossible to replicate, yet we can see it happening daily. (The use of these terms varies: self-fulfilling prophecy is described as a negative force and expectancy effect is often used as a positive force.)

The attitude to be encouraged must surely include a heightened awareness of all aspects of teaching: accurate definition of task, neutral use of language, monitoring of body language, use of discussion techniques to include all pupils, consideration of personal attitudes and of administrative decisions and so on.

A balance must be struck between realism (we know that prejudices are present in our society, not just in our schools) and idealism (if we can help pupils to maintain a balanced view of others we will have achieved something of value).

What is your culture anyway? Goffman (1959), a renowned sociologist, recommends caution in such definitions. He explains the situation in terms of the human need to describe oneself. It is necessary for us all to have a cultural and gendered identity. However, in order to consolidate essentially vague, nebulous ideas about our culture's values we may be tempted to over-emphasise the 'otherness' of other groups.

All the world is queer save thee and me, and even thou art a little queer.

(Robert Owen, utopian socialist, 1858)

Useful references

Alexander, R. (1984) **Primary Teaching.** London. Holt, Rinehart and Winston.

Allport, G. W. (1954) **The Nature of Prejudice.** Reading, Massachusetts: Addison-Wesley.

Askew, M. and William, D. (1995) **Recent Research in Mathematics Education 5–16**, in a series of Ofsted Reviews of Research. HMSO.

Batelaan, P. (1983) **The Practice of Intercultural Education.**

Bennett, R., Glennerster, H. and Nevison, D. (1990) *Investing in Skills: To Stay On Or Not To Stay On.* Oxford Review of Economic Policy. Vol. 8, No. 2, pp. 130–145 (Table 2).

Bruner, J. (1960) **The Process of Education.** New York.

Carrington, B. and Troyna, B. **Children and Controversial Issues.** Lewes: Falmer Press.

Coates, J. (1993) **Women, Men and Language.** 2nd edition. Longman.

Crocker, T. and Cheeseman, R. (1988) in *Educational Studies* 14 (1) pp. 105–110.

Delamont, S. and Galton, M. (1980) 'Anxieties and Anticipations – Pupils' Views of Transfer to Secondary School' in Pollard, A. **Children and their Primary Schools.** Falmer Press.

Department of Education and Science (1985) **Swann Report: Education for All.** London: HMSO.

Diagnostic and Statistical Manual of Mental Disorders (1994) (4th ed) (DSM-IV). Washington DC, American Psychiatric Association.

Dusek, J. B. (ed.) (1985) **Teacher Expectancies.** London: Erlbaum.

Equal Opportunities Commission and Ofsted (1996) **The Gender Divide.** HMSO.

Foster, P. M. (1991) 'Case still not proven: a reply to Cecile Wright', *British Ed Res*, 17 (2) pp. 165–70.

Gillborn, D. and Gipps, C. (1996) **Recent Research on the Achievements of Ethnic Minority Pupils.** Ofsted Review of Research, HMSO.

Glennerster H. and Low, W. 'Education and the Welfare State: Does it add up?' in Hills, J. (ed.) (1990) *The State of Welfare: The Welfare State in Britain Since 1974.* Oxford: Oxford University Press.

HMI (1983) **Race Relations in Schools.** London: HMSO.

Jeffcoate, R. (1982) **Multicultural Education: Curriculum Issues for Schools.** Unit 14 Course E354, The Open University.

National Commission on Education (1993) **Learning to Succeed.** London: Paul Hamlyn.

New Scientist, 9 March 1996, vol. 149, no. 2020, p. 7.

New Scientist, 12 March 1994, vol. 141, no. 1916 p. 22.

Rogers, C. G. (1982) **A Social Psychology of Schooling.** London: Routledge and Kegan Paul.

Rosenthal, R. and Jacobson, L. (1968) **Pygmalion in the Classroom.** New York: Holt, Rinehart and Winston.

Savva, H. (1994) 'Bilingual by Rights' in Pollard, A. and Bourne, J. (eds) **Teaching and Learning in the Primary School.**

Shan, S.-J. and Bailey, P. (1991) **Multiple Factors: Classroom mathematics for equality and justice.** Stoke on Trent: Trentham Books.

Short, G. (1991) 'Children's Grasp of Controversial Issues' in Woodhead, M., Light, P. and Carr, R. (eds) **Growing Up in a Changing Society.** London: Routledge, Open University.

Short, G. and Carrington, B. (1987) 'Towards an Anti-Racist Initiative in the All White Primary School: A Case Study' in Pollard, E. (ed.) **Children and their Primary Schools.** London: Falmer.

Stanworth, M. (1984) 'Girls on the Margins: a Study of Gender Divisions in the Classroom' in Hargreaves, A. and Woods, P. (eds) **Classrooms and Staffrooms: The Sociology of Teachers and Teaching.** Milton Keynes: Open University Press.

Tizard, B. *et al.* (1988) **Young Children at School in the Inner City.** London: Erlbaum.

Troyna, B. (1988) 'The Career of an Antiracist School Policy: Some Observations on the Mismanagement of Change' in Green, A. G. and Ball, S. J. (eds) **Progress and Inequality in Comprehensive Education.** London: Routledge.

Webb, N. M. (1984) 'Sex Differences in Interaction and Achievement in Co-operative Small Groups', *Journal of Educational Psychology* 76 (1) pp. 33–44.

Whalen, C. K. and Henker, B. (1996) *Attention Deficit/Hyperactivity Disorders* in Ollendick, T. H. and Hersen, M. (eds) **Handbook of Child Psychopathology.** 3rd edition. New York: Plenum Press.

Whyte, J. (1986) **Girls into Science and Technology.** London: Routledge and Kegan Paul.

Woods, P. (1979) **The Divided School.** London: Routledge and Kegan Paul.

Woods, P. (1990) **Teacher Skills and Strategies.** Lewes: Falmer Press.

Assessment (1)

Today I have learnt how to measure pencils.
(SMILE Mathematics Programme Self-evaluation Sheet)

LEARNING OUTCOMES

As teachers we collect, record, interpret and use the responses pupils make to an educational task. This may be a central part of daily classroom interaction or a formalised task with its own rules.

By the end of this chapter, you will have examined the purposes and methods of assessment and have done practical exercises to develop your understanding of why and how we assess, record and report pupils' progress. You should also be able to define the following types of assessment: **criterion-referenced**, **norm-referenced**, **formative** and **summative**.

REFLECTION

73

How was *your* school work assessed? Did you prefer some methods of assessment to others: practicals, oral, marking, grades, marks, levels, exams? Do you remember any assessments, formalised or not, which had a positive or negative effect on you?

You will soon realise that there are many varied ways in which we assess pupils' work and that we do so for many different **purposes**. Which of the following purposes were identified by you or your group?

- record keeping
- supporting pupils in their own learning
- measuring what pupils know, understand and can do
- screening
- providing information for parents
- motivating pupils
- diagnosing learning difficulties
- measuring or controlling standards

- ranking pupils in order
- feedback for teachers to assess their own effectiveness/success in meeting their objectives
- selecting pupils (for example for setting)
- summing up pupils' progress so far
- deciding on grades, certificates, qualifications

Assessment

List these and any other items you can think of and rank them into an order according to which you think are most commonly used. Explain your order. Now rank them in what you regard as their order of importance.

74

The purposes of assessment

Here are two questions you need to ask yourself:

- What are the purposes of my assessment?
- What is my evidence for assessment?

There are three main purposes of assessment. They are:

1 **Diagnostic** to focus on what a pupil can and cannot do and why they cannot do it, to reveal misunderstandings and learning difficulties. What level of understanding have they already achieved? We need to build on strengths and identify and target gaps.

2 **Formative** to decide what a pupil or class needs to do next, whether they're ready to move on etc. (for example to inform future teaching).

3 **Summative** to measure attainment in order to sum up a pupil's achievement and progress so far (for example for the award of a certificate or qualification or to inform parents).

There are two main categories of assessment: **criterion-referencing** refers to a means of measuring pupils' level of knowledge, skills and understanding in the context of the task set (assessment in detail); **norm-referencing** refers to means of measuring pupils' level of attainment in the context of what is considered to be normal for a particular age group (assessment overview).

Most tasks are assessed by a combination of these two methods. Instrumental music exams and driving tests are examples of assessment which are largely criterion-referenced. GCSE and A levels are examples of assessment with a major norm-referencing component.

Now put each item from the list above into one of these two categories. (Some, of course, will fall into both categories.)

Questions about assessment

As teachers we regularly need to ask ourselves:

1 **What do you regard as good practice in assessment?**
   The results should be meaningful to you, to colleagues, to pupils and to parents. The results of assessment procedures should be useful for improving professional practice. Assessment isn't something that only happens to pupils in schools. Pupils need to be made aware that assessment is an integral part of life, not just for school. Good practice ensures that children have opportunities to assess themselves.

2 **Are your methods of assessment clear to the pupils?**
   Keep your assessment system and your language as simple as possible. Can peer group assessment be used?

3 **Have you used a variety of different approaches?**
   Teachers often wish assessment to be definitive, precise and finite (to give an accurate prediction of exam performance). This is seldom possible, and there is a place for subjective as well as objective judgements. Consider using the self-fulfilling prophecy as a force for good.

4 **Have you been as consistent as is reasonably possible?**
   Moderation should be taking place within departments: 'agreement trials' for comparison, and discussion of samples of work and marking techniques.

5 **Does your assessment help the pupils improve their performance?**
   Teaching pupils to carry out self-assessment can also be valuable. A diary of progress can be encouraged – *I did well in this lesson because . . .*

6 **Does the assessment enable you to identify a pupil's strengths, and to indicate weaknesses and how to resolve them?**
   Profiling and Records of Achievement can provide added evidence and suggest additional ways forward.

7 **What do you see as the major long-term aims of assessment?**
   Recent investigations (by Ofsted and others) suggest that the results of assessment are not used for curriculum planning as much as they should be. One major purpose of assessing the level of achievement of a pupil should be to use the results to influence the planning of your curriculum in terms of teaching method and differentiation of material.

8 **Pupils need good examples on which they can model their own work.**
   These should represent differing National Curriculum levels at Key Stage 3 and Key Stage 4, and should exemplify the extremes of the ability range as well as the average.

9 **Are you clear about the purposes of your different types of assessment?**
   The two main purposes of assessment are discussed in the next section of this chapter.

The evidence of a pupil's learning is revealed in a range of forms. The most obvious is tests and exams but everyday, lesson-based assessment has the potential to provide a far wider, fuller picture of what a pupil knows, understands and can do. **Remember:** a pupil's learning may not lead to a finished product but a comment or action may, nevertheless, reveal fresh insight or increased understanding. Such ephemeral or unexpected evidence is no less important for assessment purposes. In fact, we should strive to assess what is important rather than make important that which is easy to assess.

Gardner's work on multiple intelligences gives an indication of the need for a variety of assessment instruments in order to assess the wide variety of talents that school students possess. Narrow assessment can lead to narrow teaching and restricted opportunities for learning (Gardner, 1985).

Marking pupils' work

The informal, in-class assessment of pupils' work is vitally important. Another type of assessment which involves all teachers is 'marking'. What are the aims of marking? Why do we do it when it takes up so much of our time? Sometimes it feels like the sort of ritualistic behaviour children expect of us as proof of our 'teacherliness', without them being prepared to benefit from it. Parental expectations about work being marked regularly are also a factor.

Teachers' marking, even when expressed bleakly as marks out of ten, *can* have a powerful effect upon pupils' self-esteem. Most pupils (and most trainee teachers too) like having goals to achieve, and respond well to praise as well as to positive and constructive criticism. In marking, correcting and commenting upon pupils' work, teachers are giving clear signs to the pupils about whether they are on the right track and, if not, suggesting and advising about how to improve. In this way, marking can be a very effective tool for guiding and reinforcing pupils' learning. It would be a betrayal of pupils for teachers not to provide this feedback.

Marking should give significant feedback and satisfaction. It should motivate the pupil to achieve more. There is little point in using it as a punitive exercise – you will only be punishing yourself by spending your time unprofitably. You also need to fit in with school and departmental policy on assessment, recording and reporting.

The process of marking can be used to teach useful study skills, such as:

● **Proof-reading**   Pupils can learn to check their own work by skimming and scanning, asking a friend to check it, and concentrating on details such as spelling, punctuation and numbering.
● **Drafting and redrafting**   One of the study skills associated with proof-reading is drafting: pupils can become actively involved in reworking their own material to improve it, concentrating on bigger details such as sentences, paragraphs, the presentation of ideas, diagrams and labelling.
● **Analysing the value of their work**   Has it met the criteria set by teacher or pupil? This begs the question of whether the teacher and pupils have discussed the criteria for what constitutes good work.

 We can also focus on specific issues while marking. If a pupil regularly has twenty corrections on a page, it will be necessary to establish priorities. The sequence outlined below can be followed.

1   Make an informal assessment of what is causing the problem. Is it any of the following?

● carelessness
● real difficulties with spelling, punctuation, number notation, iconic representation
● lack of understanding
● lack of required knowledge
● lack of motivation

2 Discuss the issues with the pupil and consider some of the following solutions:

- For **carelessness** it is necessary to introduce the pupil, or the whole class, to proof-reading and drafting skills. You may also need to raise your expectations of the standard of work.
- Where there are **real difficulties with recording** you might select a priority area in discussion with the pupil, e.g. correct use of the equals sign in mathematics, or certain recurrent spelling errors, such as vowel blends in the middle of words – look out for patterns. Review the process after several markings and set new targets. You can use an Individual or Group Education Plan (Code of Practice) for this purpose – (See Chapter 27 on Code of Practice). Look at Chapter 14 on differentiation for alternative means of recording.
- Where there is a **lack of understanding or knowledge** it is necessary to scaffold the task more carefully, to consider using Wood's five levels and to look again at putting several pupils together who are in similar zones of proximal development so they can support each other.
- Where there is **poor motivation** it is necessary to use marking procedures to build up an interest and reinforce the positive aspects of whatever work the pupil produces.

Remember the self-fulfilling prophecy. Comments like 'You *can* do this' or 'You *will* pass' can be a force for good.

Marking of pupils' work is also a very useful way for us, as teachers, to check up on our effectiveness and whether our lesson objectives have been met – or are even appropriate in the first place!

The marking of pupils' work is one aspect of a teacher's work which is exposed to direct and rather public scrutiny. Anyone – pupils, parents, other teachers or inspectors – can form a quick judgement about a teacher simply by looking at the way pupils' work has been marked. Unmarked work is something which annoys pupils and parents, just as incomplete work by pupils annoys teachers. In many schools, experience suggests that where teachers have entered into a 'contract' with pupils (for example in which teachers are committed to marking and returning work by the next lesson or a set number of days), deadlines for pupils to complete work are most likely to be met.

Assessment and policy

Read the assessment policy of your school. Does your particular department have a policy on marking? If not, devise a list of guidelines, preferably with the help of your mentor, explaining how good practice can lead to an improvement in learning.

75

Recording pupils' achievements

REFLECTION

What do you remember of your school reports? What did you or your parents learn from them? Did the report comments, in any way, inform, re-inforce or direct your learning? In what ways?

76

We have already recognised that it is beneficial for pupils to be involved in the assessment process. Just as trainee teachers need to reflect on and review their progress in collaboration with their mentors, so pupils should be encouraged to take responsibility, along with their teachers, for their own learning. Pupils can take an increasingly active role, as they get older, in identifying their own strengths and weaknesses and in working out ways to build on the former and eradicate the latter, so that they can identify areas, and set targets, for development. One way of doing this is through the Record of Achievement.

In many schools, the Record of Achievement is also the main means for reporting on pupils' progress and achievements. It allows pupils to become increasingly involved in the reviewing, recording and reporting of their own progress as they become more able to evaluate critically their own work. It also provides the main basis for reporting to parents (and writing references for universities, colleges and employers) over a period of time. Selected evidence of a pupil's learning is collected in a portfolio which thus provides a record of the curriculum followed and a report of progress made. In many schools, reports to parents have now been incorporated into the Record of Achievement and thus contain comments by teachers (and usually by pupils as well) on what pupils have shown that they know, understand and can do.

These comments should be as precise and specific as possible. The following phrases are useful for reporting what pupils have actually achieved:

has demonstrated	designed
planned	generated
presented	completed
read	has written
performed	collected evidence of
has shown (x) skills by	

Comments such as 'Emma should work harder' are of less value than the comment which explains *precisely* what Emma needs to work harder at, *why* work on a particular area is required and advice on *how* to make the necessary improvement.

Report comments should include both the subject-specific and the more general (examples of the latter being oral, writing and computer skills, team work, initiative, adaptability). Comments about behaviour, punctuality, presentation, organisation can be made in the context of advice or targets for future learning. These comments can be candid yet sensitive and supporting.

At Key Stage 3, assessments need to be recorded as required by the National Curriculum while, at the end of Key Stage 4, the Record of Achievement should include a statement of achievement describing personal qualities and a summary of the range of achievements, interests and experiences as well as examinations entered for and awards received. This is supported by evidence such as certificates and course reports.

Two key characteristics of the Record of Achievement are that they should enable the pupil to celebrate success, which increases confidence and the motivation to learn more, and that the teacher should share his or her interpretations and assessments of the pupil's work in order to develop the learner's awareness of the criteria upon which assessment has been based. These will make for the more autonomous learners which we want our pupils to become.

Assessment and achievement

Are you familiar with the process of assessment in your subject within the National Curriculum? For most subjects SCAA has produced 'Exemplification of Standards' documentation to help teachers assess pupils' work.

Look at the skills needed to achieve high levels of achievement in your subject. What task would you need to set for a child to show they can attain it? How would you record (assess) it?

SUMMARY

Ofsted (1995) is asking inspectors to report on strengths and weaknesses in the procedures for assessing pupils' attainment and wants information about the extent to which:

● there are effective systems for assessing pupils' attainment
● assessment information is used to inform curriculum planning

The notes of guidance provided by Ofsted ask that:

● Inspectors should evaluate whether assessments are accurate and used to plan future work and to help pupils make progress.

It is this aspect which should underpin your early efforts at assessing pupils' work. Does it 'help pupils make progress'? If the answer to this is no, then you need to review the forms and purposes of your assessment. This chapter should have indicated some of the rich variety available. The later chapter on assessment will offer you further opportunities to expand your repertoire of assessment choices.

Useful references

Gipps, C. and Stobart, G. (1993) **Assessment: A Teacher's Guide to the Issues.** London: Hodder and Stoughton.

Ofsted (1995) **Guidance on the Inspection of Secondary Schools.** London: HMSO.

Differentiation (1)

14

Everyone is both unique and yet, in certain respects, like a lot of other people ... in order to move towards a fuller appreciation of the worth of each individual we need to acknowledge any real differences between groups. (Shackleton and Fletcher, 1992)

LEARNING OUTCOMES

When you have read this chapter you should be able to give examples of the four main types of differentiation: by **outcome**, by **task**, by **process** and by **response**.

Introduction

One of the teacher's major challenges is getting to know pupils and understanding how to meet their needs. If you get that wrong, the self-fulfilling prophecy will trap the pupil in a negative cycle with loss of self-esteem and chronic failure. You will need to establish realistic expectations and continually modify these according to the evidence you collect while teaching. If you get that right you will have the key to motivating children and educating them.

Differentiation is a key term used to describe this process. The National Council for Educational Technology (NCET) defines it thus:

Differentiation is a planned process of intervention in the classroom to maximise potential based on individual needs. (NCET, 1993)

One of the constraints on this process is the curriculum. The reality of teaching now is that curriculum content is, largely, prescribed by statute (see Chapter 15 on the National Curriculum). The assessment system provides differentiation in various ways, for example different papers at GCSE or at KS3, in some subjects.

However, in any one class you may well find that a wide range of achievement levels, reading levels, behaviour problems and curriculum constraints limit the flexibility of the teacher's response. .

Types of differentiation

You will be developing many different ways of differentiating during the course of the year. At this stage a fundamental distinction can be made between differentiation by **outcome**, by **task**, by **process** and by **response**.

The last of these, differentiation by response, probably forms the major part of our teaching and enables us to monitor the match or mis-match between the pupil and the task.

Differentiation by outcome

This represents one of the commonest teaching techniques. The same task is set for the whole class, for example *Write a newspaper article on Rwanda*, or *Move from one side of the gym to the other using the apparatus provided.* Any differentiation arises naturally in the end product of the task, controlled by the capabilities of each pupil.

The **advantages** of this technique are as follows:

- easy to plan and set up
- useful summative assessment which will show you the different levels within the group (that is assessment as a pause point for assessing what pupils have learnt by this stage; see Chapter 13 on Assessment)
- pupils can be allowed to work co-operatively
- teacher assumes success for all as no criteria for failure are specified
- pupils expect less individual attention, because they accept that you want each one to work at their own level

Disadvantages might be:

- some pupils may be very restricted in what they can do without support
- not much diagnostic assessment is possible (that is using assessment to find out pupils' strengths/weaknesses in some areas)
- failure is inevitable for some because pupils measure their performance against their friends and some realise that they fall below the class average
- this perceived failure may lead to behavioural difficulties

Differentiation by task

This represents an attempt to provide work which is suitable for each pupil. For example, some maths schemes are based on work cards and activities which are carefully sequenced by small steps of increasing difficulty.

Advantages:

- work can be chosen which is suitable for each pupil
- it is an efficient way of covering the curriculum
- failure is unlikely, so that behavioural problems may be reduced
- it can be related to National Curriculum levels
- it is useful for formative assessment (that is assessing pupils' work or performance in order to form decisions about what to teach them next; see Chapter 13 on Assessment)

Disadvantages:

- pupils may slow down to avoid finishing an allotted task
- labour intensive for teacher as much organisation is needed
- work schemes for individuals may impede social learning and highlight differences
- summative assessment is difficult and needs to be carried out separately

Differentiation by process

This, at its best, combines the best of differentiation by task and by outcome because the various aspects of the process are differentiated according to the pupils' strengths.

For example, a CDT task is set to build a stool. The process of planning, research, design and so on becomes part of the assessed task and the outcome (the finished stool) also becomes part of the task, not the only measure of success.

In English, the production of a newspaper article is the end product of a process which includes research, planning, drafting and checking.

Appropriate differentiation enables you to see that a pupil may be weak on planning or checking and needs support.

Advantages:

- a highly differentiated form of teaching
- an excellent vehicle for using Vygotsky's zone of proximal development (see Chapter 6 on Vygotsky), Bruner's scaffolding and Wood's five levels (see Chapter 7 on Bruner)
- useful for helping pupils to work on their own weak areas
- excellent as a method of working with one part of a class at a time
- makes full use of pupil creativity

Disadvantages:

- makes heavy demands on the teacher
- difficult to provide for a whole class
- time-consuming way of covering the curriculum
- requires detailed record keeping

Differentiation by response

This is probably the most frequently used form of differentiation. It can be seen when a teacher is moving around a group of pupils answering individual questions. Each answer will reflect a differentiated response to that pupil's needs.

Advantages:

● provides opportunities for the teacher to give structure and advice which is specific to that pupil's needs

Disadvantages:

● very demanding of the teacher's time – each discussion with a pupil has to be seen in the context of simultaneously running the whole class

Differentiation and teaching skills

Differentiation

Use the following six areas to plan for differentiation and to deliver a differentiated curriculum initially to a group, then to a class. Write this up at regular intervals for your PDP.

78

Each of these four methods has its own strengths and weaknesses, and you will develop combinations of these and many others. Above all, preparation is necessary before you can present a properly differentiated lesson. Therefore, in order to provide differentiated learning experiences for a whole group or class, you also need to develop the following skills:

1 Recognise the variety of individual needs within a class

● Use different questioning styles (see Chapter 10 on Language Awareness)
● Familiarise yourself with the work that's been covered
● Talk to other teachers
● Ask to see the pupils' books
● Use differentiation by outcome to establish different levels of functioning (the same task is set for all, with different end products depending on each pupil's level of attainment)

2 Plan to meet those needs

● Develop a structure of lesson plans with which you and the school are happy.
● Use these plans to prepare extension exercises for the very bright, and more structured work for the less able.
● Use the departmental curriculum guidelines as a framework, and within them develop your own style of delivery.

3 Provide appropriate delivery

● Use your lesson plans to organise the whole class in terms of their educational and management needs (for example don't use group work before you are fully in control of your pupils)
● Ensure that you are thoroughly prepared, for example practise the words and actions which you will use to explain the activities.

4 Evaluate the effect of the activities

● Use your lesson plans to record what went well (don't dwell on failures, look at how to do better next time).
● Get feedback from the pupils; ask them what they thought of a certain activity.
● Consider for the future whether the activities allowed you to: a) maintain pupil control, b) meet the needs of most pupils, c) cover the necessary curriculum areas.

5 Balance the needs of the individual (including you!) with the needs of the whole group, in terms of managing pupils and resources

● Each type of differentiation has its strengths and weaknesses, for example some pupils excel in group work, some don't.
● You won't have time to do individual tutorial work with each pupil; moreover some pupils feel intimidated by such individual support.
● You must pace yourself. Some lessons will be less differentiated, for example by outcome only (same task set for all, with end products depending on each pupil's level). Some will be organisationally complex, for example group work, with some groups consolidating familiar work, leaving you free to do highly structured new work with another group. Some lessons will make heavy demands on you, for example by process, where project work or course work follows different paths of development.

6 Be realistic about your own energy

Concentrate on *one* teaching group and *one* type of differentiation to start with. For this you can use action planning techniques:

● Which type of differentiation do I want to try?
● Which group?
● For how long?
● How can I evaluate success and move on?

Teachers sometimes say that they do not differentiate, yet this is untrue. You need to develop opportunities for talking to colleagues about the many techniques which they use for meeting different children's needs, and which they often do almost automatically. In-service training for teachers indicates that they are often pleasantly surprised at how many different types of differentiation they use, when this is drawn to their attention. Moreover, such knowledge gives them more conscious control over their teaching.

Differentiation

While you watch a lesson and/or while talking to colleagues, make notes about the following and add your own items:

79

- departmental policy on setting and the mixing of boys and girls
- a particular group of pupils *before* the lesson (look for an example of differentiation by outcome)
- a group of pupils *after* the lesson (look for examples of differentiation)
- whether differentiation by task was appropriate for this lesson

SUMMARY

'Differentiation' provides a shorthand description of a complex technique which is at the heart of all teaching – making the National Curriculum and the general curriculum accessible to all.

Useful references

Ainscow, M. (1991) **Effective Schools For All.** London: Fulton.

Barthorpe, T. and Visser, J. (1991) **Differentiation: Your Responsibility.** Stafford: NASEN Enterprises Ltd.

Bates, R. (1993) **Guidelines for Secondary Schools for Effective Differentiation in the Classroom: Planning for a Whole School Approach.** Chelmsford: Essex County Council Education Department.

HMI (1993) **The Education of Able Pupils.** Edinburgh: Scottish Office, pp. 6–52.

Norwich, B. (1990) **Special Needs in Ordinary Schools.** London: Cassell.

Office for Standards in Education (1992) **Handbook for Inspection of Schools.** London: Ofsted.

Shackleton, V. and Fletcher, C. (1992) **Individual Differences.** London: Routledge.

Stradling, R. and Saunders, L. (1991) **Differentiation in Action (LAPP): A Whole School Approach.** London: HMSO.

Thomas, G. and Feiler, A. (eds) (1988) **Planning for Special Needs.** Oxford: Basil Blackwell.

Visser, J. (1993) **Differentiation: Making it Work.** Stafford: NASEN Enterprises Ltd.

Wiltshire County Council (1992) **Differentiating the Secondary Curriculum.** Trowbridge: Wiltshire County Council.

The National Curriculum

15

When the wild winds of change blow, some people build shelters and some build windmills. (Mao-Tse Tung)

LEARNING OUTCOMES

When you have read this chapter you should have a basic knowledge of the structure of the National Curriculum and some of the associated terminology.

The evolution of the National Curriculum

For almost a decade teachers in England and Wales have been struggling to keep up with centrally imposed curriculum changes.

A brief historical overview is necessary before we look at the major changes. In the mid-1980s, the Government decided to plan for the introduction of a national curriculum. This was intended to ensure that every child would have the chance to follow a broad, balanced and coherent curriculum between the ages of five and sixteen years.

The National Curriculum was introduced in 1988 as part of the Education Reform Act (ERA). Implementation of the new curriculum started but, within a couple of years, there was an increasing number of complaints. These were both about the quantity of material required to be covered and the complexity and time-consuming nature of assessment procedures.

Despite attempts to dismiss these complaints as teething problems it was finally acknowledged that revision was necessary. In April 1993 the Secretary of State for Education asked Sir Ron Dearing to *review the structure, manageability and assessment arrangements of the National Curriculum.* Dearing's Final Report (1994) followed consultations with teachers and resulted in an attempt to make the National Curriculum less cumbersome.

The body which oversees the planning, implementation and testing of the National Curriculum is the School Curriculum and Assessment Authority (SCAA).

The National Curriculum is characterised by the following age ranges:

Key Stage 1	Ages 4/5 to 7 years	called Reception, Years 1 and 2
Key Stage 2	Ages 7 to 11 years	called Years 3, 4, 5 and 6
Key Stage 3	Ages 11 to 14 years	called Years 7, 8 and 9
Key Stage 4	Ages 14 to 16 years	called Years 10 and 11

National Curriculum subjects

There are **three core subjects** – English, maths and science – to be studied by all pupils from Year 1 to Year 11 (from five to sixteen years). These are to be assessed at the end of each Key Stage by national testing (which at the end of Key Stage 4 is GCSE, graded G to A with A* for exceptional performance).

There are a further **six foundation subjects** at Key Stages 1 and 2 (from four/five to eleven years) in England: history, geography, technology (covering design technology and information technology), art, music and physical education.

At Key Stage 3 the number of subjects is increased by the addition of a modern foreign language.

In Wales, Welsh is present at all Key Stages (except at Key Stage 4 in non-Welsh speaking schools until 1999).

The National Curriculum from September 1995 at Key Stage 3

Core subjects	Foundation subjects	
Mathematics English Science	History Geography Art Music Technology Modern Foreign Languages Physical Education	* * * * ** **
Religious Education is also compulsory both at Key Stages 3 and 4		
* Optional at Key Stage 4		
** Short courses (equivalent to half a GCSE) are permissible at Key Stage 4 in technology and a modern foreign language. From August 1996 these subjects form part of the National Curriculum at KS4.		
Attainment Targets (ATs) have been reduced to simplify assessment. ATs describe key features of the curriculum, for example Attainment Target 1 in English is called 'Speaking and Listening'.		

The final Dearing Report stipulates that at least 80 per cent of the pupils' timetable at Key Stage 3 should be devoted to **core** and **foundation** subjects. This is intended to allow schools some flexibility in their curriculum delivery, for example to leave time for classics or a second modern language.

Key Stage 4 should be 60 per cent National Curriculum, leaving 40 per cent for optional studies (for example a second foreign language, vocational courses). It should be noted however, that PE, social and sex education, religious education and careers education are still compulsory to the end of Key Stage 4.

Programmes of Study and their assessment

At the heart of the syllabus in each National Curriculum subject are the **Programmes of Study**. Children's **knowledge**, **skills** and **understanding** of these Programmes of Study are to be assessed at the end of each key stage. Children's attainment will be assessed and reported in terms of **levels**. Key Stage 1 covers Levels 1–3, Key Stage 2 covers Levels 2–5 and Key Stage 3 covers Levels 3–8. Teachers may select material from a lower or a higher key stage for pupils with special needs. An additional 'level' described as 'Exceptional Performance' was introduced to enable pupils at Key Stage 3 to achieve above level 8. These 8 levels are only applicable to the first three Key Stages. At Key Stage 4 assessment uses the familiar GCSE lettered grades, A to G, with A* for exceptional performance.

New GCSE syllabuses reflecting the revised National Curriculum were introduced for courses beginning in September 1996; and examined for the first time in 1998.

How are these levels assessed in the revised National Curriculum?

Level description/descriptors (LDs), introduced in the revised National Curriculum, are designed to provide guidance on the knowledge, skills and understanding required to reach each of the levels in each subject. Teachers will produce a 'best fit' of their pupils' work to these level descriptions; in other words they will select the level description that most closely fits the work of each pupil. Exemplar materials have been distributed to schools to help teachers to recognise levels of attainment at Key Stage 3. Although some of the assessment at the end of key stages is undertaken by teachers in schools, assessment of the core subjects (English, mathematics and science) also involves national tests. In a few subjects (art, music and physical education) instead of levels there are end of key stage descriptions. These 'describe the types and range of performance that the majority of pupils should characteristically demonstrate by the end of the key stage'. These broad band descriptions are equated with a range of levels in other subjects.

Wider implications of the Dearing Review

Some of the wider implications of these recommendations are:

- There is an underlying hope to broaden A levels, perhaps offering radically different 14 to 19 alternatives, for example General National Vocational Qualification (GNVQ) levels 1 to 3 instead of the traditional academic pathways.
- Subsequently Sir Ron Dearing has reported on ways to strengthen, consolidate and improve the framework of 16 to 19 qualifications. His enquiries were, amongst other things, meant to *constitute the most searching review of the rigour of A levels for many years* (Dearing, 1995).
- The introduction of vocational courses necessitates new courses being developed: historically, the English system is weak on the vocational side.
- The balance between the vocational and academic elements of a pupil's programme will vary – one danger in this is that the vocational could be seen as second best. Any notion that work experience might be a motivational tool aimed at those pupils who have not succeeded at school might devalue the experience for all pupils.
- Will pupils with special educational needs have full access to the National Curriculum?

REFLECTION

With someone who shares your main subject, look at this subject in the revised National Curriculum. Make a note of any areas where you need clarification in school or from your Subject Co-ordinator.

80

Abbreviations

With the help of a close friend, test each other on the following abbreviations. What do they stand for? (Some of these are included in this chapter; you will have to find out for yourselves about the others.)

ERA, SCAA, LDs, GCSE, GNVQ, ACAC, NCVQ, SACRE, TA, AT

81

Adrian, PGCE Secondary Trainee

82

Adrian was introduced to the National Curriculum for Mathematics while studying for a PGCE. Once he had become secure in his understanding of his own subject, he thought he would check the National Curriculum structure in Mathematics with another subject in order to assure himself of cross-curricular consistency. The results are shown below.

Mathematics – Programme of Study

The National Curriculum for Mathematics currently consists of Programmes of Study at Key Stage 1, Stage 2 and a joint programme at Key Stages 3 and 4.

The sections into which the PoS are divided are:

Using and Applying Mathematics
Number
Algebra (not at Key Stage 1 or Key Stage 2)
Shape, Space and Measures
Handling Data (not at Key Stage 1)

At Key Stage 4, there is also a section entitled further material for those pupils who have acquired the knowledge, skills and understanding within the Key Stage 3 and 4 Programmes of Study.

Mathematics – Attainment Targets

There are four attainment targets at Key Stage 3 and 4:

Using and Applying Mathematics
Number and Algebra
Shape, Space and Measures
Handling Data

Pupils can attain one of eight levels up to the end of Key Stage 3 in each of these attainment targets. There is also an additional set of descriptions called Exceptional Performance for those pupils beyond level 8.

My confusion

At first, I was confused by the levels and the attainment targets. I was thinking that there were eight attainment targets in each of four sections. I think that this confusion arose from the fact that the attainment targets have the same name as the sections of the Programmes of Study (apart from target 2 which combines two sections of study).

In order to try and sort out my confusion I spoke to my wife, who is a Modern Languages teacher. This brought to light the fact that the structure of the National Curriculum in Modern Languages is very different. It too has Programmes of Study, attainment targets and levels, but the structure differs as below.

Modern Languages – Programme of Study at Key Stage 3 and 4

There are two main parts as shown below each subdivided into several sections each:

Part 1   Learning and using the target language (Sections 1–4)
Part 2   Areas of Experience (Sections A–E)

Modern Languages – Attainment Targets

In each of the above areas, there are four attainment targets:

- Listening and Responding
- Speaking
- Reading and Responding
- Writing

The differences

The most obvious difference is the naming of these four ATs, but this aside, the way one uses the attainment targets across the Programmes of Study is different.

Modern Languages has a very simple structure where each attainment target runs through all the areas in each programme.

Pupils must achieve in four ATs throughout the Programmes of Study. The Programmes of Study encompass the Learning and Using, and Areas of Experience.

A visual presentation of each could be as shown below.

AT	Part 1 Learning and Using	Part 2 Areas of Experience
Listening		
Speaking		
Reading		
Writing		

Mathematics has a far more complex structure where Ma1 – Using and Applying Mathematics – is the 'theme' which runs through each of the other sections. I have used two methods of illustrating this. The first is one that I devised to ease my confusion. The second is one which I found in an ATM article by Mike Ollerton, drawn by Peter Lacey. I have abridged it slightly since at the time of its conception there were **five** attainment targets.

Diagram 1

Using and Applying		
Number and Algebra	Shape & Space	Handling Data

Diagram 2

Ma 2-4 skills are represented as a number of different destinations

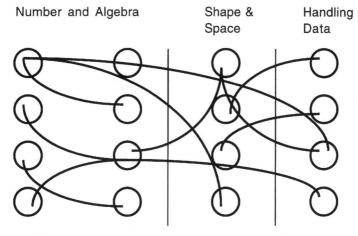

Number and Algebra   Shape & Space   Handling Data

Ma1 is about how the destinations could be connected

As can be seen, the ways in which teachers of these two subjects operate have to be very different. Teachers of Modern Languages have to make sure that pupils work within each attainment target in all language areas. Teachers of Mathematics must make little 'journeys' between different sections of the PoS to ensure competence in every attainment target.

It seems strange to me that the same language should be used to describe two fundamentally different structures. This could easily lead to misunderstandings in cross-curricular communication – something which I had assumed the language of the National Curriculum was devised to remove.

Comparing subject orders

Obtain a copy of 'A Guide to the National Curriculum' published by SCAA and ACAC (1996) and compare your subject orders with another. Make notes in your PDP.

Teacher autonomy versus central control

One of the concerns over the National Curriculum is the role of the teacher within such a centralised system. If the curriculum is prescribed and leaves little choice to the subject teacher over what to teach, then one of the main roles for the teacher is removed; that of deciding which areas of the subject are most appropriate for the group being taught. The expert teacher in the classroom is in the best position to make such decisions. The counter argument to this is that individual teachers may omit key elements because they are not enthusiastic about them or do not have experience of teaching them. The issue is therefore one of teacher autonomy versus central control, of teacher creativity versus student entitlement. There are also current initiatives to create a National Curriculum in Initial Teacher Training. This would go beyond saying that this is what must be taught in schools; it could describe how it must be taught in schools. At the time of writing it is planned that this would focus on mathematics and English within the primary school and on general teaching competences in both primary and secondary phases, with the intention to then move into the secondary core subjects of mathematics, science and English. Again there arises the same need for balance between autonomy and control.

The subject mentor requires a greater depth of knowledge and deliberative thought than is implicit in the traditional role of expert. An expert teacher is perhaps seen in some eyes as someone who makes immediate decisions in the classroom. They may not be able to put the justification for their actions into coherent form; their response is based on experience. As Schön (1987) comments:

Skilful improvisers often become tongue tied or give obviously inadequate accounts when asked to say what they do. Clearly it is one thing to be able to reflect-in-action and quite another to be able to reflect on our reflection-in-action so as to produce a good verbal description of it; and it is still another thing to be able to reflect on the resulting description.

As mentor, the teacher must become able to discuss their expertise and to help trainees to develop their own forms of mastery. It is this role which places the teacher at the heart of the process. Teachers involved in the training of new colleagues must be able to be critical about the nature of their subject within the National Curriculum. They need to become 'learned' as well as expert, with an awareness of the broader debate in their subject area as well as being an experienced teacher in their own context.

This concept of the teacher as 'learned' was examined in a presentation to the Eighth International Congress of Mathematics Education by Bloomfield and Sanders (1996). They commented as follows.

Such a democracy of learned teachers is not in harmony with notions of standardised top-down quality control or with centrally imposed curricula. It is time to emphasise that empowered learned teachers are central to improving the standards of teaching and quality of learning in schools. Their inspiration is also needed to provide the environment in which trainee teachers can develop.

If there is to be any form of agreed curriculum, then there must of necessity be some restrictions on teacher autonomy. However the need for a looser structure allowing scope for learned teachers to exercise their creative judgement seems to outweigh the need to impose total uniformity. A feature of our individual societies is perhaps the degree to which we allow teachers to be independent. In making creative decisions about the curriculum, we have to avoid the trap of restricting the creativity of those who implement the curriculum. We must allow teachers the chance to be learned.

SUMMARY

After a decade of upheavals the revised National Curriculum is now being implemented. All pupils will study the core subjects of English, mathematics and science. A further six foundation subjects are also to be studied, with the addition of a modern foreign language at Key Stage 3. Pupils' knowledge, skills and understanding for each level, in each subject, will be assessed by comparison with a range of standard level descriptors, introduced in the revised National Curriculum.

It is intended that the revised National Curriculum be implemented and then left to develop undisturbed for five years. If this happens, schools will be able to decide whether it is possible to fulfil Dearing's wishes for a less prescriptive, more flexible curriculum in which schools have more control of their own curriculum planning than they did under the original National Curriculum.

Useful references

Bloomfield, A. and Sanders, S. (1996) **Redefining Teacher Education for the Zero-based Mathematics Curriculum.** ICME-8, Seville.

Dearing, R. (1994) **The National Curriculum and its Assessment: Final Report.** London: School Curriculum and Assessment Authority.

Dearing, R. (1995) **Review of 16–19 Qualifications: Summary of the Interim Report – The Issues for Consideration.** London: HMSO.

Department of Education and Science (1985) **Better Schools.** London: HMSO (ERA Primary and Secondary Curriculum, pp. 9–24).

Department of Education and Science (1988) **National Curriculum Task Group on Assessment and Testing: Full Report and Summary.** London: HMSO.

HMI (1991) **The Curriculum for Five to Sixteen Years: HMI Curriculum Matters No. 2.** London: HMSO.

House of Commons (1988) **Education Reform Act.** London: HMSO.

Kelly, A. V. (1990) **The National Curriculum: A Critical Review.** London: Paul Chapman.

National Curriculum Council (1991) **Curriculum Guidance Nos 3–8.** York: NCC.

Ollerton, M. (1993) **Content with Process?** MT145 Derby, ATM.

Schön, D. (1987) **Educating the Reflective Practitioner.** San Francisco: Josey-Bass.

School Curriculum and Assessment Authority (1995) **An Introduction to the Revised National Curriculum.** London: SCAA.

School Curriculum and Assessment Authority (1996) **A Guide to the National Curriculum.** London: SCAA.

Managing Your Lessons

16

If the rules of expected behaviour in a classroom are clearly and consistently drawn up and the child is given an opportunity to act in the classroom like an intelligent individual, this type of treatment becomes a technique by which the child may develop self-reliance, dependability and initiative. (Virginia Axline, 1969)

LEARNING OUTCOMES

When you have read this chapter you should be able to list the major findings of the Elton Report and describe five characteristics of an effective teacher. You will be able to consider some of the major features of rules, rewards and punishments.

In terms of study skills, you will be using cross-referencing to make the best use of other chapters.

Introduction

We read regularly in the newspapers about the breakdown of discipline in schools. Newspaper editors seem to delight in stories about classroom disorder, perhaps because we ourselves find such articles fascinating! Wish fulfilment from our own school days . . . ?

Your own behaviour

Attempt to recall some of your own bad behaviour – or that of someone else if you were a model pupil. How did pupil and teacher feel?

84

There are indeed frightening and even life-threatening incidents taking place in our schools, but these are rare and are not usually the events which teachers report as being stressful. The reality of school life is much less sensational with a number of recurring problems which have a cumulative effect. Teachers often feel that they are being beaten down rather than beaten up.

Research describes three major recurring problems:

1 *talking out of turn*
2 *disturbing other pupils*
3 *coming unprepared for lessons (no pen for instance) (Elton Report, 1989)*

There are several reasons for the high stress factor in these behaviours:

- it is difficult to teach if pupils are talking or disturbing others
- it is difficult for pupils to learn if others are talking or disturbing them
- management issues arise: telling off the talkers, sorting out the ill-equipped ones, and so on
- long-term issues then arise in terms of covering the syllabus (can't be done), and motivating pupils (boredom sets in if the teacher is too busy to teach you because of disciplining others)

  Lesson management

85

Consider the following true story and analyse the likely/probable differences between the two teachers.

A gifted and experienced drama teacher did a simulated drama exercise on bullying with Year 10 pupils. He did a very relaxed introductory talk, to which the fourteen to fifteen year-olds responded creatively, generating problem solving devices and implementing them in the form of role play. The teacher's input appeared minimal. The trainee who observed the lesson was inspired by it. Being very interested in social issues he decided to try a similar lesson on drugs. He gave a relaxed introductory talk, to which the group reacted very negatively. The pupils refused to take it seriously and ridiculed the trainee. In a subsequent lesson senior management had to be brought in to restore order and to deal with the pupils' demands for the restoration of their drama teacher.

1   List three differences between the two teachers:

Trainee	Experienced teacher

During the first few lessons with a new class, experienced teachers behave differently from new teachers. Experienced teachers use teaching material which is highly structured and does not demand much input or maintenance by the teacher, who is therefore free to establish a firm 'presence' – make good eye contact, work out who the lively characters are and decide on seating arrangements for instance.

The new teacher, in contrast, believes that the key to a responsive, well disciplined class lies in the presentation of stimulating, exciting curriculum material. Wragg and Wood (1984) look at these issues in some detail.

2   Make notes on your personal and professional views of these contrasting approaches.

NB   Two mentors were working with this trainee. One approved his drugs lesson plan and the other vetoed it. The event caused the school to re-think their mentoring arrangements.

What is an effective teacher like?

There are many different styles of teaching and pupil management, but research suggests that there are certain powerful features which are common to most good teachers:

Being prepared

- by being ready for the pupils' entry before the lesson (not always possible)
- by knowing how to cope with interruptions (pupils arriving late is the fourth most annoying event as listed in the Elton Report)
- by knowing what you are going to teach and having good lesson plans ready
- by developing what Kounin calls 'with-it-ness' – scanning the room, making eye contact, noting possible disturbances, knowing the pupils, sensing the atmosphere
- by having work ready for those who finish early

Being confident

- by posture (for example confident body language)
- by use of gestures (for example not too much hand flapping)
- by eye contact and other 'non-verbal signals' (for example be assertive but not confrontational)
- by being in possession of the teaching space (there should be no no-go areas)

Being a good manager of resources

- by developing pupil responsibility for giving out books, collecting work, and so on
- by teaching a sense of responsibility for property
- by knowing what resources are available in your department and using them appropriately.

Being aware of environmental factors

- is the temperature too high or too low?
- is the blackboard clearly visible to all?

Being in control

- be a quiet, firm disciplinarian, believing that praise is more powerful than criticism
- remember that the work ethic and high levels of educational achievement are the keys to success.
- remember that pupils are individuals, who need to feel good about themselves and need individual attention

Recent research carried out by the National Foundation for Educational Research (NFER) for the National Commission on Education found that only half the pupils interviewed reported being praised for good work by all or most of their teachers (Keys and Fernandes, in Moon and Mayes, 1994).

How can you develop effective teaching?

By watching others

- You will learn a lot by watching experienced teachers.
- You can pair up with another trainee and spend time observing each other's lessons, in a spirit of mutual support.

By gaining experience

- Your course is designed to enable you to build up experience gradually by observing and then running small groups, then teaching a class. Also, if possible, you will participate in team teaching.

By establishing your own expectations

- You should decide what you expect of the pupils, ensure that your expectations are compatible with school rules, and make them clear to your pupils.

By deciding how to develop your personality with the pupils

● The Elton Report research points out that teachers spend more time scolding bad behaviour than praising good behaviour. Why do we do this when it simply wears us out?

● Giving well thought-out praise for good behaviour and for good work will make you a strong, effective teacher and allow you to define pupils' performance positively instead of negatively.

Rules, rewards and punishments

86

You have already considered **class rules** (in Chapter 4 on Skinner). See if you can remember the five you decided upon by writing them down. Remember they need to be short, clear and some should be positives. For example, *Listen to the teacher* instead of *Don't talk* – listening is an active skill, unlike 'not talking'.

Now consider **rewards**. How many suggestions can you find in this chapter? List them. (Look also in Chapters 8 and 9 on Motivation and Adolescence for ideas about rewards. This cross-referencing between chapters is necessary for you to make full use of this book.)

Remember that **praise** from you is one of the best rewards, if you respect the following rules: praise should be specific (to something the pupil has done), sincere (and not delivered according to a formula) and acceptable to the pupil (quiet praise may work better for some pupils than public announcements of excellence). (Brophy 1981)

Now consider **punishments**. Make a note here of the punishments which were used when you were at school. Did they work? Make some brief notes about how punishments can be made fair and effective, referring back to Chapters 4, 8, 9 and 12 on Skinner, Motivation, Adolescence and the Self-fulfilling Prophecy.

Subject-specific issues

87

Each subject makes different demands on the pupils to behave appropriately. In Modern Languages, for example, a quiet classroom could be read as a danger sign! The noise level is often high when effective communication is being developed. However, a high noise level can also be threatening to the teacher and may be misunderstood by both pupils and colleagues. Consider the balance which you must achieve between keeping order and being creative. Can you find an example which is characteristic of your subject?

SUMMARY

Many discipline incidents are trivial, but they can accumulate to make you as a teacher feel powerless. Most of the elements discussed in this chapter focus on how the teacher copes. The appropriate use of praise cannot be over-emphasised as an effective way of getting the best out of pupils. The major features of effective teaching have been discussed (being prepared, being confident, being a good manager of resources, being aware of environmental factors and being in control). When considering behaviour in schools it is also necessary to look more closely at two other major elements: the **pupil** and the **school**. Chapters 8, 9 and 12 on Motivation, Adolescence and the Self-fulfilling Prophecy are useful in this context. Analysis of whole-school issues will emerge in Part 3.

Useful references

Axline, V. (1969) **Play Therapy.** New York: Ballantine Books.

Brophy, J. (1981) **Teacher Praise: A Functional Analysis.** Review of Educational Research, 51 (1) 5–32.

DES and Welsh Office (1989) **Discipline in Schools: Report of the Committee of Enquiry Chaired by Lord Elton.** London: HMSO.

Fontana, D. (1994) **Managing Classroom Behaviour.** Leicester: British Psychological Society Books.

Kounin, J. (1970) **Discipline and Group Management in Classrooms.** New York: Holt, Reinhart and Winston.

Moon, B. and Mayes, A. S. (eds) (1994) **Teaching and Learning in the Secondary School.** London: Routledge.

Robertson, J. (1989) **Effective Classroom Control: Understanding Teacher–Pupil Relationships.** London: Hodder and Stoughton.

Scherer, M. (ed.) (reprinted 1992) **Meeting Disruptive Behaviour.** London: Routledge.

Wragg, E. and Wood, E. (1984) **Classroom Teaching Skills.** London: Routledge.

Planning, Preparation and Presentation (1)

Teaching is a very complex activity and, as with many other professions, involves a considerable degree of decision making, problem solving and 'orchestration' of knowledge and technique. (Clark and Yinger, 1987, p. 97)

LEARNING OUTCOMES

By the end of this session you should be aware of the necessity for clear, detailed lesson preparation, and some of the major techniques for achieving this.

You should be able to plan and prepare aims and outcomes for a short lesson, using a lesson planning guide. You should also be aware of presentation techniques and you should have examined the sequence of events from the start to the finish of a lesson and studied how teachers manage them. You should be able to describe the switch signals you want to use, and expectations you have of each of the five phases. (Expectations can be described in terms of pupil behaviour, noise levels and so on.)

Introduction

Ofsted (1995) reported that the lack of explicit long-term course or topic planning, as well as the lack of specific lesson preparation, are frequently identified as contributing to work of poor quality.

The HMI report 'The New Teacher in School' (DES, 1988) cited inadequate planning as a major determinant of 'poor' and 'very poor' lessons in secondary schools.

The most serious weaknesses were insufficient attention to planning and either lack of clear objectives or objectives that are misconceived, with the result that pupils often saw no progress in what they were being asked to do (DES, 1988, p. 22)

Features of 'good' or 'excellent' lessons observed were

. . . first and foremost, thoughtful planning and preparation, in which the choice of content, the use of a range of resources, and a variety of activities and teaching approaches were carefully considered. (DES, 1988, p. 22)

Thus the DFEE expressed the view that newly qualified teachers should be able to '. . . produce coherent lesson plans which take account of NCATs

(National Curriculum Attainment Targets) and of the school's curriculum policies ...', and when doing so '... ensure continuity and progression within and between classes and in subjects' (DFE, 1992).

The plan for a lesson, unit or course should be the result of a considerable degree of thinking on the part of the teacher.

Lesson planning

Discuss lesson planning with your mentor. You and your mentor may find the following outline of activities helpful to follow.

Early lesson planning – Ray the Mentor's approach

Ray Keeley is a Head of Special Needs

> 1 As a first step I planned a lesson using my own lesson planning proforma.
>   I gave the trainee a blank proforma and a list of areas to focus on and asked her to observe me teaching the lesson and to complete the proforma.
>   After the lesson we compared my original plan with the trainee's version, using the area of focus as a prompt for discussion. We explored our different perceptions of how the lesson progressed.
> 2 Secondly, we planned a lesson together and I conducted it. She was able to give more detailed analysis of this second lesson because she knew more about it through the joint planning. More specifically she noticed the changes I made and could guess at the reasons for them.
> 3 Our next step was for the trainee to begin to contribute to the teaching of some classes by either sharing the lead, splitting the group, using a circus of activities or team teaching.
>   We decided on our course of action and I involved the trainee fully in the planning of the lesson. I explained the context of the lesson, its objectives and then encouraged the trainee to suggest learning strategies and resources.
>   We carried out the lesson and then discussed the extent to which our objectives had been achieved.
> 4 Our final stage was jointly to plan a part of a lesson (15 mins?) for the trainee to deliver whilst I observed.

The sequence which Ray described gives you a framework for planning and beginning to teach, and this can be modified according to your level of experience and the challenges you face.

Lesson planning guide

When you plan a lesson there will be a number of general issues to consider as well as subject-specific issues. The following will give you some helpful guidelines to lesson planning, especially if you use the relevant chapters in this book.

● Make yourself familiar with the context of the lesson you are planning. Where does the lesson fit in the general scheme of work? How does it relate to the National Curriculum Programmes of Study? What is the general ability level of the group you will be teaching? How can you find the answer?

● What do you want the pupils to have done and learnt by the end of the sequence of lessons (or topic) and by the end of the particular lesson which you are planning? To what degree do you want to differentiate? How will you ensure continuity and progression?

● Build in assessment from the word go. What type of assessment will you use, for what purpose and at what point? How will your assessment relate to the National Curriculum requirements (if appropriate)?

● What are your aims and objectives for the lesson you are planning? State them clearly and then check back to see whether the activities which you have planned match with your intended outcomes. How will you let your pupils know what their objectives for the lessons are?

● Think carefully about the sequence and timing of the activities in the lesson. Pay attention to variety and try to build in variation in pace. Are there opportunities for whole class teaching, group work, pairwork, and so on.

● Do you intend to set homework? If so, at what point should this be done? Do you know whether pupils have the necessary equipment/ textbooks to be able to do the homework?

● Are there any key issues of classroom management to consider? Will you need to use teaching aids? Where are they kept and how will you use them? What do the pupils need? Consider each stage or phase of the lesson, including the structure of your beginning and end.

Planning your lesson

89

Plan a fifteen minute lesson in your subject, using these materials to guide you. You will find an example of a lesson planning sheet which you can modify below.

You will probably find that you need more space than has been provided here.

Do you believe that you need a new column called **'Teacher activity'** or would you fit this information into **'Organisation'**?

Lesson Plan

Activity ...... Estimating & Measuring Angles .....   Lesson No ...... 6 of 12 ......   Class .... 8Y ....   Date .... 14.11 ....

Learning outcomes ......To correct misconceptions about angle size. ....

Aims: To see if practical lesson helps with class management.
: To get class under control & get out alive.

Materials/resources needed .... Sheets with several angles on to be cut out. ....

Scissors & glue. Large gin and tonic.

Timing/phase	Pupil activity	Organisation	Teaching points	Comments: Teaching style Assessment Differentiation Special needs
5–10 mins	Registration. Use Number cards to settle them.	Whole class. Mentor starts lesson.		
10–25 mins = my 15 minute lesson	Cut out angles. Arrange in order of size & stick them in their books. Measure them & describe them (acute, obtuse etc).	Desks already arranged in 2 clusters on either side of room. I will choose groupings.	Mentor & I to do different groups & swap over pupils when ready. Contrast angle sizes.	I will use differentiation by response & pair pupils with those at similar levels.
25–40 mins	Change to mentor's task.	Changing tasks must be peaceful.		

Evaluation ...Achieved task to varying degrees. ....

Reasonably well behaved. Jo (Mentor) started & finished lesson which had a calming effect on me & the pupils.

Adrian

Lesson structure

Watching successful experienced teachers in action tends to provide student teachers with little explicit guidance on successful lesson management skills, since such teachers make everything look too easy. It is only when such teaching is contrasted with that of teachers where problems arise, that the difference in what they do becomes evident, and the skills used by successful lesson managers can be described. (Kyriacou, 1991)

Newly qualified teachers will be expected to create and maintain a purposeful and orderly environment for the pupils . . . (DFE, 1992)

Newcomers to teaching regard successful class management highly. Long hours spent lesson planning, marking and completing written course assignments can be tiring but are not as stressful as a lesson which goes out of control.

REFLECTION

90

Read through the following checklist, noting your acceptance or rejection of the statements. If you have the opportunity discuss them with others. Some of these will be relevant prompts for evaluations at the end of a lesson. You may find that your experiences change, or support, your views.

Discipline is the most serious problem facing schools today.

A systematic approach to discipline would be useful.

Teachers are trained to deal with behaviour problems.

Male teachers cope better with behaviour problems.

If you are a good teacher you should be able to handle all behaviour problems with no help from more experienced staff or parents.

Teachers have rights in the classroom.

Teachers have the right to establish a learning environment which meets their needs.

Teachers today risk burn-out.

Young teachers make the best teachers.

Teachers have no right to support from parents.

More behavioural problems occur in large classes.

Teachers have the right to the active support of their Head Teacher and senior staff.

Only experienced teachers should be given known difficult classes.

All pupils can behave appropriately in the classroom.

It is useful to send home positive notes to parents.

Teachers must ensure there are negative consequences every time pupils disrupt.

All pupils know how to behave when motivated to do so.

Teachers should consistently reinforce appropriate behaviour.

Well-structured lessons increase opportunities for learning and decrease opportunities for disruptive behaviour.

Lesson phases and switch signals

Hargreaves *et al* (1984) divide lessons into five phases:

1 The **entry** phase
2 The **settling down** or **preparation** phase
3 The **lesson proper** phase
4 The **clearing up** phase
5 The **exit** phase

Lesson phases

As you work through this chapter, prepare a checklist of the major issues in your subject, using these five headings. Include practical steps for managing them. Build on this resource bank of strategies as the year proceeds.

91

The entry phase

Rules operate to ensure that the teacher and pupils are assembled within the appropriate space, be it classroom, laboratory or sports hall.

Hargreaves lists three rules:

● Pupils must sit down or remain close to their seat.
● Pupils may talk to other pupils but they must not shout or scream.
● Pupils must cooperate in the distribution of equipment.

REFLECTION

How else might you manage the entry phase in PE for example? How does pupil age affect these rules? What rules may operate if the teacher does not implement the first and second of the above points? Is the situation different in PSE or tutorial lessons?

92

Using signals

Observe a colleague's lesson. Use an observation proforma (see Chapter 1). How much time is there between the lesson bell and the actual start of the lesson? What do pupils do while they are waiting? Are there any signals to mark the start of the lesson? Are there any activities or introductions to prepare the pupils for that lesson's work – for

93

example, a recap of last lesson's work or a short exercise, demonstration or task?

The settling down phase

Transcript

T: Right 9R can we have that chair . . .

S: Miss Karen's got my//

T: Alright Stephen. Karen? Hang on a minute . . .
Right can we make a start. Who's missing?

Several: (confused shouts)
(general noise)

S: Karen's got my bag.

T: Wait a minute. Right Stephen. What's the matter?

K: Nothing I never did anything to him he always . . . swinging it around . . . its not fair you//

R: Have you seen my book? Oi, Miss have you . . .

T: Karen ssh you'll have a turn in a minute. Just give him his bag back.

(general commotion)

Commentary

How do we address groups and individuals? Some groups have strong feelings about this.

If we ask a general question we can expect several people to answer at once. Are we then going to sound annoyed with those who were trying to help and what about those who can use this opportunity to continue their personal conversations?

Karen has interrupted here but feelings are running high so the teacher takes probably the only course open.
Would you object to being interrupted like this? Or is it sometimes best to ignore things?
'You'll have a turn' reassures the child that she will be listened to, if in the past the teacher has kept this type of promise.

REFLECTION

Compare the beginning of the following lesson with the one above

94

Transcript

T: Morning. Oh that's nice, Sam. James have you got yours? Good. On my desk . . .
(Children are chatting as they place bags under the tables. Some are reading the sheet on the benches.)

T: Let's begin. Jane. Parmjit. In front of you you have a sheet with instructions for the experiment we are going to do.
All got one. Good.

Yes, Sara. It will be good, this one, you'll enjoy it.
(Some laughter, including Sara)

Commentary
Greets the children as he lets them into the lab. Accepts work with a quiet word of appreciation.
They expect to put their bags out of the way. Safety rule.
This a positive, fast start. The two girls are required to pay attention.
Teacher uses this opportunity to scan whole class.
Pre-empts Sara.
An indication here of a good rapport.

REFLECTION

Consider Hargreaves' three rules listed on page 160. From the impression gained from these brief transcripts could you identify features here of successful management of the beginning of lessons?

95

The teacher's 'Good morning' or 'Sit down' serves as a switch-signal to end the entry phase and start the preparation phase. Ideally it should be enough to use one or two switch-signals to indicate a change from one phase to another.

The lesson proper phase

The lesson proper usually falls into several sub-phases.

In the first sub-phase the teacher is very active – explaining, demonstrating or describing.

Rules:

● Silence is expected

This is often the opportunity for teachers to engage and motivate their pupils. It is also the most demanding of a new teacher's skills of exposition.

The discussion of different types of circuit was pertinent and appropriate but tended to be delivered as a lecture with insufficient involvement of the pupils. A more animated delivery with ample, structured questions would engage the class more effectively. Straight descriptions may be accurate but it is much more interesting to use analogies and images to reinforce a message. (Subject Mentor's written comment on a PGCE student)

96

Explaining your subject

Choose an idea or concept, a term or an action from your subject and plan how to explain it. Decide if you will need to demonstrate, if it will require props, involve the use of an OHP or whiteboard. Watch out for having to explain something else first!

Find out where your idea/concept fits into your subject's National Curriculum.

In the second sub-phase, pupils take the active role, having been assigned a task, for example writing, reading, groupwork or solving problems.

Rules: There are two common rules in this second sub-phase:

● There is no loud talking or shouting
● The talk is work-related or relevant to the task

The third type of sub-phase is a combination of the first two with both teacher and pupil actively involved, for example question and answer sessions or discussions

Rules: Hargreaves gives the following rules for this sub-phase:

● On the whole, it is the teacher who asks the questions and the pupils who contribute the answers.
● Pupils should be willing to volunteer answers.
● That a pupil is willing to volunteer an answer should normally be signalled to the teacher by hand-raising.
● Pupils must answer when called upon to do so and normally should not shout out an answer on their own initiative.
● If the teacher does not allow the pupils to take the initiative several pupils must not call out their answers simultaneously.
● Pupils must not offer an answer whilst another pupil is answering.
● Pupils must not talk to each other when the teacher is talking or a pupil is answering a question.

The clearing up phase

Hargreaves maintains that clearing up follows on naturally. Also, this fourth phase is signalled by clear switch-signals such as 'Put your rulers and pencils away'.

Rules:

- Talking is allowed.
- Co-operation with teacher and helper pupils is expected.

The exit phase

When the teacher is ready the exit phase is signalled by such switch-signals as 'Right, away you go'.

Rules:

- The teacher, not the pupils, decide when exit is allowed.
- The pupils are expected to leave quietly, without crushing each other.

A trainee said of a teacher she had observed:

People say he's good – my mentor told me to watch him but I can't see what's so special. He didn't do a lot. I didn't think the lesson was that exciting or anything. For some reason the kids just behaved themselves. The same ones that are really sneery with me were so polite and nice I couldn't believe it. I'd thought they always behaved like they do with me. It made me mad to be honest.

The teacher said:

What Debbie didn't understand was that I worked really hard with that group.

The phrase *I had to work hard* with particular groups comes up frequently in teacher's reflections of lessons.

A group of teachers identified these factors, in no particular order, that constituted working hard during a lesson.

> Having everything to hand
> Making decisions very quickly
> Constantly scanning the room
> Anticipating difficulties with the work
> Differentiating on the spot
> Anticipating difficulties between pupils
> Being cheerful
> Feeling well-disposed towards individuals
> Listening properly
> Being firm, confident and positive
> Jumping on the first person out of line
> Being flexible
> Not losing your temper, or feeling defeated
> Avoiding whole-class sanctions
> Not jumping to conclusions
> Intervening quickly before there's an argument
> Good pace and timing – not letting an activity drag on or finishing it before the majority of pupils have finished.

Other groups would come up with other lists and frequently the items seem contradictory.

REFLECTION

97

Can you account for the contradictions in the list above? What action can be taken if the class does not respond quickly or fully to a teacher's signal that they are beginning the lesson?

There is no one right answer:

- You may calmly praise those who are responding.
- You may firmly call by name one or two individuals who are not responding.
- You may by body posture (for example standing **directly** in front of the class) begin either to address the class using an attention-seeking phrase such as 'I am waiting', or fold your arms and wait for silence.
- You may begin the lesson with an exceptionally interesting pronouncement delivered above the noise. 'Today we are going to set fire to things' (a burning fuels experiment) then drop the voice 'But only if I can hear myself think'.
- One teacher wrote SILENCE in big letters on the board. It worked. Maybe it will only work as long as it has novelty value.

Teachers develop their own style and the management can be quite subtle. Imagine the teacher speaking in an angry mood, in a hesitant manner or in a pleasant and assured tone and the differences it would make to these critical points.

Self-appraisal

98

Now analyse your own style: have you developed switch signals (for example *Okay! Right! And stop!*)? Are you developing ways of moving pupils smoothly from one activity to the next? Keep a record of them and add more as you go.

One trainee's mentor made this written comment on a lesson he watched.

The initial questions were not demanding enough and the pupils appeared to lose interest. Unacceptable behaviour was promptly tackled but in a rather bad tempered way.

A teacher's intonation, the pace, pitch and volume of what he or she says, can all affect pupils' reactions.

I've mentored three trainees this year with voice projection problems. The first was quite unusual. Gary never finished an explanation or instruction . . . He mumbled a lot, on a monotone. The children were always asking, What have we got to do? We suggested he prepare his explanations carefully before the lesson by practising on tape and playing it back to himself. Luckily, he had a partner who played the role of an uncomprehending 15 year-old and he improved dramatically.

(Mentor of a PGCE Geography student)

If teachers are not happy with the response of a class group they have several courses open to them. Schools have various procedures in place to help support teachers or classes who are having difficulties.

Support

While on your first placement in a school find out what support is available. Listen carefully to conversations that involve managing classes. Can you collect different teachers' views about how, and in what circumstances, staff can use the school's support systems?

99

SUMMARY

An experienced mentor, reflecting on the qualities of trainees who do well, said:

Many successful teachers, faced with difficulty managing a class, can hold two seemingly contradictory ideas in their heads at the same time. I am not to blame for this situation, and, What can I do to improve things?

Your developing understanding of Switch-Signals and lesson planning will help you to begin to develop the 'practical wisdom' of which Richard Smith writes: the applied combination of knowledge, theory, skills, perceptions and emotional responses.

Useful references

DFE (Circular 9/92, 1992) cited in Mawer, M. (1995) **The Effective Teaching of Physical Education.** Longman.

Gray, J. and Richter, J. (1988) **Classroom Responses to Disruptive Behaviour.** London: Macmillan.

Hargreaves, D. *et al Rules in Play* in Hargreaves, A. and Woods, P. (1984) **Classrooms and Staffrooms.** Milton Keynes: Open University Press.

Kyriacou, C. (1991) **Essential Teaching Skills.** Oxford: Basil Blackwell.

Laslett, R. and Smith, C. (1984) **Effective Classroom Management.** London: Croom Helm.

Wilkins, M. and Kyriacou, C. (1993) *The Impact of the National Curriculum on Teaching Methods at a Secondary School* in **Educational Research**, vol. 35, No. 3, pp. 270–276.

Evaluation and Reflection (1)

18

A thousand mile journey starts with one step. (Taoist saying)

LEARNING OUTCOMES

At the end of this chapter you will have more understanding of how to evaluate your teaching. The activities will help you in your development as a reflective practitioner by explaining why evaluation is important.

Introduction

Although evaluation of your teaching during your training year can often feel as if it is 'done to you' by observers and mentors, it is essential that you take an active role in evaluating your own work. By this stage in the course you will be developing your Professional Development Portfolio (PDP), using the guidelines in your course documentation. You need to check regularly with your mentor whether you are keeping a good variety of evidence, to record your development as a teacher.

Your teaching must be judged by the effect it has upon children's learning either in the short term or long term. When you are teaching a particular skill, effectiveness can be judged easily. However, on occasions you will be seeking to change pupils' attitudes to learning or to develop their metacognitive skills (their ability to learn how to learn).

Preparation

Discuss with your mentor a number of lessons you have observed or taught. For each lesson try to identify the main learning points for you in your professional development.

REFLECTION

100

One of the main aims of your course is to help you to become a **reflective practitioner**, a teacher who reflects on their practice. This term is taken from Donald Schön's work (1987), and is considered to be a feature of good teaching. Becoming a truly reflective practitioner will probably take you several years and can be achieved by using teacher as researcher methods. You will find yourself reflecting on your practice in all the following areas:

- planning and preparation
- lesson presentation
- provision for differentiation
- lesson management
- development of a positive classroom climate
- assessment of pupils' work

The aim is to judge the success of a lesson and to learn from the experience in order to make our teaching better in the future.

Feedback

Whatever your view of good teaching you will need to gather evidence with which to judge the effectiveness of your own teaching. One of the chief sources of information available to you from the start will be the feedback you receive from your mentors – experienced teachers accustomed to the pressures of teaching and aware of the individual pupils in the group you are teaching.

Receiving feedback won't be easy for you. You will have put a lot into the lesson and may feel defensive about your performance. Remember that your colleagues will feel equally responsible for your progress – the important thing is to learn from their observations. It is not just a professional courtesy to seek the opinion of your mentor; it's a real opportunity to learn more about teaching. Your mentor will no doubt see things that you miss, if only by virtue of their greater experience and having time to observe.

There is much to be gained, both from immediate feedback and advice and from taking the opportunity to **reflect** on the discussions you have with your colleagues.

In looking for evidence to evaluate your teaching you will be able to use the strategies outlined in Chapter 1 on methodology as 'Teacher as researcher and writer'. For example, if you are trying to gauge the effectiveness of a lesson involving group work and discussion, you could use systematic observation techniques. Whoever is observing your lesson (be it your mentor, a departmental colleague or another trainee) could be asked to record pupil time on- and off-task.

Early problems and the value of reflection

101

After you have read the case study below, make notes about any difficulties you are experiencing. Choose one area to analyse with your subject mentor. Remember that you should pay attention to the positive features of your teaching as well as considering what can be improved.

Mark has been training as a teacher for about two months. After his degree course he spent a year doing a variety of jobs and worked as a volunteer in a local youth club. He decided that as he enjoyed working with young people and felt enthusiastic about his subject – physical education – he should consider going into teaching. He applied during the following year and carefully saved some of his earnings to prepare himself for being a student again!

Mark entered his training course feeling fairly confident and enjoyed working alongside the experienced teachers in the department. He was aware that not all young people are enthusiastic about PE but this did not seem to be a big problem in the school where he was working. He knew he had to develop his understanding of a range of games and sporting activities and that he had to learn the specialist skills for teaching gymnastics and athletics during the year.

By November Mark had started teaching his own groups. Not all of them were going well. The weather had deteriorated and the pupils were a lot less keen to go outside into the cold wind than they had been earlier in the term. Quite a few had started 'forgetting their kit' and although Mark carefully followed departmental procedures about this, he felt sure that less forgetting would have gone on with the normal teacher. The preparation for lessons and the packing away process seemed to take longer than it should and he was finding that it was difficult to cover all the learning he had planned for each lesson.

Mark's subject mentor realised that he was embarking on a self-destructive sequence and sat down with him to identify the positive points of his teaching. Mark was able to acknowledge that he was achieving success with his younger groups, where participation and discipline was not a problem. His mentor encouraged him to adopt with the older groups techniques that he was using successfully with younger ones, for example making the organisation of equipment a part of the lesson, and to adapt his lesson plans for a week to work on the consolidation of skills, rewarding co-operative behaviour with a chance to take part in a game for the last part of the lesson.

At the end of the next week Mark was able to identify positive improvement in the attitudes of several of his pupils and to feel that both he and the pupils had enjoyed their lessons more. Gradually, he was succeeding in winning back some of the 'forgetters' and he began to approach the lessons in a more determined and positive frame of mind himself.

M Lesson observation and feedback

It is vital that you and your mentor develop a way of working which permits you to seek and receive regular and frequent lesson and feedback. There are many ways of achieving this evaluation.

A Mentor's approach to observing the trainee and giving feedback

Jill Rundle: Subject Mentor

The trainee and I planned the lesson which I was to observe. We determined a focus for the observation and discussed each other's preferred styles of teaching.

I used two columns on my observation sheet. On the left hand side I recorded an objective, chronological list of the events of the lesson. I used the right hand column to note objective comments alongside particular events.

At the end of the lesson I wrote a few notes as a general summary, gave the trainee a few words of encouragement and arranged a time to discuss the lesson fully. On one occasion she was upset about a lesson which did not go according to plan: I briefly pointed out three successes, asserted my belief that there was plenty of good material there and, later, spoke privately to her general mentor to check that there were no other problems.

When I gave the trainee my observation notes I folded them over and I asked her initially only to read the objective comments. In this way the trainee was able to comment on the events of the lesson from her point of view before my own comments could influence her in any way. It was interesting to compare her perceptions of the lesson with my own.

After a thorough discussion we were able to identify strengths demonstrated. Finally we set and recorded targets for the next lesson.

Joint target setting

Six guidance points for mentors and trainees. We should aim to set targets together which are:

- measurable
- attainable within a week or two
- specific (and do not degenerate into general goals)
- set by the trainee, with some guidance if necessary
- limited to three
- realistic, given the resources and classes available
- written down (form in Appendix 1) and kept for reference
- reviewed and re-appraised weekly

Keeping a record

It is important that you keep a record of your reflection and evaluation of teaching episodes. However, there is a risk that this will become a chore, completed for its own sake rather than for the effect it has upon your professional development. Some graduates are less experienced (or perhaps only too experienced) in writing at length and see the act of writing as a barrier rather than a tool to aid reflection.

There are alternative ways of keeping records. Try dictating your ideas onto tape at the end of the day: write the key points up later when you have time. You might prefer to talk to another trainee instead and record your conversation. The important thing is to record, analyse and question. Don't forget that your mentor is there to help as well. Taping some of your discussions with your mentor may help you recall key points.

Keeping a notebook handy to jot down critical incidents is another solution. Moments of real success or failure, which bring insight into some aspect of your learning to teach, can be recorded in brief note form at the end of a lesson. These are just short reminders for you – if the incident is important enough, they will be sufficient to jog your memory.

What should you record?

Telling you what to record means there is a danger of doing the reflection for you, defeating the point of the exercise. Wood's five levels of support (see Chapter 7) might suggest that letting you get on with it will not necessarily lead to reflection on your behalf either.

  Evaluating lessons

Discuss with your mentor some successful lessons you have observed or taught. Use the following questions to assist you in the evaluation of the lessons:

102

- **What** happened?
- **What** effect did it have?
- **Why** did it happen?
- **How** can I make sense of it?

- **How** could it be different?
- **How** might I (we) have behaved differently?
- **What** would I do next time?

Your questions might be applied to a moment, a lesson, a sequence of lessons or even to a school placement.

REFLECTION

103

While you read Maria's words below, consider possible concerns about being watched.

On being watched

Maria is a Science teacher (NQT). These are her views on being watched during her first year of teaching:

I have to think about the lesson a lot more. Last year because I was on the course I really enjoyed getting feedback. It's nice to take time out to look at what you've achieved and think: I did this wrong, that wrong. I learnt about what to do to improve my lesson. You don't often get a chance to think about it. I'd love to go round and look at other people and see what they're doing. That's what's nice about having trainees in. Last term there was a trainee in school. It was nice watching what she did that worked. She comes up with different ideas for worksheets and things like that and sees exactly what the teacher misses. It's totally different. You think that you see every-thing and then when you see someone else doing it you realise that you see about 10% of what goes on. I'm still used to being observed. However with people who haven't been observed for three or four years you have to be really careful.

SUMMARY

During the course of your training you will need to have faith in your ability to learn and therefore to change. By recording your self-evaluations and reflections you will be able to chart your changing perceptions of your own per-formance, as well as the changes in your teaching, and the develop-ment of your professional relationships with pupils, mentors and col-leagues.

Useful references

HMI (1988) **The New Teacher in School.** London: HMSO.

Kyriacou, C. (1993) *Research on the Development of Expertise in Classroom Teaching During Initial Training and the First Year of Teaching* in **Educational Review**, vol. 45, No. 1, pp. 79–87.

Martin, S. (1995) *Promoting Reflective Practice Amongst Mathematics Novice Teachers: Are the Perceived Benefits Related to Novices' Learning Styles?* in **Proceedings of the Day Conference Held at the University of Birmingham.** London: British Society for Research into Learning Mathematics.

Ofsted (1993) **Framework for the Inspection of Schools.** London: HMSO.

Schön, D. (1987) **Educating the Reflective Practitioner.** US: Jossey-Bass.

PART

2

Develop Your Teaching

Introduction

That transition from the back to the front is one of the longest walks that you make, because the children have got used to seeing you at the back and suddenly one day you're there at the front. Both you and the pupils, have got to settle yourselves in.

(Jenny, PGCE trainee 1993–94)

By now you will have completed the induction period and established yourself in school, spending time in lessons both as a non-participant observer and as a participant observer. You may have tracked a pupil throughout the school day, in order to experience at first hand the variety of teaching and learning styles to which a pupil is exposed. You will have used a combination of methods for collecting and analysing information, and you will have been teaching individuals, groups and possibly whole classes.

During your time in school you will have encountered many different examples of the goodness of fit between a pupil's needs and the learning context; you will also have seen pupils struggling or switching off. You have begun the task of analysing how children learn – a journey of exploration which will last throughout your teaching career.

Part 2 will help you to put this knowledge into practice: the major emphasis is on you as teacher, and as a teacher-researcher using critical evaluation. You will be using the activities to look again at assessment and pupil management, and to reconsider areas such as planning, preparing, delivering and evaluating lessons.

In order to help you to plan, implement and reflect, materials have been drawn from a variety of sources: recent government documents, educational literature and research, pupils' beliefs, case studies and teachers' voices.

Chapters 19 to 25 and Chapter 30 can be used in school with other trainees, with your general mentor and/or your subject mentor. One approach which can be used within such sessions is that of controlled, documented 'brainstorming'. This can lead to planning, implementation and reviews and by using techniques such as Brainstorming you will also focus on aspects of professional practice which you would like to develop, for example encouraging pupils to think. Coping with Stress and Securing a Teaching Post also, perhaps understandably, belong here.

ACTION RESEARCH

Teacher as Researcher

19

Action research is small-scale intervention in the functioning of the real world and a close examination of the effects of such intervention. (Cohen and Manion, 1994)

In Part 2 you will be consolidating the methodology techniques you first encountered in Part 1. The chart below will help you to cross-reference between Part 1 and Part 2 and you will make different use of these research methodologies, because you will be aiming to improve your own practice. We call this **action research**. One way of achieving this would be to plan three lessons, teach them and review your successes. You would modify your second and third lessons with particular reference to the areas covered in this textbook – Chapters 19 to 25 and Chapter 30.

Action research is a term which is used frequently and has virtually no meaning in some contexts. Yet it is a valuable pursuit, which enables you as teacher to take control of your teaching and make it better, developing your understanding of your own practice and using your planning, teaching and evaluation as an experimental circle of research. Having identified an issue which you wish to work on through your teaching, you will proceed through a process which follows a sequence like this: observation → solution → action → reflection → modification (as in Kemmis and McTaggart, 1982).

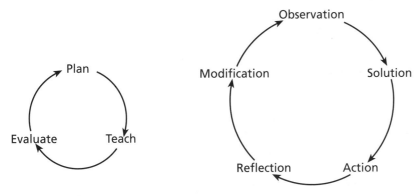

The original model of 'action research' and the term itself were developed by Kurt Lewin, a social psychologist. Elliott describes Lewin's model, which has more steps to it than that of Kemmis and McTaggart (above) but which may reflect more accurately the to-ing and fro-ing of our attempts to improve our own practice. Lewin's model runs as follows. In brackets are some possible applications to the field of education:

1 identifying a general idea (curriculum or management focus)
2 reconnaissance (find facts within department)

3 general planning (study section from a Programme of Study: PoS)
4 developing the first action step (plan first lesson)
5 implementing the first action step (teach first lesson)
6 evaluation (reflect with mentor)
7 revising the general plan (prepare for second lesson)

A spiral then evolves in which you develop the second and then the third action step. You can replace 'step' with 'lessons' and conduct action research on a series of three lessons.

Elliott suggests that implementation of an action step is not easy – monitoring the extent of the implementation is advisable before the effects can be understood. It is certainly true that your actions in a lesson are difficult to disentangle from the events which led up to them and the effects which those actions then have. Consider the following: a pupil uses bad language within earshot of the teacher. The teacher chooses to ignore it. What will happen now? That pupil may desist from such testing behaviour, or decide to become even more outrageous. Many complex factors will have determined the teacher's first decision and if the teacher had chosen to act differently the subsequent chain of events might have been completely different. When conducting action research into your own teaching, you need to acknowledge these complexities, and be honest about the subjective element of your analysis.

In other words, your action research should fulfil three functions:

● it should help you to improve your own practice
● it should also enable you to present theoretical conclusions
● it should be discussed with colleagues and made accessible to them.

This is 'systematic enquiry made public' (Stenhouse, quoted in Rudduck 1985) and the assignment as set out below would make it possible. Action research is also context-bound and should contribute to your self-evaluation.

Managing the Learning Environment
3000 Word Assignment

Introduction
For this assignment you will be required to analyse a sequence of lessons which you have taught during your First School Placement Module.

The Task
You should submit a critical analysis of your chosen sequence of lessons in the light of your experiences and your background reading.

You should pay particular attention to the following key areas:

• Planning and preparation
• Lesson presentation
• Provision for differentiation
• Lesson management
• Development of a positive classroom climate
• Assessment of pupils' work
• Reflection and evaluation

You should indicate how your analysis will inform the planning and preparation of subsequent sequences of lessons. In short what have you learnt?

Guidance

1 Three lessons will give you plenty of material.

2 The lessons should be with the same class or large group.

3 You can include as an appendix to your analysis (not part of the 3000 words) a *selection* from the following:
lesson plans and evaluations; examples of children's work; feedback on your lesson(s) from the Training Manager or Subject Colleagues; . . .

4 Your analysis should stand on its own merits without reference to the appendices.

Assessment Criteria

Please refer to the generic list of criteria in the Course Handbook.

References

Kyriacou, C. *Essential Teaching Skills*
Kyriacou, C. *Effective Teaching in Schools*
Perrott, E. *Effective Teaching*

You should look for additional evidence to support your arguments.

School-based initial teacher education is characterised by its practical emphasis. We believe that this is the best way to learn to teach. However, it is vital that your mentors support you in reflecting on your practice. Edwards and Brunton use Vygotsky's ideas to clarify the relationship between mentor and trainee. Vygotsky believed that learning takes place first in a social way between individuals (intermental level) and is then internalised in a personal way (intramental level). This reflection in and on practice can take place during a lesson, after a lesson, or over coffee in the staffroom, as well as during mentoring sessions. Moreover, your learning can influence the development of others:

The more mentoring I do, the more I realise what I do, and therefore in a way the more effective I am as a mentor. It sort of feeds round in a circle. The more I think about my teaching, the more I can explain to them how I teach, and hopefully the more effective I become. (Jo, Subject Mentor)

In conclusion the use of action research in this controlled way will help you and others to develop.

Useful references

Cohen, L. and Manion, L. (1994) **Research Methods in Education.** 4th Edition. London: Routledge.

Edwards, A. and Brunton, D. 'Supporting Reflection in Teachers' Learning' in Calderhead, J. and Gates, P. (1993) **Conceptualizing Reflection in Teacher Development.** London: The Falmer Press.

Elliott, J. (1991) **Action Research for Educational Change.** Milton Keynes: Open University Press.

Kemmis, S. and McTaggart, R. (1982) **The Action Research Planner.** Geelong, Victoria: Deakin University Press.

Rudduck, J. and Hopkins, J. (1985) **Research as a Basis for Teaching. Readings from the Work of Lawrence Stenhouse.** London: Heinemann.

Suggested Plan for Action Research on Three Lessons

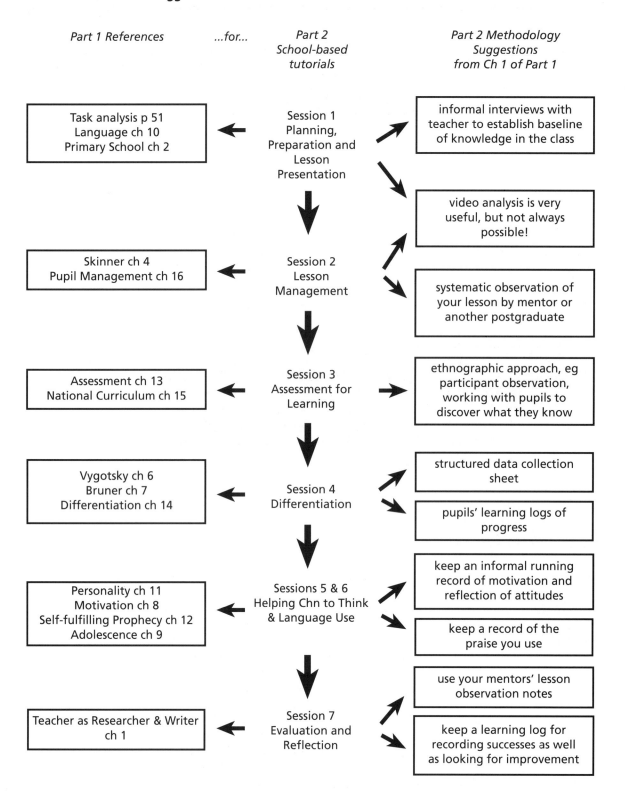

| *Part 1 References* | *...for...* | *Part 2 School-based tutorials* | *Part 2 Methodology Suggestions from Ch 1 of Part 1* |

Task analysis p 51
Language ch 10
Primary School ch 2

Session 1
Planning, Preparation and Lesson Presentation

informal interviews with teacher to establish baseline of knowledge in the class

video analysis is very useful, but not always possible!

Skinner ch 4
Pupil Management ch 16

Session 2
Lesson Management

systematic observation of your lesson by mentor or another postgraduate

Assessment ch 13
National Curriculum ch 15

Session 3
Assessment for Learning

ethnographic approach, eg participant observation, working with pupils to discover what they know

Vygotsky ch 6
Bruner ch 7
Differentiation ch 14

Session 4
Differentiation

structured data collection sheet

pupils' learning logs of progress

Personality ch 11
Motivation ch 8
Self-fulfilling Prophecy ch 12
Adolescence ch 9

Sessions 5 & 6
Helping Chn to Think & Language Use

keep an informal running record of motivation and reflection of attitudes

keep a record of the praise you use

use your mentors' lesson observation notes

Teacher as Researcher & Writer ch 1

Session 7
Evaluation and Reflection

keep a learning log for recording successes as well as looking for improvement

Planning, Preparation and Presentation (2)

20

I'm expected to learn by osmosis.

I have to show I can plan lessons but everyone in the Department teaches from an already written Scheme of Work with detailed lesson plans. They say, Don't reinvent the wheel. Use these. (PGCE trainees)

I gave him absolutely everything he needed. I told him exactly what to do and he still couldn't manage it. (Subject Mentor)

LEARNING OUTCOMES

By the end of this chapter you will have used some planning and presentation techniques. You will be able to structure a lesson, using a lesson planning guide, assess reading material and compose effective worksheets. You should be developing links between your own schemes of work and the relevant sections of the National Curriculum Programme of Study in your subject.

Introduction

 Newcomers to teaching often feel that they are given insufficient guidance. Many appreciate that the task of planning a lesson is so vast that they don't know where to start. The difficulty is not that there are too few parameters, rather that it is difficult to successfully gauge where those parameters are. Planning involves research and an exploration of the boundaries in the initial stages. Experienced teachers are attuned to all sorts of signals and, rather like the driver who does not think about every gear change, they only have to work on the map of the journey. This automatic practice may account for why some practising teachers are poor at explaining the planning process to new teachers. Eraut (1994) believes that we should be wary of this 'automatic' model, because he believes that we should acknowledge the importance of planning and accept that expert teachers may make mistakes.

Unless you have made the plans your own by working them through in your head, by understanding where the children are in their learning, and why you are doing what you are doing, the lesson may well be disappointing, even though the plan looks good.

Remember, you will be planning lessons in the context of particular classes, in a particular school. The teachers already working in that situation will have internalised this part of the planning process.

There are a number of general and localised factors which will influence not just the content, but the delivery of your material, and which should be explicitly planned for.

REFLECTION

Think about how the following have influenced the lessons you have observed. You may wish to add to this list.

104

The National Curriculum (Refer to the chapter on the National Curriculum)	Programmes of Study
	Attainment Targets
	Examination Syllabus
The School (This is a key function of school familiarisation programmes)	Whole School Policies
	Department Policies
	Existing Schemes of Work
	Resources available
	The Catchment
The Class (This is a key function of observation programmes)	Class routines
	Class interests/behaviour
	Class and teacher expectations
	Individual Needs
The Teacher (Self appraisal)	Subject knowledge
	Presentation and delivery techniques and skills
	Preferred teaching style
	Interests
The Wider World (a variety of events and circumstances from outside can influence planning)	Political trends
	National and Local Events
	Topical issues
	The weather

The Case Study which follows shows how subject knowledge and the context can be combined to inform the planning of a Scheme of Work. It may seem most relevant to those training to teach English although it does illustrate the interplay of factors which may be taken into account in any subject.

Planning a scheme of work

105

Sarah, a trainee, had to plan a Scheme of Work for a Year 9 English class. Look at what Sarah has said about her planning for this class in the light of the **National Curriculum**, **the school**, **this particular class**, **her personal preferences** and the **wider world**. Were there any unintended outcomes that Sarah could use to inform future work with this class?

I had to teach Romeo and Juliet, a set text for the SATs, to a class of mixed-ability Year 9 pupils. They are a noisy group but very interested in topical issues. They will discuss things that interest them but there are some difficult characters in the group. A group of girls are excessively interested in boys and make-up; often in trouble but above average ability. The class teacher told me that the leader of this group is a really talented writer. Many children in this class have had problems in their families, which has affected their school work or their attitude. One boy is statemented as a non-reader. He has a teacher supporting him in one out of the two lessons a week I have with this class.

I decided to concentrate on a few major aspects of the play, feuds between families, the theme of fate with the star-crossed lovers, and the poetry.

The family conflicts I thought they would understand, but I was a bit worried, as this is a Catholic school with several Irish children in the class, about tackling the Protestant/Catholic parallels, you know.

The role of fate I thought would appeal particularly to the girls, who spend a lot of time reading their stars in magazines and who were interested in relationships with friends and so on. But I wanted to feel I was teaching some real literature. It's the poetry I really love, and I wanted to give opportunities to get some really good work.

I started with a description of the personalities associated with various star signs. This was an unexpected opportunity to teach vocabulary! Lots of the words such as reckless and impetuous they didn't know. I then got them to write a personality description of a best friend, a bad teacher, a good parent, themselves. These characters I later compared to Romeo or Juliet, the Capulets and Montagues, Mercutio, the friar and the nurse.

The difficulty with teaching Shakespeare seemed to me to be that I was the only person who knew any thing much about Shakespeare and I thought this would bore the children who couldn't be very active. The class teacher suggested I find out what the class collectively knew about the play first so I brainstormed on the board, accepting anything. I was amazed. We even got one or two quotations.

The other stroke of luck I had was the case in the news of a 14 year-old girl who had left Essex to marry her Turkish boyfriend. The class got into a deep discussion, arguing about the characters in this story. The newspapers even used Romeo and Juliet in their reporting. The fact that shocked me the most was that the more emotionally mature of the group took the view that what a teenager did was the teenager's affair, that parents generally were too interfering. They were, however, very critical of a parent who would let their child leave home at 14, or marry at that age. And most surprising of all they weren't aware of any contradiction in what they were saying.

Scheme of Work

Title:- 'Romeo and Juliet' by William Shakespeare   Key Stage 3   Time to complete

Class.................

Aims: To familiarise pupils with a prescribed text by Shakespeare.
To explore plot and character in R&J.
To study the language of Shakespeare.

Note:- *In Key Stage 3, . . . pupils should be introduced to . . . a play by Shakespeare (p 20)'*

Objectives:
- Enable pupils to follow the plot of the play, exploring the sequencing of events.
- Identify the major themes of the play.
- Explore the motivation of the major characters.
- Produce a variety of written and spoken outcomes.

Skeleton Plan

1   Pre-reading activities, introducing ideas to be explored later through the text:- Family conflict using role play cards and/or an episode of a soap.
2   Star signs and their associated personalities – ideas of fate and destiny.
3   Brainstorming and DARTs (Directed Activities in Reading and Thinking) to understand plot sequence.
4   Language study including language change, and language form.
5   Explore the themes of love and fate. Look at how these are conveyed in the language.
6   Character profiles and roles.
7   Analysis of particular scenes, drawing together character, theme and language study.
8   Examination practice.

Assessment:

Assess by National Curriculum level descriptors in each AT and record according to Dept. policy. Differentiation by response, complexity of ideas manipulated and written and spoken outcomes. Structure discussion and written work, encouraging progression through questioning technique and development of argument.

Specific planned opportunities for Speaking and Listening (AT1):

In pairs, groups and whole class. Opportunities for role play, argument and debate. Some of the tasks require analysis of character and situation and encourage the development of reasoning.

Reading (AT2):

Shakespeare text. Vocabulary work, reading and using adjectives precisely to describe character.

Writing: (AT3):

Short descriptions and a formal essay.

Resources

Textual:
Visual:
Audio:
IT
(Abbreviated in part – for guidance only)

Once Sarah has a Scheme of Work she can confidently plan individual lessons. The numbers on the skeleton plan will correspond roughly to the lesson or small sequence of lessons.

Lesson Plan *(possibly 2nd in Scheme)*

Date   **Time**   **Class details**

Notes:

Aims:

Learning Outcomes (Objectives): ....

Resources:

Textual: Class set of 'Star Signs'
                     Set of templates for writing the four descriptions

Visual:

Audio: Tape of the prologue?
IT

Methodologies

Timing	Organisation	Pupils' Activity	Teaching Points	Comments
10 mins	Sheets on desk before pupils arrive. Pupils sit in pairs, facing the front.	Read sheet. Each child compares their character to that described under their star sign. Discuss with partner.	Give meanings of unfamiliar adjectives used to describe character traits.	Make note of those whose vocabulary is particularly good or poor.
10 mins	Teacher lead	Whole class discussion: Is character predetermined by the stars?		Could extend whole class discussion if goes well.
20 mins	Individual work sheet/template prepared with four headings and space for sign/ symbol.	Write brief description of characteristics of:- 'Myself', 'Typical Parent' 'Ideal Friend' and 'A Bad Teacher' as model given on sheet.	Looking for the choice of adjectives to describe characters. The sign should be symbolic of the character. Explain. Encourage good presentation.	Ideas introduced here, to be noted later roughly are: Myself = Romeo or Juliet Parent = Capulet /Montague Friend = Benvolio/ Mercutio Teacher = Nurse/ Friar
5 mins	Class facing the front	Listening to teacher: Reading out examples of work.	Finish work sheet of 4 characters for homework.	Display finish sheets.

Assessment: ....

....

Evaluation: ....

Lesson Plan *(possibly 3rd in Scheme)*

Date   **Time**   **Class details**

Notes:

Aims:

Learning Outcomes (Objectives): ....

Resources:

Textual: OHT of the Prologue for Romeo and Juliet

Visual:

Audio: Tape of the prologue?
IT

Methodologies

Timing	Organisation	Pupils Activity	Teaching Points	Comments
15 mins	Groups of four, label A, B, C, D. Rough paper.	Write role play cards. A: character traits of an imaginary teenager. B: the same C: character traits of an imaginary parent D: character traits of an imaginary aunt/uncle.	Try to use some of the vocabulary from last lesson.	
10 mins		Role play situation – A has fallen in love with someone C finds totally undesirable. C confronts A. B and D observe. B advises A and D advises C.	Extension – hot seat very good performers. Explain carefully. Check for understanding. Teacher moves from group to group. Characters must not change roles they have written themselves.	Opportunity for oral assessments.
10 mins	Class face the front.	Class feedback. How true to life was it?		From comments judge depth of understanding
10 mins	OHT of the prologue from Romeo and Juliet.	Class listen to teacher reading/tape?	Elicit issues of rights, family feuds, prejudice between racial, social and religious groups. Draw points together. How different characters react in different situations. Advise class will start with prologue next lesson.	

Assessment:..

....

Evaluation:...

Recording schemes and lesson plans

Discuss Sarah's Scheme of Work and individual lesson plans, possibly with a colleague. What format is used in your department for recording schemes and lesson plans? Compare and contrast Sarah's plans with your own. Would you prefer another model?

106

Scheme of work

Work out the aims and objectives and opportunities for assessment from this lesson plan (1–8 in Schemes of Work).

107

Do you think the children would be able to see the point of the lessons? Are there a variety of activities? What will they be able to do, or know, by the end? How will the teacher know? Are there opportunities for assessment?

How could achievement be recorded? (See Chapter 13 on Assessment.)

What continuity and progression is there?

For more help with planning refer to Active Learning in Chapter 39, Group Work in Chapter 6 and Chapter 14 on Differentiation. The 'must', 'should', 'could' chart below, will also help with your planning.

When planning a lesson, the following checklist can be useful:

● What do the pupils already know?
● What do I want them to know (in other words my long-term aims and my short-term objectives)?
● How long do I have?
● How will I structure, sequence and finish the lesson?
● How will I present it?
● What equipment/facilities do I need?
● What will the pupils actually do?
● How will I evaluate the lesson?

This checklist can be viewed differently, using the mnemonic SACK:

Skills: what will they be able to do?
Attitudes: how will I motivate them? How will they collaborate with each other? How will their beliefs change?
Concepts: what ideas and thinking patterns will they develop?
Knowledge: what will they actually *know*?

A third way of approaching your planning is by considering these categories: knowledge, concept, skill and teaching and learning, in terms of the levels **must**, **should** and **could**.

● **Must** represents what each pupil needs to achieve, or know already – a baseline.
● **Should** represents what the majority of pupils should achieve.
● **Could** represents a level to be reached by the most able pupils.

Here are two completed examples of this. The danger of this approach is that it oversimplifies a complex situation. Despite this, such a grid structure can help you to clarify your ideas while planning. Before using this approach you should be clear about whether you are planning a single lesson or a sequence of lessons – this grid can be used for either.

Possible focus: Year 7 – Designing an item for sale at Christmas Fayre (textile)
(Research – Design – Make – Evaluate)

	MUST	SHOULD	COULD

Knowledge	Single design
	Use of materials
	Textiles: materials
	          glues
	          joins
	How to devise a design
	Follow instructions
	Design knowledge
		Repeated patterns	More complex patterns or designs

Concept	Creativity – imagination research/design/make/ evaluate ──────────────────→		Market forces – demand
Skill	(Sewing) ──────────→ Sticking Cutting Design skills Research skills (in class – what kind of item will sell?)	Sewing Details Process Devising questionnaires	Lace skills (already learnt) (by outcome) Analysing
Teaching & Learning	Teaching of basic skills of construction Research skills need to be taught, eg questioning Design – drawing	Extending skills of ──────────→ construction Designing questionnaire E V A L U A T I N G D E V E L O P I N G C R E A T I V I T Y	

Possible focus: Year 7 – Compose a piece of music (in a group) which should reflect either or both the movement & sound of an animal

	MUST	SHOULD	COULD
Knowledge	Be aware of contrasting pitch, rhythm and structure Be part of performance	Use pitch/rhythm to compose melodic line, with accompaniment, showing texture, timbre and dynamics Perform Evaluate process	Notate composition Direct performance Evaluate their own and others
Concept	Pitch Time Structure	Pitch Duration Structure Timbre Texture Dynamic	Relationships between concepts
Skill	Recording Process – graphic – written form Limited performance skill e.g. simple rhythm, or ostinato melody	Notation – graphic & musical Performance – recognition of ensemble Evaluate process	Full notation Use of IT in recording composition
Teaching & Learning	Individual teacher help Group work Discussion – social skills Take part in performance	Group work Lead discussion Ref to previous knowledge – C of A Present perform & record	Support of others Organising group performance Record & revise

Preparing and presenting material for teaching

A mentor wrote about a trainee's lessons:

John has used some imaginative and creative approaches to topics. For example, he has made jigsaws of the structure of the skin and periodic table game cards. The cards were of excellent quality. This is potentially a very difficult class with a significant specials needs demand but the lesson was delightful, even magical. Much of the success was due to the meticulous planning and the provision of entirely appropriate material. All the activities were inclusive and all the written material was accessible.

Some of the difficulties that children experience in composing effective written language and in understanding books and workcards derive from the differences between written and spoken language. (K. Perera, 1984)

The language of a textbook, for example, often has to include **specialist vocabulary** that children need to learn. It is estimated that a reader can normally comprehend a text as long as s/he recognises a reasonable percentage of the words.

REFLECTION

Choose a school textbook. Look at it critically. What is it that you like about it? Are there any features you think are poor? What Key Stage is it intended for?

108 Some years ago it was common for teachers to talk about 'readability' and there are reputedly fifty ways of measuring the degree of difficulty of a text. One, an adaptation of the Fogg Index (1952), illustrates the point:

Readability formula

● Select, at random, at least three one hundred word passages from the book.
● Count the number of sentences in the hundred words to the nearest complete sentence.
● Calculate the average number of words in a sentence.
● Count the number of words of three or more syllables in the hundred words.
● Add the average sentence length to the number of words of more than three syllables.
● Multiply the total by 0.4. This will be the American Grade level for which this text is suitable.
  six years old = Grade 1.
● Repeat, as checks, with other passages.

Readability formula

Using the formula find out the reading age of the textbook you looked at.

Although this method may have its uses, it is likely that you have found it an unsatisfactory way of evaluating the appropriateness of the book. It is worthwhile clarifying the reasons for that dissatisfaction because it enables us to look at our *own teaching materials* critically and improve them. Record your findings.

Even if the reading age approximates to your impressions, it is not just the word and sentence length that makes a book 'readable'. Many linguistic and visual features *in conjunction with each other* make books and worksheets accessible. An acknowledgement of the importance of how interested the reader is, how much s/he needs or wants to read the book and the fact that word length is not a reliable indicator of reading complexity has led to these formulae being used less frequently. Our instincts about 'readability' are often sound enough, but the idea raises interesting issues.

REFLECTION

How much should the reading needs of one or two children influence our choice of materials for the majority?

How do we improve reading ages if we never make demands on our readers?

DARTs

There are several techniques loosely termed DARTs (DARTs is an acronym for Directed Activities in Reading and Thinking, or Directed Activities in Reading Texts) that can help children engage with the material we want them to understand. DARTs were originally developed by Lunzer and Gardner (1984). For example:

● Pupils create their own questions to ask about a text.
● Pupils supply words missing from a text (Cloze procedure).
● The text is split into sections and the children reassemble it in the correct sequence.
● The pupils rewrite the text in another form, for example having read about the Industrial Revolution, they write a story about a mill worker.

Other ways of introducing and familiarising pupils with the terminology of your subject:

● Explain the terms, or let children guess the meanings, before they read the text
● Explain the derivations of the word and mention other words that are from the same family. TV and films are a source of enlightenment
● Write a glossary
● Play word games

Recording reading

While tracking a pupil through the school day, record how much, what type and for what purposes a particular child has to read in one school day.

111

Reading difficulties

Blank out every fifth word of a page from an unfamiliar text book. This exercise is easier if you work in a pair and prepare a photocopied text in this way for each other. How difficult is it to understand now? A child with a reading difficulty may be faced with text of this level of difficulty several times a week.

112

Common features mentioned as making a text-book and/or worksheet readable:

The layout (graphological features)

- the typeface and the size of the letters
- clear headings
- bold print or italics to highlight selected words or sentences
- use of colour, including colour-coding
- An 'easy on the eye' handwriting style. Letters formed conventionally.
- Illustrations, diagrams, tables, matrices, flowcharts
- Paragraphs clearly marked, bullet points, symbols, numbered instructions
- White space
- Line length
- Gaps. Where
  lines are split can make
  it harder or . . .
  Where the lines are split
  can make it **easier** to read.
- Signposting, showing pupils the way around the page. Demarcation of instruction and information.

Despite recommendations for clarity, it is worth remembering that children can follow cartoons easily. These are surprisingly complicated and require somewhat different reading skills. They do not always read left to right, for example, and have their own conventions. Children are also very familiar with the type of matrices that appear in football tables or other forms of statistics even when the print is small.

Vocabulary and grammar

- Synonyms (words with a similar meaning) to support difficult vocabulary which is in brackets (parentheses)
- A limited number of unfamiliar words
- Inclusive language: 'We looked at volcanoes **last week**'
- Written instructions in the active rather than the passive: 'You must heat the water' rather than 'The water must be heated'
- The use of simple sentence constructions
- Standard English **grammar**, conventional punctuation and accurate spelling

Assessing a worksheet

Look at one of your own worksheets critically. Write a worksheet using some of these techniques to make your meaning clearer or to introduce new terminology or to test the children's understanding of the topic you have taught.

113

As you sequence the lesson's activities think about how you will present the content to the children.

What variety of tasks are there? Will the change from one activity to another necessitate changing the layout of the classroom or the grouping of the children? How will you control or direct the pace of the lesson so that the children's interest and motivation is sustained?

SUMMARY

It is essential that you plan what you will do, that you plan what the children will do and that you know why. How the reality matches up will depend on the quality of that planning.

A well-planned lesson will have taken account of:

- the interplay of a range of factors, some of which may be outside our control but much of which can be anticipated
- the production of accessible teaching and learning materials
- a lesson structure suited to the needs of the children
- an appropriate delivery that interests and challenges

Just because a lesson is unsuccessful once does not necessarily mean it will not work in another situation with another group. Teaching parallel classes in the same year may highlight how the interplay of factors and personalities produce differing outcomes.

Useful references

Eraut, M. (1994) **Developing Professional Knowledge and Competence.** London: Falmer Press.

Lunzer, E. and Gardner, K. (1984) **Learning from the Written Word.** Edinburgh: Oliver and Boyd.

Pupil Management (2)

21

But all subsists by elemental strife,
And passions are the elements of life
(Alexander Pope)

LEARNING OUTCOMES

During this chapter we will be looking at pupil management in ways which will help you consider your own personal style; we will discuss techniques and strategies and attitudes. Many of these will enable us to share common ground with each other, yet it is your individual style and personal learning which are the keys to your success. There are many different acceptable solutions to discipline issues. Techniques and strategies are useless to you unless you find a place for them in your way of teaching and your unique and individual way of being with pupils. Your individuality also needs to integrate with the school system within which you are working, and to support your development as a subject specialist.

Pupil management involves managing yourself in order that pupils can derive maximum benefit from your teaching.

Jonathan

Jonathan, a twenty two year-old newly qualified music teacher, is having difficulty with a boisterous bunch of sixth form boys. Reconciling himself to the fact that he may not gain the respect of such pupils until he has established himself more securely within the school, he is also learning something else from the situation:

114

When I am really concentrating on my playing, I lick my lips. These characters sit near the organ in chapel and after a week or so I realised that they had noticed. I don't do it now. It took a supreme effort of willpower but I don't lick my lips any more.

115

Now note any aspects of your behaviour in front of a class which you find difficult to come to terms with e.g. being 'bossy', being firm in a way which makes you unpopular, making sweeping generalisations about a subject area, which you know will help some of the class, but which you know to be simplistic.

There is a new person here ... 'me as teacher', whom you may not always like. You may need to adopt new strategies to help you with this role.

List three teacherly changes in behaviour which you believe are consistent with your personality and would not surprise a friend?

Self control

You will have natural reactions towards pupils because they are fellow human beings, yet these reactions need to be considered carefully; you may find some pupils a pleasure to teach, others seem the opposite, and with the less easy ones you may find it easier to point out inappropriate behaviour than to praise good behaviour.

Self protection

You need to develop strategies for protecting your personal feelings; becoming really angry may mean that you lose control of the situation. Feeling angry but only showing a controlled displeasure may be more effective, even if it means playing a part. It is a delicate balance between protecting your private self, achieving some personal satisfaction from teaching and also maintaining your own dignity and that of the pupils (Furlong and Maynard, 1995).

Satisfying the self

Once you have established a professional relationship and are relatively confident about your control of the class, you are able to switch appropriately between your personal and professional self; sharing a joke without losing distance is a simple example of this complex phenomenon.

Appropriate actions

Consider the following scenario and make a note of your reactions. What would you do in this situation? Why would certain actions be more appropriate than others?

116

I was on dinner duty yesterday and something really bad happened. It was windy and cold and I was just getting ready to go in and get a quick cup of coffee and grab my books . . . it's a long walk to a double lesson and if I don't get there in good time I can't get them back down from the ceiling. Anyway I was just turning away thinking I'm glad nothing has happened, and I saw this very big kid, whom I'd never seen before, really laying into this skinny kid whom I taught last year, and who wouldn't hurt a fly. Well I couldn't ignore it, especially as some other characters were wandering over and showing a bit of interest. So I walked over to the big kid and before I even had time to open my mouth he shouted 'F*** off' right in my face and ran off. Loads of kids must have heard what he said and they were all looking at me. So I . . .

What would you do? Would you . . .

- go after the big kid
- find out the big kid's name
- report the incident to the Head of Year
- report the incident to the Headteacher
- or?

Appropriate actions

It is not advisable to chase after a pupil. The other pupils will be able to tell you whether he attends the school and what his name is. Reporting the incident to the Head of Year would clearly be necessary, who can then report it to others if appropriate. It is important to check that the boy is alright. You should retain a sense of personal dignity and calm: the situation was not of your making. Being sworn at was not an attack on your status and your action may have helped to defend the 'victim'. At no time should you take sides: your assumptions about the 'skinny kid' may be inaccurate and your objective judgement will be valuable in supporting other staff to resolve the problem.

Crisis in class

117

Now consider the following incident.

Year 10 and going alright, in fact going very well and I was really enjoying myself. So much so that I didn't even wonder how everything could possibly be so great, and when would it all go wrong? I just happened to notice that Jane had her head down on her arms and looked as if she was asleep. I went over to speak to her and noticed just as I started to say something, that her eyes were open and she looked a bit as if she'd been crying . . . but by then I'd already started saying something like 'Come on, Jane, you've been doing so well recently and I'm so pleased with your work. Pay attention now.'

And all hell broke loose . . . she went completely bananas, she shouted 'P*** off' and threw her chair at the wall. Then something else happened . . . I think she swept her books off the desk and something else happened but I don't know what it was – all I know is that there was a little scream from the girl next to her. And I just thought . . . I'm a bit out of my depth here and she's such a lovely girl usually and she started to rant on about teachers all being the bl**dy same and she couldn't cope. (I thought, nor me.)

What would you do? Would you . . .

- send her out
- send for a member of staff
- try calming her down
- ask her friends if they know what it's about
- or?

Note your reasons for adopting a certain course of action and rejecting another.

Appropriate actions

It would probably be unwise to send her out: she is so upset that she might storm off and is not responsible for her actions. Sending a reliable pupil to bring a colleague might be advisable if Jane does not calm down. You may find it difficult to calm her, yet her friends should be able to achieve this on your behalf. They will also be able to give you some more information about Jane. Alternatively, you may decide to send her out and report the incident immediately to senior staff. If, exceptionally, she continues to rave, you could take the rest of the class out of the room. Try to give the impression that you are calm and be responsive to the needs of the class.

REFLECTION

Compare these two viewpoints with a colleague and decide on the relative advantages and disadvantages of each. Note them in your Professional Development Portfolio.

118

Working alone

I've had to be seen to be doing something . . . If I had to be going, cap in hand, to any-body else to sort out any problem in class . . . If the children see you doing that then they obviously feel that teacher who you sent them to, they are important, they sort out all the problems, and I think that works against us. I personally do not send people to senior members of staff because I don't want to lose face in front of kids because my own belief is that I've got to create an atmosphere in the classroom where learning can take place and I want to have the power to be able to make that happen.

(Male Geography teacher)

Working in a team

The majority of staff are keen to get the place running nice and smoothly for their own sake and they talk about the problems that they've got. We tell each other solutions that we've got, and we show how we do that sort of thing and most of them are not afraid to ask for help. Even the better teachers, you know, they say, I've got this prob-lem here. How would you cope? (Male)

The interviews in this Reflection are based on *Discipline in Schools* ('the Elton Report') 1989, published by HMSO.

The Elton Report

We discussed the main findings of the Elton Report in Chapter 16 and it is worth looking back to Managing your Lessons to refresh your memory. At this point it is useful to consider the main findings about the ways in which teachers can wear themselves out. Research which was carried out for the Elton Report shows that four main areas cause teachers most con-cern: **pupils talking out of turn**, **hindering others**, **coming unprepared for lessons** and **arriving late for lessons**.

It is also worth considering that we may be able to reduce some of this repetitive and tiring behaviour if we analyse other aspects of our teaching styles. The chart shows an interesting and thought-provoking relationship

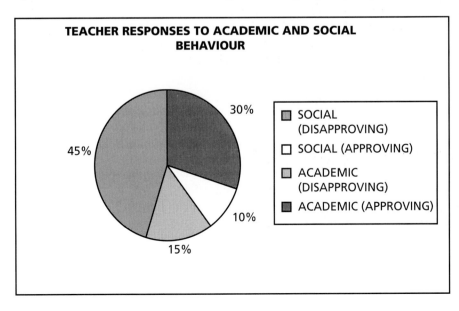

TEACHER RESPONSES TO ACADEMIC AND SOCIAL BEHAVIOUR

30%

45%

10%

15%

- ▣ SOCIAL (DISAPPROVING)
- □ SOCIAL (APPROVING)
- ▦ ACADEMIC (DISAPPROVING)
- ▪ ACADEMIC (APPROVING)

between our approving and our disapproving reactions to pupils; we respond much more to bad behaviour than to good behaviour (three times as much). This finding is consistent across many schools and with many teachers and it is worth asking ourselves whether it is productive to respond more to bad behaviour. Perhaps the way we respond to inappropriate behaviour is one of the factors which keep it going. It may not be possible to ignore bad behaviour, but it should be possible to increase our responses to good behaviour, to show that we are pleased with what we see.

If we use more praise to support good behaviour, this response will be more consistent with our responses to academic performance. The graph on page 197 shows the reverse to be true – we respond three times as much to inappropriate academic performance as we do to appropriate academic performance.

Lesson organisation and management

Twenty five years of research on lesson management show that we react to pupils' bad behaviour in such a way that they are in control, instead of the teacher being the active determinant of the desired classroom environment. We tend to take away rewards as a form of punishment which leaves us with no motivators. Two separate systems need to operate – reward and punishment. Moreover, we underestimate the power of our personalities to motivate. You will find it useful to review your progress in the following way.

Audit

Make a proforma with the following headings:

1 How do I organise and manage my classes at present?
(Perhaps use the colloquial headings 'Getting them in, getting on with it, getting on with them, getting them out', or 'Entry/exit phases, teaching style, relationships with pupils/whole class')

2 Are there any areas which I would like to alter/improve? For example, switch signals?

3 The characteristics of my department's/whole school approach are as follows:

4 Which of the above can I make more/better use of, or add to?

5 Planning: how does this fit in with my lesson planning?
(Design a lesson plan sheet to use this term which always includes your discipline routine, adapted to school practice. Start with 'entry phase'. Refer back to Chapter 17. An alternative to designing a new lesson plan sheet would be to incorporate your key routines into the lesson plan sheet which you have developed and used up to now. Keep a representative sample of such lesson plans in your PDP with successes and failures and targets.)

Subject specific issues

Good pupil management also involves teaching your subject well and appropriately. This is not easy. Are you noticing any conflicts/friction within your view of your subject? For example, in English, do you see the most important strengths of English as being an academic study of literature ... or is it English as a means of expressing feelings, beliefs, values and developing as a person, or is it about basic communication skills?

Elbaz (1983) holds that if you believe strongly in all of these, you may need to keep them separate in order to carry on. The balance can become distorted if you are teaching pupils with special educational needs because they need a great deal of support with basics. Sophisticated differentiation techniques will be necessary to teach literature in ways which are not patronising. Would this shake your faith in your subject knowledge and subject application by opening up a chasm between your love of the subject and your love of teaching? Look at this situation with regard to your own subject and consider solutions available to you.

It is possible that there are, or will be, unresolvable tensions in your teaching which may at times lead you to consider leaving the teaching profession. Yet contradictions and paradoxes are inherent in all our lives – it *is* possible to educate and support pupils even if your results fall short of your ideals, and the ensuing tensions can be productive.

Given the complexity of the analysis and the complexity of teaching, it would be unrealistic, to say the least, to expect a smooth transition from theory to practice. Indeed it would be undesirable (Stones, 1979)

Without some sort of tension or mismatch between our ideal lesson and the actual lesson there would be no development.

REFLECTION

R

120

Being confident and clear about teaching your subject is a vital part of achieving and maintaining an atmosphere which is conducive to learning.

Look back at Chapter 5 on Donaldson and reconsider her concept of 'human sense'; making knowledge accessible by giving examples from everyday life.

Consider PGCE trainee Helen's idea for teaching exterior angles. She drew a tent and put the angle outside the tent. This is a good example of human sense, embedded in a clear iconic way.

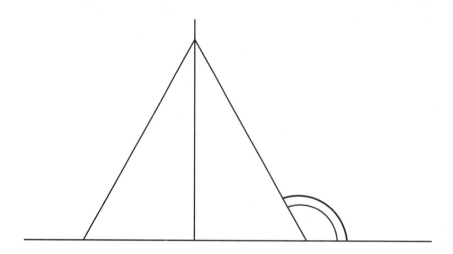

Yet it can be possible to distort teaching material by using an example which in fact is not typical but rather is unique, which gives an unbalanced view or is actually irrelevant.

To take an example of 'human sense' with a mathematical flavour that doesn't always work, the sum $4a + 2b + 3a = ?$ This can be represented as a manipulation of apples and bananas, which is quite an attractive example in that it seems real. It provides the instrumental understanding which makes it possible for a pupil to get the right answer. Yet these apples and bananas present potential difficulties for the learner when faced with more advanced uses of letters as variables. We can see that $a \times a$ (a^2) has no meaning for a learner still playing with the fruit because you cannot square fruit. Long-term relational understanding has been sacrificed in a spurious attempt to provide human sense.

Understanding can be achieved through substituting numbers for letters to show that algebraic expressions give the same values no matter what numbers are substituted for a and b. This takes longer than apples and bananas but leads to deeper understanding. Short-term success may lead to long-term failure. Human sense when misapplied is not always a useful solution.

Professor Lewis Wolpert reports that, after a presentation at the Royal Institution on 'The Unnatural Nature of Science', a member of the audience commented that he would like his epitaph to be 'He tried to understand economics all his life, but common sense kept getting in the way'. It was James Meade, a Nobel prize winner in Economics.

It is worth using the Bruner concept of the spiral curriculum to guide you; you will need to learn how to present your subject matter simply in some classes. For instance, open questions could be used to provide a scaffolding so that, in responding to the questions, the learning actually comes from the children themselves. But this simple version should not have to be unlearned, rather it needs to be used and built on and understood differently as you provide your pupils with deeper understanding. This will not always be possible but it is well worth striving for it. Remember also that you need more than words:

The fact that teacher and taught use the same word may mislead the teacher into thinking that the meaning the learner takes from the word is much the same as his own

(Stones, 1979)

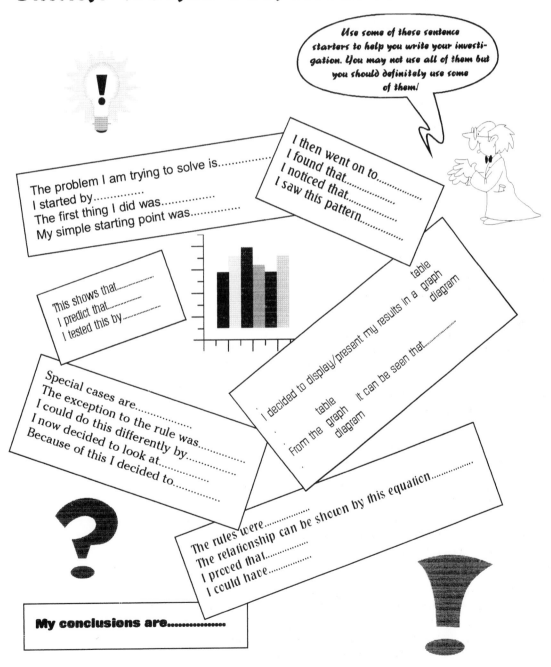

Explaining

With your mentor, develop over an agreed period, for example the next half-term, a repertoire of different ways of using words to give explanations that help pupils to understand. Remember Bruner's belief that any subject can be taught to any age group without distortion (Bruner, 'Actual Minds, Possible Worlds'). Collect these in your Personal Development Portfolio, in note form, with a brief reference to the lesson plans where you are able to use these applications.

Build into your examples Bruner's ideas about enactive, iconic and symbolic representation, and use any other ideas and structures to help you: Gardner's multiple intelligences for example. You may find that you make use of metaphors and other devices to clarify your explanations.

At every point, consider how these techniques fit into your personal style.

SUMMARY

It will take time to develop your personal style of teaching. In the process of doing so, you would be wise to consider both disciplinary and subject specific issues. Moreover, the relationship between these two is complex: your decisions about setting up group work, for example, should be informed by both. It is vital for your development as a teacher that you review regularly the stage that you have reached.

Useful references

Bruner, J. S. (1966) 'On Cognitive Growth' in Bruner, J. S., Olver, R. R. and Greenfields, P. M. (eds) **Studies in Cognitive Growth.** New York: Wiley.

Bruner, J. S. (1986) **Actual Minds, Possible Worlds.** Cambridge Mass: Harvard University Press.

Elbaz, F. (1983) **Teacher Thinking: A Study of Practical Knowledge.** London and Canberra: Croom Helm.

Furlong, J. and Maynard, T. (1995) **Mentoring Student Teachers: The Growth of Professional Knowledge.** London: Routledge

Gardner, H. (1983) **Frames of Mind: The Theory of Multiple Intelligences.** London: Heinemann.

Stones, E. (1979) **Psychopedagogy.** London: Methuen.

CHAPTER

Assessment (2)

22

Assessment is an integral part of effective teaching and learning. It is a continuous process. The methods used to assess pupils' work will vary from school to school and differences of approach will be found both within Departments and Year Groups. These methods, their frequency and purpose will, of course, be compatible with the school's aims and objectives, curriculum policy and national policy legislation.

(Derek Plumb, Deputy Headteacher)

Assessment through teaching

Skilled observation, thoughtful listening and perceptive questioning, as well as more conventional marking, are needed to assess the outcomes of pupils' work. These outcomes may include the following types of evidence:

- **oral** – questions, discussion, presentation, role play, debate, audio
- **written** – notes, lists, diaries, questionnaires, scripts, poems, essays
- **graphic** – diagrams, drawings, graphs, printouts, photographs, video
- **three-dimensional** – models, sculptures, constructions
- **physical** – co-ordination, manipulative skills

The wider the range of evidence of pupils' work which we seek, the greater the opportunities for pupils to demonstrate the full extent of their achievements.

We can consider critically the traditional emphasis on the ability of pupils to memorise and reproduce knowledge, and focus more on thinking and problem solving. Vygotsky believed that we should use tools and aids for reflecting and supporting learning. His beliefs are consistent with the development of assessment which allows the use of tools and auxiliary aids, for instance assessment through teaching and course work.

  Assessment context

For this exercise you will need to have available one piece of work produced by a pupil in your school and any supporting teacher records.

122

1 Describe the piece of work and explain to colleagues the context in which the work was produced:
How did it arise? Was it part of a topic/during a visit? What was the purpose (aim) of the particular activity?

2 Next, present any information you have about the pupil (teacher records, reports, grades) and explain how it relates to the work and illuminates the pupil's achievements.

3 Now, consider the following questions with your colleagues:
- What does the evidence reveal (progress, achievement, attainment)?
- Is the evidence representative of the pupil's overall progress and achievements? If not, why not? What is missing? (for instance evidence of oral contribution, group work)
- Is there one piece of information which points a way forward for this pupil? What is it? How might this information be assessed and used?

4 Finally, consider the types of evidence/information which have been presented and note which could be used to show:
- progress over time
- significant achievements
- particular learning difficulties
- what should be taught next

This exercise will have illustrated the extent to which assessment is an integral part of teaching and learning. In fact, all teaching involves a continuous assessment of the pupils' knowledge and understanding. By asking questions and noting responses, the teacher is continually monitoring the pupils' progress (as well as his or her teaching). Teachers need to diagnose and give immediate responses to individual pupils' difficulties. These informal classroom assessments are important because they enable a teacher to make adjustments to the style of teaching and allow the learning process to be finally tuned. Assessing feedback from pupils is also a useful way of measuring the effectiveness of lessons.

In these ways, assessment is part of the dynamics of teaching and is crucial to the on-going dialogue between teacher and pupil. The more the pupils understand the assessment procedures, the criteria for success and how to progress further, the more responsible they will become for their own learning.

A   Gathering evidence

123:

Consider the ways of gathering evidence for assessment given below. What can you add to the list:

- checklists
- observational notes
- class discussion and review
- teacher's use of questions
- tests
- questionnaires
- videotape
- audio tape
- examples of pupils' work
- pupils' self-reports

- ....

- ....

- ....

- ....

R **REFLECTION**

Is it possible for you to involve pupils actively in the assessment process at this stage? Discuss the following points with a colleague:

124:

- Assessment is often seen as the last stage of the learning process before a new piece of work is started.
- It can be argued that pupils should be involved right from the start in understanding the criteria on which they are being assessed.
- Examples of good pieces of work can be discussed with pupils.
- Lists of criteria for success can be elicited from the class, to involve them in the assessment procedure.
- Assessment can be used for setting targets within the learning process and used as a means of development.
- Tension may develop here between the National Curriculum and pupil participation in assessment: a formative, profiling concept of assessment may be replaced by a more traditional summative model.

Developing the independent learner

One way to develop pupils' responsibility for their own learning is to involve them directly in assessing what they have learnt and how. As they get older, they are more likely to be motivated if they can identify their own needs and discuss how they can improve with their teachers. In order to make this possible, you should ask, and discuss in pairs, the following questions:

- Are you, and then the pupils, clear about the **purposes** of your different types of assessment?
- Are your **methods** of assessment clear to the pupils? Is your assessment system and your language as simple as possible?
- Are the criteria for gaining an A or a B (or Level 6 or Level 7 or whatever) as clear as possible?
- Are your pupils familiar with examples on which they can model their own work? Such examples should represent differing National Curriculum levels giving pupils a clearer idea of what is expected.
- Is your assessment as consistent as is reasonably possible? An extremely valuable exercise during a teacher training course is for the trainees to compare their assessment of pupils' work with more experienced colleagues.
- Does your assessment help the pupils improve their performance? Teaching pupils to carry out self-assessment can be valuable. Pupils can record their progress and keep a record of how they worked in a diary or learning log. (I did well in this lesson . . .)
- Have you used assessment to set targets for the pupils' future learning?

However pupil-centred an assessment policy is, teachers still need to make their summative judgements about pupils' progress, for example for parents, employers, universities and colleges. Such summative assessments can only be valid if they are based on the continuous formative assessments which are an integral part of the teaching and learning process.

Coursework

125 GCSE coursework forms up to 30% of the final grade in many subjects. It is formative in that it can indicate to teacher and pupil how far the latter has come and how far he or she has to go to achieve the grade of which they are capable in the terminal exam. It is summative in that it constitutes part of the work on which the final GCSE grade is based. As you read through 16 year-old Anna's report, consider the problems she experienced with this system.

I think coursework is basically a good idea as it removes some of the pressure of the exam BUT – in my experience there were some problems . . .

IN MATHS: Everyone had to do broadly the same pieces of coursework so we all copied and helped each other. The last sections of these pieces of coursework were individual but once you had understood the first bit (with someone else's help) they weren't at all difficult.

One of the pieces of coursework had to be done on a computer and involved using and creating simple programs. I was completely computer illiterate at the time and the school computers that we had (very limited) access to are useless, so I got a friend to do the first bit for me on her computer (in exchange for me helping her on another piece of coursework) and from that I worked out how to do the individual part on my own.

IN ENGLISH: We weren't told which pieces of work could be considered as coursework and, as our teacher was ill and away a lot, we didn't do very many pieces of work. Also, we had no say in what was submitted as coursework and we ran out of time towards the coursework deadline and weren't given the chance to correct spelling and punctuation errors (which we had been told we would have).

IN GEOGRAPHY: We had to do a study on a plan for developing local sports facilities. This was quite an interesting and relevant topic for a study (although we did get a bit bored of it by the end).

We had six months in which to complete the study and it was virtually spoon-fed to us.

I sent off letters, did some research and made loads of notes at the start of the study and then forgot all about it until the last week. I worked on it for almost six days and completed it on time. I got full marks.

I was lucky that I had done the initial work and paid attention at the beginning but others who hadn't, and had left it as late as me (or even later) got very low marks, simply because they hadn't bothered. It all appeared so easy, and it was but you did have to do the work!

IN ART: Nearly all our lessons were spent doing projects which could become pieces of coursework. We had no real motivation and little encouragement or guidance during the lessons; also there was a very relaxed atmosphere in the classroom (and a few disruptive pupils) which meant that very little work was done.

For art we also had to do a special study on a subject of our choice. We had a long time to do it in and again, everyone left it until the last minute.

Choose one subject which Anna discusses. Analyse the problems which she encountered. How could they have been resolved?

SUMMARY

Assessment is an essential and integral part of the teaching and learning process. However it must be assessment for a purpose which helps to increase pupils' knowledge, skills and understanding. Poor assessment can be harmful to pupils' progress in learning. A variety of assessment tools will help to support variety in teaching and learning and reflects the range of intelligences shown by pupils.

Useful references

Gipps, C. (1994) **Beyond Testing: Towards a Theory of Educational Assessment.** London: The Falmer Press.

Gipps, C. and Murphy, P. (1994) **A Fair Test? Assessment, Achievement and Equity.** Milton Keynes: Open University Press.

Differentiation (2)

23

Differentiation is the process whereby teachers meet the need for progress through the curriculum by selecting appropriate teaching methods to match the individual child's learning strategies, within a group situation. (John Visser, 1993)

LEARNING OUTCOMES

By the end of this session you should have built on what you learnt from Chapter 14, the first Differentiation chapter, heightening your awareness of different approaches to planning for differentiation. You should have developed a collection of practical examples relevant to your subject. You should have considered Vygotsky's zone of proximal development, Bruner's scaffolding and Wood's five levels in the context of differentiation.

Introduction

Differentiation is an integral part of good teaching, yet experienced teachers continue to request guidance on how best to balance the demands of the curriculum, the needs of the group and the needs of the individual. Why do teachers believe that it is important to work on differentiating their teaching? Major reasons include:

- Teachers are aware that they often differentiate unconsciously, and therefore cannot always build on their own strengths in a conscious way. The process of mentoring can help both teachers and trainees, in different ways, by offering opportunities to talk, explain, share and understand.
- Teachers wish to raise educational attainment levels, and this is not possible by teaching to the level of a so-called average child.
- The Elton Report (1989) presents evidence that poorly differentiated lessons can contribute to behaviour problems (although the report acknowledges that behaviour problems are complex and not necessarily caused by inappropriate teaching).
- Ofsted guidelines for the inspection of schools consider that the quality of teaching can be seen in terms of 'suitable' differentiation, and should focus on special educational needs being met throughout the ability range.
- The Code of Practice specifies guidelines for meeting special educational needs and emphasises differentiation as a major responsibility

for teachers at Stage One of the five-stage model for assessment of special educational needs.

● Using active planning to meet pupils' needs is a major source of job satisfaction, professional motivation and departmental strength. Moreover, pupil entitlement to the National Curriculum is a key issue.

There have always been two major types of problem with differentiating the curriculum:

● Some pupils cannot *read* well enough to be able to follow the work.
● Some pupils cannot *write* well enough (a) to be able to complete the work, and/or (b) to allow you to assess their work in some useful way.

Often, both these problems combine to impede the progress of the same pupil.

REFLECTION

R

126

Review the following from Chapters 6 and 7 *before* working on this material:

Vygotsky's zone of proximal development, Bruner's scaffolding and Wood's five levels apply to individuals. How can they be implemented in a class of 25 to 30 pupils?

Consider the following quote:

Student diversity is not a liability in a problem-solving organisation . . . it is an asset, an enduring source of uncertainty and thus the driving force behind innovation, growth of knowledge and progress. (Skrtic, 1991)

This is a fine expression of the high standards and professionalism of teachers, but how can we resolve the tension between the needs of the individual child and the demands made by a whole class?

Ann Lewis (1992) defines differentiation as '. . . the process of adjusting teaching to meet the learning needs of individual children'. She describes eleven different ways of differentiating the curriculum in the classroom: content, interests, pace, level, access, response, sequence, structure, teacher time, teaching style and grouping. In your teaching you will have realised that most of our efforts at differentiating material consist of combinations of different types of differentiation techniques. In the following case study you will be able to find examples of some of these types.

Attempts at differentiation

C

127

There are two complementary types of evidence for you to consider in this activity: a lesson observation form and then accompanying extracts from the discussion of the lesson. First, look at the lesson observation form on page 211.

Find the section of the lesson where Laurence experienced particular difficulties with differentiation and see if you have any different solutions for how to avoid it happening. Have you experienced anything like this in your own subject?

LESSON OBSERVATION FORM

TEACHER Miss Laurence A	**DAY/DATE:** 22 May	**TIME:** Period 2
SUBJECT: French	**GROUP:** 7N	**OBSERVER:** Mr Steve L (Subject Mentor)

Room Plan	Focus of observation
Difficult room non specialist	Differentiation

Time	Sequence of events	Observer's comments
9.50 9.55 9.56 10.00 10.03 10.15	Students arrived late from previous lesson Students a little noisy but LA settled them quickly using French Oral task involving all students giving places in town. Took register and had all students say something. Where students were absent others said so in French. Continued to ask for oral recognition of places in town. Use books if necessary. Moved to exercise using textbook and tape. Task explained in French. Repeated in English when students did not understand. A little noise – LA brought to order in French. Explained new structures/vocab in French. Only a few understood: immediately Laurence found other examples until many understood.	 Good idea. All students on task. Writing for slower students. Be careful with accents café près English don't know where they go and which way – need a clear model. Seemed a little 'irritated' when students did not understand. Students seemed to find this difficult to start with but soon got it. Students swapped books to correct. Good idea. Well done! Asked them to make notes in books – really give them time.
10.25 10.36	Written exercise based on worksheet of town plan. 2 different exercises students could choose. Eventually LA used English. Students still confused; led to some chatting. LA had to work hard to keep order. Packed away Nothing really happened during this time in terms of learning French. Oral activity recapping vocab given sentences in English asking students to translate. Lesson finished on time.	Good idea to differentiate. Students found the explanation of choices difficult but listened very carefully. They were certainly on task initially. May have been better to hand the worksheet out first rather than put it on the wall or hold it up! Worked with more able mainly. Could have used Flash Cards perhaps. Some students not involved – off task. Students left in orderly fashion.
10.40		

Summary

The final task was rather complicated and the students were confused. May have been better to present it in small stages having given the worksheet. Generally the lesson was well planned. Activities flowed well.
There was a good atmosphere in the room. Students were on task most of the time. Lots of good work and learning took place.
The final activity was a good idea as it was differentiated but it was not thought out clearly enough in terms of presentation.
When things go wrong – try not to get flustered.
If they don't understand the complex, graded task – settle for something 'doable'.

Now use the mentor's summary and the transcript, to illuminate your understanding of Laurence's problems with the lesson from 10.25 to 10.40. You will be able to find discussion of differentiation by pace, by task and by outcome. Why did this final activity fail?

Transcript of mentoring session

S: Do you think it was clear to them who should do what?

L: No (both laugh)

S: Because that was my feeling. I wasn't sure if you were saying 'Everybody should do all of this', a kind of chain of events – first do this, then do that, ... or 'you lot should pick that activity'? Was it up to them to make the choice?

L: One thing they all had to do was to fill in the map and then say what was in the town and then they could expand or choose to do dialogue. It's true that it's really up to them to choose what they feel like doing. I didn't intend to say 'well do this, then this, then that'. I wanted them to choose as much as they could.

S: Yes, I thought it was a very good idea. There was nothing actually wrong with the materials you had or with the idea because that's exactly what you've got to do: you need to differentiate in that way and give children the chance to reach their own levels. And don't not do that ever again just because it kind of went wrong. That's exactly the sort of thing you need to be doing.

Something I've seen and used myself is an A4 format. If it's a task for everybody you have perhaps 'Tout le monde' or something like that and then you might have 'choisis' and then you might have arrows: 'Tout le monde commence ici', and then a sort of flow chart feel to it and then I think what you're doing is reinforcing the instructions graphically. That works quite well if you're using that sort of differentiated task.

It was quite complicated. It seemed simple to you because you created it. You know whenever you try to explain anything to anyone you think 'oh why don't they get it?' But it certainly wasn't obvious to me what they were supposed to do. And I was trying hard. And I think they were too. They weren't trying to be awkward (both laugh). You have a good relationship with that class which you've built up and they were trying. You can try to keep doing this kind of thing in a kind of flow chart presentation and as you say what you could do is have one of them in an OHT [Overhead Transparency].

L: I think it'll be interesting to see what they've actually produced. I know some of them won't produce anything.

Children are different?

128

Consider Laurence's final point: there are many possible reasons why different children produce work of such a wide variety. Look at the register of a class you work with. In your Professional Development Portfolio list 3 to 10 pupils you know who have different learning needs. Summarise these needs and how they can be met. Use first names only, for confidentiality.

First name (maximum ten names)	Needs	Differentiated provision

You should also consider a group of pupils whose needs can be met as a group – summarise their needs and how they can be met. Look at Chapter 27 on the Code of Practice for Group Education Plans.

Differentiation appraisal

129

Consider the honesty and analytical self-appraisal which Laurence showed. Try to use this approach yourself to describe a subject specific type of differentiation you have seen during lesson observation or while teaching.

How successful was this? What factors determined its success or failure?

Begin to build up a picture of the factors which can help or hinder effective differentiation at the levels of the individual, the classroom and the whole school. Keep notes on this topic in your Personal Development Portfolio, and update your knowledge on differentiation through the year.

S U M M A R Y

An important area for later consideration is that of 'inclusion'. The 1944 Education Act stated that all pupils should have access to the Curriculum. The inclusion style has been an integral part of sports teaching for many years: it embodies the belief that differentiation by outcome is the most effective way of including all pupils. There is now renewed debate across the curriculum about the tension between differentiation and inclusion. Can differentiation create a dangerous exclusivity?

Useful references

Daniels, H. (1993) *'Educational Responses to Diversity: Responsibilities and Choices in Differentiation'* in **Curriculum**, vol. 14, no. 3, pp. 157–162.

DES and Welsh Office (1989) **Discipline in Schools: Report of the Committee of Enquiry Chaired by Lord Elton.** London: HMSO.

Differentiating the Secondary Curriculum (1993). Trowbridge: Wiltshire Education Support and Training, Education Department.

Kerry, T. (1993) *'Teachers Learning Differentiation Through Classroom Questioning Skills'* in **Journal of Teacher Development**, vol. 2, no. 2, pp. 81–92.

Kyriacou, C. (1991) **Essential Teaching Skills.** Oxford: Basil Blackwell.

Lewis, A. (1992) *'From Planning to Practice'* in **British Journal of Special Education**, vol. 19, no. 1, March 1992.

Skrtic, T. (1991) *'Students with Special Educational Needs: Artefacts of the Traditional Curriculum'* in Ainscow, M. (ed.) **Effective Schools for All.** London: David Fulton.

Visser, J. (1993) **Differentiation: Making it Work.** Stafford: NASEN Enterprises Ltd.

Helping Children to Think

24

My brain is worn out, can you use yours?

LEARNING OUTCOMES

This chapter will give you the opportunity to explore the value of positive expectations. By the end you should have looked closely at a variety of ways of developing and maintaining a positive climate and developed strategies which can be integrated into your own personal teaching style.

Introduction

The findings . . . suggest that children tended to make better progress, both behaviourally and academically, in schools which placed an appropriate emphasis on academic matters. This emphasis might be reflected in a well planned curriculum, in the kinds of expectations teachers had of the children they taught, and in the setting and marking of homework. It is also relevant, perhaps, that when we asked pupils what they thought were the most important goals or functions of schooling, they consistently selected 'instrumental' goals such as examination success and preparation for jobs.

. . . It also appeared that frequent disciplinary interventions in the classroom were associated with worse behaviour. Once again, it is difficult to disentangle cause and effect, as the teachers' interventions were designed to deal with behaviour which disrupted the class. Nevertheless, it does seem that a form of teacher response which results in innumerable interruptions to the flow of the lesson and which involves constant checking and reprimand may serve to perpetuate pupil disturbance. (Rutter et al, 1979)

This extract is from research carried out in twelve secondary schools during three years of fieldwork. Much of the evidence which was analysed indicates that the 'ethos' of a school contributes significantly to the success of the pupils. Rutter's researchers concluded that teachers who seek to create a good learning environment must focus on educational goals, more than on pastoral issues, so that the latter serves the former and does not become an end in itself. Arriving late to teach a lesson because you have been counselling a pupil in distress: this may happen occasionally, but not frequently. In Part 3 you will be looking more at the factors which contribute to a good learning environment throughout a school. Now we will focus on your personal role in developing a positive learning environment.

130

Read the testimony of Catherine (a pupil aged 14) below about what makes a good teacher. Underline the key points she makes about her ideal teacher. Circle any features you think may be problematic and discuss them with your mentor.

I think good teachers are those who communicate well with their classes. They have a good 'working relationship' with their pupils and are respected by them. By 'communicate' I mean the way in which the teacher addresses that class, talks to the individual pupil and sets work. My best teachers are those who are interesting people and are able to convey what they are attempting to teach in an interesting and captivating fashion.

I have found that good teachers are those who are not shy or intimidated by a class of teenagers, but are confident and 'raring to go'. These teachers are generally nice people who have a friendly nature and an unpatronising and patient manner. I think teachers should always be 'approachable' and make sure they have the confidence of their pupils. They should not try to be too nice as this leads some pupils to take advantage of their good nature and 'get away with murder' in class. It also helps if the teacher does not have a flat and expressionless voice because this is a guaranteed and immediate 'turn off' for pupils. I have found that my best teachers are those who are willing to give up some of their free time occasionally, for example lunch hour, to assist me with my work.

Small scale research on pupil learning is being carried out by Professor Jean Rudduck, Director of Homerton College, Cambridge. In the *Times Educational Supplement* of 6 October 1995, she lists the major points made by 90 secondary aged pupils from three secondary schools. Consider the close similarities between Catherine's views and this list of features of good teaching practice from Rudduck's research findings:

● teachers being available to talk with pupils about learning and school-work (and not just about behaviour)
● teachers recognising pupils' readiness to take more responsibility as they grow older and engaging with them in as adult a way as possible
● teachers being sensitive to the tone and manner of their discourse with pupils, as individuals and in groups, so that they do not humiliate them, criticise them in ways that make them feel small (especially in front of their peers) or shout at them.
● teachers being seen to be fair in all their dealings with all pupils and realising that one important aspect of fairness is not prejudging pupils on the basis of past incidents.
● teachers ensuring that they make all pupils feel confident that they can do well and achieve something worthwhile

We can see the importance of a teacher's communication skills in fostering an atmosphere which is conducive to pupils' learning and their well-being. This is reflected both in Catherine's testimony and Rudduck's research evidence. Yet we also know that it is artificial when one person communicates with thirty.

Communication in lessons

Language in lessons is not normal conversation. With luck and good judgement it can have the best features of real discourse and sometimes, for example, in class discussion, the worst, with either everyone shouting at once or even more unnerving, a class who do not talk at all.

Lesson language is not like conversation because:

- of the large number of participants
- one person at least has preplanned
- one person is directing the conversation
- most participants speak only when given a turn
- one person has more status than all the others
- the person with the most power chooses the topic
- digressions and interruptions are barely tolerated
- the person with the most power controls the turns
- the atmosphere depends upon all the participants co-operating

Lesson language

Recall a lesson that didn't go very well. Did any of these classroom language factors have an influence? Use this list to form the basis of a checklist? Which of these factors do you feel influenced you the most when planning the lesson for that particular class?

Which of these factors did you feel influenced you the most when delivering the lesson to that class?

Did any of these factors produce unexpected outcomes, problematic or pleasant? What effect did these factors have on your planning for the next lesson?

Vygotsky believes that language provides the shape for thinking: that we develop ideas by talking about them, and only then do we internalise them in thought. For Vygotsky speech is a form of action.

Impressive language

You will no doubt already have completed a classroom observation of a teacher whose use of language you found impressive. Negotiate another observation and use the following features of good practice for developing an analysis of *why* and how that teacher makes good use of language.

- clear explanation
- teacher asking questions that make pupils think about others
- demonstrations
- breaking the task down into manageable chunks
- co-operation between pupil and teacher, for example the demonstration, the use of 'we'
- humour
- clear switch signals

Why do you think that these characteristics are important in helping the teacher to develop positive attitudes to learning?

The role of teacher, and the systems set up by the school institution confer some status and by the time pupils start secondary school they are aware of the conventions of classroom discourse. However, in practice this is often not enough. Power and status are not the same. Power is about subjugation, status is about recognition. We need children to recognise us as a resource, a main source of knowledge in the classroom.

- We must know our subject. (**Subject Knowledge and Understanding**)
- We have to explain it so that children can understand it. (**Planning, Teaching and Class Management**)
- We also have to assess to ensure successful and effective learning. (**Monitoring, Assessment, Recording, Reporting and Accountability**)

REFLECTION

133

The inter-relation between knowledge, power and status can be thrown into high relief by the able pupil. The following incident is by no means a frequent occurrence, but highlights the role of subject knowledge in relation to status and mutual respect.

Sharon was a pupil in a High School taking pupils from Y8 onwards. She was in her first few weeks at the school and was a couple of minutes early for maths. After a brief hullo, she asked 'Sir, did you know that aleph-zero plus aleph-zero is aleph-zero?' Fortunately I was able to answer yes! What followed was a brief discussion about aleph-zero (the cardinal number of the set of counting numbers) and how Sharon came to know about this concept. Her parents were both lecturers at the local university and she had been watching Open University degree programmes on television at the weekend.

Sharon was clearly testing me out, but what happened was that subsequently she was able to work at a higher level in her mathematics lessons, because her knowledge and love of the subject were now out in the open.

This conversation with an extremely able pupil could have ended very differently with the teacher using power to avoid discussion and thereby losing the respect of the pupil.

How do you cope if you don't know what aleph-zero is? What strategies are there in your subject which don't shut out Sharon and pupils like her from discussion with the teacher.

Beware the defensive response such as 'Not now, dear' or, as a historian might say: 'It's not my period'. Consider that you may be able to re-frame the situation by exchanging teacher–pupil roles: 'Tell me about it. Can you explain it to me?'

If you still do not understand, have another try later. After all, not all pupils understand everything you tell them the first time.

Prompts/Questions/Statements

How would you set about tackling this one?
What do you think?
Why does it work?
Convince me that you're right.
Convince the group that you're right.
Make up a problem of your own.
Describe how you got the solution.
What other questions could you ask?
Share your ideas with your partner.

Try to foster a climate for conjecture, unlike this teacher's comment at a parents' evening: 'Jenny asks a lot of questions – perhaps she should go into a lower set'.

REFLECTION

134

What type of people do you avoid at parties? Why? It may be because they violate what are called Grice's Maxims, named after H. P. Grice (1975) who postulated that conversation depends upon co-operation and that in our interactions we behave as if there are a set of conversational rules, or maxims.

1 **Maxim of quantity.** We give the information that is required, but not more than is required.
2 **Maxim of quality.** What we say we believe to be true. We don't say what we know to be false. (Yes, we know everyone lies but we normally behave as if people are telling the truth.)
3 **Maxim of relation.** What we say is relevant to the purpose.
4 **Maxim of manner.** What we say is clear and unambiguous.

Which maxims do you break? We all break them of course, but it is difficult to see how sarcasm and irony, for example, can work unless we operate as if maxims exist and can therefore be broken.

The application of these ideas in the classroom is multi-faceted. Children are learning to operate conversations themselves. They are learning all about reading between the lines. They understand that people don't always mean what they say. Other children will take what we say literally. They may be very hurt by an adult joke, in the same way that a teacher may feel hurt by a casual remark of a child.

We have to manage interactions in classrooms as far as possible according to certain rules, including the principle of politeness. In addition, the degree of formality has to concur with the standards expected of us by the position we are in. If we take account of these considerations we will be able to set up a positive atmosphere for learning and thinking.

Challenging children to think

Children rather than the teacher should do most of the thinking. For example even with an exposition phase during a traditional lesson, the teacher instead of asking for short easy answers, can ask children to take the whole of the next stage themselves by working on a scrap of rough paper and then discussing with a partner what they have done. This work can then be discussed by the whole class. Agreed answers are usually easier to talk about with the rest of the class.

As the focus must be on children's thinking, the teacher must foster this atmosphere of possibilities by challenging pupils to think. This can be best achieved through using a variety of techniques; oral, organisational and interpersonal. Some strategies are listed below for focusing on thinking skills.

Body language/movement/strategies

If you want children to think and talk, you need to create a classroom environment where on-task thinking and talking is encouraged. There are many ways of doing this: for example real group work where groups are expected to reach agreed responses. It also helps to be aware of where you stand to receive replies. It may be important to move to the child to listen to a quiet reply, which is tentative, indicative of emerging thought. You can indicate openness by body language. Firmly crossed arms, rigid posture and severe looks do not foster independent thought and certainly do not invite open responses or questions.

SUMMARY

At times, fostering a climate where creativity and thinking skills are paramount will seem too challenging for new teachers. Surely it is safer to get children to behave sensibly first. It is quite understandable that a new teacher will focus on class management initially and look for survival strategies. However in the long run it is essential that children are encouraged to think, to discuss and to create. We must focus on educational goals and foster their attainment by the climate we establish.

Useful references

Grice, H.P. (1975) **'Logic and Conversation'**, in P. Cole and J.L. Morgan (eds) *Syntax and Semantics 3*. New York: Academic Press.

Kyriacou, C. (1991) **Essential Teaching Skills.** Oxford: Basil Blackwell.

Marsland, D. (ed.) (1987) **Education and Youth.** London: Falmer Press.

Nelson-Jones, R. (1993) **Practical Counselling and Helping Skills.** 3rd edition. London: Cassell.

Rutter, M. *et al* (1979) **Fifteen Thousand Hours: Secondary Schools and their Effects on Children.** London: Open Books.

Language Awareness (2) 25

. . . the relation of thought to word is not a thing but a process, a continual movement back and forth from thought to word to thought. (Vygotsky)

LEARNING OUTCOMES

When you have read this chapter you will have a greater understanding of the forms and functions of language used in the classroom and you will be more appreciative of your role in classroom interactions.

Introduction

Language enables us to communicate our needs, to voice our opinions, to share ideas and to be creative. Language, thought and action develop in complex interrelationships.

Teachers must be aware of the implications of the language they use in the classroom. Appropriate techniques of communication can avoid the frustration and misunderstandings caused by a poorly thought-out approach.

We must guard against assuming that children can, or should, use language in only one way. We all have a range of speech styles. We don't always speak or write in the same way all the time. Sometimes we are conscious of the variation. For example, in an interview we take care with both the content and the expression of our speech. We choose safe topics, we use a more formal speech style and we try to ensure that our intonation conveys our enthusiasm and competence. Back among friends our expressions change.

Types of language

How many different types of language, written and spoken have you used today? On page 222 is an example of a chart you could make.

Speech event/Audience	Writing Task/Reader	Features
Shouted to the children to get up		Imperatives! Loud.
	Left note for partner saying I'd be late.	Informal. Slang. Abbreviations

A major concern to new teachers is the challenge of adapting language for your audience. Every teacher has to face this challenge throughout their career, as their audience changes.

REFLECTION

How informal should we be? Should we use pupils' nicknames? What is our attitude to pupils swearing? What personal questions are we prepared to answer? Do we correct children's speech?

136

There are so many language roles to fulfil that it takes some initial thought to get the balance right. This also applies to children. Teachers who have known a taciturn child in school are surprised to hear that on work experience the same child is gregarious, or that the confident, articulate child is shy and silent in the workplace.

Teacher talk

The functions of teacher-language are somewhat different to the ones we normally use as adults talking and working with our peers. For example, there is the question and answer exchanges that in some ways are more like the language used by caretakers of small children: they have a high number of questions to which the adult already knows the answer and ideas are often simplified and repeated with an exaggerated intonation. However, it requires a spirit of genuine inquiry and interest in the children if teachers are going to lead purposeful discussion. One way of avoiding the accusation of being patronising is to ask more open than closed questions. Instead of 'What do we call this?' teachers often use more open forms such as, 'Why do you think that's happening?' More open forms can help a teacher to assess pupils' prior knowledge and understanding.

'Teacher-talk' can be acquired as any other interactional skill. Many newcomers to teaching adapt their language readily, others benefit from having some features initially highlighted for them.

Mentors' comments to trainee teachers illustrating some of the functions of teacher-talk

*See it from the child's point of view. You think they know far more than they do. You really need to **explain the basic terminology**.*

*Teaching this should be fun. Can you **use your imagination** to adapt the material? Couldn't some of them be farmers and some of them road builders?*

*You could have accepted Laura's comment, 'Pencils'. You asked what symbols could you use in a pictogram? I know you were thinking of people here, but drawings of pencils would have represented the idea just as well and would have validated her contribution. I think **you were generalising** and **Laura was thinking of the concrete example you'd given**.*

*I had to smile at the **threat**. When you said, 'Do you really want to stay here all night?' Someone was bound to say 'Yes!'*

We need to know what we are using language for and how it is likely to be interpreted by our pupils. Earlier chapters on the work of educational theorists, for example Donaldson's **'human sense'** and **'disembedded thinking'**, can offer us useful insights into teacher and pupil language.

Language analysis

From your lesson observations note examples of the actual words, and types of sentences: **statements**, **questions**, **commands**, used in the lesson to:

137

Explain
Instruct
Inform
Persuade
Entertain

Note how these major purposes are combined to motivate and control. This activity may be broken down into small, manageable examples of dialogue or a mentor may consent to having a lesson recorded on audio tape for you to analyse.

Teachers who are particularly successful, can combine and manipulate language functions and styles fluently. The language they use *appears* to approximate to normal conversation and has a personal style and attractive delivery that children can relate to.

Language development

As teacher you will need to provide opportunities for children to develop their language. Often our role is to make children aware of the appropriate variety of language to use, in particular circumstances, for example examination style writing.

The first and most important way in which language competence develops is through use. Children rely on interactions with other speakers to acquire language. The teacher has an important role to play in this process by providing specific, planned opportunities for children to talk and listen, in pairs and groups, across friendship, gender and ability groupings. The talking should have a purpose, for example to hypothe-sise, to solve problems or to express opinions. There should be opportuni-ties to read in order to understand factual information and opportunities to read for implicit meaning, sometimes 'between the lines'. Children need to write for specified audiences and purposes for a variety of media. They also need opportunities to create their own 'language' (or images) to express ideas and thoughts, whether that is in writing, speech, dance, film, art or music.

Language opportunities

138

Do you plan to provide any or most of the following? Are they mentioned in your subject's National Curriculum? For your Professional Development Portfolio you could compile a list of the different language opportunities you have offered children.

Are you providing opportunities for:-

Listening ☐,   speaking   ☐,   reading ☐,   writing. ☐
Working in groups ☐   across friendship ☐   and gender. ☐

Are you providing opportunities to use different forms of language:-

letters ☐	essays ☐
reports ☐	investigations ☐
debates ☐	role play ☐
tape recording ☐	video making ☐
project evaluations ☐	oral presentations ☐

Are you making language forms explicit. Do you

encourage drafting and redrafting of work?
teach vocabulary?
teach the conventions of the subject discipline? e.g. setting out an experiment
provide examples?
provide model answers?
teach writing and layout conventions? e.g. use of the passive, paragraphing
use headings and subheadings?
show children ways of using tables, graphs etc?

Are you using Information Technology?

Word processing
Software packages
Spreadsheets
Data bases
Graphics packages

Do you need to target any of these for development?

SUMMARY

M

- The teacher's choice of language plays a central role in the classroom.
- There are a number of ways that teachers can use language to encourage children's learning and to foster positive relationships in the classroom.
- We should repeatedly provide opportunities for children to *use* language for a variety of purposes and audiences in a range of contexts.

Useful references

Carter, R. (ed.) (1990) **Knowledge about Language and the Curriculum.** London: Hodder & Stoughton.

Cox, B. (1991) **Cox on Cox: an English Curriculum for the 1990s.** London: Hodder & Stoughton.

Crystal, D. (1987) **The Cambridge Encyclopedia of Language.** Cambridge University Press.

Halliday, M. (1974) **Learning How to Mean.** London: Edward Arnold.

Jackendoff, R. (1993) **Patterns in the Mind: Language and Human Nature.** Hemel Hempstead: Harvester Wheatsheaf.

Langford, D. (1994) **Analysing Talk.** London: Macmillan Press.

Pinker, S. (1994) **The Language Instinct.** New York: William Morrow.

Perera, K. (1984) **Children's Writing and Reading: Analysing Classroom Language.** Oxford: Basil Blackwell (particularly pages 325–328).

Sutton, C. (1981) **Communicating in the Classroom.** London: Hodder and Stoughton.

Tough, J. (1985) **Listening to Children Talking.** School Curriculum Development Committee.

Trudgill, P. (1975) **Accent, Dialect and the School.** London: Edward Arnold.

Trudgill, P. (1983) **Sociolinguistics – An Introduction to Language and Society.** London: Penguin Books.

Domains of Thinking

26

Only Connect. (E. M. Forster)

LEARNING OUTCOMES

When you have read this chapter you should be able to define, and give an example of each of the following: prior knowledge, schema (mini-theories and mind maps), alternative frameworks and the difference between domain-specific and domain-general knowledge.

Introduction

Vygotsky and Bruner view the learner as a social personality, seeking and needing support from more competent learners. This provides an alternative to Piaget's view of the learner, which emphasises a solitary individual constructing their own reality.

Piaget's theory of the development of logical thought needs to be examined critically in the light of psychological research into the structure of young people's knowledge. Piaget concentrated on the development of logical structures in the mind, yet it is now recognised that we need also to consider people's **prior knowledge** if we are going to be able to understand how they think.

Prior knowledge has two parts: first, factual information about various subject areas and second, knowledge of problem-solving rules and procedures. In order to solve a problem, we need to know how it fits in with previous problems and which thinking skills to use. We will be making use of existing knowledge, as well as trying to develop new skills.

REFLECTION

139

Consider the calculation 19 × 23. There are several ways of tackling this. Individual students will have their own strategies; two examples of which follow.

Strategy A

1 Some will use the standard written algorithm:

```
  23
  19×
 230
 207
 437
```

However even this 'standard' approach will have variants.

Strategy B

2 Learners who feel more at home with number and have a relational understanding of number will see the problem as

19 × 23 is 20 × 23 take away 1 × 23
i.e. 19 × 23 = 460 − 23 = 437

Strategy 1 is representative of instrumental understanding; a routine or algorithm to be followed requiring little awareness of what underlies the layout of the calculation. The answer could be found without a deep understanding of place value.

Strategy 2 is typical of a learner who has made links in their learning, who connects different elements in a structured way. In short this is a strategy indicative of a deeper relational understanding of number. The learner is able to use prior knowledge; the distributive nature of multiplication and addition and key number facts (2 × 23 = 46) to solve a new problem.

Domain specific and domain general learning

It seems that learning and reasoning skills (schemata) develop as a result of repeated experiences in a knowledge area or **domain**. If the subject matter is familiar, as in Donaldson's concept of 'human sense', it is easier to work out which schema to use. The word 'schema', with the plural 'schemata' or 'schemas', is used to describe the patterns, models or examples which we store in our minds – past experiences which enable us to predict and solve new problems.

A learner driver experiences many T-junctions in practice and also learns about them from the Highway Code. This combination of practice and theory enables the driver to store up a **schema** of how to recognise any T-junction and how to drive the car into a T-junction.

Claxton calls these 'mini theories' and 'mind maps'. Donaldson describes Piaget's analysis of them in the Appendix to *Children's Minds.*

There is also evidence of a developmental trend. Overton *et al* (1987) worked with 9 to 18 year-olds on the two Wason problems (the cards with vowels and odd numbers or beer and age). Half of the 14 year-olds, two thirds of the 16 year-olds and three quarters of the 18 year-olds could do the familiar content problem. A similar trend emerged for the abstract content problem, but with consistently lower success rates (see Chapter 5 on Donaldson for a look at the Wason problem).

These results, and many similar to them, are giving rise to debate. Do adolescents inevitably become better thinkers as they mature (Piaget), or do they become better thinkers as they encounter or are taught more examples which they can then use (Vygotsky)? It seems highly likely that the truth involves a combination of these two proposed explanations.

There must also be other factors involved. The information processing abilities of younger children are probably less efficient than those of older children. Younger individuals may fail to absorb and consider all the information in a problem and thus fail to recognise the similarity of the problem to any of the schemata they already possess.

A 12 year-old looking for the fenced/unfenced symbols on a moorland road on an Ordnance Survey map may miss them, while busily seeking something that looks like a fence. The symbols are continuous/dotted line respectively. Experience of map work and more flexible conceptualisation of 'fencing' would have helped the child find the appropriate schema for 'limits' in their mind and then pick out the words 'fenced/unfenced' beside the appropriate symbol. The words were there in the key but the child didn't 'see' them.

Siegler is making a major contribution to this area, in developing the belief that many aspects of children's knowledge are rule bound: 'if this … then that …'. A feature of his theory is the 'information processing' model – as Meadows indicates (1993), this is not necessarily a useful way of conceptualising thinking. The complexities of perception, spatial awareness, motivation, prior knowledge and current attitude cannot be encompassed by an information processing model. Yet, it does seem clear, as Siegler proposes, that children learn better within the confines of a subject (domain specific) than at a decontextualised level (domain general).

Adey, Shayer and Yates (1995) find, in their work on the development of higher order thinking, that pupils make better progress if the thinking is contextualised within a curriculum subject. Their science project can be taken as evidence of domain specific, yet very powerful thinking, which they believe will also make it possible for the child to think better in other subjects. A subject area is, however, necessary as an arena for cognitive development (Keil). Case, on the other hand, argues that a knowledge base is merely a vehicle for thought, not a powerful structure which helps thought to develop at what Case believes to be a domain general level. As teachers we have much anecdotal evidence (and Adey *et al* provide evidence of this in their research) that pupils frequently do not generalise thinking skills from one area of the curriculum to another, and can even fail to generalise within a subject area.

Here we can look to Vygotsky and Bruner for classroom inspiration in the **zone of proximal development** and the concept of **scaffolding**. Vygotsky's notion of mediation is also valuable: we can 'mediate' or communicate meaning by selecting appropriate stimuli, presenting them clearly and intervening in the process of learning if necessary. One way of achieving mediation is by using psychological tools such as language, signs, gestures, images: this can be achieved at whole class level although much more accurately on a one-to-one basis. Feuerstein's theory of mediation postulates that three features of mediation must be present: the significance of the task must be clear to the learner, as must its purpose beyond the here and now, and there must be a shared intention. Williams and Burden (1977) discuss this model of learning further.

Alternative frameworks

Another area of research about learning which is extremely important for effective classroom teaching is that of **alternative frameworks**. Sneider and Pulos (1983) believe that school children develop very clear ideas about cause and effect developed from observation, personal experience and adult information. Often these ideas are wrong, yet they are difficult to change and can get in the way of the pupil accepting the right interpretation. One approach to challenging their own ideas is to have an active session.

Many infant and junior age children believe that the cats' eyes in the middle of the road light up as their vehicle approaches and switch off after the car has passed. Children can produce eye witness evidence of this which is very difficult to disprove.

Most adults, including teachers, are unaware of these beliefs and have forgotten what they themselves believed as children. There are many examples. Such things as adequate notions about gravity or about the shape of the earth are even harder to develop and may still be inaccurate by the age of 14 (Driver *et al*, 1990). These inaccurate alternative frameworks can, on the one hand, obstruct the teacher's attempts to explain 'how things really are' and, on the other, mislead pupils into using alternative frameworks which are inappropriate, for example 'switching on' to explain cats' eyes.

Implications for the classroom

The teacher needs to be able to 'scaffold' a situation which is new, so that the pupil recognises those elements which are familiar and compares prior knowledge with new material. (See Chapter 7 on Bruner for a discussion of scaffolding.)

For the map symbols example given above, it would be useful to:

- help a class working with Ordnance Survey symbols to consider what a fence actually does: it acts as a limiting edge to separate two areas
- show the class worked examples of some of the Ordnance Survey sym-

bols, including fences; the teacher needs to be able to remember what it was like to be that age, and think about a fence as a three dimensional object with panels or slats

- teach the class the specific skills involved in map reading

More generally, this implies that:

- the teacher should give the class the opportunity to identify and explore their difficulties, for example by working with some partially completed examples in order to tease out the incorrect alternative frameworks
- classroom discussions are valuable for exploring the implications of each other's alternative frameworks; such discussions would first, help a teacher to find out what students believe and secondly, help pupils develop a questioning attitude to their own beliefs.
- textbook language needs to be 'translated' for students; models are often not recognisable in the real world without the help of a more expert view
- teachers should be sensitive to pupils' different learning styles and the different approaches needed

Different teaching styles

140

Make observations of two lessons which are very different in teaching style. It could be that the same teacher will deliver two completely different lessons. You will need to develop a proforma to help you look out for contrasts and comparability. Headings could include: use of language, use of gesture, use of signs or images.

SUMMARY

In conclusion, pupils enter school with many pieces of **prior knowledge** and **schemata**.

If the subject matter is familiar, as in Donaldson's 'human sense', it is easier to work out which schema to use. Even a 4 year-old will start school with some useful emergent prior knowledge about numbers: number as sequence ('I get the third cup'), number as place ('My house is number 44'), and number as label ('That bus is number 69').

It is probably ill-founded to regard either Piaget's concept of 'formal operations' or Donaldson's 'disembedded thought' as the peak of the formal education process. It seems much more likely that we develop a set of different schemata or mini-theories or mind-maps which help us to understand new situations and solve new problems.

There is a complex relationship here between **domain-specific** and **domain-general** knowledge. For example, we learn to understand arbitrary road markings which shape our behaviour because we can think symbolically. The ability to think in symbols is **domain-general**, in other words we all use symbols in many applications including reading or following diagrams for instructions. Road markings, however, are **domain-specific**, or marks which have a particular meaning for road-users.

By secondary transfer each child will have much more knowledge – some of which will be useful, some of which will be false – based on alternative frameworks, such as their interpretation of observation, personal experience and adult information. Some of this knowledge will be **domain-specific** (for instance how to conjugate a French verb), some of this knowledge will be **domain-general** (for example prior knowledge about how to make patterns with any language, including our own, or with numbers). The issue with domain-specific and domain-general knowledge is that we often do not make connections between, for example, French and English, thereby restricting ourselves to many unconnected chunks of knowledge.

The implications of this for teaching are that we should never assume that *They've done this, so they know it, and they can use it next lesson in a slightly different form* – pupils will not necessarily make such connections. We may have to make those connections for them and with them repeatedly.

Useful references

Adey, P. S., Shayer, M. and Yates, C. (1995) **Thinking Science: Student and Teachers' Materials for the CASE Intervention.** London: Nelson (2nd edition).

Anderson, J. R. (1990) **Cognitive Psychology and its Implications.** New York: Freeman (3rd edition).

Case, R. (1985) **Intellectual Development: Birth to Adulthood.** New York: Academic Press.

Claxton, G. (1990) **Teaching to Learn.** London: Cassell.

Driver, R. *et al* in Lee, V. (ed.) (1990) **Children's Learning in School.** London: Hodder & Stoughton.

Hope, J. A. and Sherrill, J. M. (1987) *'Characteristics of Unskilled and Skilled Mental Calculators'* in **Journal for Research in Mathematics Education**, 18, pages 88–111.

Keil, F. C. (1989) **Concepts, Kinds and Cognitive Development.** Boston: MIT Press.

Overton, W. F. *et al* (1987) *'Form and Content in the Development of Deductive Reasoning*, in **Developmental Psychology**, 23, pages 22–30.

Sneider, C. and Pulos, S. (1983) *'Children's Cosmographies: Understanding the Earth's Shape and Gravity'* in **Science Education**, 57, pages 205–221.

Williams, M. and Burden, R. (1977) **Psychology for Language Teachers.** Cambridge: Cambridge University Press.

The Code of Practice

27

To rely upon definitions and categories to suggest remedies is to divert attention from observations of the individual and his or her circumstances. There are no easy solutions, so we have to think. (McManus, 1989)

LEARNING OUTCOMES

This chapter will build on the introduction to the Code of Practice in Chapter 1. It will give you examples of Stages 1 to 3 of the five-stage Code of Practice and help you to see the tensions between the child's needs, the school's needs and the administrative structure of the special needs recommendations which are in the Code of Practice.

The Code of Practice on the Identification and Assessment of Special Educational Needs

The Code of Practice is a document published by the Department for Education, which is intended to provide **guidance** for the Special Educational Needs component of the 1993 Education Act. The 1993 Act updates and generally replaces the 1981 Act, and states that a child has special educational needs if s/he has a 'learning difficulty' which calls for 'special educational provision' to be made. On 1 November 1996 the 1993 Education Act was repealed and special education law was incorporated into the consolidating Education Act of 1996.

At some time during their school years, about 20% of the school population may need special provision; the government believes that most of **this provision can be met by school resources**. Only about 2% of pupils will have **a statement of special educational needs** maintained for them by the LEA, with extra funding. Over the last thirty years there has been increasing emphasis on **integration** into mainstream for pupils with SEN and fewer places in segregated settings (special classes, units or schools), with, unfortunately, no transfer of funds from special to mainstream. The concept of 'inclusive education' (all children have the right to attend their neighbourhood school) is therefore an ideological position in theory and a financial and professional pressure in practice.

A child has special educational needs if he or she has a learning difficulty which calls for special educational provision to be made for him or her.

A child has a learning difficulty if he or she:

a) *has a significantly greater difficulty in learning than the majority of children of the same age*

b) *has a disability which either prevents or hinders the child from making use of educational facilities of a kind provided for children of the same age in schools within the area of the local education authority*

c) *is under five and falls within the definition of the points above or will do if special educational provision is not made for the child.*

A child must not be regarded as having a learning difficulty solely because the language or form of language of the home is different from the language in which he or she is or will be taught.

Special educational provision *means:*

a) *for a child over two, educational provision which is additional to, or otherwise different from, the educational provision made generally for children of the child's age in maintained schools, other than special schools, in the area*

b) *for a child under two, educational provision of any kind.*

(The Code of Practice, 1994, DFE)

The Code recommends a five-stage model.

Case studies of Stages 1, 2 and 3 are given here. At Stage 4 a full psychometric and educational assessment is carried out, to establish whether the pupil can have a statement of SEN. During this time (assessment and administrative procedures take at least six months) the child should continue to receive Stage 3 support. At Stage 5 the LEA agrees that it has a legal duty to make special provision: it is to be hoped that adequate funding will be made available at this point to meet the pupil's needs.

Stages 1, 2 and 3

Work through these Case Studies to come to an understanding of the first three stages, and compare them with the pupils you know.

141

Stage 1

If a teacher is worried about a pupil not making good enough progress, Stage 1 of the Code of Practice is the appropriate first step.

Stage 1 (Educational): Sanjay

A well differentiated curriculum should be in place and the teacher should be assessing through teaching. If Sanjay is nevertheless not making adequate progress the teacher will use the Stage 1 to do the following: put extra support into place, contact the parents and ask for their support, make a note of the strategies proposed and the time scale. If this is a learning problem, a sixth former may give Sanjay some extra help, for example.

Stage 1 (Behavioural): Moira

A behaviour intervention would be started if the form tutor began, for example, to receive some complaints about Moira's poor behaviour and apparently poor motivation. If Moira does not respond to clear, consistent rules and appears to understand but not follow a well planned school behaviour policy, then she may need to be monitored by the Special Educational Needs Co-ordinator or form tutor. Moira may need to agree to come and see that member of staff on a Monday morning to try and set up a better attitude for the week.

Stage 2

Stage 2 (Educational): Sanjay

After one or two terms at Stage 1, Sanjay is not improving. His reading age is just above the cut off point for specialist support and his spelling is poor. Mild learning difficulties seem to be present in most subjects and the gap between him and his peers will widen if action is not taken.

At this point therefore the Special Educational Needs Co-ordinator needs to be aware and an Individual Education Plan (IEP) must be established. Parents, SENCO and (probably) form tutor will be involved. The IEP will focus on alternative means of recording his work, as Sanjay's spelling is poor and will need to be reviewed half termly.

Stage 2 (Behavioural): Moira

Despite one term of monitoring, Moira is becoming increasingly disruptive. She has been ejected from French several times and is doing very little homework. She has been cheeky to two of the school meals supervisory assistants in connection with some bullying incidents of younger children. In an attempt to pre-empt escalation of the problem, Moira is being put into detention and being told off. On her past record it seems that this is not effective, and her behaviour will probably deteriorate even more. At the meeting with parents to set up an

IEP, the positives are stressed. Moira responds to structured praise and it is hoped that this can be used productively in her IEP. Fortnightly reviews are to be held when possible and the IEP will be used to keep a log of good behaviour as well as bad.

Update: Two terms after the Stage 2 was started on Sanjay, he has not improved educationally. He still does not meet the County criteria for a statement of special educational needs, but will be moved on to Stage 3, with educational psychologist involvement.

Two terms after the Stage 2 was started on Moira, her work and behaviour have improved markedly, partly because of involving the parents. By putting her back onto a Stage 1 the SENCO still has the opportunity to monitor.

Stage 3

Stage 3 (Behavioural and Educational): Wayne

Wayne was a Year 7 pupil who did not settle at secondary transfer and refused to do anything that three of his subject teachers wanted him to do. His Head of Year soon put him onto a Stage 3 IEP without going through the usual monitoring and reviewing at Stages 1 and 2. A Behavioural Support teacher took him out of class once a week to play games and he was relaxed and happy when receiving individual attention. Unfortunately this did not generalise to his classroom behaviour. Together the educational psychologist and the form tutor met Wayne's mother and discovered that Wayne's father had a severe heart condition. After heart bypass surgery which had seemed successful, he suffered a relapse. Wayne's increasingly defiant behaviour happened at the same time as the father's relapse. The educational psychologist recommended that the teachers should give Wayne choices, that is ask Wayne to do one of two things, give him a limited choice at all decision points in a lesson – instead of telling him to do something. Educational and psychometric assessment indicated that, at that time, Wayne should not be given the choice of reading unless he was to be supported. This was because his reading and spelling levels were those of a 7 year-old, although his understanding was good. It seemed likely that Wayne's inappropriate behaviour had masked his poor educational attainments: sometimes children are so difficult to manage that they succeed in hiding their educational needs. Wayne's reading age was low enough to merit a Stage 4 Statutory Assessment. He will receive some school-based learning support. His emotional needs are difficult to support. The school staff are attempting to support Wayne without making unreasonable concessions: by looking at the whole child, home situation, educational, emotional and social needs, they are able to understand the emotional turmoil he is experiencing and are also now in a better position to support him with a structured literacy programme.

A statemented pupil

142

Consider a pupil you know who has a statement of SEN. Describe her/his needs to a colleague. What form does the provision take? Does it help the pupil or the teacher much? Is it adequate?

Consider a pupil you know who does not have an SEN statement, but whose additional educational needs are acknowledged and who receives support from within the school's own resources. How does this work?

The term 'additional educational needs' is used by the government to allocate resources to local education authorities through the Education Standard Spending Assessment (SSA). The term reflects a concept of SEN which includes children from disadvantaged backgrounds or from ethnic minority groups, who are considered to have needs greater than those of the general population. We are using the term here as West and Sammons do in their writings, to refer to those pupils who are perceived to have educational needs over and above those of others in their school/class (especially SEN and English language needs). Clearly it is vital to recognise that these concepts of SEN and additional educational needs are context-related to a large extent: different schools with variations in intake, provision and school development plans will make different decisions.

Reading the Code

143

There is no substitute for reading the Code of Practice. It is readable and even interesting. The legally binding sections are typed in blue. Every school has at least one copy.

In order to help you to focus on the major issues, the SWOT sequence will be used here (Strengths, Weaknesses, Opportunities, Threats). You need to be critical of the way in which the following points are grouped: the categories reflect the hopes and fears of many professionals, yet there is room for manoeuvre; some schools may be able to turn weaknesses into strengths and threats into opportunities, often with your help.

Strengths of the Code of Practice

- It ensures the legal status of SEN procedures: governors must present annually to parents the school's SEN policy and procedures, and have a statutory duty to 'have regard to' the CoP.
- Resources allocated by schools to children with SEN must be clearly described, reviewed and 'transparently' funded.
- The CoP places special educational needs high on the agenda for all schools, and Stage 1 of its (recommended) five-stage model emphasises differentiation. The child's teacher or tutor will: 'provide special help within the normal curriculum framework, exploring ways in which increased differentiation of classroom work might better meet

SPECIAL EDUCATIONAL NEEDS REGISTER (1)

SCHOOL:

PUPIL	D.O.B. & YEAR	Category						Stage 1 DATE SNS21	Stage 2 DATE SNS2	Stage 3	
		L	B	PH	HI	VI				DATE SNS3	DATE SNS-R

SPECIAL EDUCATIONAL NEEDS REGISTER (2)

Name	D.O.B.	Form	Recommended by	Date	Problem area(s)			Discussed with Parents	Action	Review dates
					Progress or Development	Behaviour and Adjustment	Physical and Sensory			

the needs of the individual child' (CoP, page 23). This is recorded and monitored/reviewed/amended through an IEP.

● CoP recommends that records of differentiation be kept. This can be interpreted along Ofsted lines, in other words that you keep records on differentiated groups, three being adequate for general purposes.

● Within CoP the Special Educational Needs Co-ordinator (SENCO) is given an enhanced role, with a preventive and a supportive element. This can and should be seen as a way of building on already existing good practice, and as a way of strengthening the role of the teacher, as opposed to de-skilling subject specialists by imposing the knowledge of outside experts. The SENCO needs to set up and maintain SEN registers, for Stage 1 (initial cause for concern) and for Stage 3 (LEA information). Above are 2 examples of SEN registers.

● CoP recommends that **schools should work together**, to pool resources, and to ensure co-ordinated SEN provision within their area. They should cluster for the purposes of

1 developing their SEN policies
2 sharing expertise for meeting staff development needs
3 enabling special school staff to take their expertise into mainstream and vice versa
4 and having meetings to pool ideas over issues of common concern e.g. efficient methods of transmitting SEN information from primary feeder schools to the secondary school, without prejudice to the pupils concerned.

Weaknesses of the Code of Practice

- **Financial:** The integration into mainstream of pupils with SEN is advocated in **a piece of legislation which does not make available any extra funding for the implementation of such a demanding task**.
- More pressure is being put on schools to meet the needs of children who, ten years ago, might have had **more support in mainstream**, or attended special provision. Staff must now record and review the school's support through IEPs. The more able child is not discussed in the Code, yet many teachers could teach very clever children better, and Ofsted inspections work at such provision.
- Very limited funding was available for implementing the Code of Practice. The DfEE would argue that there is no need for training because there are no statutory duties; yet schools are being put under pressure to fulfil the recommendations of the CoP, and Ofsted inspections will look for evidence of this. The recent Ofsted report on the Code of Practice was critical of the lack of training provided for SENCOs. Lewis, Neill and Campbell (1996) found that only two-thirds of secondary schools have salary policies that recognise the responsibilities of the SENCO.
- There is no common approach to resourcing special educational needs as part of LEAs Local Management of Schools formulae (West and Sammons, 1996). There are variations between LEAs in the proportion of the budget allocated to SEN and in the factors used to identify such needs (Sammons, 1993). There are also resources which are allocated to schools as part of an 'additional educational needs' component, but these resources are not 'hypothecated' – which means that LEAs are not forced to spend that money directly for meeting the needs of the children with additional educational needs. The Code does not include children with English language needs, yet some LEAs include such needs in their LMS formulae.
- **Any change process is time consuming and stressful**, and the CoP is based on the expectation that schools will make changes. These changes include putting the CoP on the **Senior Management Team (SMT)** agenda and the **Whole School policy agenda**; all this takes time and time is money.
- The emphasis on individual education plans (IEPs) may in fact serve to fragment a school's desire to meet the needs of pupils, instead of encouraging policy shifts on support for learning, curriculum, staff development and staff co-operation. Lewis *et al* (1996) found that many schools had been interpreting the Code too rigidly, which can discourage teachers from developing appropriate and innovative approaches.

Opportunities within the Code of Practice

- **Parental involvement** is emphasised: research shows that standards improve when schools involve parents.
- The Code of Practice puts **good teaching** fair and square in the centre of the picture by its emphasis on **differentiation** and on good **curriculum-based collaborative work** between subject specialists and SENCOs.

- The **Individual Education Plan** (IEP) (on pages 242–3) have been superseded by the Action Plan (AP), before the CoP. Both the IEP and the AP fulfil, generally speaking, the same function – **focusing on the pupil's special needs in a practical, mostly curriculum-related way**, co-ordinated by the SENCO and facilitating collaborative work among staff, and with parents. The IEP is now being proposed by the CoP as a way of differentiating the curriculum for a pupil about whom we have serious concerns (some SENCOs will support staff well at this point). The IEP signifies that the pupil is at stage 2 of the Code of Practice stages.
- **Senior Management Team** involvement in the above areas is emphasised by the CoP, as is **governor** responsibility.
- **Pupils' opinions** about their special needs are to be asked for, taken seriously and integrated into any planning, if at all possible. This is in line with the spirit of the Children Act.

Some pupils have strong views about in-class support, about being 'extracted' for support and about their priorities for being helped. A recurrent example of the last point is the pupil who works painfully slowly, never completes work and seems sluggish and unmotivated; it could be that the major factor is handwriting. Some teenagers are so determined to produce acceptable written work that they may need a crash course in handwriting on their IEP, not a short course of counselling sessions.

Threats of the Code of Practice

- The quality of provision will not necessarily be improved by this legislation. Support service expertise is relatively expensive and schools may look at cheaper options in order to provide more hours of support. This may not always be the most appropriate solution. Moreover a sample of schools has identified between 1.5% and 53% of pupils as having special needs. Even given differences in catchment area, this is a huge range.
- There is a danger of **bureaucratic patterns** developing, which may be self-defeating; the Stage 3 register which has to be maintained by each LEA, may generate a lot of extra work for SENCOs without any tangible benefit to the school. (Stage 3 represents the point at which outside agencies become formally involved, and this may sometimes lead to statementing procedures.)
- More pressure is being put on class teachers and pastoral heads to be accountable for interventions which they undertake. This should raise standards but SENCOs will need **good management skills** in order to support rather than to overload their colleagues.
- Who will **audit** all this and help schools to review their progress annually in a constructive, creative and financially sensible way?

The SENCO

Make an appointment to have an informal discussion with your school SENCO. Use this activity as a focus for the discussion. One of the major problems for all schools is the increased administrative demands made on the SENCO by the Code of Practice. What is the value, for you as a subject specialist, or as a member of the pastoral team, of a Stage 3 register (a list of all pupils with special needs)? Look at the examples of a pupil with a hearing loss, but no special provision except for twice termly visits from a peripatetic teacher for the hearing impaired, and a pupil with Social Services Department involvement.

144

Individual Educational Plans (IEPs)

The IEP should set out the following:

- nature of the child's learning difficulties
- action – the special education provision
  the staff involved, including frequency of support
  special programmes/activities/materials/equipment
- help from parents at home
- targets to be achieved in a given time, and review date, set by SENCO
- any pastoral care or medical requirements
- monitoring and assessment arrangements

Setting up an IEP is not particularly difficult, but what comes after that can be problematic, in other words maintaining it, reviewing it and deciding what to try next if it doesn't seem to benefit the pupil. If existing school records can fulfil the role of IEP, no new IEP for children with SEN is needed.

- Look for examples of intervention in the chapters on differentiation, teaching and learning styles and behaviour difficulties.
- Parental involvement is recommended, but according to the CoP, however, inviting a parent to work on a child's spelling or tables would not be adequate intervention for an IEP; there must be school teaching input.
- If you started too many IEPs the pressure on you would be excessive and would fragment your teaching style. Up to 10% or three in a class would be realistic.
- An alternative at Stage 2 is group IEPs. These would need to be monitored and reviewed for each individual in the group.

IEPs

Look at the two examples of IEPs on pages 242 and 243.

145

Individual Education Plan

Name: Neil _____   DOB:_____   SEN Stage: SpLD 2

Tutor Group: 7 _____   Subject: Literacy

Baseline/Strengths

Neil recognises his difficulties with reading and spelling in lessons. He's reading below his chronological age and has considerable spelling problems, especially with vowels, initial blends, double consonants and word endings. Neil doesn't use cursive writing and finds punctuation hard.

Actions Agreed

Reading and spelling with handwriting in workshop.
Ensure Neil gets the main ideas of lessons, particularly in difficult texts.
Keywords (in back of exercise books?)
Praise & reassurance

Intended Outcomes

Improving literacy skills and development of cursive writing
Ensuring access to curriculum – key words to give him hooks to hang information on
Raising self-esteem

Resources
Workshop
– books
Charles Cripps
Hand for Spelling
Word processors for presentation

Personnel
Helen (Workshop teacher)
Ann (SEN teacher)

Timescale for Action
2 months

Review Date
Jan 1997

Signed: _____   Class Teacher_____   Date: 6/11/96

Helen E. pp. SEN Co-ordinator

Consider the following:

- Short-term and long-term purposes of IEP
- How to avoid excessive administrative overload
- How to ensure that all relevant staff are involved
- Your school's responses to the need for IEPs
- How monitoring and review procedures are managed

In answering these questions it would be useful to discuss the issues with colleagues in your department/faculties and the SENCO. Look at the Teacher as Researcher chapters (Chapters 1 and 19) for guidance.

An alternative strategy would be to use a **group in-class support plan** in line with Ofsted's recommendation that many classes can be put into three groups for general differentiation purposes.

INDIVIDUAL EDUCATIONAL PLAN

NAME OF PUPIL _____ DATE OF BIRTH _____

YEAR _____

DEFINITION OF DIFFICULTY

1. Physical Handicap   Sensory Impairment

    Learning Difficulty   Emotional/ Behavioural Difficulty

2. Description of Nature of Difficulty

CLASS/SUBJECT TEACHER

STAGE   PLAN   Type of strategy required:

Organisational   YES/NO   Motivational   YES/NO   Teaching   YES/NO

Material   YES/NO   Behavioural   YES/NO

Brief description of strategy(ies) to be adopted, specifying programme:

Date strategy started   Signed

Position

Evaluation of strategy:

Date of evaluation   Signed

Position

Parents informed   Discussed as far as possible with pupil

Need to advance to Stage   YES/NO

Group in-class support plan

146

Design a group in-class support plan below. Select from one of your classes a small group of pupils about whom you have serious concerns. Focus on one practical aspect of differentiating their curriculum which you could set yourself and them as a half-term target.

Differentiating the CoP

147

Look at the case study on **Differentiation and the Code of Practice** below. Consider the raw data here. Find out as much as you can about this Year 7 class, decide what you know about their needs in any area of the curriculum which demands reading skills, and decide what you would do to meet their needs. Consider what information you can find out from a reading test. Does this depend upon which reading test?!

Name	Reading age
Anita	16.5
Jane	8.6
Esther	7.3
John	7.8
Rachel	16.6
Michael	8.5
James	8.3
Susan	16.0
Penny	16.0
Pamela	9.0
Peter	12.6
Narish	10.5
Winston	7.9
Yasir	9.6
Dieter	16.3
Jane	9.9
Jonathan	11.8
Mohammed	16.0
Kelly	10.3
Jason	8.2
Ahmed	11.6
Jade	16.8
Freda	12.3
Daniel	16.3

Strategies

148

The case study on page 244 is a real class. Now select a class you are teaching at present. Use the information you have about them to develop strategies for grouping them, for example using a group IEP.

Here are three more **opportunities** within the Code of Practice to round off this section:

● The CoP provides the impetus to **re-consider school policies**, reviewing and assessing as part of a positive approach;
● working on SEN policy can influence many aspects of **provision for all pupils**, for example literacy and numeracy across the curriculum, (as emphasised in the new National Curriculum)
● it can influence policies about in-class support and policies about use of laptop computers for dyslexic pupils . . . and many more.

SUMMARY

The Code of Practice has a tone of voice which challenges schools to meet the needs of all pupils better. It also officially recognises specific learning difficulties (including dyslexia) and emotional and behavioural difficulties. Specific target setting, monitoring and reviewing of progress are probably more effective than before. Yet the major challenge of the Code of Practice remains unmet. This relates to the improvement of the school as a learning school, in which pupils, teachers and parents need to work together. Such a poorly resourced piece of national legislation must beg the question of how SENCOs can improve the learning of all pupils without the mechanism and the funding to influence the whole school. School development plans should reflect the intention to improve team work, co-operative planning and collaboration in policy making and in lessons.

Useful references

Department for Education (1994) **Code of Practice on the Identification and Assessment of Special Educational Needs.** London DFE.

Department of Education and Science (1978) **Special Educational Needs (The Warnock Report).** London: HMSO.

Landy, M. and Gains, C. (1996) **Inspecting Special Needs in Schools.** London: David Fulton.

Lewis, A., Neill, S. R. St J. and Campbell, R. J. (1996) **The Implementation of the Code of Practice in Primary and Secondary Schools: A national survey of the perceptions of special educational needs co-ordinators.** London: National Union of Teachers. Report available from NUT, Hamilton House, Mabledon Place, London WCH 9BD.

Lewis, A., Neill, S. R. St J. and Campbell, R. J. (1997) **SENCOs and the Code: A National Survey,** in Support for Learning, vol. 12, no. 1.

McManus, M. (1989) **Troublesome Behaviour in Class.** London: Routledge.

Phillips, S., Crockett, P. and Louvre, A. (1995) **Special Educational Needs: Putting the Code to Work: Secondary Edition.** Manchester Metropolitan University and Pitman Publishing.

Sammons, P. (1993) **Measuring and Resourcing Educational Needs: Variations in LEAs LMS Policies in Inner London.** Clare Market Papers, no. 6 (London Centre for Educational Research, London School of Economics).

West, A. and Sammons, P. (1996) **Children with and without 'Additional Educational Needs' at Key Stage 1 in Six Inner City Schools – Teaching and Learning Processes and Policy Implications.** British Educational Research Journal, vol. 22, no. 1.

Stress

28

Usually I take one day at a time. Lately several days have attacked me all at once.

LEARNING OUTCOMES

Experienced teachers often feel as if 'several days are attacking' them, so don't be surprised when you do too.

When you have read through this chapter, you will have examined some of the factors underlying stress. You will have begun to analyse whether you are at risk from 'burn out' caused by the pressures of teaching and realised that there are strategies available to you which can help you to avoid stress-related illness.

Introduction

Teaching is potentially a very stressful occupation, which can place both the novice and the expert teacher at risk from stress-related illness. When faced with an external physical threat we have a choice: to stay and fight or to escape – the 'fight or flight' model. Our body responds to these reactions of challenge by producing physical feelings needed to deal with an attack, by another person for example. Work-based threats to our state of well-being cause the same responses even though these may not be at all appropriate. The accumulation of these responses without the release of 'fight or flight' can in the end cause stress-related illness.

Stress in itself may not necessarily be bad for a person. It can help to produce optimum performance in a challenging task: for example in a major sporting event or a public performance (music or drama), an interview or a lecture. Indeed it may be necessary to monitor stress responses so that such optimum achievement is possible; in other words to raise adrenalin levels before the event. Many sports people are obsessive about preparation, going through a set routine to the extent of being superstitious about trivial things. Superstition itself is a response to fear and a means of trying to manage in difficult circumstances. We all have our own threshold of stress which may be set low in some individuals (quick to feel stressed) and high in others (slow to feel stressed). We develop our own coping mechanisms to deal with stress as we perceive it.

REFLECTION

Develop the habit of reviewing your teaching situation. If you ask yourself: 'What's wearing me down this week?' you will be half way to a solution for reducing stress. Here are three examples:

149

- Minor misdemeanours by pupils can become very wearing (see Chapter 16 on the Elton Report for a list of behaviours – pupils talking out of turn, arriving late and so on). You may be accepting too high a level of disruption and, if so, this needs to be discussed with your mentor.

- One of the characteristics of a good teacher is the ability to take account of many phenomena simultaneously: stress can result when you are learning how to do that. If the challenge of preparing and teaching your lessons has become uncontrollable, re-assess the situation.

- If either of the above two situations arise, you will face the dilemma (stress-provoking in itself) of having to decide whether you are showing weakness by 'owning up' to a problem, or whether you can become even stronger by asking for advice. Having decided on the latter course you may then feel that your voice is not being heard. If that were to happen, you would need to seek advice elsewhere: ask for a meeting with your mentor and the senior member of staff responsible for your training. Now turn this reflection into action to strengthen your development. As you work through this chapter, you will be able to consider how to find solutions. Remember, above all, to celebrate your own successes and those of others, and to enjoy the community of support which the school can offer you.

The four faces of stress

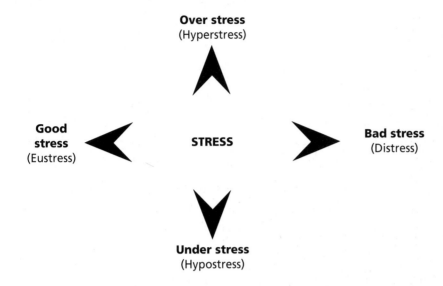

Selye's framework above shows one way in which stress can be interpreted. If asked about stress our initial reaction is to regard it as a negative factor in our lives. This framework allows for alternative interpretations. Over-stress is when the demands exceed our capacity to respond: there is no way in which we can complete the workload. Under-stress when the work is insufficiently challenging; routine paperwork with no stimulating aspect. Good stress is when we have the challenge of a potentially interesting lesson; bad stress may come with the sudden surprise of the cover lesson from hell which drops in your lap late on a Friday afternoon. We need therefore a response to stress that achieves a balance between under-stress and over-stress; with as much good stress as we need and as little bad stress as we can manage. The match between the person and the environment needs to be such that a little tension is there but not too much; there is challenge, but not so much that one cannot possibly cope.

Another way of viewing stress is the performance against stress curve as seen on page 250. It indicates where the development of stress overload occurs and how good stress can eventually become unhealthy and negative. This curve is of course still dependent upon individual factors; the shape of the curve and the point on the curve at which the critical change takes place are neither of them absolutes. The characteristics of the curve will reflect the characteristics of the individual concerned, for it is not the situation in itself which determines the level of stress, but the way in which we interpret events.

Individuals react differently to the same external stimulus. US Executives were studied in the midst of company reorganisation. Whilst half fell victim to stress-related illnesses, the rest were able to cope and remained positive and cheerful. The difference was attributed to a 'hardy personality' characterised by the three attributes: commitment, control and challenge.

● **Commitment** to themselves, their job and their family
● Feeling of being in **control** of their lives
● Seeing change as a part of life and a **challenge** (Kobasa, 1985)

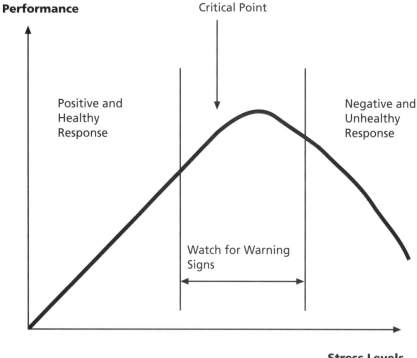

To a certain extent you will have been examined for this robustness during the interview for your course; it's not easy to determine this of course, but you might for example have been asked about what mechanisms you have for coping with difficulties. Teachers, like others in the caring professions, need to have or to develop this 'hardiness'.

To achieve this response to change and pressure, one needs to perceive threat as a challenge. The difficult part is to prepare oneself in such a manner that this is possible. The first step may be to examine your own lifestyle to see if you are at risk from stress. There are many factors which can be indicative of potential stress-related illness. The examples of questions below are taken from a stress audit in *Coping with Stress in Caring* (Bailey, 1985) as cited in Cook, 1992).

Stress Audit

> **1** Are you drinking, smoking or eating more than usual?
> **2** Do you have difficulty sleeping at night?
> **3** Are you more touchy or argumentative than normal?

So how do you manage with the pressures on you during your time in school? What actions can you take which will replace habits that lead to stress? The following list of strategies is adapted from Cook (1992).

● Be over-prepared when possible, yet attempt to incorporate flexibility
● Take the time to listen to others. You won't be the only one with concerns or solutions. Give others time to think and explore ideas.

- Be more patient. Perfection isn't always possible and instant perfection certainly isn't. Don't forget to be patient with yourself as well as others.
- Become more aware of how obsessional you are about time. Deliberately plan to spend some time enjoying someone's company, enjoying talking about things other than work.
- Plan time for reflection. Consider a weekly review of how your plans are progressing; get feedback from others especially your mentor. This reflection is a central part of your course.
- Maintain or even broaden your interests – read novels, go to the cinema, do things which demand your whole attention. Activities which demand your attendance because others are expecting you are very useful here; team sports or dance or orchestra or . . .
- Be aware that deadlines encourage 'hurry up' behaviour; be realistic and only create deadlines when necessary. You will probably find that the task of teaching creates enough without building in too many extras of your own!
- Learn to say NO if you wish to protect your planned use of time. Ask for advice from your mentor if experienced teachers expect you to help them. You will need to manage your time.
- Breathing spaces during a busy working day will allow you time to reduce stress by relaxing or deep breathing and recovering before starting again. This is a really difficult one if you are teaching. You will already have recognised that breathing space is not easily obtained while you are teaching.
- Relax; take opportunities during the day and night to relax, remembering that like all skills, it takes time and practice to become really effective.

There is no correct way of course. You may well need to become professional enough to realise that teaching may be incredibly demanding but 'It's just a job after all'!

Burn out

Burn out is a stress induced syndrome, which has three major aspects: emotional exhaustion, depersonalisation and reduced personal accomplishment. As ever there are individual factors at work here and some teachers are more at risk than others. The performance/stress curve also indicates that there can come a point where overwork leads to ill health; it suggests that performance cannot continue to meet demand and that a critical point can be reached after which performance decreases.

Many teachers believe that self-sacrifice is necessary to demonstrate loyalty and commitment. This is clearly unwise and counter-productive, since a prime need in schools is for stability. Stability and hence success is achieved through teachers being healthy and being in control. If you are a good, caring teacher, having someone replace you temporarily because you are ill, does nothing to improve your students' learning! You need to monitor your level of stress in order to avoid illness.

Time management: use your time effectively

Work smarter not harder; it's important not to cope with additional demands by just working harder. There are many ways in which our use of time can be better managed. It may be that the way in which you work could be more efficient. Fontana (1993) emphasises the benefits that arise from effective time management; long-term planning, greater job satisfaction, less stress, more personal time with the opportunity to 'switch off' from work.

REFLECTION

There are many strategies which can help you to avoid working excessively. For example:

150
- Set aside a block of time to complete any major task
- Prioritise tasks by listing what has to be done
- Work at the best time of day for you

Work with a partner and extend the list given above, but also give examples of what they might mean in practice for you.

For example: *Work at the best time of day for you*
Wherever possible I always try to arrange to complete routine tasks in the afternoon leaving the morning for more creative work. When *do* you do your marking and when do you plan lessons?

Avoiding stress-related illness

The following list is not meant to be exhaustive of all possible techniques for avoiding the dangers of stress. You may want to add your own.

Get a life!

Teaching can seriously damage your health, as can any other job which demands a lot of you. You need to develop or maintain interests which take you away from work and allow you to switch off. It is particularly valuable to have friends and hobbies outside teaching, which enable you to become absorbed in them and to stop worrying about work. There is more to life than work.

Physical rest and relaxation

Can you relax? Find a time in the day to be quiet and calm. If you have something stressful looming up, you need to take the time to be calm beforehand. Find a technique which helps you to relax in school; a massage or a warm bath are probably not options available to you in most schools!

Separate work and home

You may need a chance to unwind before going home, perhaps by doing a different activity before being the person you are at home, such as walking the dog or playing in the staff five-a-side.

Do more of what you like and less of what you don't

Is your job letting you do what you want to do? Are there any alternative ways of sharing out the work in the department, which allow everyone more of what they do well? There are people who are good administrators: there are even people who enjoy paperwork! Work as a team to promote everyone's job satisfaction. You may also be able to plan ahead so that you get a job which suits you better, not necessarily a more stressful post. It may be that other options arise because your personal situation has changed. Don't change for change's sake however. There is little point in exchanging a stressful job for a worse one.

Build up your support network and be supportive of others

Colleagues can be incredibly supportive if you allow them to be so. They can provide you with many things:

- a new way of seeing the situation
- new skills to overcome a problem or raise your professional self-esteem
- recognition of your value as a teacher
- constructive feedback on your teaching
- emotional support when things are difficult
- just listening
- an escape from your worries for a while

REFLECTION

Build up your own list of ways to avoid stress-related illness. There are many stresses built into your learning to be a teacher. Make sure that you survive the course and just as importantly survive the hazards of teaching throughout your career.

151

SUMMARY

It helps to work with friends. But there will be some people who don't hit it off and will never be able to support each other. The best advice is to seek those who you can support and who can support you. Some teachers will however prefer to do things on their own. You should respect this and not try to force them into a group.

Useful references

Bailey, R. (1985) **Coping with Stress in Caring.** Oxford: Blackwell Scientific.

Cherniss, C. (1995) **Beyond Burnout: Helping Teachers, Nurses, Therapists and Lawyers Recover from Stress and Disillusionment.** London: Routledge.

Cook, R. (1992) **The Prevention and Management of Stress.** Harlow: Longman.

Cooper, C. and Davidson, M. (1991) **The Stress Survivors.** London: Grafton.

Cooper, C. L. and Travers, C. L. (1996) **Teachers Under Pressure: Stress in the Teaching Profession.** London: Routledge.

Fontana, D. (1989) **Managing Stress.** British Psychological Society. London: Routledge.

Fontana, D. (1993) **Managing Time.** British Psychological Society Books.

Kobasa, S. (1985) in **The Stress Survivors**, Cooper, C. and Davidson, M.

Selye, H. (1956) **The Stress of Life.** New York: McGraw-Hill.

Securing a Teaching Post

29

Before I secured my first post I had interviews for several jobs. I felt like the old saying 'Always the bridesmaid, never the bride'. But I didn't give up.

(The early experience of a successful Headteacher)

Introduction

Your choice of where you want to work can be based on several factors. You may wish to return home or remain in the area where you have trained or been on teaching practice. The more flexible you are the more opportunity you will have to find a post. If you are fixed to an area where few vacancies occur, you could consider a temporary (supply) contract in the first instance. Fixed-term contracts are increasingly common for Newly Qualified Teachers (NQTs).

Where are jobs advertised?

The Times Educational Supplement published on Fridays is the biggest source of vacancies. Jobs are also advertised in the *Guardian* on Tuesdays and the *Independent* and the *Daily Telegraph* (mainly independent schools) on Thursdays.

Some schools and Local Education Authorities (LEAs) advertise in local and regional papers. If you do not currently live in an area of interest, a friend or a relative can help by scanning the papers regularly.

Some religious and ethnic newspapers carry teaching post adverts, for example the *Church Times*, *Jewish Chronicle*, *Catholic Herald*, *Universe*, *Methodist Recorder*, *Asian Times* and *The Voice*. The Catholic Education Service also produces a weekly vacancy sheet.

Many LEAs produce lists of vacancies that they send directly to your college or university (found either in your department or careers service) or you can obtain them by sending stamped addressed envelopes to the LEA Education Offices or equivalent.

A number of LEAs produce recruitment literature/brochures and sometimes videos. These may be available in your institution.

First Teaching Appointments Procedures, published by the Association of Graduate Careers Advisory Service (AGCAS), should be kept by your careers service. The Unions also produce valuable information in a similar format, for example *Obtaining Your First Teaching Post* (NUT) and *Finding Your First Teaching Post* (NASUWT). Your own HEI (Higher Education Institution) may produce their own materials. Most jobs applied for by Newly Qualified Teachers in LEA controlled schools are on the Common Professional Scale (CPS) where good honours graduates receive two mandatory scale points.

How to apply – the procedures

There are three different application procedures for teaching posts, namely 'pool' applications, 'general' applications and specific vacancies.

LMS (Local Management of Schools) has affected 'pool' procedures, so the traditional pool where the LEA estimates the number of vacancies likely in September and recruits are appointed 'to the Service of the Authority' (usually after interviews around Easter) is disappearing. Sometimes it is only in June and July that schools are allocated to successful applicants.

It is now more likely that a firm contract of employment is offered only after applicants are interviewed by the school.

Schools may rely on the LEA pools for their recruits. So if you are considering that authority, remember to apply for the pool. In other LEAs the pool may only handle some of the vacancies, so there can be specific vacancies advertised by the schools also.

These are known as general applications or 'open' applications where there are opportunities for applying to an LEA asking to be considered for suitable vacancies. Be sure to specify in the form or letter of application any preferences you have for type of school or location. Interviews are normally held in the school where the vacancy has arisen.

Specific vacancies in individual schools invite applications directly to the school, according to the instructions in the advertisement. These posts are advertised in the local or national press or are sent directly to your institution.

Most LEAs advertise their 'pool' arrangements in December and January and 'general applications' are made in the Spring term. Specific vacancies occur all year round but start from late January and reach a peak in April, May and June (the final date by which current teachers have to resign to change jobs is the end of May).

If a school encourages applicants to visit before applying it is good practice to do so if it is possible. It indicates real interest if you make the effort. If you wish to visit, telephone to make arrangements. You may be invited to an individual appointment or invited at a time for other potential candidates. Try to visit during a school day as you will get a better feel for the school that way. Remember that there is no such thing as informal contact with a school!

How to apply – the application

Some of the worst applications and CVs which tutors and certainly careers advisers see are those written by potential teachers! First impressions are crucial. Many applications are rejected immediately due to:

● Poor or illegible writing, or typing errors
● Cluttered or confusing presentation
● Bad spelling, grammar and punctuation
● Incorrect spelling of names, especially Headteachers or Schools
● Poorly answered or unanswered questions

Your written application is where you market yourself – it is your bid for an interview! Like all good bids it needs planning and research and to be presented properly. Therefore you need to spend time drafting a good curriculum vitae (CV) and a strong supporting statement.

If you remember to be positive and use action words, you should shine. Examples of action words include:

achieved	demonstrated	increased	pioneered	revised
accomplished	devised	initiated	planned	solved
advised	directed	inspired	prepared	started
analysed	documented	installed	presented	streamed
approved	edited	instructed	produced	structured
arranged	enlarged	interpreted	promoted	succeeded
collaborated	established	introduced	proposed	supported
compiled	evaluated	invented	proved	supervised
completed	expanded	investigated	recommended	taught
co-ordinated	generated	led	reported	trained
created	implemented	managed	researched	translated
defined	improved	organised	resolved	utilised
delivered	inaugurated	persuaded	reviewed	wrote

There are two types of written application. Either the LEAs or school's **application form** or your **curriculum vitae**. A curriculum vitae needs to be accompanied by a **covering letter**.

Application forms

Under pain of sounding patronising, there are some fundamentals about application forms. Apart from completing the form accurately, neatly, thoroughly and winningly, you must:

● Read the form and accompanying literature carefully
● Photocopy the form and write a draft
● Construct an effective supporting statement
● Follow the instructions – if it says use a black pen, do so!
● Handwriting needs to be legible
● Check your spelling and grammar
● Leave no sections blank – write 'not applicable' as it shows you have read the form
● Check dates for gaps and inconsistency
● Keep a copy so you can refer to it later, perhaps on the way to the interview

Ask a friend, a careers adviser or tutor to check your form as they may notice errors that you have missed. This is best done at the draft stage.

Apart from details of your education the form will ask for details of your teaching experience, employment, leisure and interests, and referees. Besides the supporting statement, you will be asked to disclose any criminal background and to consent to the recruiter checking the accuracy of the response with the police. The Rehabilitation of Offenders Act requires this.

Letter of application

For more and more jobs the application involves sending a CV with a letter of application. All the basic comments made about the application form apply to the letter. It is your opportunity to market yourself as a new teacher to the school. A tip here is to focus on what will make you a good teacher in that school! Some pointers about the letter of application:

● The letter can be hand-written or word-processed. Bearing in mind your CV will be word-processed, it may be helpful to hand write the letter (it will give the school an example of your handwriting). However if your handwriting is not a strength, word-process the letter.
● Aim to use one side of good quality A4 paper, two sides maximum
● The content should include:

An introductory paragraph telling the reader why you have applied to that school/LEA.

An outline of your course of training, main subject and subsidiary. Emphasise the curriculum areas you would like to develop.

Details of your teaching experience and practices, mentioning ages taught, type of school, background of pupils. Don't forget to mention your experience with children.

An outline of your beliefs about education and why you would like to put them into action. Remember you are not writing an essay about the philosophy of teaching! You are describing how you see yourself as a teacher.

Details of any interests, activities or non-teaching work experience that you feel will enhance your teaching, especially if it includes examples of work with children.

Applications

Prepare a letter of application and ask a senior colleague to go through it.

152

Curriculum Vitae (CV)

A CV presents the basic information that would be included on an application form. CVs should usually be typed/word-processed, run off on a good printer (laser is best) and not exceed two sides of A4 (do not print on both sides). The following headings provide a guide.

Name
You may wish to indicate gender if you have a name that does not make this obvious, for example Robin

DfEE number
If you know it at the time of application

Date of birth
Marital status
Optional

Schools and colleges attended
Give brief details of your education from the age of 11

Qualifications
List your qualifications stating level, subject and grade for GCSE and A levels, University/College Course – Degree (main subject, dissertation). PGCE students should include information on the content and class of their degree.

Other qualifications
Music, sport, Duke of Edinburgh award, first aid certificate.

Teaching experience
Give details of school teaching practices and attachments, with names of schools and dates. Include any other teaching experience you have had, e.g. vacation work.

Other work experience
Give brief details with dates of previous full time or vacation employment together with part time and voluntary work. It is a good idea to indicate what your responsibilities included and skills acquired.

Interests and activities
This section should tell an employer something about you. Don't just list interests, give some details. Interests relevant to teaching are particularly valuable.

Other information/additional skills

Give details of specific qualifications or skills such as computer expertise, driving licence, languages.

Referees

You should choose your referees with care. It will be expected that you give at least one referee who can comment on your teacher training. If you have the choice select a person who can comment on both your academic ability and your teaching performance whilst on school experience.

Always ask the person you wish to name before listing them as a referee. Tell them when you apply for a post so that they are not unexpectedly deluged with requests for references.

The second referee ideally should also know you from a teaching situation, for example a headteacher, head of department or form/class teacher from one of your placement schools. Again, it is important to ask their permission before naming them and ensure that you give them a copy of your application material. If in doubt over who to give as referees, consult your Course Leader for advice. There are variations between courses as regards the best procedure to follow.

The interview

The interview is the most important part of securing a job. As you have already persuaded them that you are worthy of an interview, the next stage is to convince them that you are the best candidate for the post.

Preparation for interview

If you have visited the school before applying you will have already gained useful insights. For example, about the school's catchment area, the standard of work on notice boards, the attitude of the children to visitors. You may have some clues to issues that will be raised in interview. It may help you to formulate questions you want to ask at interview.

Re-read your application and highlight the topics you feel will be discussed. Anything you have written in your application is a possible area for explanation.

Teaching at interview

You may be asked to teach a lesson in which case you need to plan carefully, preferably with assistance from your subject specialist colleagues, in school, college or university.

153

The interview itself

A typical timetable for the interview day includes a morning in the department and preliminary interviews with key staff, such as the Head of Department.

Many schools will invite a smaller number of candidates to the formal interview after the preliminary informal interviews held during a morning session.

After you have arrived in plenty of time, dressed in your best interview garb, you will probably be introduced to the other candidates. You may be given a tour of the school and introduced to the other staff members. You are being assessed even during this exercise. It is an opportunity to appear interested and enthusiastic.

You may have been informed who is interviewing but there is no set rule about the composition of an interview panel. The only surprise would be if there were less than three people involved. If there are two interviewers it will be the Headteacher and the Chair of Governors. In secondary interviews the Head of Department is usually the third member. There have been rather extreme cases where there have been five (and many more) people on the panel.

Try not to appear nervous, or worse too laid back. Try to be yourself and to be interested and interesting! Therefore monosyllabic answers do not impress. Try to give some thought to your answers and answer as truthfully as possible. The panel is attempting to gather information about you, but it is not a cross-examination.

Humour is allowed in interview as long as it is not flippant or arrogant. There is a fine line between confidence and over-confidence.

There are a range of questions asked often in teaching interviews. Ask any one who has been involved as an interviewer or interviewee in teaching and they will tell you the most common. At the end of the interview you will be asked if you have any questions. Two short questions is the limit. An answer such as 'I think you have covered everything I had thought about' is perfectly reasonable.

The interview is likely to take twenty to thirty minutes.

Before the end of the interview you should be clear in your own mind whether you will accept the post. If asked whether you would accept the post if offered, answer honestly.

Practising

Ensure you have at least one 'mock' interview with senior colleagues before you have a real one.

154

Appointment

If you are verbally offered an appointment which you accept, a written confirmation of appointment will follow. You then make your acceptance in writing. It is courteous to inform your referees and the correspondents for your outstanding applications that you have secured a post.

Post-interview

Failure to get the job

Try to control the feelings of disappointment and rejection. The school made a choice based on many criteria – it is not a personal decision about you.

If a de-brief is offered take the opportunity immediately, if possible. A later de-brief by telephone may also be available. Although it may sound a painful experience, any advice offered at this point could help you to secure a post at your next interview.

The de-brief is likely to be conducted by the Head of Department or Subject Adviser and comments may focus on some of the following issues:

- documentation: CV/letter of application
- interview performance: length and quality of answers
    body language
    eye contact
    attitude – too laid back, over-confident, vague, aggressive, inflexible
    knowledge of current issues
    knowledge of subject issues/NC requirements
    knowledge of school – did you read the information sent to you?
    indication of personal abilities, skills and interests outside the classroom
    indication of what candidate can offer the school

Interview panels are not too worried about nervous candidates, but they like to feel that you really want to teach in their school.

Travelling expense forms should be offered to unsuccessful candidates.

All applications, references and any other personal information are destroyed after the interviews.

SUMMARY

Securing a teaching post requires organisation, commitment and determination. It will probably involve you in some disappointment before you succeed. When you get the job, you will be feeling elated and perhaps go away without asking all the questions you meant to ask if successful. Most schools will expect you to return towards the end of the Summer Term to spend a day or two familiarising yourself with what is expected of you. For some of you this will be the first permanent job; for others the first post in a new career. Whatever your previous experience the first teaching post will be a tremendous opportunity, but also a very demanding one.

Evaluation and Reflection (2)

Few people say 'I am here'. They seek themselves in the past and see themselves in the future. (Georges Braque)

LEARNING OUTCOMES

By the end of this chapter you should be able to evaluate your continuing development as a teacher. You can look back and reflect on how much progress you have made and you can look forward and set targets for yourself. You will also have had the opportunity to do an 'active learning' task which highlights the effectiveness of good reflection and is at the end of this chapter.

Introduction

It is likely that increasingly you will be alone with classes. Much of your teaching will be independent and you will be expected to take more responsibility for the quality of the teaching and learning. This section aims to give you support in the continuing task of becoming a reflective practitioner and a better teacher.

Improving your evaluation skills

155

Mark, whom we first read about in Chapter 18 on Evaluation and Reflection, is feeling happier with his progress as a teacher and now wants to concentrate on developing his skills in specific areas of the curriculum. Overleaf is an example of an evaluation sheet that he used to help him work on an area of his teaching that he enjoyed but still felt needed improvement. In many ways he is still commenting from his own perspective rather than being aware of pupils' learning. Consider your own stage of development as you work through this Case Study.

YEAR 8 GYMNASTICS LESSON 2 OF 6

Aim: to develop a sequence of movements using balance, working first individually, then in pairs.

Planning and preparation

This worked well; I allowed adequate time for different sections of the lesson and the pupils completed the sequences I had planned.

Lesson presentation

All pupils seemed to grasp the idea very quickly. By reminding them of balances we had learned last week, they built on this well.

Provision for differentiation

Lesson management

Used most able to demonstrate last week's skills; planned pairs to give support to less confident.

All went smoothly, including the getting out and putting away of equipment, with responsibilities clearly allocated.

Development of a positive climate

Good; pupils accepted that supporting others was part of the purpose of the lesson.

Assessment of pupils' work

No formal assessment attempted; my main concern was to ensure that all went smoothly.

R E F L E C T I O N

What kind of evaluative comments would you expect if Mark were focusing on pupils' learning rather than his own teaching?

156 After discussion with his mentor, Mark agreed on a number of targets for development.

Targets

Next lesson:

a) Plan an assessment sheet for pupils to use to assess one another.

b) Organise group work so that one member of the group has specific responsibility for assessment of others' work at each stage.

c) Concentrate on commenting on qualities of work being achieved by groups in order to assist with development of assessment skills.

d) Plan future lessons to incorporate assessment opportunity for me as teacher.

Evaluation

Choose a lesson to evaluate. Use general headings like those used by Mark, then focus on a particular competence, (after discussion Mark has chosen assessment) or you could concentrate on the progress of an individual child.

One approach to this task is to ask yourself:

- What is happening now?
- What would I like to happen?
- What steps can I take to achieve my goal?
- How will I know that I have got there?

This approach to evaluation by focusing on a particular competence or on an individual child, should help you to gain a greater depth of understanding, which should then be used in future planning.

The context of self-evaluation

The position you are in has particular tensions. You may not find yourself in complete sympathy with the philosophy of the school. You haven't the status of a permanent member of staff and the children are likely to recognise you as a newcomer to teaching. You are also a newcomer to the department and the staffroom. Occasionally, trainees are given conflicting advice from colleagues, often well-meaning, but which can cause confusion. There may be a history of conflict or tension between staff of which you are unaware. It can be difficult to find yourself involved in staffroom micro-politics of this kind.

Taking over other people's classes can be awkward for you. Teachers prize highly their relationships with classes. Some teachers and pupils find those relationships hard to give up. Some children are loyal (temporarily) to the class teacher. Children may mistrust change and teachers may be drawn into popularity contests. Conversely, some teachers suspect that the class will prefer a new, exciting teacher and they feel threatened and become over-critical. Perhaps a teacher has had to struggle hard with a class and doesn't look forward to the consequences of a break in that understanding.

New teachers, observing lessons, may forget that even experienced teachers feel vulnerable to criticism, real or perceived. Oiling the wheels of harmonious relationships by thanking people for letting you into their class or just a comment about something you found helpful or enjoyable can make a difference to working relationships.

Similarly, experienced teachers need to be truly supportive. It can be difficult for anyone to admit they are having a problem with a particular group if the response is smug or dismissive. '11XY are no trouble with me', is not a helpful thing to say, although it may comfort the teacher who says it.

Against this complex backdrop, some trainees, having made a good start, do not seem to make progress beyond what they do well naturally. Having acknowledged the difficulties, we have to rely on a concept of profession-alism and, by developing professional skills, move forward.

Blockages to professional development may be poor listening skills and ineffective target setting. Targets need to be achievable but ideally they should stretch the individual a little. Targets cannot be imposed – they should be agreed and conflicts, as far as possible, need to be resolved.

REFLECTION

158

It is common for trainees to experience difficulties, not all of which are of their own making. The following state-ments are all negative ways of viewing the school place-ment. They represent a response to the situation which places the problem anywhere but with the trainee. Think carefully how you would act if you were in danger of believ-ing such statements. What effects would these beliefs have on your teaching and on your relationships with colleagues?

Statement	Action to be taken	Effect on teaching performance?
I wouldn't choose to work in the type of school I am in.		
The children know I am a student.		
I don't understand the whole school documentation, for example the prospectus or handbook.		
I am a relaxed easy-going person and cannot discipline pupils.		
The school staff seem too busy to talk to me.		
The advice I am given is often contradictory.		
My school never uses IT properly.		
All the Department seem to get on very well together and ignore me.		
I'll never be as good as they are. It all seems so easy for them.		
The usual teacher can't keep control, so how can I do it?		

Work to be done with a mentor or another colleague

Consider now the ways in which you could 're-frame' these beliefs in order to find a solution which would be acceptable to all parties and which would enable you to finish your school placement successfully.

 **Sally and Dean**

The following comments were made about two trainees, Sally and Dean. At this stage both were finding teaching a challenge, but were able to come to terms with this after receiving support. How does this compare with your progress?

Sally

We ask trainees to list their requirements for lessons for each week, giving it to us the previous Friday morning. Lists should include textbooks, worksheets and equipment – the more detail the better. In Sally's case the list is late and incomplete. I had to tell her it won't do. Her lessons just are insufficiently planned. But every time we tried to tell her as sympathetically as possible she'd cry. Tom found it difficult to handle and he'd end up back-pedalling so as not to upset her.

Dean

Target setting was impossible. If I said anything that could be vaguely interpreted as a criticism he'd become very aggressive in tone. He'd say, What do you mean by that exactly, in such a way that I didn't bother to make any suggestions. And according to him, everything was going swimmingly. We could be having a riot in there and he'd be oblivious and say how wonderful it was.

Sally and Dean both gained their teaching qualification. Sally talked with the School Mentor and with her tutor but the real turning point came when she dealt with a serious breach of discipline without help and gained the respect of staff and children. Her increased self-esteem allowed her to feel more in control. Dean was shocked by a warning of failure. He really liked working with children and was determined to succeed. He took target setting and review very seriously thereafter.

Most schools have a senior teacher who is centrally responsible for the smooth operation of Initial Teacher Education within the institution. Ask for their active support to make your experience in school as happy and rewarding as possible. They will be able to help you with forming professional relationships with colleagues and in identifying your targets for professional development.

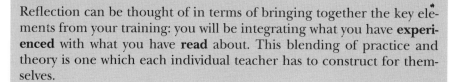

SUMMARY

Reflection can be thought of in terms of bringing together the key elements from your training: you will be integrating what you have **experienced** with what you have **read** about. This blending of practice and theory is one which each individual teacher has to construct for themselves.

Useful references

Calderhead, J. and Gates, P. (1993) **Conceptualising Reflection in Teacher Development.** Lewes: Falmer Press.

Schön, D. (1987) **Educating the Reflective Practitioner.** San Francisco: Jossey-Bass.

Tabachnich, B. R. and Zeichner, K. (eds) (1991) **Issues and Practices in Inquiry-Oriented Teacher Education.** Lewes: Falmer Press.

The Learning School

Introduction

When trainees come back into my sessions after being on placement, it is really obvious that their confidence has grown. Their body language, the authority with which they discuss ideas and their mutual respect all provide evidence of this growth.

(Subject Co-ordinator)

At this stage you should be relatively comfortable in your school, developing your teaching, having some pastoral experience and becoming a member of a team, be it departmental or faculty. You would be wise to use this opportunity for looking at your current understanding of the school and exploring whole-school issues. You will find that some administrative issues will have unexpected effects on policy. You will come to a better understanding of your subject teaching and of your care for pupils if you study the school as a learning environment.

The chapters in Part 3 fall into two categories: Chapters 31 to 36 provide you with areas of interest at the whole-school level as well as at individual teacher level. Chapters 37 to 40 will enable you to continue to develop your teaching. Teaching the Big Ideas (Chapter 36) provides a link between the two, as it covers areas of major importance to every pupil, every teacher and every school.

Sue Goble and Mike Francis, Deputy Headteachers in Gloucestershire, suggest that in the learning school, teachers must also be encouraged to develop as learners themselves, to have ideas, to experiment, to take risks and to participate in active and broadening debate. For the school this implies

- creating opportunities for teachers to discuss and develop ideas for improving pupils' learning experiences
- overcoming insecurity, where it exists, which leads to teachers feeling vulnerable when asked to discuss their teaching practices or when they are observed in the classroom
- creating an environment in which ideas and innovation are encouraged, valued and shared
- developing a style of leadership which encourages collaboration in order to establish an open commitment to learning at all levels (Goble and Francis, 1996)

Every teacher should participate in the development of a 'learning school'. In Part 3 we will show how these ideas can be implemented.

Practitioner Research

31

Action is a series of desperate acts which allows you to retain hope. (Braque, 1971)

LEARNING OUTCOMES

When you have worked through this chapter you will be in a position to develop a case study research project of whole school issues. It is vital that you familiarise yourself with these techniques because you will need to use them throughout your teaching career.

What is research? The following serves as a useful working definition: *asking yourself a question to which you do not know the answer, and then looking at how to answer it.* There is no point in asking a question if you know the answer. It is also quite possible that you may not find a satisfactory answer; the process will give you a lot of new knowledge, and both process and knowledge are more important ultimately than the end product. You will be a teacher practitioner, involved in practitioner research. As such you will be a 'key player' in the research process and you will need to follow certain ethical guidelines carefully (see list on page 283).

Our primary objective as teachers is to improve the effectiveness of our pupils as learners. You have considered the individual pupil's learning and thinking styles in Part 1 and you have analysed the major issues facing you as the teacher of a class in Part 2. Now we will be looking at the whole school and integrating our knowledge of the pupils, the teaching, the staff and the ethos into a clearer understanding of department and whole school policies and their implementation. There is always a difference between setting up a system and implementing it. You will notice this when you are looking at policy and practice at a whole-school level.

What is the relationship between policy and practice?

Schools, like political parties, have policies on many things, and so do individual professionals. An example of a school policy is that on exclusions. Policies on the exclusion of a pupil from school have changed in accordance with recent changes in legislation. Certain procedures have to be followed before a pupil can be excluded. Indefinite exclusions are no longer an option. Central government decrees may have 'knock-on' implications for schools. Losing the option to exclude indefinitely may cause a revision of school behaviour policies.

At an individual professional level, our practice may be inconsistent with school policy. When asked for a solution to a problem, we may say, *my policy in that situation, is to* ... However this may simply reflect one person's characteristic problem-solving technique and may not be consistent with departmental policy or school policy. You may find discrepancies between what people do, what they believe should happen, and what the policy document actually says.

What policy document? Some of us may not know what the department or school policy is on certain matters. There may not be one.

Policies are intended to ensure that all those involved can follow certain guidelines and be consistent. In this section you will be looking at school issues of policy and practice which go beyond the classroom. You will also find that you want to look at the impact of these issues on individual teachers and pupils. The extent to which you concentrate more on the policy or more on the classroom, will depend on your interests and your school. The assignment below shows a structure which you could use. You can produce a good assignment with no classroom observation, or one with only a brief analysis of county policy. However, all the elements listed as four 'key areas' in the assignment outline must be addressed at some level in your finished work.

3000 WORD ASSIGNMENT

Introduction

For this assignment you will be required to analyse an area of school life which is of particular interest to you in your professional development. It will be a much more useful document if your project informs developments within your parent school. You will be expected therefore to negotiate your choice of project with your Training Manager.

The Task

You should submit a critical analysis of your chosen area of school life in the light of your experiences and your background reading. You should set your chosen area firmly within the context of your main school placement.

You should pay particular attention to the following key areas:

- your parent school's policies and practices in your chosen topic
- national policies and directives, and county ones if appropriate
- theory into practice i.e. research and literature relevant to your project
- theory from practice: i.e. what you have learnt which is useful to you in your professional development as a teacher

---

WHAT are you working on?
WHY are you doing it?!
HOW will you collect information?
WHEN? What is your timetable?

Guidance

1 You are encouraged to work with other postgraduates on this assignment.
2 You can include, as an appendix to your analysis (not part of the 3000 words), a limited selection of material including policy documents (regional and/or national), lesson plans if appropriate, examples of pupils' work . . .
3 Your analysis should stand on its own merits. Refer to your appendices to show more detail.
4 The topics covered in this reader are intended to guide you. Other topics can be chosen, in negotiation with your Training Manager.

References

- Teaching and Learning in the Secondary School ed. by Bob Moon and Ann Shelton Mayes, Routledge, 1994
- Ofsted Handbook for the Inspection of Schools, HMSO, 1993
- Research Methods in Education, 4th Edition, by Louis Cohen and Lawrence Manion, Routledge, 1994
- A Teacher's Guide to Classroom Research by David Hopkins, Second Edition, Open University, 1993
- Doing Your Research Project: A Guide for First-Time Researchers in Education and Social Science by J. Bell, Open University Press, 1987

Jack

160

Consider the case study of Jack in Part 1, Chapter 11. This was a true case, analysed with due care and attention to the specific problems experienced by Jack and his teachers. We have added to that a discussion of more general issues about this kind of situation and the approaches which may work, using some ideas from counselling etc. To make Jack's case study into an appropriate study for Part 3, it would be necessary to incorporate analysis of the material which follows in the textbook, for example the 'no blame approach', and link this directly to national, county and school policies on behaviour. In order to achieve that, you would probably interview the form teacher and the head of year and possibly do some classroom observation. Consider Jack also in Chapter 33, where we look further at his situation.

You would be using the technique for data collection called triangulation, that is comparing and contrasting different viewpoints and different types of data in order to obtain a full and useful picture. As in triangulation in map work, the different viewpoints can be used to cross-check your findings.

The data types could be as follows for Jack:

● interviews with Jack, form tutor, head of year and mother
● record of classroom observation
● analysis of national, county and school policies on behaviour

You might then be able to try to formulate an understanding of the situation and make some suggestions for the way forward.

Case study practitioner research

The case study approach will involve you in similar processes to those of Part 1. You will be 'taking some snapshots' of an area which is of general professional significance to all educational institutions and which has particular relevance to your school. Therefore your concluding analysis will inform your professional development, although your specific conclusions will be more directly applicable to your parent school. The case study will allow you to collect different types of information and evaluate them in order to gain a better understanding of your chosen area of study. Your analysis will probably be qualitative rather than quantitative. You will be collecting data from three main areas: what do people tell you about what they do, what do you see them doing and what does documentation tell you about the situation.

Focusing on your subject

Goble and Francis describe the following ways in which teachers can be encouraged to try out aspects of Gardner's theory of multiple intelligence:

- moving a language class out of the classroom to a place which enabled more freedom of movement for all their lessons
- conducting all oral work in context, using gesture, bodily interpretation, as well as voice in receiving and producing language
- using visual stimuli as often as possible to accompany voice and action
- using rhythms to increase pace and fluency of response, for example songs, raps
- pupils only working at tables/desks for written and reading work
- including as much group interaction as possible with the emphasis on making others 'look good'

You may also like to consider the '10 dimensions of a learning organisation', which Green quotes from Pedler, Burgoyne and Boydell in The Learning Company (1991), Goble and Francis suggest.

1 **Physical environment** – the amount of and quality of space and privacy afforded to people for their preparation, planning and review.
2 **Learning resources** – the numbers, quality and availability of resources for personal and professional development.
3 **Encouragement to learn** – the extent to which people feel encouraged to have ideas, take risks, experiment and learn new ways of doing old tasks.
4 **Communications** – the degree to which the flow of information is open and free and people are encouraged to express ideas and opinions.
5 **Rewards** – the recognition given for good work and the reward for effort (which does not have to be financial).
6 **Conformity** – the balance between the expectation to conform to rules, regulations and policies and the acceptance that people can think for themselves.
7 **Value placed on ideas** – other people's ideas, opinions and suggestions being sought out, encouraged and valued.
8 **Practical help available** – the extent to which people help each other, lend a hand, offer skills, knowledge and support whenever they are needed.

9 **Warmth and support** – the friendliness of people in the organisation and the degree to which they support, trust and like working with one another.

10 **Standards** – the emphasis placed upon quality in all things where people set challenging standards for themselves and each other.

Curriculum-based case study work provides an excellent opportunity for a subject department to examine practice. It is a way in which a trainee can help more experienced colleagues to consider and evaluate alternative approaches to teaching and learning. Schools involved in initial teacher training have welcomed the depth of case study research made possible by a trainee teacher's interest and insight. However you must be clear about the difference between case study research and action research. We recommend case study approaches, which the school may subsequently use to develop action research.

Information Technology

161

Andrew, a trainee, wanted to explore IT in the curriculum. Any use of IT to support teaching will have two sets of learning outcome: one in terms of increased understanding of the subject domain, the other in knowing more about IT – how to use a particular computer, particular software, or an increased awareness of the variety of roles which IT can play. Hopefully this awareness will develop into a clear understanding of the many uses which IT can serve, then a general confidence and competence using a wide variety of IT techniques to fluently solve problems which the pupils may face. Developing IT capability has implications for both the design of learning activities and for the deployment of IT resources.

As a trainee teacher of mathematics I can see this use of IT as:

● *A subject support tool* in that it aids me in teaching maths as opposed to teaching about some applications of IT
● *A cognitive support tool* in that it helps thinking and its development. It did this by holding information, doing calculations and checking hand calculations, helping the pupil to represent the information in different ways and to translate between representations.
● *IT skills*, e.g. keyboard skills, are developed.
● *A knowledge domain* – how IT can be applied to a number of problems.

Used in the right context therefore I can see the real benefits of using IT to assist me in teaching maths. People have been aware of the possible benefits for some time. The Cockroft report, Mathematics Counts (HMSO, 1982) recognised that 'the availability of low cost calculators, and microcomputers had very great implications for the teaching of mathematics.'

What, though, are the attractions for the student that I noticed in the lesson and can relate to the literature.

Students can solve problems more quickly and with less effort by allowing computers to do the work, for students can solve more problems in a limited time. Thus, they can see the topic from a wider viewpoint, leading to a deeper understanding of the topic. This method does not hinder students from developing mathematical thought. What is replaced by the computer has, in essence, little relation to the development of it. If the input to the system is correct, the results from the system are free from the mistakes which students might make during tedious calculations by hand.

(Howson, 1988)

There are of course points to be aware of. Since computer systems return wrong answers to incorrect inputs, it is very important to instruct pupils not to believe the answers from computers absolutely. There are other dangers that are still causing much debate within education – 'the wide spread use of computers, or even sophisti-

cated calculators, will lead to the view that arithmetic is no longer a necessary skill to acquire'. (Howson, 1988).

The fear has even been stated that the more able students who might have gone on to the higher reaches of mathematics will be enthralled by the attractive alternative of entering a field (computers and IT) which is in an explosive stage of development and where the opportunities to make your mark are much greater.

'One has to hope that mathematics, by its power and beauty, will still attract intellects of quality in the future and that not all of them will be seduced by the computer.'

(Fletcher, 1985)

Care does have to be taken in ensuring that the main teaching point is not submerged beneath the enthusiasm for IT. Can understanding the factors that make IT attractive be used to enhance a better learning environment away from computers? Using a computer is a doing exercise. The pupil is, or feels that, they are in charge of their own learning. Response times are fast and non-judgmental, they are challenged but not threatened. The children can work independently, in pairs or small groups. There is a good cross fertilisation of ideas. If one pupil gets stuck advice can be on either side of them from their peers in their own language. If they have a good idea or solution to a problem it is amazing how quickly the word goes around the class. Tasks are more easily differentiated and all pupils should be able to produce a piece of well presented work that they can take pride in. All of these can be remembered for most lessons to enhance good teaching practice and to improve the learning environment.

The following cautionary note from Pimm is applicable for all IT learning. He wonders whether the subject matter (in Pimm's case mathematics) is buried so deeply in the computer tools that the students using the tools will miss the subject relevance. He also proposes that a screen image is a particular kind of dynamic symbol.

Computers generate screen images which are dynamic, interactive symbols – a very new class of symbols. (Pimm, 1995)

Andrew used these ideas to interview the Heads of Key Stage Curriculum areas. He collated their responses about the strengths and weaknesses of IT and his analysis was used to resolve some problem areas within the school's existing IT provision.

Talking to people about what they do

This is perhaps one of the most interesting aspects of working in a school community. Structured or semi-structured interviews can be prepared (solo or group), or questionnaires. Record the content of casual chats in note form if you have the person's permission.

How to prepare for an interview

Jim (trainee)

162

I was starting some research about behaviour management in my parent school. This focus emerged after discussion with my training manager, because I'm interested in improving my discipline of classes an the school has just had some INSET on assertive discipline, an Australian INSET 'package' which is strongly influenced by behaviour modification. My training manager suggested that I could approach the Head of Year 9 for an interview and another pastoral head. So I went along to Mr B (Head of Year 9) and he said he'd do an interview, as long as I kept it to 20 minutes and he also asked for an idea of the areas to be covered, beforehand. (The other Head of Year gave the interview without asking about topics or questions.)

In fact it did me good to prepare questions beforehand, so that I knew what I was doing. I used my discussion with my training manager to formulate the questions, because she's interested in the area – another member of staff would have been better for some other topic, for instance appraisal or European initiatives. I wrote the questions down with space in between for making notes, and I audio-taped it as well (after getting permission from the interviewees). (If I'd had more time to get organised, and if I'd realised the potential, I'd have videotaped it, I think, because it was interesting to see the unfolding of one person's strongly held views about his job, as well as his views about assertive discipline and behaviour policies. It wouldn't always happen like that, though.)

I wanted to be able to make notes during the interview so that I could concentrate on the discussion as it developed and come back to certain information later if I wanted to, to ask further questions. The audio-tape was for listening to later, to see if I'd missed anything. It would have taken hours to transcribe the interview word for word and really that wasn't necessary, as I got all the main points and could summarise them. But the audio-tape was useful for transcribing some things which the interviewees stated in such a clear way that I used some of their statements in quotation marks in my project write-up (with their permission). If they'd wanted to retain confidentiality, I would have asked if I could use their views, but without attributing them to anyone. They both asked to see the finished assignment.

Perhaps I should have asked my training manager if I could use the ideas she gave me about assertive discipline, to write about her views as a member of the senior management team. On this particular topic I think she would have said that she didn't want her opinions discussed with other staff – the assertive discipline training was so recent and had proved so controversial that she did not want to pre-judge the issues.

Re-read and consider which decisions were ethical and which were practical. Go through Jim's text again, underlining the practical decisions and ringing the ethical ones.

Looking at what people do

The setting

You will want to look at what people do, as well as talking to them about what they do. There are two recurrent formalised settings within the school for looking at what people do – meetings and teaching situations. There are many other areas, of course, such as people on playground duty, people in the staffroom and pupils at play.

Your approach

In some of the above settings you may want to be a participant observer, for example team teaching with, or partly supporting a colleague whose work is of relevance to your project (PSE, behaviour management, form tutor lessons, in-class support work and so on). The role of participant observer might be useful for allowing you to experience at first hand the issues which you're discussing with that colleague. If you feel that 'taking part' will be too demanding in your role as practitioner researcher, you may choose to be a non-participant observer. If you are attending meetings or shadowing someone on break duty, you may choose to be a non-participant observer, in order to maintain some distance from the events unfolding before you.

Your recording of data

In Part 1 you developed some techniques for classroom observation, and these can be used here, if appropriate to your topic. Ethnographic open-ended and context-dependent approaches are also useful, (see Part 1).

Systematic observation could be useful if you want to record specific events (such as how often does a particular statemented pupil ask the support teacher for help?)

Audio-taping and video-taping both need to be used with care. You should collect only a small amount of raw data and if you tape for half an hour you should use that data effectively and economically. Take certain quotations for use, make notes about any patterns which may develop during a half hour sequence, but do not analyse/transcribe the whole tape unless you have a whole weekend to devote to it!

Looking at documents

This project provides you with the opportunity to look at the relationship between policy and practice within your school. One part of this task will involve you in studying documentation of different types.

You will need to develop your own way of making sense of documents, and using a highlighter pen is one way! There are other ways of 'having a dialogue with the document'. You can work on the left hand side and the right hand side of your working surface (page or screen). Make notes on the left hand side for fact and the right hand side for opinion. Using different colour pens can be useful. Consider whether the document is a statement of intent, or a proposal for consideration, or whether it is a description of existing practice.

You will be:

- collecting information
- forming opinions
- deciding on how policy and practice are linked or discrepant
- making notes

This will help you to compare your conclusions with what you see in the school.

What do we mean by documents?

Policy documents

School-related, for example on discipline, on PSE, equal opportunities, assessment recording and reporting; examples are school brochure, school bulletin, school development plan, subject/departmental plans and records, schemes of work, governors' reports.

LEA policy documentation

For example early years screening, implementation of the code of practice, child protection guidelines.

National policy documentation

For example 1993 Education Act, the code of practice for SEN and circulars from the DfEE.

Classroom resources as documentation

For example pupils' work, textbooks, handouts, any curricular material given to pupils for their use.

Documentation

Ask for permission to look at the school's policy documentation on the area of interest to you, for example Information Technology. As you read through it, decide how you would develop this work in a way which would be helpful to the school and useful for your professional development. Contrast it also with Jim's research approach on page 277.

Using questionnaires

Devising the questions

You will need to use the teaching skills you have developed in class for wording closed questions or open questions, as appropriate. You can use a scale for structuring responses (very often, often, rarely, never). Alternatively you can request yes/no responses, as long as you word the questions carefully. You may wish to invite people to add written comments for some responses – but remember how precious their time is.

Response levels

- Giving a questionnaire out to a group of pupils or a group of colleagues and asking them to fill it in there and then will ensure that you get a response! Consider whether it will be a true or forced response.
- Sending questionnaires is less likely to produce a good level of return and may not be appropriate for this piece of work, given that you are in school.

Promise anonymity

Decide if this seems appropriate or necessary.

Time it sensibly

If you are evaluating an INSET course, will you evaluate half way through or at the end?

Process it clearly

Use graphs to compare data. Quantitative statistical analysis is not necessary and in most cases would be inappropriate. However if it is appropriate you can of course use it.

Pilot the questions

This will check that they work.

Getting started

These are some examples of titles:

- A Comparative Study of the Transition from Key Stage 2 to Key Stage 3
- GNVQs: The Way Forward at School?
- European Initiatives at School
- The Role of the Form Tutor
- Spiritual Development
- Investigation into Induction Policies for New Members of Staff
- Control and Discipline in Schools
- The Appraisal System at School

- School Discipline: Policy and Practice
- An Insight into the Provision of INSET
- The Reporting of Bullying and its Effect on Pupil Access to a Whole School Bullying Policy
- The Organisation of Marketing: Links Between Schools, Industry and Commerce

Keeping a record as you go

Suggestions for record keeping are outlined below.

Keep a research diary

This may contain ideas and thoughts and questions, noted quickly so as not to forget them. Your research diary jottings may also contain factual information which you need to transcribe later to your project write-up, but which needs to be combined with other information. Events in lessons may need to be noted down too. Make sure that you know which jottings are fact, which are ideas and which are possibilities to follow up. Later you will be able to examine these events in greater detail and find out why they were a 'salient moment' for you or your colleagues. Mason (1992) suggests that their significance depends on subjective factors:

Certain aspects of an event or situation stand out and are attended to while other details are not even noticed. The aspects of an event or situation which make it stand out are principally aspects resonant or dissonant with past experience or present expectation. (Mason, 1992)

Be honest with yourself

Be honest with yourself about your opinions, personal feelings and reflections as a way of minimising bias in your work. You cannot get away from bias, however, so you need to state your own views as an integral part of your research. There will be a lack of depth of understanding and knowledge on your part. You need therefore to approach this task with caution and humility.

Complex institutions like schools are not particularly responsive to change (Fullan, 1982) and you should not set yourself up as a change agent. Any institution like a school, hospital, local authority can take on dragon-like characteristics and eat 'hero innovators' for breakfast (Georgiades and Phillimore, 1975). If, however, you build on observed good practice in school as the key to creative understanding, you will be able to provide a critical analysis with suggestions which may help the school to move forward. The school which grows and changes is one which makes use of true collegiality – working together in effective ways which can be seen, directly or indirectly, to improve the nature or degree of pupils' development.

Working together means that some teachers will be influencing others with their views. In your capacity as a teacher in training involved in a very small scale research project, you will be in a position to advocate change.

Teachers engaged in curriculum development or otherwise involved in content innovations must put their advocacy in perspective. If these teachers try to sell a product without recognising that it may not be the most important thing on other teachers' minds, and without being sensitive to the need for other teachers to come to grips with the sense of the innovation, they will be doing exactly what most developers or advocates of change do – confusing the change with the change process. It is this tendency that led me to form the proposition that the more an advocate is committed to a particular innovation the less likely he or she is to be effective in getting it implemented. The reverse is not true: commitment is needed, but it must be balanced with the knowledge that people may be at different starting points, with different legitimate priorities and that the change process may well result in transformations or variations in the change.

(Fullan, 1991)

Moreover, all change is traumatic and the process of changing your views about your chosen area of research may involve you in 'passing through the zones of uncertainty ... the situation of being at sea, of being lost, of confronting more information than you can handle' (Schön, 1971). Nor is it necessarily true that working together is always the best way forward. Little (1990 cited in Fullan, 1991) argues that solitary working habits are necessary and valuable too. This is relevant for this project, when you need sometimes to stand back and evaluate situations critically.

By the time you have finished, you will also know more about an area of professional interest to you. Practitioner research is conducted by teachers in their own classrooms and schools. One of the main purposes of this project is to help you and others to improve practice. Practitioner research will give you some of the skills you will need in order to do this.

One of the advantages for the school in your being there is that you are not as deeply committed to existing practice. It may be that your questioning can help colleagues to become more aware of the decisions that are made. The negotiation you undertake in school over the choice of your study may help to highlight this process.

Ethics for school research

- Negotiate ideas, title and initial access with your general mentor. Ensure that you get permission from the people whose opinions you want. Committees and groups may need to be consulted, and their permission sought.
- Organise access to key participants. Ensure that others who may be interested can talk to you if they want to contribute, perhaps throughout an announcement at morning briefing.
- Accept and maintain responsibility for confidentiality (do not use pupils' surnames – only give names of staff and only attribute opinions to them after checking it with them).
- Be aware of the audience you are writing for. Practitioner research is for your benefit and for the school's benefit, and therefore you are writing it so that it will be constructive and useful for you and for colleagues.
- Obtain permission for using quotations; these may emerge from transcripts, casual comments, audio or video extracts or opinions or recommendations which you find in reports.
- Go back to people to check up on whether you've got your views straight about the following types of issues: their job descriptions, their views about policy and practice, their professional perceptions of school situations and analyses. Have you been fair and accurate? Is your text relevant?
- Keep your general mentor and other interested parties up to date with developments – you don't want to waste your time barking up the wrong tree or following inappropriate lines of enquiry.
- If you want to observe a colleague teaching or in a meeting, obtain their permission first.
- Maintain your right to carry out your work. If you satisfy the above criteria, you would be entitled to continue and complete the assignment – barring unforeseen developments and subsequent veto by your general mentor.

Useful references

Bell, J. *et al* (eds) (1984) **Conducting Small-scale Investigations in Education Management.** London: Harper & Row/The Open University (this book contains a useful chapter on keeping a research diary).

Cohen, L. and Manion, L. (1994) **Research Methods in Education** 4th edition. London: Routledge.

Fullan, M. (1982) **The Meaning of Educational Change.** Ontario: Teacher's College Press.

Fullan, M. (1991) **The New Meaning of Educational Change.** London: Cassell.

Fullan, M. (1993) **Changing Forces.** Lewes: Falmer Press.

Georgiades, N. J. and Phillimore, L. (1975) 'The myth of the hero-innovator and alternative strategies for organisational change' in Kiernan, C. C. and Woodford, F. T. **Behavioural Modification with the Severely Retarded.**

Hopkins, D. (1985) **A Teacher's Guide to Classroom Research.** Milton Keynes: Open University Press.

Mason, J. (1992) **Noticing: A Systematic Approach to Professional Development.** Unpublished research paper available from the author at the Centre for Mathematics Education, the Open University, Milton Keynes.

McNiff, J. (1988) **Managing a Better School.** London: Routledge.

Moon, B. *et al* (eds) (1990) **Judging Standards and Effectiveness in Education.** London: Hodder and Stoughton.

Pimm, D. (1995) **Symbols and Meanings in School Mathematics.** London: Routledge.

Potter, D. and Powell, G. (1992) **Managing a Better School.** London: Heinemann.

Schön, D. (1987) **Educating the Reflective Practitioner.** San Francisco: Jossey-Bass.

Sherman, R. R. and Webb, R. B. (eds) (1988) **Qualitative Research and Development.** London: Heinemann.

Stenhouse, L. (1978) **Curriculum Research and Development in Action.** London: Heinemann.

Working with Colleagues

32

One of the scandals of our schools is the way in which we have continued to allow teaching to be such an isolated and private activity. (Brighouse, 1991)

LEARNING OUTCOMES

Teaching can be a lonely profession. Schools are normally arranged so that an individual teacher has responsibility for a group of students. This chapter will help you to learn about the nature of groups and their importance for you working as a teacher in school. You will find out about what makes an effective group and begin to consider the role of the leader. Although on occasions it is necessary to reflect alone on experience, overall you will become a better teacher by contributing to a team.

Introduction

Every teacher is a member of several groups within the school. Some groups are 'official'; for example the department led by a Head of Department or a year team of tutors led by a Head of Year. Other groups are 'unofficial'; the group of people you usually talk to at break; the colleagues you meet outside school on a regular basis. Other groups exist outside school for the teacher. One group every teacher deals with is the class of pupils.

The advantages of groups

Handy and Aiken (1986) listed the following four advantages for schools:

- Groups set higher standards for themselves and for the individuals within them than the individuals would on their own.
- Groups are very kind to their members once the forming and storming stages are over.
- Groups are flexible. It is easier to change the membership of the group or its purpose or its standards than it is to change the personnel or structure of the whole organisation.
- Groups allow individuals to reach beyond themselves, to be something that none of them could have attained on their own and to discover ways of working with others to mutual benefit.

Johnson Abercrombie (1960) highlights the value of a group as a testing ground. 'We become aware of discrepancies between different people's interpretations of the same stimulus and are driven to weigh the evidence in favour of alternative interpretations.'

REFLECTION

Can you reflect on your experience of working in schools and try to identify a particular example of a group which operated in one or more of the above ways?

164

Individuals within groups

Why do individuals contribute to groups? What value is there to the individual? Handy and Aiken list five general ways in which individuals use groups:

- to share in a common activity
- to promote a cause or idea
- to gain status or power
- to have friends and 'belong'
- because it is part of their job

REFLECTION

What needs are fulfilled for you as an individual by the groups you belong to?

Can you identify the above five uses in the groups you have joined?

165

The life cycle of a group

Many of the groups you join will be already established and as a trainee teacher or a newly qualified teacher, your task will be to join in smoothly. However on other occasions you will become part of a newly-formed group. You will have already done this on the course on several occasions. Sometimes a group will be formed for a temporary purpose; for example to prepare for a one-off event or deal with a one-off problem.

What are the stages that a group goes through from birth onwards? There appears to be a clearly defined growth cycle, which can be described in four stages: forming, storming, norming and performing. According to Handy and Aiken (1986) they have the following meanings:

- *Forming – an edgy process of sniffing each other out, in which each individual makes his or her mark and displays a little of their agenda*
- *Storming – a period of conflict, sometimes about the aims of the group, sometimes about the aims of individuals, in which the first easy but false consensus is challenged*
- *Norming – a resettling into an acceptable way of working with goals and roles more understood and accepted*
- *Performing – a mature and sensibly productive phase which allows argument and discussion but within an agreed set of objectives.*

New groups

Do you recognise any of these stages taking place in a newly formed group, which you have been in recently? One case you might consider is the group of trainee teachers in your school or within your subject on the course. Write down any examples you have noticed.

166

An example of a very condensed life cycle of group dynamics might be a new group, set up to produce a policy statement within a short time scale (one month). The group may meet for only three meetings in this time. The group could well comprise several individuals who did not know each other at the start so there is no pre-formed sub-group. The first meeting might contain lots of 'This is where I'm coming from' sentences or guarded position statements. Towards the end of the first meeting these positions start to become more challenging; 'Surely we're really here to ... otherwise we are wasting our time!'. Later this becomes calmer and more accommodating of others: 'I can see that might be true for your area, but we need to consider all aspects. Don't forget the change in Sue's department over the last 12 months!' At last there's the task taking over: 'We need to produce a paper and this is our agreed framework ... now what about this for a rationale? Does it present a balance of what we have agreed?'

Being a new member of an established group

As a newcomer to a group you may well become aware of a similar accelerated dynamic process going on as the group tries to adjust to allow your active participation.

- The group appears to welcome your contributions, at times unreservedly.
- The group challenges your assumptions and reminds you of group norms.
- The group accepts your views and accommodates them to produce new group norms.
- Full acceptance ... your ideas are treated on their merits.

An alternative strategy unfortunately is to ignore the newcomer from the start.

Being a newcomer

167

As a newcomer to a department in school, you are going into just such an established group. You may therefore have experience of some of these processes. Can you recall any and record them in your learning log? Record in your Professional Development Portfolio your plans for becoming part of a department.

Another established group, which you would be advised to join is the relevant local subject association in your area. It is to be hoped that this will be another example of an established group, which will be keen to welcome new members and to give them the chance to contribute ideas.

Conflict and disagreement

Conflict and disagreement within a group about the *task* is not only desirable but essential for the achievement of the best solution to a problem. There are dangers in working too closely within a group. The possibility exists of going along with the group because it is more comfortable to do so.

Many agree that among one's most shameful memories are of saying that black is white because other people are saying it.

(Doris Lessing 1986, cited in Fullan and Hargreaves 1995)

There is a need for solitary reflection as well as group activity; a need to 'unwrap' one's own ideas as well as to contribute to others, to develop a personal stance as well as help to form a consensus. These demands appear to be contradictory. In fact both independent thought and group discussion are interdependent; each can contribute to the other. 'As one engages in interactive professionalism it is essential that development and change are grounded in some inner reflection and processing' (Fullan and Hargreaves, 1995).

One of the dangers of the school subject department is that a small group of like-minded people form a group that becomes cosy, insular and inward looking. Solutions are only sought from a limited range of 'acceptable' options; acceptable that is to the department members. Such a group may possibly be very good friends and get on well together, but there may well be a shortage of new ideas and old ones are insufficiently challenged. The need here is for the group to seek ideas and challenge from outside the department, but the ease and comfort of existing practices make this difficult. Effective small departments look to outside larger groups for stimulus and challenge; for example to other departments, to other schools or to local and national subject associations.

Often in these circumstances there is a need to concentrate more on process: 'How can we meet to look at this problem in a new way in order to solve it together?' Time constraints and familiar habits often preclude creative discussion. Problems are therefore resolved by the group members readily accepting a solution proposed by one person, even when the solution is a mismatch to the problem. INSET (In-Service Training) can facilitate the process of problem solving by forcing the group to rethink their approach. The external 'expert' can create the space to think more divergently by challenging accepted norms or providing new ideas, which need to be put into operation. However the effect may well be short-lived!

The Department

A head of maths describes how her department operates in a way that ensures that individual experience benefits the whole department:

168

Department staff meet together formally once a month. Many administrative details have to be dealt with in these meetings, but we have made it a priority that time is spent discussing the teaching of mathematics. We discuss and share mathematical ideas and examine pupils' work. Staff in the department are prepared to lead discussions and INSET activities relating to their particular responsibility. Staff also report back on any country or nation-wide courses that they have attended so that the whole department can benefit from any new knowledge. (Harrington and Banks, 1994)

Can you identify in the above passage those elements which contribute to group maintenance and those which contribute to growth and change?

Examples from meetings

Give examples from department or year group meetings you have attended which are concerned with the maintenance of existing behaviour, seeking new solutions to problems or new problems to solve.

169

Successful groups

What makes for a successful group? If the small cosy group doesn't function effectively or produce creative solutions to problems, why is this? What sort of mix makes for a productive group?

Belbin's Balance

Belbin (1981) lists eight personalities that a successful and productive team should have.

- **The company worker** – has organising ability, is hard working and self-disciplining. He or she is conservative, predictable and dutiful and can lack flexibility.
- **The chairman** – is calm, self-confident and controlled, with a strong sense of objectives, unprejudiced and not necessarily particularly clever.
- **The shaper** – provides the drive to the group and a readiness to challenge inertia or complacency, is highly-strung, outgoing, dynamic but also impatient.

- **The plant** – is the genius of the group, providing imagination and knowledge. He or she is individualistic, seriously unorthodox and often unrealistic.
- **The resource investigator** – is extrovert, enthusiastic, curious, with the energy to challenge and contact new people, but can easily get bored.
- **The monitor-evaluator** – provides judgement, discretion and hard-headedness, is sober, unemotional and prudent, but can be dull.
- **The team worker** – is sensitive, mild and able to respond to people and promote the team spirit, although he or she can be indecisive in crises.
- **The completer-finisher** – is the perfectionist, painstaking, conscientious and orderly, as well as having a tendency to worry about little things.

Clearly these are overlapping categories and the list is not meant to be mutually exclusive. It is likely that any individual would fit into several of the categories and may take different roles in different groups. Belbin believed that most people have a preferred major role, but also a subsidiary one. A balanced group would need all eight roles but could contain less than eight people.

REFLECTION

What do you think of this model? Do you think it has any validity? Can you identify any of the above roles within your behaviour in groups?

170

Of course, one's role may be affected by the nature of the group and of the task it has to perform. You are probably aware of the different personalities you adopt in different groups.

There are simpler classifications of roles. A much simpler model would have two personality types:
one concerned with the *task* – getting the job done
one concerned with the *group* – getting the process right.

The group leader

The more managers adapt their style of leader behaviour to meet the particular situation and needs of their followers the more effective they will be in reaching personal and organisational goals. (Lazarus, 1980)

When the troops continually gather in small groups and whisper together the general has lost the confidence of the army. (Sun Tzu, 4th Century BC)

In this chapter we have not talked at length about the role of the leader. Hersey and Blanchard (in Handy and Aiken, 1986) defined a cycle of four basic leadership styles.

- Telling (high task and low relationship)
- Selling (high task and high relationship)
- Participating (low task and high relationship)
- Delegating (low task and low relationship)

This model is useful and merits brief explanation.

- 'Telling' is the initial instructional stage, where your mentor tells you about the job.
- 'Selling' is the process of further induction, where you are given inspiration about the importance of your role and of the contribution which you can make to it.
- 'Participating' is the phase when you are becoming familiar with the job by doing it, and with direct participative support.
- 'Delegating' is the point at which you are trusted enough to take on tasks and do them: some may not agree that delegation is 'low task, low relationship', because there may always be the need for the boss to step in, monitor progress and give advice. The senior partner delegates responsibility but not accountability. This means that the relationship should be good and should be based on trust.

The style which is most appropriate depends not on the leader but on the maturity of the individual in terms of the given task. If an experienced individual is given a task which is very unfamiliar to them they may well need telling rather than delegating. There are parallels here with the early trainee-mentor relationship! One may have worked elsewhere for ten years, but teaching takes one back to the role of novice very quickly.

Some **small** groups function well if meetings are chaired by a different 'leader' each time, but this is unusual in a school setting where hierarchies are usually firmly established.

Expertise in teaching is often seen as only applicable to the teacher's role within the classroom – when the teacher is working with a group of children rather than working with colleagues. We need to redefine this notion of expertise and replace it with one that expects the expert to share good practice and reflect upon experience in partnership with fellow teachers. These are precisely the qualities that one looks for in an effective mentor and in a useful member of professional groupings.

Fullan and Hargreaves (1995) put this unequivocally:

Teacher leadership, defined as the capacity and commitment to contribute beyond one's own classroom, should be valued and practised from the beginning to the end of every teacher's career. There are few more basic things to fight for.

The learning school

One of the ways in which a whole school can make real the aim of working collaboratively is to develop the notion of a learning school.

Headteachers can take a leadership role in moving towards the culture whereby the school becomes seen as a centre of learning for pupils, for teachers and for the community.

The school will need to develop a shared vision of what constitutes a coherent definition of learning for all three groups. It may well be that there would need to be some realignment of some teachers' views of learning to encompass this wider vision. The narrow assessment strategies employed at GCSE have focused attention upon a limited range of skills and understanding. This has restricted the profession's views of what constitutes both intelligence and learning. Several have challenged this narrowness of vision; Claxton talks of two kinds of intelligence, whilst

Gardner's work on multiple intelligence has shown the limitations of traditional strategies. By identifying linguistic, musical, logico-mathematical, spatial, bodily, kinaesthetic, interpersonal as the seven intelligences, Gardner argues for a change in schools' perceptions of what constitutes an effective curriculum and challenges traditional views of teaching and learning. Trainees and newly qualified teachers can be an important part of this challenge to tradition. The focus within most training upon reflective practice indicates a desire to hold established and innovative practice up to scrutiny. By being part of a learning school, where such debate is encouraged, such reflection is seen as central to the teacher's role, not an inconvenient afterthought.

SUMMARY

Teaching is normally a team game. You will be a better teacher if you contribute to a team. You will need the support and encouragement of your colleagues in both official and unofficial groups. It is most worthwhile to consider your role within groups. How can you both *be and be seen as* a constructive influence within the group? Without being seen as positive by your colleagues, you might find your ideas are ignored irrespective of their real value. As in most aspects of teaching, both process and product are important. However even as you work within a group there will be occasions when individual reflection is necessary.

Useful references

Banks, J. and Harrington, A. (1994) **The Mathematics Department**. Milton Keynes: Open University.

Belbin, R. M. (1981) **Management Teams: Why They Succeed or Fail.** London: Heinemann.

Brighouse, T. (1991) **What Makes a Good School?.** Network Educational Press.

Fullan, M. and Hargreaves, A. (1995) **What's Worth Fighting for in Your School.** Milton Keynes: Open University.

Gardner, H. (1985) **Frames of Mind.** New York: Basic Books.

Handy, C. and Aiken, R. (1986) **Understanding Schools as Organisations.** London: Penguin.

Johnson Abercrombie, M. L. (1960) **The Anatomy of Judgement.** Hutchinson.

Lazarus, R. S. (1980) **Organisational Psychology.** Prentice Hall.

Lessing, D. (1986) **Prisons We Choose to Live Inside.** CBC Enterprises.

Bullying and Better Behaviour

33

It was not what Hooper really did, as to what he might do, it was how he could make him feel. (*I'm the King of the Castle* by Susan Hill, 1974)

LEARNING OUTCOMES

This chapter will enable you to consider a variety of solutions to bullying and many different ways of developing good behaviour in schools. You can use these to formulate your own professional approach to improving relationships among pupils.

REFLECTION

Can you remember bullies when you were at school? Make a note of 3 characteristics of bullies and 3 factors which make a person into a bully.

171

Jack

In preparation, re-read 'Jack' in Chapter 11.

Now consider this discussion with Jack, his mother, his Year Head and Form Tutor, after a Stage 1 exclusion.

172 *Jack seems courteous, charming, articulate and apologetic.*

What's the problem?

He's been like this with adults many times before, without reducing his bullying behaviour.

What's the solution?

Take time to let him and his mother talk. Carl Rogers maintains that most people know the answers to their own problems and that they need the chance to express them. Time is a rare commodity but worth it. Jack is in deep trouble. So let us take time over this.

For the first minutes, Jack presents himself almost as a victim who has to act big or else he will be bullied himself. He then goes on to complain about lunch-time supervision: it is inadequate, in his view, and leaves large areas of the school unsupervised, thereby allowing opportunities for bullying.

What's the problem?

First, the Year Head feels furious, because Jack is implying that other people should operate a bully-proof system, and he seems to be blaming others for the untold suffering which he has inflicted on many children. Secondly, it is not possible to improve the dinner-time supervision (staff morale is low, supervision is undertaken partly by low-status non-teaching staff, and the school campus is big).

What's the solution?

It may be necessary at this point to explain to Jack that he has to take responsibility for his own actions. Yet it is also worth asking him what he thinks could be done to improve the situation and to help him. At this stage Pervin's ideas are useful – 'Am I me or the situation?' – maybe there is something in what Jack is saying (an interaction between the environment and the personal characteristics of the individual). Mother reports at this stage that Jack's father is a silent man who according to his wife was very unhappy at school and can't help Jack with his problem.

Jack explains that he would very much like more individual contact with teachers – he suggests that he might undertake some tasks for the teachers in the lunch hour.

What's the problem?

The Form Tutor feels stunned and manipulated: Jack has taken up hours of punitive supervision time and may soon be put on a Stage 2 exclusion – yet he's asking if he can help the teachers . . . ridiculous!

What's the solution?

To help one keep cool it may be useful to consider Rogers' belief in the motivational power of respect: would it be worth swallowing one's pride and giving Jack 'conditional positive regard', that is warmth and respect given only when the person responds appropriately? After all, Jack is saying that he likes and respects the staff.

Further discussion of this request reveals that Jack is well aware of the fact that, if he is helping teachers, he is away from danger zones where he and his gang can bully. He also states that he would like to work with Year 7 pupils who experience difficulty with their work!

What's the problem?

Perhaps Jack is just manipulating the situation – trying to please adults and get himself off the hook.

There are organisational implications here which have to be negotiated between Form Tutor and Year Head: is it worth the effort?

What's the solution?

It may be worth implementing both Jack's requests: however, this co-operation by staff should then be used as a motivator to address the other areas of the problem, for instance peer group (gang and victims).

Suggested approaches

173

Develop your thinking in this area by working on one of the following approaches. Discuss Jack with your mentor and make notes on the discussion *or*
Analyse ways in which you believe Jack could be helped to work better in class *or*
Build up a collection of supportive mechanisms for working with the bullied and the bullies.

Factors which may increase the risk of children being bullied

● Those who are seen to be 'different' (red hair, glasses, a stammer). The literature suggests that bullying is less vindictive where the victim cannot change the stigma (for example physical disability) as opposed to those who can, in the attacker's view (for example obesity or poor co-ordination).

● Children of an ethnic minority, who are shown to be liable to hurtful and pervasive forms of racism, through name-calling. Where parents of all race groups have complained to Head Teachers about this problem, common responses include:
 – no problem in our school
 – recognition of a problem, but not a racial one
 – claims that parents and children are over-reacting

● Clumsy children are identified as being at 'high risk' for being victims of bullying (Olweus, 1978, found that 75% of boys identified as victims had co-ordination problems).

● Provocative victims are those children we may have encountered who appear to provoke attacks from others. However, most victims of bullying are passive victims.

● Non-telling. For a child subjected to bullying attacks over prolonged periods, the seeking of help is reduced in line with the child's increasing belief in being inferior, or that name-calling is valid. Such children are able to hide their suffering in their shame of being so unpopular.

● Situational factors. Here, a child may be more vulnerable due to environmental factors both within and outside school (for example narrow corridors, distant changing rooms, poorly supervised classrooms or lonely paths near the school).

Preventive strategies in schools

The following strategies have proved successful in counter-acting bullying.

Counter-acting bullying

As you work through these strategies, make notes in your Professional Development Portfolio. Relate them to your own experiences of how schools deal with bullying. Your notes will cover some of the following issues:

● Have you seen this working?
● Do you think this is a good idea?
● Do you have doubts about this?
● Would you like to discuss this with colleagues at school?

You can use these headings to guide your notes.

Talk, discuss, dramatise in situations which allow pupils to 'thrash out their problems' with the staff and with each other. Conflict should be handled constructively, with a focus on perspective-taking and amicable resolution of situations.

Induction days involving incoming Year 7, and Year 8 pupils and facilitating open discussion for concerns.

Such days may serve to identify children at risk, for example those without friends, afflicted with some 'stigma' or unusual feature, poor communication skills, school refusers, of minority ethnic origin, family out of catchment area. Induction during initial weeks should include map drawing, identification of relevant rooms and faces, a 'befriender system', a careful pairing and grouping of children.

Contract/school policy in which all staff members (supported by the LEA) declare firmly that bullying in school, in any form, will not be tolerated and, indeed, will be dealt with firmly. This document should be familiar to all pupils, parents, staff, governors and LEA employees.

Class contract established by Year 7 pupils and signed by the teacher and all pupils. Such a contract should be mainly devised by the pupils themselves and serve as useful reference point and method of reinforcement if, and when, bullying incidents arise over the school year. With each school year the contract could well be re-examined and reworded.

False excuses must not be accepted but must be challenged: 'It was only a joke', 'Not everyone was laughing!', 'It was an accident' should not be accepted unless pupils behave in a manner appropriate to the occurrence of an accident.

Tell someone what happened – then **qualify** it. Pupils are requested to **write down** their account of the incident as they perceived it. This report is then presented to the culprit as a 'warn off' with the statement that the whole thing is now **on file**. Pupils very much dislike something negative being recorded in this way. Further, **make the incident public**, perhaps in school assembly, without naming names, but reminding pupils of the class contracts, which they all have signed, the school contract and the school rules.

The emphasis is on fast and efficient lines of communication, to deal with incidents quickly before secondary problems arise. The method for collection of relevant information and dissemination to all interested parties is crucial if further occurrences are to be prevented.

Parents are urged **not** to stay away from school 'until it is all sorted out'. Further, they are encouraged to contact the school to communicate any anxieties in the initial stages before crises develop.

Further, parents of accused bullies are always involved. For parents unwilling to come to school, exclusion may follow unless an appointment is made that day – save in exceptional circumstances, and senior staff must make themselves available to accommodate parents' working hours.

Photograph of the incident or its consequences where physical aggression has occurred. This is important for file records and is also effective with parents of accused bully.

Supervision: there must be emphasis on staff being **punctual** to lessons and on the maintenance of **active**, **vigilant supervision** for the identification of incidents in their early stages. Specifically, the following are highlighted:

- constructive but informal supervision, with evident staff presence, chatting to pupils and being watchful of activities around the building
- more structuring of breaks and lunch-times (offered games/activities); observation work, including video to highlight problem areas; support and possibly training offered to dinner supervisors
- identification of 'high risk' areas (toilets, cloakrooms, libraries, showers) with these points marked on a map for staff employed on duty or on spot checks. Older, more responsible pupils could also help with this supervision
- supervision on school bus; spot checks by teaching staff, 'lollipop' staff, parents or others, in target spots within close proximity to the school

It is obvious that the LEA and the governing body need to offer not only verbal and moral support for this supervision, but also adequate staffing and money!

Teacher attitudes: teachers as bullies – research points in particular to the number of teachers observed to make remarks to pupils pertaining to such things as physique, appearance, race or family. There is evidence also of scapegoating particular individuals or applying rules inconsistently, all of which serve as negative role models in maintaining bullying forms of behaviour.

It is significant that jokes and nicknames used by teachers may seem witty and humorous in class, but are then picked up and open to cruel exaggeration in the playground.

It is important that schools identify the occurring conflicts between teachers and situations in a non-threatening way. *Vice versa*, teachers who are being bullied by pupils may require school support (alteration in composition of groups, in-service training to offer insights, observers in the classroom to analyse social groupings/relationships/reactions).

Class Management and PR

During the year, collect some examples of successful solutions to bullying, or, even better, ways of avoiding bullying. This pupil support work should become more of a priority as you begin to feel increasingly confident with your mastery of your subject knowledge and teaching, as part of your PR (Professional Requirements).

Each child is unique and therefore it would be glib to suggest that you can use magical formulae to help the bullied. Yet it is realistic to believe that by having high expectations of pupils' ability to behave well and support others, you can achieve small miracles.

'No Blame'

Read the following and make an appointment with a member of the pastoral team to discuss this approach. A form tutor or a head of year will be able to tell you about school initiatives and you can request involvement and write it up for your Professional Development Portfolio. Discussion of this 'No Blame' approach offers an opportunity for discussion, even if your school is not using it. Do not try to bring about change. Use the opportunity to learn from experienced colleagues by listening and watching. Are there drawbacks to this approach?

The 'No Blame' approach

The 'No Blame' approach is popular at the moment and can be successful: Pikas (1989) seeks to develop a common concern by working with the bullies, individually, to discuss the suffering caused by their actions, and develop positive proposals for the future.

Maines and Robinson (1991) take this 'No Blame' approach further by telling the bullies in a group about the specific effects of their actions and seeking to elicit a 'common concern' shared within the group. Open-ended discussions about possible solutions often lead to children apologising to their victims privately and seeking to make amends. Maines and Robinson recommend that work with groups of pupils can follow a sequence thus:

Group work

1 agreement that bullying takes place and that it is undesirable;

2 extending the definition of bullying to a range of behaviours and to discussion of passive onlookers;
3 teaching something about group processes;
4 working in groups;
5 giving opportunity for creative work to express feelings about bullying;
6 problem solving: 'What can we do?';
7 prepare for further work.

Problems with this approach

1 it is time-consuming to set up and maintain;
2 many teenagers want retribution – 'an eye for an eye, a tooth for a tooth';
3 Jack's problems in class are different and therefore need to be resolved differently;
4 some standard punishment system may need to be maintained and ideas may conflict here;
5 some victims cannot bear to become involved.

Advantages of this approach

1 it invites staff and pupils to concentrate on improving behaviour, rather than simply attempting to react to bullying;
2 it can be used to develop a whole school ethos and trust, and better behaviour;
3 it encourages creative, social problem solving;
4 it should make it possible for victims to change.

This approach is an attempt to foster a school climate in which victims of bullying can talk about their difficulties and where perpetrators and onlookers can help to devise solutions.

It is based on the belief that bullying is an interaction which establishes group identity, dominance and status at the expense of another, and it is only by the development of 'higher values', such as empathy, consideration, unselfishness, that the bully is likely to relinquish the bullying behaviour and function differently in a social setting. If the preventive policy depends on policing the environment, forbidding the behaviour, encouraging the victims and punishing the perpetrators, then no lasting change can be expected.

1 Ideally, the victim will tell a parent who will talk (with the victim) to the teacher. Otherwise, the victim will talk to the teacher, alone or with a friend.
2 The victim should be encouraged to explain how he or she *feels*, not only what happened.
The teacher takes notes and agrees *what* they can tell the group. The focus will be on the *effect* of the incident on the victim.
3 The teacher takes the victim's story to a group of young people including the bully and also some 'nice' pupils who joined in or did nothing to stop it. The victim is given the choice of attending this meeting – about 25% will choose to do so; the other 75% would prefer the teacher to represent their views.
At this meeting the teacher:

● Explains that nobody is going to be punished.
● Describes how awful it is for the victim.

- Lets the 'nice' pupils take control of the situation and think up ideas to make things better for the victim.
- At the end of the meeting, the teacher STRESSES that, if there are further occurrences of unacceptable behaviour, serious action will be taken.

4 The teacher should see the victim about a week later and discuss how things have gone. There should then be a follow-up with other pupils.

Bullying

177

A tall, strong boy (Year 8) has been systematically bullying his peers 'when lining up for lessons, in certain parts of the playground etc.' Recently a charismatic, virtuous Year 8 boy seems to have decided to form a small, elite vigilante group and bring the boy who is doing the bullying under control. The latter comes to you in fear, but continues to intimidate the others when he can.

Analyse the situation and discuss possible solutions.

SUMMARY

There are pupils who are labelled as bullies and pupils who are labelled as victims. Every staffroom contains teachers, also, who can be described in these ways. All are losers who become involved in a relationship which is characterised by misuse of power, and schoolchildren believe that bullying often goes unnoticed. You need to establish and maintain an environment in which there is mutual respect and in which learning and teaching can take place. Focusing on good behaviour, attitudes and beliefs is ultimately more effective than trying to stamp out bullying.

Useful references

Maines, B. and Robinson, G. (1991) **Stamp Out Bullying.** 71, South Street, Portishead, Avon, BS20 9DY: Lucky Duck Publishing.

Olweus, D. (1984) 'Aggressors and Their Victims: Bullying at School' in Frude, N. and Gault, H. (1984) **Disruptive Behaviour in School.** Wiley.

Pikas, A. (1989) 'The Common Concern Method for the Treatment of Mobbing', in Roland, E. and Munthe, E. (eds) **Bullying: An International Perspective.** London: David Fulton.

Tattum, D. (ed.) (1993) **Understanding and Managing Bullying.** Heinemann.

16 to 19 Education

34

Now I'm studying in the Sixth Form we're looking at topics in a much broader and deeper way – and I want to go back and look at some of my GCSE material again in more depth. The time management of all this is difficult though! (Deepinder)

LEARNING OUTCOMES

16 to 19 education is a complex and rapidly changing area. Indeed, by the time you read this there are likely to be further developments, which are not yet in the public domain. This chapter aims to raise your awareness of some of the challenges of this phase of education and increase your knowledge of recent issues.

Introduction: Becoming a student within 16 to 19 Education

Education and training between 16 and 19 are bridges between compulsory statutory education and the worlds of work and further and higher education. (Sir Ron Dearing: Summary of Interim Report, Review of 16–19 Qualifications, 1996)

Educational experience demonstrates that learning seems to work best where the learners themselves achieve a happy balance of clear vision, self direction, high quality support and a real sense of achievement and development. (Patrick Whitaker, 1995)

We believe that the understanding of the problematic nature of much 'knowledge' and the process of self-critical problem-solving based on real evidence is the basis for life-long learning and development. (Ashcroft and Forman-Peck, 1994)

Reasons for staying on in education

'I want a good job and you can't get that without paper qualifications these days'
'I am looking forward to the experience of higher education'
'I may as well stay on . . . and my parents want me to'
'I wasn't going to stay on, but my school made it sound so attractive – like they couldn't do without me'
'I was told I'd be on the scrap heap without further qualifications'
'There aren't any jobs and I don't rate the training schemes'
'I suppose I'm really staying on because I like learning'
'I enjoy school'
'I didn't really consider any other option'

REFLECTION

178:
- Where and why did you continue your education and did this work for you?
- Who helped you make your choice of destination and subjects?
- With hindsight could this have been more informed?
- Would you have chosen differently?

Pupils into students

179 Interview a Head of KS4 or Year 11 and a Head of Sixth Form and ask them for their thoughts on how turning 'pupils' into 'students' might best be managed. Of course many 11 to 16 schools now refer to those in their charge as school 'students' and expect them to be independent learners. What are the essential transitional changes faced by school students at 16?

How to ensure progression from pupil to student is the fundamental challenge of post 16 education.

It is also the most difficult challenge and one for which there is no easy answer. The following comments should help to start you thinking about the way you teach post-16 and the way you treat the students.

As an NQT, I found that the most difficult task was to manage the tension between ensuring my students had enough subject knowledge whilst at the same time encouraging them to think, question and work independently. It would have been so easy to spoon feed them through a diet of lectures and note taking. Encouraging them to take the lead in lessons, setting up structured discussions, testing their knowledge in various ways and showing them how to make and use worthwhile notes are all teaching strategies I have experimented with. Before I taught this age group, I thought that the great bonus would be that they had all chosen to stay on and would therefore have a love and enthusiasm for the subject. Of course this is true in some cases but the majority need to be encouraged and motivated through a variety of different teaching strategies. I was told by a more experienced colleague to teach post-16 students as though they were simply older Year 11s and not to worry if the transition from 'pupil' to 'student' took a very long time. 'Above all', he said, 'convince them that you are treating them like adults even though they may behave like children.'

(An NQT in Gloucestershire, Autumn 1996)

Yes, I do find the transition from GCSE to A level hard. It is not so much the standard of work though, more the amount of it, the long deadlines and the frightening sense of being left on your own. There is no quick and easy answer as to whether you have 'got it right'. The teachers are helpful but they seem to expect too much too quickly.

(Year 12 student, Gloucestershire Sixth Form)

Conflicting needs

180 Consider the comments made opposite by post-16 students about their learning needs and the qualities most prized by their teachers. How far are they compatible? Where are the conflicts?

Ten Tips for Teachers post-16

1 Sense of humour.

2 Reliability.

3 Ability to relate naturally, to communicate with students, not try to be 'one of us'

4 Ability to relate on a personal/social level.

5 Lively and interesting lessons to maintain student enthusiasm.

6 Thorough knowledge of subject essential and preferably knowledge of subject related careers

7 Mutual respect established through discipline, although this should not be excessive.

8 An awareness and understanding of other demands on a student's time.

9 The ability to explain away difficulties without patronising the student.

10 Be prepared to work outside teaching hours for one to one tutoring if necessary.

Successful students start here

1 Show initiative, independence and responsibility in the way you learn.

2 Meet deadlines – work at time management.

3 Adopt a questioning approach.

4 Don't be afraid of making mistakes – and learning from them.

5 Understand what is required of you: the syllabus coursework demands and so on.

6 Be able to make a competent oral presentation.

7 Read around the subject.

8 Learn and practise the skills of note taking.

9 Use study time constructively.

10 Acquire basic IT skills.

Summary of major changes to 16–19 education

'A little learning is a dangerous thing'

Sir Ron Dearing published his review of the 16–19 qualifications framework in March 1996. This report, widely regarded as the most fundamental review of English education since 1945 was broadly welcomed by politicians from all political parties and most teacher organisations.

(The Dearing Report on 16 to 19 qualifications: An update by OCEAC and MEG)

In all, 'Sir Ron Dearing made 198 recommendations. Those most likely to affect schools and colleges are outlined below:

1 A national framework of qualifications at four levels: Advanced, Intermediate, Foundation and Entry.
These levels will 'include the three main qualification pathways of GCSE/A level, GNVQ and NVQ. This framework is designed to be easily understood and will give explicit recognition to the equivalence of academic, applied and vocational pathways' (SCAA 'Inform', June 1996).

2 An emphasis on the 'key skills' of communication, application of number and information technology for all 16 to 19 year-olds and ways of validating this.

3 Replacing the current AS with a revamped model, the 'Advanced Subsidiary' examination representing the level of achievement expected from one year of post-16 study.

4 Measures to increase participation in mathematics and science courses post-16 as well as moves to ensure standards are maintained at A level both within and between subjects.

5 The revision and relaunch of the National Record of Achievement.

National Award	Academic	Applied	Vocational
Advanced Level	AS and A Level	Advanced GNVQ	NVQ Level 3
Intermediate Level	GCSE Grades A*–C	Intermediate GNVQ	NVQ Level 2
Foundation Level	GCSE Grades D–G	Foundation GNVQ	NVQ Level 1
Entry Level	Common to all pathways: Grades A/B/C. Equivalent to NC Levels 3, 2 and 1 but made relevant to post-16 age group. A* is the top grade.		

Government targets

Sir Ron Dearing's review was commissioned as one way in which the Government might address the targets it had set for the nation in producing an internationally competitive work force by the year 2000. These targets are:

1 60% of young people by the age of 21 should achieve two A levels, an Advanced GNVQ or NVQ level 3.

2 85% of young people by the age of 19 should achieve five GCSEs at Grade C or above or an intermediate GNVQ or NVQ level 2.

3 75% of young people by the age of 19 should achieve level 2 competence in communication, numeracy and information technology; and 35% should achieve level 3 competence in these core skills by age 21

(White Paper 'Competitiveness: Forging Ahead')

Other major developments

● GNVQs first proposed in the 1991 White Paper: 'Education and Training for the 21st Century' were intended as an avenue towards both employment and higher education.

To provide students with a programme that has sufficient academic rigour to give the necessary skills and knowledge for entry to higher education, linked with a clearly defined vocational area which includes work with a large practical and problem-solving element.

All GNVQs have the same basic structure: mandatory units in the designated vocational pathway (for example Art and Design) plus a number of optional units. Accreditation is available at pass, merit and distinction level and assessment takes place through end of unit tests and the compilation and assessment of a portfolio of evidence. Where GNVQs differ most radically from other current post-16 qualifications is the emphasis on core skills and the style of teaching and learning. GNVQ students need to be involved in action planning to devise assignments which will meet exam board criteria. The 'teacher' role is far more that of a facilitator and the emphasis put on extensive tutorial sessions with individual students reflects this.

● Modular A levels have become increasingly popular in recent years. There is considerable debate over whether they can maintain the 'gold standard' of A level qualifications.

● The increased emphasis on market forces in education means that competition between schools at sixth form level or between schools and colleges is inevitable when a post-16 student is worth just under £2,500 to the institution he or she chooses to attend.

Subject specific issues

The following questions and issues can be revisited throughout your course. Keep a record of your thoughts in your PDP.

181
● Follow up the issue of modular A levels by considering the modular and linear syllabuses in your subject specialism. What advantages and disadvantages can you see? Talk to students, teaching staff and the examinations officer in your school to gain as wide a perspective as possible.

● GNVQ and A levels require different teaching and learning styles. Investigate the different approaches, what is common to both and what they might usefully learn from each other.

● What 'key skills' can you identify in your subject area? Could you devise a way in which they might be assessed.

● Teaching and tutoring post-16 is widely regarded as a particularly attractive option. What particular **challenges** would post-16 students pose for you?

● Ask if there is any work being done on 'value-added' in your institution and, if so, find out as much as you can about it. Choose a small number of students and conduct your own 'value-added' survey on them. Could the information be useful? How might you use it?

Guidance and choice at 16+

182
Post-16 education is currently provided by a variety of institutions, often located in close proximity to one another. Students are able to choose which school or college to attend and their freedom of choice inevitably generates a degree of competition between providers. In this competitive environment it is therefore essential that schools become more fully aware of the costs being incurred and the effectiveness of their provision. (Effective Sixth Forms: Ofsted)

The following 'case study' is based on real students in a real situation, but is a lighthearted look at a serious practical and ethical dilemma currently being faced by all post-16 providers. You can use the material for discussion. It can also be developed as role play with colleagues or even with students which then gives rise to even livelier discussion. It is essential that you read 'A little learning is a dangerous thing' and 'Other major developments' on pages 303 and 304 *before* you begin this exercise.

The following students are all seeking post-16 institutions. What advice would you give them as:

- A dispassionate observer?
- The Head/Head of Sixth of one of the particular institutions listed here?

Academic Anne is a school year ahead of her chronological age. Predicted 9 grade 'A's at GCSE she could do any A levels she wanted. She says she is committed to an academic post-16 education and, although quiet and unassuming, might well aspire to Oxbridge. At present, Anne is looking towards 'Arts' A levels although other subject areas are keen to poach her.

Goodtime Gordon is a favourite with pupils and some staff. His pleasant, affable manner and native wit provide a useful smokescreen for the thinness of his knowledge. Able, but idle, he is confident of 'A' grades at GCSE whilst his teachers are resigned to Cs. Gordon's parents would like him to follow in their footsteps and enter the medical profession. Gordon has not given a moment's thought to his future career but he does find it easier to keep his parents happy!

Maverick Margaret is, as her name suggests, unpredictable both academically and personally. She enjoys giving the impression of an individual who has grown out of school and who has opinions and values at variance with the institution. Paradoxically, she works best in structured 'old fashioned' lessons with 'strict' teachers. She knows she is unlikely to gain Maths at a 'C' but she could get all the rest between an 'A' and a 'C'. Apart from Maths, her weakest subjects are the practical ones.

Aspiring Asiya is a modern girl with strict Muslim parents. They have high aspirations for Asiya and want her to become a lawyer as they assume she will do well in her GCSEs. Asiya is not so sure. She knows that she excels at practical subjects and those with a strong coursework component where her hard work pays off.

Wide Boy William really enjoys practical work and his part-time job but refers to most classroom lessons as 'boring'. He has a very bright sister and parents want him to follow in her footsteps. William's teachers have predicted him 'A's in Art and Technology and a 'D' or 'C/D' in all of the others. William's first love is sport.

Able Albert works extremely hard, is predicted mainly 'A's and thinks that one day he would like to go to university. He is under pressure to leave at 16 and get a job as money is extremely tight. Albert has never known his father but he does know that his mother would hate him to leave home. Albert cannot decide what to do as he knows he has ability as a linguist but also feels responsible for his mother.

Dizzy Diana is an entirely creative 'darling'. Constrained by formal education she is longing to express herself, but at what and how she is at a loss to say, being too wrapped up in new ideas to consider such boring details as what to do after GCSEs. Diana is likely to do well in subjects which interest her but terribly in others.

Jittery James suffers from an acute lack of confidence as a result of a stammer and being small for his age. This has improved considerably in Year 11, although he still does not believe he has the capacity for further study. His teachers are confident that, providing he does not crumble in the exams, he should gain almost all 'B's and 'C's, although French is a weakness. He has no idea what he wants to do and his parents are anxious that above all he should be happy.

Abbeyfield is an inner city comprehensive, struggling to maintain its post-16 provision in the face of local FE colleges. It has small numbers doing A levels and a larger (75) number on GNVQ courses.

Broadmead is a small selective state school in a city with many different kinds of post-16 providers. It has a high academic reputation and a large proportion of the Year 11 students stay on into the sixth form to study A levels. There is no one-year course.

City College is a large sixth form college with both full time and part time students. Apart from its mature students, it takes most of the students from a variety of local schools who wish to study post-16. It offers a wide range of courses including A levels, Advanced and Intermediate GNVQs.

Deerside College is an enormous FE college serving a wide area. There are huge numbers of full and part time students of all ages and a plethora of different courses.

Eadon High is a large 11 to 18 comprehensive with a strong sixth form tradition which it wishes to preserve. The majority of students are on A level courses but 3 GNVQ courses are also established and available for one year students.

Question: How do you resolve the difficulty of giving unbiased advice based on the needs of the student, with the need to maintain viable numbers in your subject/institution? Clearly there are no absolute answers as to which 'typical' student should go to which 'typical' institution. However, you could argue that there are better or worse places for each of the students listed above.

SUMMARY

Post-compulsory education has in the past seemed relatively stable in comparison with the major changes within 5 to 16 education brought about by the introduction of the National Curriculum. If the aims of the Dearing Review of 16 to 19 education are to be met, the change within this phase of education will be as dramatic. Teachers will need to work within a rapidly changing framework and to be adaptable. Such adaptation may not always be comfortable or easy for experienced teachers.

This chapter can only hope to be a taster of the issues and experiences involved in teaching post-16 and to give you some idea of the demands and dilemmas facing schools and colleges. Post-compulsory teaching is a richly rewarding area where the challenge is to provide a high quality education which meets the needs of young people both for Further and Higher Education and in the world of work, into the millennium and beyond. The concluding passage indicates that perhaps change is not as great a challenge for the trainee as for the expert.

A lot of teachers are tired of constant change in education and have grown cynical over the years with constant change . . . a new thing is brought in and you wonder whether it's going to last more than three months or a year. I can understand that . . . What's quite interesting is that I've come into the profession and all of this change and all the things that are going on are just part of it . . . It's just all part of the job.

(PGCE English trainee)

Useful references

The following publications may be of use to you in finding out more about the complex and ever-changing area of post-16 education.

'Review of Qualifications for 16–19 year olds: summary report'. Ron Dearing, March 1996. SCAA Publication (0181 561 4499).

'Effective Sixth Forms'. Ofsted (1996). HMSO Publications Centre (0171 873 9090).

MacFarlane, E. (1993) **Education 16–19 In Transition.** London: Routledge.

Hayward, G. (1995) **Getting to grips with GNVQ.** London: Kogan Page.

Glover, L. (1995) **GNVQ into Practice.** London: Cassell.

National Council for Vocational Qualifications, 222 Euston Road, London NW1 2BZ (0171 072 1958).

Ashcroft, K and Forman-Peck, L. (1994) **Managing Teaching and Learning in Further and Higher Education.** London: The Falmer Press.

Halsall, R. and Cockett, M. (1996) **Education and Training 14–19. Chaos or Coherence?** London: David Fulton.

Whitaker, L. (1995) **Managing to Learn.** London: Cassell.

In addition, the various examination boards will supply you with information about their latest developments in response to The Dearing Review.

Tutoring – The Pastoral Process

35

Tuesday September 14th

We've got a new form teacher. His name is Mr Lambert. He is the kind of teacher who likes being friendly. He said, 'Consider me a friend, any problems to do with school or home, I want to hear them.'

He sounded more like a Samaritan than a teacher. I have an appointment to see him after school tomorrow.

Thursday September 16th

Barry Kent has made an appointment with Mr Lambert to talk about his family problems! I hope Mr Lambert has got twenty four hours to spare. Ha! Ha! Ha!

Friday September 17th

Nearly everyone in our class has made an appointment to see Mr Lambert about their family problems . . .

Mr Lambert is going about the school biting his nails and looking worried. He has stopped taking people to the café.

(*The Growing Pains of Adrian Mole* by Sue Townsend; 1984)

LEARNING OUTCOMES

When you have read this chapter, you will have explored the role of the form tutor within the pastoral care system of the school. You will have focused on the tasks of a tutor and you will have examined the pupil–tutor relationship.

Introduction

Towards the end of their course, trainees often feel that they are well prepared to teach their subject, but that their experience of tutoring is limited. A trainee is likely to have observed registration, visited some PSE (Personal and Social Education) classes and talked to various pastoral managers, for example the person responsible for Primary School liaison.

What pastoral care experiences have you had? Record them in your Professional Development Portfolio and add to them as you work through this chapter.

183

All these activities are a useful introduction to tutoring. You also bring other skills to the tutor role that you may be less conscious of. Highly regarded trainees are often those who participate in the school as a community. For example, they spend time talking to pupils outside lessons, they 'pull their weight' on the school trip, in the school play or on the sports field. They are good communicators who have formed effective working relationships with a range of teaching and non-teaching colleagues. They have been noted for their concern for the individual child. These characteristics, summed up in part by the competence descriptor, 'Further professional development', are reliant on the same skills needed in tutoring.

Despite recommendations that newly qualified teachers are not given a tutor group, this is not always possible, and in many schools it is accepted practice that an NQT has particular responsible for a class of children – they are form tutors.

Some teachers welcome this role, while others see it as a chore.

Much of your effectiveness as a tutor will depend on the importance you attach to your role. Tutoring is the 'chalkface' of pastoral work in schools. For example, the task of taking the register is sometimes a way of getting to know pupils. Absence notes are also more than just administration. They can give you insight into the child's life outside school.

Absence notes

Consider this absence note:

John will be away from school for the next two weeks because he has a chance to go on holiday with his aunt. I know this is in term-time but we have had domestic problems recently and the break will do John good.

184

Yours sincerely,
Gladys Andrews

As a tutor how do you respond to the above note?
a) Are you familiar with school policies and procedures concerning absence?
b) Are your responses affected by your own attitudes towards optimum school attendance?
c) Would you refer this to another colleague?
d) Would you discuss this with the child concerned?
Discuss absence notes with a form tutor.

A tutor's immediate reaction to the student can convey powerful messages that can strengthen or undermine relationships. For example, we know that bereaved children may need to talk about their loss, some children need to be as 'normal' and as inconspicuous as possible and until they have control of their own feelings. It is also wise to hold back from implying that a child's absence is unjustified, or that a child is lying, until at least, you know more about it.

Exchanging information

185 Find out how the school manages the exchange of information between the pastoral and the subject staff about students' welfare and their academic progress. Are these the same or different systems and procedures?

Tutors' reports

Curriculum development since the early 1980s has concentrated on programmes of study and on how children's progress can be assessed. It has been largely left to the school to decide how best to match the curriculum to the individual. This is an important aspect of the pastoral process – ensuring individuals engage with the curriculum successfully. Behaviour problems may be the result of an inappropriate curriculum for that child. Tutors need to be informed of their students' progress and behaviour. Monitoring and reporting student progress across the curriculum is a fundamental principle of pastoral work. It is normally the tutor who writes a summative comment to parents to accompany a child's school reports.

Tutors' reports

Consider these examples of tutors' reports. To what extent do they reflect a tutor's interest in the student's academic, personal, and social development?

186 William's immaturity and high rate of absence is hampering his progress. Both need to change dramatically if he is to achieve a level of success. He needs to develop a more positive attitude to school. He must also try to curb his silly behaviour during lunchtime.

Debbie is quietly confident with a good sense of humour. She relates well to others and is always courteous. She is organised and well-presented. Debbie has a good attendance record and is always punctual. I was pleased with her involvement in community work this year. Debbie is a valuable member of the group.

Daniel is doing well. His Maths and Science grades this term are impressive. He achieved excellent marks in a recent Biology practical examination. He needs to spend more time on his weaker subjects: his French homework is not completed with the thoroughness we have come to expect from him. If he continues to work hard, he can look forward to some pleasing results in the Summer.

These examples could reflect a tutor's approach to their role. They may also reflect the type of relationship that exists between tutor and student. As with all reporting, evidence should exist to support a statement. We need to guard against placing constructions on behaviour which have not been tested through talking with the student. It is important to recognise the whole range of students' achievements and experiences so that the reporting process encourages the child's self-esteem and is positive and motivating. If changes are desirable, possible strategies for moving on need to be offered. It is the tutor who, in most schools, compiles with the child, over a period of time their Record of Achievement. The quality of that record is heavily reliant on the interest, the commitment, and the interpersonal skills of the tutor.

Tutor responsibilities and tutor attitudes are the practical application of the pastoral aims of the school. Two important principles traditionally inform pastoral care in school; the education of the whole child and the role of teacher *in loco parentis* (in place of the parent). The education of the whole child entails, for example, helping the child to make informed decisions and encouraging a concern for others (in other words moral education). *In loco parentis* means that a teacher behaves towards a child as a caring parent would. The professional equivalent of a parent's 'caring' must be a concern shown equally for all students regardless of a teacher's personal likes or dislikes.

REFLECTION

187

One school lists the aims of its pastoral care policy as:

- to establish and maintain an appropriate relationship with every student
- to encourage a caring and orderly environment
- to monitor student progress across the curriculum
- to offer support and guidance for achievement and personal and social development
- to establish a positive relationship with parents.

How does each of the following tutor tasks, recorded by a Year 9 tutor in one half term, further the aims of the school's pastoral policy?

- taking the register
- dealing with incidents of bullying
- leading a session on road safety awareness
- listening to a distressed child
- organising fund raising for charity
- looking after a sick child
- planning an assembly
- picking a team for an inter-form competition
- filing absence notes
- putting up form notices
- liaising with SEN department
- attending pastoral meetings with Head of Year
- monitoring a child's progress by parent's request
- attending a case conference
- talking to parents about their child's GCSE option choices
- setting targets for a disruptive child

The number of these tasks, and how an individual tutor does them will depend on the pastoral system within the school, the skills/inclinations of the tutor and the age of the class.

REFLECTION

188

What are the difficulties with each of these profiles?

The following describes a school system where the tutor has a high profile role:

The tutor stays with the same group of children throughout their school career. They are expected to play a large part in the induction process in Year 7. Confidential information on pupils will come to them. They are the person with access to all their pupils' records and they are responsible for updating them, filing letters and copies of reports. Subject colleagues will be expected to inform them about curriculum and discipline matters. The form tutor will be the first point of contact with home. They will be responsible for writing all letters home, including those about misbehaviour, and they will be present at any interview with the parents, and/or other welfare agencies. They will deliver health education programmes, vocational and careers guidance.

Indicators of a school where a tutor has a more subordinate role would be:

Tutors mark the register but do not follow up absences. Vocational and careers education is centralised. Senior staff deal with all problems, transgressions, interviews with parents and other agencies.

REFLECTION

189

What are the advantages and disadvantages of the following students' perceptions of tutors?

– he always sticks up for us.
– she phones my mum everytime I miss a day . . .
– I can talk to Mr X about anything. I've told him things that I won't tell anyone else.
– Miss X always has the best behaved class. You don't dare do anything wrong.
– Mr X is honest with us. We know he thinks Mrs Y is useless and should be able to control us.

How would you wish to be perceived by pupils in your tutor group? Does it differ at all from how you wish to be perceived by the other children you teach? And how does it change with the age of the pupil?

Most schools fall somewhere between these two tutor-role descriptions above. As a tutor you are likely to have the support of a Head of Year or a Head of House and to be a member of a pastoral team. It is sensible, and in your own interests, to find out, early on, what the accepted practices are in your school. Some managers, for example, have strong feelings about who contacts parents, whether by phone or letter.

I once knew a teacher who wrote to a boy's parents about his poor behaviour in class not knowing that the child's mother was dying. Luckily, the teacher showed the letter to the boy's tutor and it wasn't sent. It would have caused unnecessary upset.

(A Year Head)

Most schools insist on all correspondence being checked by a colleague. Without a clear understanding by everyone of the roles, responsibilities and tasks of the tutor the possibility exists of a role being adopted or projected onto the tutor which is inappropriate, unrealistic or even dangerous. There can be no complete confidentiality in the student–tutor relationship. There are circumstances, for example when a child alleges abuse, when a tutor needs to follow a procedure set down in the Child Protection Act.

Establishing and maintaining an appropriate relationship with every student in your tutor group is a demanding task. According to Hopson and Scally in their 'Lifeskills' teaching programme effective relationships are characterised by Respect, Genuineness and Empathy. By 'respect' we mean tutor behaviour which conveys to the pupil that they are worthwhile and valued. Children notice simple courtesies, such as asking how they are when they have been poorly or remembering what they told you last week about their family. A tutor who is thought of as 'genuine' will seem to be open and trustworthy. They are not defensive. What they say will be consistent with their tone and with their body language. A teacher who shows 'empathy' can see the world the way the child sees it. They reflect back to the child feelings they are picking up, 'You must have felt very angry'. They share experiences of their own.

Effective tutoring balances the relationship between the tutor and the group on the one hand and the tutor and the individual on the other. The group relationship is not the accumulation of numerous one-to-one encounters but the result of the tutor's lead in modelling respect, genuineness and empathy; the kinds of behaviour we need to encourage in students if they are to develop the skills of making good relationships.

A 190 Changing expectations

Find out how children's expectations of their form tutor change, from the time they arrive in secondary school, to the time they leave at the end of Year 11 or 13. Use teacher-researcher methods (for example small group interviews or questionnaires, for pupils).

What different roles, tasks and activities do tutors undertake according to the age and or stage of development of the pupils? You may wish to discuss this with pastoral managers, Year Heads or experienced tutors (you can use semi-structured interviews, perhaps five questions as a basic structure for open-ended discussion, for staff).

The focus of this chapter largely excludes discussion of Personal and Social Education courses. Most schools locate PSE within the tutorial system because of the obvious congruence between pastoral objectives and those of such courses, with their emphasis on personal development, health education and citizenship. The content of PSE can provide the tutor with the foundation for exploring issues with individuals. It can enhance a tutor's credibility in responding to, for example, an individual's health concerns. Similarly, a tutor who teaches a Careers module within PSE can be more effective in the area of vocational guidance. Further references to structured PSE courses can be found at the end of this chapter.

PSE

191

Find out if your school has a Personal and Social Education programme of study? How does this relate to the work of the tutor?

Teachers are often concerned about having the right answer to students' worries and concerns. This is an unrealistic expectation. The tutor's role is to enable the student to explore the issue and consider his/her options and possible courses of action.

Jo

192

You have a Year 10 tutor group who are taught by ten different subject teachers. Mid-way through the year, three teachers in the same week tell you that, Jo, a bright student who is expected to achieve high grades at GCSE, has failed to meet their recent course work task deadlines. Jo's attendance has been very good until the last two months, during which you have seen an increasing frequency of one-day absences. Jo is an out-going, popular student and you have not observed any change in outward behaviour recently.

● Is this information a sufficient basis for counselling and guidance?
● What else do you need to know?
● Who else do you need to communicate with?
● What would your strategy be in Jo's case?

Of course, the pastoral process is not exclusive to the tutoring system. Sensitivity to student need and effective differentiation should be a feature of every lesson. But a subject teacher is unlikely to have sufficient opportunity to go beyond recognising that there is a problem with a particular student in their own subject. The form tutor will have an overview of how the pupil feels about all their work, and what other factors, for example, problems at home, may be influencing an individual's progress. The tutor can go beyond counselling and offer structured support and guidance.

Developments in the National Record of Achievement and reporting and the recent SCAA publication, 'Skills for Choice', suggest a significant role for tutors in the guidance process. Key issues include action planning and self-presentation, in which students are encouraged to take responsibility for their learning and behaviour, assess their achievements and identify areas for progress. A tutor's role in these processes include the ability to:

- build relationships that encourage openness
- communicate clearly, precisely and sensitively
- set appropriate standards and expectations
- help students to identify weakness and ways of developing skills
- help students to review progress through constructive feedback.

To help students implement 'Skills for Choice' tutors need a broad understanding of the educational experience for pupils across the curriculum from a pupil's perspective. This understanding could help not only their tutoring skills but improve their own subject teaching.

SUMMARY

- Pastoral care is concerned with the education of the whole person. It has four interrelated dimensions: welfare, curricular, administrative and disciplinary. These aspects of pastoral care must be seen in the wider social and cultural environment.
- Pastoral care requires all teachers to make effective and supportive relationships with the children in their care, and with other interested parties; parents, welfare agencies and support staff.
- Schools have structures and systems to administer and monitor pastoral care. Most see the form tutor as having a key pastoral role in the school.
- Good practice in tutoring has applications for all teaching.

Useful references

Marland, M. (1974) **Pastoral Care.** Heinemann Educational Books.
Hopson, B. and Scally, M. (1980) **Lifeskills Teaching Programmes.** Lifeskills Associates.
Schools Curriculum and Assessment Authority (1996) **Skills for Choice.** SCAA Publications.
Lang, P. and Marland, M. (eds) (1985) **New Directions in Pastoral Care.** Oxford: Basil Blackwell.

Further reading

Adams, S. (1989) **A Guide to Creative Tutoring.** London: Kogan Page.
Bulman, L. and Jenkins, D. (1988) **The Pastoral Curriculum.** Oxford: Basil Blackwell.
Clemett, A. and Pearce, J. (1986) **The Evaluation of Pastoral Care.** Oxford: Basil Blackwell.
Hamblin, D. (1986) **A Pastoral Programme.** Oxford: Basil Blackwell.
Hamblin, D. (1978) **The Teacher and Pastoral Care.** Oxford: Basil Blackwell.
Housego, P. and Parsons, J. (1989) **Guidance and Tutoring Skills.** Pergamon Educational Productions.

Teaching the Big Ideas 36

The child's current values are challenged and the possibility is opened up of aspirations that lie beyond. (Donaldson, 1992)

LEARNING OUTCOMES

When you have completed this chapter you will have an understanding of how your subject(s) can contribute to a pupil's spiritual, moral, social, personal and cultural development. You will become aware that it is the big ideas behind the subject, the central organising principles or the fundamental applications to the real world that become important when dealing with these aspects.

Introduction

How, then, do we help children to understand goals that are quite far from their own present lives and not readily displayed? How do we give them any notion of what it would be like to achieve power as a mathematician, say, or as any kind of theoretical thinker? Or, again, how do we give them some sense of the experience that comes with developing spirituality as it aspires towards transcendence?

. . . If we are wise enough and sufficiently serious about the enterprise, our schools can offer intermediate goals in a well-planned sequence so that each achievement is also an opening which reveals new challenges not too far out of reach. The sequence, though, must not be rigid, still less rigidly enforced, and must never come to resemble in practice that dreaded image of hoops to be jumped through. The teacher is not a ring-master. Neither, however, is the teacher merely a consultant. The teacher is one who knows what lies ahead and also how to get there. The teacher has new desires to offer – and new techniques for learning how to satisfy them . . . (Donaldson, 1992)

What are the big ideas that your subject tries to convey to pupils? Is it just a list of facts and skills examined at the end of Key Stage 4 by a narrowly constituted examination? If that were the case it would be hard to justify its place within the curriculum. All subjects must play a part in developing the whole child. Some subjects may appear to outsiders to fall short of this aim; usually science and mathematics are seen as fallible in this respect. However within science one must think about the moral dimension when considering technological or scientific change; mathematics can develop reasoning and logic to such an extent that it is possible to contemplate the infinite.

The formal inspection framework of Ofsted allows for such holistic considerations. Section 5.3 of the 1995 Ofsted Framework for Inspection is concerned with pupils' spiritual, moral, social and cultural development. In an earlier attempt to differentiate between these terms, Ofsted (1994) offered the following descriptions.

Spiritual development relates to that aspect of inner life through which pupils acquire insights into their personal experience which are of enduring worth. It is characterised by reflection, the attribution of meaning to experience, valuing a non-material dimension to life, and intimations of an enduring reality. 'Spiritual' is not synonymous with 'religious'; all areas of the curriculum may contribute to pupils' spiritual development.

Moral development is concerned with pupils' ability to make judgements about how to behave and act and the reasons for such behaviour. It requires knowledge and understanding and includes questions of intention, motive and attitude. Pupils should be able to distinguish 'right' and 'wrong' as matters of morality from the use of the words right and wrong in other contexts.

Social development involves pupils' progressive growth in knowledge and understanding of society in all its aspects: its institutions, structures and characteristics, including economic and political organisation, principles; and life as a citizen, parent or worker in a community. Through this gain in knowledge and understanding pupils should acquire the competencies and qualities needed to play a full and active part in society.

Cultural development refers to pupils' increasing understanding and command of those beliefs, values, attitudes, customs, knowledge and skills, which taken together, form the basis of identity and cohesion in societies and groups. It also involves: a variety of aesthetic appreciation; opportunities for pupils to develop and strengthen their existing cultural interests; and having access to a breadth of stimuli which might develop new insights and interests.

Spiritual development

Religious education can clearly make a considerable contribution to pupils' spiritual development. However many people mistakenly assume that the world 'spiritual' is equivalent to 'religious' and that their subject has nothing to contribute to a child's spiritual development. SCAA (1995) list many aspects of spiritual development: beliefs, a sense of awe and wonder, experiencing feelings of transcendence, search for meaning and purpose, self-knowledge, relationships, creativity, feelings and emotions.

These are some of the ways in which opportunities for pupils to experience spirituality and hence promote their spiritual development can be provided. These more open definitions of spirituality allow all subjects to contribute. Clearly people will differ in their interpretation of these aspects and some may ascribe causes to these which are based on belief in God. It is not our place here to restrict belief. We prefer to assert that the list of aspects of spirituality include some of the deepest reasons for teaching and learning any subject.

Spiritual development

Reflect on your experience of observing and teaching your subject over the past few weeks. Write brief notes for your portfolio of an incident where your subject contributed to a pupil's spiritual development, where a sense of 'awe and wonder' was developed. Discuss this with your colleagues.

Your subject and SMSC

Taking your main subject, try to identify specific ways in which the subject makes its contribution to each of the four strands of SMSC: spiritual, moral, social and cultural.

Examples could include:

Spiritual   *History:* a sense of time and awareness of the complexity of historical causes
Science: the size of the universe
Mathematics: $e^{i\pi} + 1 = 0$
Euclid's proof that $\sqrt{2}$ is irrational

Moral   *Science:* atomic power
Geography: comparisons between economically developed and developing countries

Social   *Physical Education:* importance of rules, teamwork
Mathematics: number as a means of communication

Cultural   *Art:* the impact of graphic design
Music: the place of music in contemporary society
English: the influence of literature on language and culture
Mathematics, Science, Technology: 'the contribution of many cultures to mathematics and to scientific and technological development' (Ofsted Framework, 1995)

Build up within your Professional Development Portfolio a log of examples where a contribution to SMSC was made. These should be from your own teaching and from your observations of other teachers. A sample of subject specific ideas can be found in the table on pages 320 and 321:

POSTGRADUATE SECONDARY COURSE 1996–97

Subject	Spiritual	Moral	Social	Cultural
MATHEMATICS	Liked for the sake of knowledge. Enduring reality – always existed, always will, description of the world, discovery or invention, astronomy beliefs, flawless?	Pay increases. Lie using statistics – interpretation, judgements, motives behind	Mean, median, mode – statistics, politics. Everyday business maths – using and applying fairness, unbiased	Number doesn't mean same to all 1, 2, many. Maths is a universal foreign language, techniques and rotation the same
SCIENCE	Theories of the universe/evolution. Awe and wonder – in complexity of nature.	Genetic engineering – do we have the right to determine life? Holocaust – the nature of nuclear weapons/energy	Good lab practice – group work (co-operation). Safety. Development of skills. Application and following rules.	Development of science in society and other cultures – relates to *spiritual* – the ideas of paradigms (T Kuhn)
GEOGRAPHY	People and their relationship with their environment. Issues relating to conservation.	Decision-making e.g. where to locate a factory. Appreciation of differences between rich and poor.	'Social Geography'. Knowledge of societies – their own and others in the world.	Different cultures 'Cultural Geography'. Contrasts between countries.
MODERN FOREIGN LANGUAGES	Awareness of spirituality through the study of: culture, history, literature. Discussion of spiritual issues in target language.	Breaking down barriers/prejudices. Political, environmental, economic issues raise moral questions.	Communication. Team work, pair work, mixed sex groups. Self-confidence. Self-esteem. Opinions.	European Dimension. Study of: customs, values, attitudes, beliefs. Projects. Exchange visits.
RELIGIOUS EDUCATION	Reflection (personal/corporate). Ability to QUESTION.	Comparison of moral codes and development of one's own.	Respect. Tolerance.	Recognising contributions of World Religions to society development.
HISTORY	The whole experience of humanity. Philosophy – understanding philosophical debates. e.g. Reformation and Discovery of the Americas.	Being aware of debates and attempt to make judgements. Awareness of responsibility e.g. Holocaust.	Understanding how society works – media, political. Knowledge of different cultures/gender issues. e.g. 'Women'	Changes and development of expression in Art, Literature, Science. e.g. History of Islam – developing respect and understanding of different belief systems.

MUSIC	World Music. 'Passions', Masses, Oratorio, Requiem.	Works that are connected to moral issues e.g. war, characters.	Composition, Performing, Team Work, Appraisal, Extra Curricula, Communication, Social Events.	Different cultures recognised within Music Universal.
ART	Individual expression – in a visual language responding to reflection of yourself and the world.	Heightened awareness of the world around us. Discovering moral issues through the work of other artists e.g. propaganda, war, gender.	An alternative means of communication – in response to our society and time. Purpose of Art in society – religion, politics, etc.	Awareness of multi-cultural Art and issues. Own cultural identity. Aesthetic appreciation (Ofsted).
PHYSICAL EDUCATION	Positivity. Self Esteem/Confidence. Religious beliefs.	Adherence of rules/laws (consequences of actions!!). Consequences of actions. Growth of the self.	Teamwork — Co-oper-ation. Mixed Gender. Group Rules.	National Identity. Patriotism. Dance – different activities. Religious beliefs.
DESIGN TECHNOLOGY	Expression of inner thoughts/ideas/designs. Through the way an *individual* would react to a problem.	Quality of persons self, evaluation of ideas. Goodness of fit, does it really help someone. Effect of design on environment.	Designing to improve quality of life. Designing to improve communication between people. Considering wider impact of one product/design.	Understanding of how products cannot be designed for one particular ethnic group. Transfer of developed world technology to help those in third world (appropriate technology).
ENGLISH	Poetry – representation of beliefs, values and emotions. Development of imagination – creative writing.	Discussion stimulated by variety of texts. Topical issues in fiction/non-fiction.	Speaking and listening skills. Social interaction. Study of texts – empathy with character.	Multi-cultural texts. Cultural heritage. Language study – accent and dialect.

Peter: The Big Ideas

195

Use this case study to focus on your knowledge and experience of other subject areas. Make notes in your Professional Development Portfolio of lessons which you have observed or participated in, that were significant in terms of the spiritual, moral, social or cultural dimension.

One of my college tutors advised me that

To create excitement and fun you should often introduce the BIG IDEA, set a problem and then have the confidence to allow the pupils to solve the problem in their own ways. By managing the environment the enthusiasm of the pupils will not be compromised because they will own the task and the solution.

(Mathematics Subject Co-ordinator)

Another tutor advised us

It is always prudent to unpick lesson plans from apparently well structured work schemes with good resources, so that you can deliver a well paced lesson with enthusiasm and conviction. Teaching style is and must be a very personal matter.

(Science Subject Co-ordinator)

Personal philosophy on my approaches to science teaching

From personal experience and following a large number of observations during my PGCE year, I have formed the opinion that a large number of humanities teachers have a different approach to teaching their subject in both style and direction, when compared to science teachers.

Direction

In humanities, the introduction to a topic could be as broad as 'Let us consider the major causes for the second world war'. This immediately will produce images of some sort in the mind of any student by comparison with current affairs, because the effects of war produce emotions (Donaldson's human sense?). Subsequent lessons are then focused around this framework with the BIG IDEA holding the interest and with differentiation being provided through different levels of depth and breadth in specific areas.

In science, the introduction of a topic is very often at the level 'this term we are going to study electricity and magnetism'. This very seldom produces any emotion in many pupils except, in some cases, panic or lack of interest. On many occasions I have heard pupils say 'you have lost me there sir' in a science class, only to have the 'facts' repeated in a different way with the addendum 'It will all make sense when you do the practical'.

In humanities there is a 'Big Idea' to start with from which all the topics hang and this holds the thread of interest.

With science, all the topics can tend to lead up to a future understanding of the 'Big Picture', with the interest being held by hope of future enlightenment.

Style

In one geography lesson I was privileged to witness, the class lesson on Volcanoes involved the construction of a 2 metre replica of an active volcano and its substrata. The 'curriculum detail' was delivered to students during construction not only by the teacher but by other students *'No silly it can't go there because ...'*.

In a history lesson the curriculum content 'Mediaeval Life' was delivered through the construction of a mediaeval market in full detail with all the noise and hubbub.

With science it is easy to fall into the trap that the activity lesson is the practical. I feel that as science teachers we could often present our lessons differently.

Making a contribution

196

Work with two other people from different subject areas (possibly from the same school). Try to compare the relative contributions to the four strands of your subject and theirs.

Mark on a diagram like the one below where you would place your subject and the others. Try to agree on your placing of the 3 subjects. This may be difficult!

No Discernible Contribution		Major Contribution
	SPIRITUAL	
	MORAL	
	SOCIAL	
	CULTURAL	

Documentary evidence

197

Comparing the documentary evidence with practice is one of the purposes of an Ofsted inspection.

Look at the documentation you have for your school and identify ways in which the school indicates that it contributes to pupils' SMSC development. Does this happen in practice? Is it reflected in your observations and teaching experience?

Possible sources of documentary evidence

- Aims and objectives
- School development plan

- School policies
- School prospectus
- Staff handbook
- Schemes of work
- Pastoral care arrangements
- Links with the community

REFLECTION

Read the following passage from the 1994 Ofsted Framework for Inspection. What styles of teaching and learning have you used/observed/experienced that 'encourage an increasingly mature response to personal experience and social issues'?

198

A school exhibits high standards in these respects if its work is based upon clear principles and values expressed through its aims and evident in its practice. Pupils display a capacity for reflection, curiosity and a sense of awe and wonder, as well as an ability to discuss beliefs and to understand how they contribute to individual and group identity. Relationships will be open and consistent; pupils will be confident and treat each other with mutual respect. The planned curriculum and the school community will provide a range of opportunities for pupils to extend their personal experience and their social and cultural understanding. The content of the curriculum and the styles of teaching and learning will encourage an increasingly mature response to personal experience and social issues. The code of practice promoted and observed in the school will be based upon personal qualities founded on a moral code and effected through all that the school does. There will be positive links with industry and with the wider community.

Changes to the Framework for Inspection

It is unfortunate that some of this richness of language is lost from the latest Ofsted Framework for the Inspection of Schools (1995). Section 5.3, Pupils' spiritual, moral, social and cultural development, indicates that judgements should be based on the extent to which the school:

- provides its pupils with the knowledge and insight into values and beliefs and enables them to reflect on their experiences in a way which develops their spiritual awareness and self-knowledge;
- teaches the principles which distinguish right from wrong;
- encourages pupils to relate positively to others, take responsibility, participate fully in the community, and develop an understanding of citizenship; and
- teaches pupils to appreciate their own cultural traditions and the diversity and richness of other cultures.

Whilst the essence of earlier descriptions is there, what is lost is the sheer delight for us as teachers in reading in an official document on inspection that good practice is exemplified when 'pupils display a capacity for reflection, curiosity and a sense of awe and wonder'. Most teachers begin with a strong sense of mission and sometimes this idealism can be forgotten in a career that can be stressful and is always demanding. There is still a place for the teacher's own reflection, curiosity and awe and wonder. Here is an example from mathematics:

The spiral is a dynamic image; an image that moves and changes. On the computer screen it can be changed by using a pointer manipulated by the mouse. In this image the lines radiating from the central point have lengths 1, $\sqrt{2}$, $\sqrt{3}$, $\sqrt{4}$, $\sqrt{5}$ . . ., built up in a succession of right angled triangles. This infinite sequence could continue indefinitely with an infinite subset of irrational numbers within this sequence. This Pythagorean Spiral was drawn using a software package:

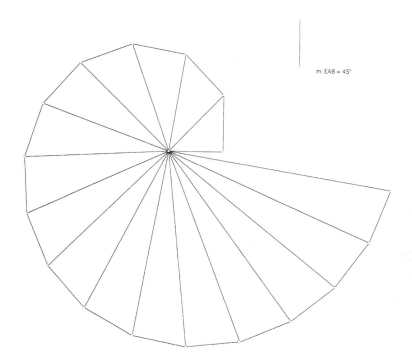

m EAB = 45°

There is the excitement here of creating a beautiful form with repeating and changing shapes. This spiral conjures up memories of natural forms, being similar to and yet different from a shell. To the mathematician within all of us, it illustrates the link between number and shape, between abstraction and reality, which is at the heart of mathematics.

SUMMARY

We have invited you to think of the many ways in which your subject can contribute to SMSC. Other areas of school life (for example the pastoral and tutoring systems) have a contribution to make as well (see Chapter 35).

Useful references

Donaldson, M. (1992) **Human Minds. An Exploration.** London: Penguin Books.

Ofsted (1994) **Framework for the Inspection of schools.** London: HMSO.

Ofsted (1995) **Framework for the Inspection of schools.** London: HMSO.

SCAA (1995) **'Spiritual and Moral Development of Young People' SCAA Discussion Papers No. 3.** London School Curriculum and Assessment Authority.

SCAA (1996) **'Education for adult life: the spiritual and moral development of young people' SCAA Discussion Papers No. 6.** London School Curriculum and Assessment Authority.

Lesson Planning and Preparation (3)

Sometimes you get the feeling they haven't worked out how the time is going to be spent. If they do plan it properly you feel more able to do your best. (John, Year 10)

LEARNING OUTCOMES

By the end of this chapter you will have considered ways of achieving continuity and progression in your lesson planning. You will meet examples of planning a sequence of lessons within the framework of the National Curriculum and you will consider the difficulties involved in delivering a spiral curriculum which has real progression.

Introduction

Here is evidence from the SCAA Document 'A Guide to the National Curriculum' (1996) page 9:

Planning

The programmes of study provide the basis for planning teaching, learning and assessment during each key stage and they set out the knowledge, understanding and skills that should be taught to pupils as their minimum statutory entitlement.

It is for schools to decide how and in what depth to teach the material contained in the programmes of study. No methodology is implied; it is a matter for teachers' professional judgement to decide the most effective and efficient way of teaching the National Curriculum.

Decisions on the depth of treatment of aspects of subjects are also for the professional judgement of teachers. Not all aspects of the programmes of study need to be taught in the same degree of depth or detail. It is also left to teachers to decide whether to include material from outside a programme of study in order to develop the school curriculum.

When teachers plan from the programme of study, they will need to consider:

- *ways in which different sections of the programme of study interrelate;*
- *what pupils were taught in the corresponding section of the programme of study at the previous key stage and what they will be taught in the next key stage;*
- *how to revisit some aspects of the programme of study to consolidate earlier work;*
- *how to ensure there are sufficient opportunities for differentiated work for pupils of all abilities.*

It is likely that teachers in primary schools will begin to plan using a whole school approach. In secondary schools, planning usually takes place within subject departments. In both primary and secondary schools, teachers will also formulate their individual plans. (SCAA/ACAC, 1996)

It is also necessary to add the following to the SCAA list:

● how to create a coherent sequence of topics
● provide ways to extend the topic beyond the confines of the National Curriculum

You will note from the above that individual departments have considerable freedom in planning their own schemes of work, even though they must make continual reference to the National Curriculum programmes of study. Continuity, progression, consolidation, differentiation and assessment must all be taken into account when planning schemes of work, and it is to these issues which we now turn our attention.

Lesson planning

199

The following is a case study which illustrates the processes involved in 'backward' planning a sequence of lessons in the topic area of 'house and home' in French. It was written by Jill Rundle, a mentor.

When I first started to teach I found no problem in planning and delivering individual lessons in isolation. My problem was that I didn't consider the links between one lesson and the next, nor did I really consider the lesson in relation to the whole topic. Therefore there was very little continuity or progression in my teaching.

As an experienced teacher I now plan 'backwards'. I look at the whole topic or sequence of lessons and ask myself 'what do I want the pupils to have done and learnt by the end of this topic – what will be the final outcome?' I also consider differentiation, i.e. whether the final outcome will be the same for all the pupils in the class. The answer is usually 'no' – there are some things which all pupils must achieve, others which most pupils should achieve and others which some pupils might achieve. (See the must, should, could grids in Chapter 20.) At this point I also consider how, what and when I should assess pupils' progress, and what measures I might take if progress is not as great as it should be. I am then able to plan a series of lessons which always have the 'end product' in mind so that the links and points of progression come naturally.

Case study: Yr 7 French: Ma Maison

End of topic/sequence outcomes (6–8 lessons)

A   Labelled section of exterior of house
B   Plan of inside of house with rooms labelled
C   Brief written description of outside and inside of house (in FL)
D   Tape in FL of description

What should pupils be able to do?

All

A, B, C, D
minimum for C and D

Ma maison est grande et moderne. Il y a trois chambres, une salle de bains, une cuisine et un salon.

Most

A, B, C, D
for C and D add:

La porte d'entrée est + colour/il y a un jardin, un garage + other rooms e.g.
entrée, débarras/au rez de chaussée/au premier étage

Some

A, B, C, D
as before

but for C:

write a letter, add some questions e.g. ta maison est grande? Tu as un
jardin? Il y a combien de chambres? and add a dialogue to D, using questions
above.

Minimum assessment points

<u>Listening</u> – identify houses of different appearances. Identify rooms.

<u>Speaking</u> – pronunciation of rooms, short talk about house.

<u>Reading</u> – identify pictures/plans of house from sample written descriptions.

<u>Writing</u> – spellings of room vocabulary. Short descriptions of outside/inside of
house.

I am now able to make an outline plan for my first lesson.

Lesson 1 (outline plan only)

Objectives:

1) different size/age of house and other features
2) set homework, introduce whole topic with pictures – FL

1) introduce different types of houses – adjectives of size/age and extra fea-
    tures (use magazine pictures/photos)

2) listening comp (tape) to identify individual houses from pictures

3) pupils repeat vocabulary

4) pupils work in pairs, describing pictures to each other using model
    Ma maison est . . . et . . .
    La porte d'entrée est . . .
    Il y a . . . (et . . .)
5) record vocabulary
6) homework. Using vocabulary – draw picture of own house, label features.
    Resources: tape recorder and tape; magazine pictures; flashcards of
    houses; homework sheet.

(The following lesson will revise vocabulary learnt so far and will move on to the
next stage, introducing rooms, etc.)

One difficulty which can occur in MFL (modern foreign languages) because of the special nature of language learning is that pupils will 'revisit' topics which they think they have 'done' before. Each time you 'revisit' a topic you will be using vocabulary already learnt, but also extending the use of language.

REFLECTION

200

Consider your own subject area in KS3 and KS4. Are there any topics which recur within or across the two key stages? How might you ensure that revisiting these topics does not result in too much repetition for your pupils, bearing in mind that you will almost certainly have to review basic work covered in the topic area before extending pupils' learning to the new material? Compare your subject with that of another trainee teacher in a different subject area, and also discuss these issues with your mentor.

Peter: an NQT

201

Now read the following case study written by Peter, a newly qualified teacher of science. Does your own subject lend itself to an approach such as this? You may need to refer to Chapter 36 on SMSC.

I am an NQT at a grant maintained secondary school with a non-selective intake policy. After being warmly welcomed in September and having filled my marking register with the names of all the year groups I was to teach, I advised my general mentor that my only priorities were

1) To deliver the syllabus
2) Be in the right place at the right time
3) Survive till Christmas.

By half term my stress level had reduced sufficiently for me to be able to take stock of where I was and the mistakes that I had made in the pace and content of my initial lessons. It left me feeling dissatisfied with my first attempt. Reviewing both the style and content of my lessons, I discovered that I had 'delivered' the National Curriculum and the topic in a very traditional manner.

Following a week in which I was lucky to have a very successful set of lessons where both pupils and teacher not only enjoyed the sessions but also produced a good learning outcome for the pupils (good end of topic results for all), I decided to restructure the style and content of my lessons.

I revised my own lesson sequences in three simple moves

1) Identify the 'big ideas' in electricity and magnetism.
2) Place these big ideas in a sensible sequence.
3) Photocopy the national curriculum requirements and the course module requirement. Cut up these documents into their separate topics, group them and paste these groups under their related big idea.

This produced from each big idea, a series of lessons for one term, which not only covered all the course and national curriculum requirements, but also had continuity and flow to suit me.

From this list (below) I identified the different styles I wished to use to present each lesson, with the abilities of the target audience in the front of my mind.

On this framework I was then able to hang the 'active learning' tasks (games) identified elsewhere in this text. These tasks were often hectic but very effective. 'GOT THAT NOW, SIR'

<u>Electricity and Magnetism</u>

A sequence of topics to cover both concept areas and national curriculum requirements.

1) BIG IDEA **Particle theory** with specific reference to 'free' electrons in metals. Pupil response: 'Stolen from Chemistry!!'

a) The model of induction and electricity as a flow of charge. <u>Approach; use electron game</u>

b) Basic electricity rules. Series and parallel circuits, components, effects of component changes. $V = I \times R$ <u>approach; electricity as water flow in a central heating system. Voltage as pressure current as volume of flow.</u> 'What is he on about?'

c) Electromagnets with reference to particle theory.

d) Transformer theory with reference to induction. <u>Approach; electron game</u> 'The man is mad'

e) Motors and generators. <u>Approach; practical. Relate back to induction theory.</u>

2) BIG IDEA **The National Grid**

a) Generation of electricity

b) Household electricity including wiring a plug, ring main and safety. <u>Approach; practical session</u> 'Thank heavens. Proper practicals.'

c) Paying for electricity (Units) Electrical safety <u>approach; classwork</u>

3) BIG IDEA **logic**

a) Logic gates and their uses. <u>Approach; classwork and practical</u> 'Thank heavens. Proper practicals.'

b) Problem solving with components <u>approach; classwork and practical</u>

c) Theory of input, process and output, relative to components and their operation. Examples LED, solenoid, relay, LDR, thermistor, transistor, diode etc.

4) Practical lessons to cover topics listed.

5) Questionnaires for elicitation; what is current understanding?

6) Test papers; for summative testing.

Using these approaches

202

Now take a topic in your own subject area. Try the 'backward planning' or the 'big idea' approach in order to plan a series of lessons within the topic. Pay particular attention to continuity and progression between lessons, and try to build in assessment from the beginning. Also consider whether the topic will be 'revisited' at a later stage and, if so, how you will make the link between revisiting what has already been covered and extending your pupils' learning.

SUMMARY

These two case studies reflect the duality of approach needed within lesson planning. There is a difference between global planning 'the big ideas' and detailed differentiated planning 'what should individuals/groups achieve at each stage'. Teachers need to be aware of these two aspects if their teaching is to be effective. Both global planning and detailed preparation need to be rooted, of course, in the relevant National Curriculum Programme of Study. Detailed planning without vision may be efficient but ultimately worthless. Vision without detail will become disorganised and disheartening for all parties. Teachers should use the three Ps of playing, planning and preparation. Playing is the free brainstorming stage (playing) of generating new approaches and identifying big ideas. It is as valuable as the more detailed stages of planning and preparation. This creating and shuffling of ideas can happen anywhere. You do not have to be sitting down with paper or word processor. At its best it can be lateral thinking as you seek alternative approaches to familiar topics.

Useful references

Capel, S., Leask, M. and Turner, T. (1995) **Learning to Teach in the Secondary School.** London: Routledge.

Cohen, L., Manion, L. and Morrison, K. (1996) **A Guide to Teaching Practice.** London: Routledge.

Pupils with Difficulties

Things fall apart, the centre cannot hold. Mere anarchy is loosed upon the world.

(W. B. Yeats)

LEARNING OUTCOMES

In this chapter you will be considering different types of behaviour problems and solutions: a child who challenges your authority will need different limits and rewards from a child who is attention-seeking or one who is lacking in motivation. You will find ideas here about understanding, planning and implementing a variety of interventions. In 'Listening for answers' you will also be introduced to 'brief therapy': a way of helping the pupil to plan and implement improvements. All these approaches can be linked to the Code of Practice.

Building bridges not walls

How do we feel about pupils who create major, recurrent, predictable management problems in our lessons? There are always a few who make us feel inadequate, unattractive and incompetent. There are two reasons for this: first, they behave in ways which cause us to malfunction as teachers, and secondly, they transmit to us, in subtle and often not so subtle ways, their own feelings of inadequacy and low self-esteem. It is in this situation that you say to yourself 'Why should you make an effort for this pupil, who makes life so difficult for me?'. At this point you should be thinking of ways to build bridges, not walls. You do not wish to become trapped in the self-fulfilling prophecy of allowing a pupil to control your lesson or permitting pupils to leave your lesson without learning something useful, life-enhancing or interesting. It is self-interest which motivates you partly, in the knowledge that most pupils can have the last word if they try hard enough. Your belief in the power of human nature to do good is tempered by the knowledge that hatred is corrosive: you will survive longer with this difficult class or difficult individual if you show respect, stay calm and endeavour to be consistent, assertive and positive.

In difficult situations it is easy to lose respect, feel uneasy and be inconsistent, reactive and negative.

Sophie

C

203

Sophie is a pain: *Acting out, disrupting the rest of the class, making it difficult for several of the teachers to provide a learning environment for the others.*

The minute she walks in to the lesson there is a different atmosphere than when she's away – which is very seldom – it's a lovely class. The pupils know I can't control her and they resent this. I resent it too. I don't seem to be able to control the situation – I find myself trying to ignore her completely when I'm trying to teach and she's chatting away and even worse openly doing the opposite of what I'm asking the class to do.

She seems to want to have the last word . . . and she often succeeds. The other day for instance, she said something really loudly when I was doing a question and answer session, without putting her hand up. I tried to be firm and said 'Sophie I want you to put your hand up and wait for me to give you permission to speak'.

She said: *'The others don't'.*

Me: *Well mostly they do.*

Sophie: *Yeah, like Jimmy, he always shouts out.*

Me: *When was that? I don't remember.*

Sophie: *All the time, like yesterday.*

Me: *Well, I will sort him out next time.*

Sophie: *I bet. Anyway, even if I put my hand up you never ask me to say my answer.*

Me: *That's ridiculous, I do.*

Sophie: *You didn't yesterday.*

Well by now I was really worn out and I told her she wasn't listening to me and she just smirked and I was really fed up. I can't think of anything good she's ever done in my lessons.

Writing a script

A

204

How can a situation like this be avoided? Write yourself a script, starting with a pupil you know who you have difficulties with, or Sophie.

Sophie: I can't do this thing and it's stupid anyway.
Me:

Now list 4 or 5 ground rules to avoid this situation happening:

Sophie is certainly attention-seeking. It would seem that her attention-seeking is a deliberate confrontation with discipline. She seeks to disrupt, unlike some attention-seeking pupils who appear to want and need a great deal more attention than they can have in a full class (of whom more later). A pupil like Sophie needs less attention and more clear limits.

Here is one way of achieving success with confrontational pupils who need very clear limits:

Improving behaviour

1 Decide which behaviour you want to change first, and what you want the pupil to do instead.

2 Discuss this with the pupil calmly and quietly, in terms of Point 1 above.

3 Explain what rewards the pupil will receive for behaving appropriately.

4 Explain what punishments the pupil will receive for behaving inappropriately.

5 Clarify the time scale. If there is little or no improvement after for example three lessons, the punishments will become more severe and will include involving senior staff and then parents.

The key to this approach is planning.

When does the problem occur?	What behaviours are taking place?	What specific, appropriate actions are needed?
1) Joe: Group work	Picks arguments with pupils in his group	Have a specific task within the group. Follow group rules. Respond to group leader. Respond well to group success.
2) Jenny: Working alone	Disturbs others. Takes too long to settle down to work	Stay in her place. Organise herself. Talk about work. Respond to quiet praise from teacher.

Behaviour plans

Now write a behaviour plan for a pupil you have had problems with. If there are many problems, choose one priority to start on.

205

When does the problem occur?	What behaviours are taking place?	What specific, appropriate actions are needed?

You may find it useful to consider different solutions for three types of problems:

1 Pupils like Sophie who experience behavioural difficulties because they seek to challenge your authority. They need very firm limits:

ignore them, reward others, deprive them of free time, isolate them, remove their audience, then use praise, in addition to the clear strategies of which the Sophie case study is an example.

2 **Pupils like Joseph (see IEP on page 339) who are attention-seeking because they genuinely want a lot more attention than they can have.** It may be necessary initially to consider giving such pupils a lot of attention. This can be done in the following ways:

- at the beginning of the lesson, when the group is assembling, a brief chat
- at the start of a piece of work, move quietly to that pupil and give support even before it is requested
- use senior staff to increase the amount of attention which can be given – praise for work, even given outside lessons
- gradually change your behaviour so that you give attention which is conditional upon a pre-arranged amount of work being done
- check your own responses: it is easy to say to attention-seeking pupils 'Not now, I'm busy'. This makes them even more desperate. Teach them to seek your support at certain times during the lesson.

3 **Pupils who have behaviour difficulties because they are lacking in motivation:**

For these pupils the following strategies are useful:

- make sure that you present yourself as a committed professional with standards and ideals and a love of the subject
- make sure that the pupil really can do the work – check for understanding, numeracy or literacy problems or difficulties with handwriting
- ensure that you give immediate, acceptable and appropriate praise for work done – even for small amounts
- discuss with the pupil some ways in which the work can be 'chunked' into small sections
- sometimes group work is useful, because of peer group pressure to complete the task
- consider involving others to support this pupil, for instance sixth formers
- discuss a sequence of short-term goals e.g. three small pieces of coursework could lead to a medium-term motivating goal such as time on a computer
- help the pupil to integrate his or her own interests into the work
- follow up homework with the form tutor's support

With all types of behaviour problems therefore, you would be wise to plan three stages of support, which may correspond to Stages 1, 2 and 3 of the Code of Practice (see Chapter 27). The intervention will differ, depending on the type of problem.

Stage 1

- Discuss your concerns with the pupil, balancing firm, consistent limits with positive support.
- Explain that you will review it after one or two weeks, and describe what you hope to achieve.
- Focus, with the pupil, on your concerns, explaining what the rewards and punishments will be, and that rewards will never be cancelled out by punishments, but that you will have to become more strict if the agreed improvements have not taken place.
- Concentrate on building a relationship of trust.

Stage 2

- Involvement of colleagues. If the situation does not improve, the pupil already knows that you will be seeking involvement of colleagues such as the form tutor and/or Head of Year.
- This may take many different forms: back-up support for removing the pupil; back-up for in-school 'suspension'; back-up for giving praise and counselling or development of an Individual Education Plan.

Stage 3

- Involvement of parents and colleagues (as above). This is an area in which you will probably not become actively involved as a trainee. It would be valuable to sit in on discussions between parents and colleagues if possible.
- At this stage the pupil's progress needs to be emphasised, so that positive developments can be built upon. It can be very difficult to find something good to say about a pupil, but this is vital if a relationship of trust is to be achieved between school and home. Honesty about the pupil's problems is also necessary. Establishing priorities, developing and maintaining effective communication, for example by regular telephone calls, will help to support the pupil.

Stage 1 and 2 action plans

206

Consider again the pupil for whom you drew a behaviour plan on page 335. Now decide whether that pupil is primarily attention-seeking or in need of limit-setting or in need of motivation. Write a Stage 1 and Stage 2 IEP for later discussion with your SENCO.

Individual Education Plan for behaviour improvement

The Code of Practice recommends using IEPs for behaviour problems as well as for learning difficulties. The Code of Practice considers that pastoral staff, such as Heads of Year, Heads of Section or form tutors, should work with SENCOs to share responsibility for establishing, monitoring and reviewing behavioural IEPs. This includes working with the pupil and with key staff and the parents to negotiate priorities and develop realistic, achievable goals.

Look at the two different IEPs presented below and on page 339.

INDIVIDUAL EDUCATIONAL PLAN

NAME OF PUPIL _____   DATE OF BIRTH _____

YEAR _____

DEFINITION OF DIFFICULTY

1.   Physical Handicap   Sensory Impairment
     Learning Difficulty   Emotional/Behavioural Difficulty

2.   Description of nature of difficulty

CLASS/SUBJECT TEACHER

STAGE	PLAN	Type of strategy required:			
Organisational	YES/NO	Motivational	YES/NO	Teaching	YES/NO
Material	YES/NO	Behavioural	YES/NO		

Brief description of strategy(ies) to be adopted, specifying programme:

Date strategy started   Signed

Position

Evaluation of strategy

Date of evaluation   Signed

Position

Parents informed   Discussed as far as possible with pupil

Need to advance to Stage   YES/NO

So far we have focused on individual behavioural difficulties: often you will find that it is necessary to rethink your behaviour management for the whole class. Here is some material from a training programme (Assertive Discipline) which will provide you with some interesting ideas.

You must bear in mind that the material which follows is designed to help you teach lessons and maintain good discipline: there may, however, be unfinished business which you will need to sort out with a pupil after the lesson or later in the day. Therefore these techniques will enable you to reduce the amount of time which can be wasted in a lesson – yet there will also be the need for you to acknowledge that a subsequent discussion with a pupil may be necessary.

INDIVIDUAL EDUCATION PLAN

STUDENT'S NAME: *Joseph* TUTOR GROUP: *9SR*

REFERRED BY: DATE: *14.10.96*

PARENT/CARER: TEL:

Nature of difficulties: *Joe disturbs lessons by shouting out inappropriately. He frequently comes to lessons without books and equipment. He becomes frustrated when faced with more demanding tasks and interferes with other children's work.*

Strengths: *Keen to please. Likes praise and lots of attention. Enjoys practical subjects, drawing and computer studies.*

Outside agencies involved:

Targets	Strategies
Help Joe focus on his own work. *Minimise disruptions to lessons.* *Future targets: to increase Joe's concentration span and improve work output.*	*Joe to carry a report card.* *Teacher to award ticks for appropriate behaviour.* *1 Enter classroom quietly* *2 Bring a pen* *3 Stay in seat* *4 Raise hand to speak* *Complete set of ticks rewarded by ½ hour on computer in study*
Roles and Responsibilities	**Time commitment**
Joe to present class teacher with report card at beginning of lesson. *Class teacher to record ticks and sign card.* *SEN assistant to supervise Joe in study.* *Joe's parents to countersign report card.*	*Initially 2 weeks*

Date commenced *16.10.* 1st Review date *30.10.*

Review arrangements:

Meeting with H.O.Y. and Mrs and Mrs _____ *14.11.*

Signed _____ Stage _____

Assertive Discipline

Assertive Discipline is an Australian training 'package', which is efficiently marketed and strongly behaviourist in flavour. It is based on the belief that rewards are the most powerful and morally acceptable form of motivating pupils to behave well and work well. There are many good ideas in Assertive Discipline, which you can develop, although it is designed for whole school implementation.

CRITERIA FOR RULE SETTING

1 Use a maximum of 5 rules, the number varying according to year level and teacher requirements.

2 Rules must be **clear** and **observable**. Be precise; define the behaviour.

3 Rules can be negotiated if a teacher so chooses. However, teachers need to feel comfortable with negotiation and avoid manipulative negotiation if they wish to negotiate rules. Both teacher and students must feel comfortable with the outcome. The program can be effective with either teacher–determined or negotiated rules. The teacher must retain the right of veto and the right to change rules.

4 Write rules in a positive way wherever possible: instead of 'Don't talk unless given permission', put 'Ask permission to speak by putting your hand up except in group discussion'.

5 Teach the rules to students with the same care given to a crucial academic issue. This applies even if the rules have been negotiated.

6 Head teacher/senior staff must agree to the rules or an acceptable alternative must be negotiated.

7 Parents are informed of the rules.

8 Have a visible display of rules. This can be a photocopied sheet in the front of the secondary student's file.

9 Rules apply throughout the whole of the school day.

10 If rules change, repeat steps 5 to 7. An effective discipline plan is dynamic and responsive to changing needs.

11 Rules must not violate a student's best interest, must facilitate the learning process and be developmentally appropriate, in other words achievable.

Examples of five good rules are as follows:

1 Follow instructions
2 Complete all your work
3 Ask permission if you need to leave the lesson
4 Work independently and do your best
5 Keep your hands, feet and possessions to yourself

Assertive Discipline Criteria

CRITERIA FOR NEGATIVE CONSEQUENCES/PUNISHMENTS

1 You must feel comfortable with the consequences. They must be effective and able to be applied consistently.
2 Consequences must be something students don't like but not psychologically or physically harmful. Demeaning, humiliating consequences or corporal punishment are not acceptable.
3 Consequences must be provided as a choice.
4 Reference to rules or consequences must be made in a matter of fact manner and voice.
5 The head teacher/senior staff must approve of the consequences or alternatives negotiated.
6 The parents must be informed of the consequences.
7 Students are informed of the hierarchy of consequences and the recording system.
8 Use a consequence a maximum of 3 times.
   Don't continue using something that is ineffective. Give the new system time (a week?) before deciding if the consequences are appropriate or not. If not, notify pupil and become tougher with that individual. If consequences change for a child, inform the parents and head teacher how and why.
9 Start afresh each day.
10 Consequences must be consistent with school policy.
11 Include a Severe Clause for major problems, such as calling senior staff immediately.

Praise and rewards

Punishments are only effective if applied consistently and confidently, and if balanced by rewards. We do not praise and reward pupils enough.

In order for your positive responses to be meaningful, they need to be:

1 Responses you are comfortable with (you may be comfortable praising a child, but not giving him sweets for appropriate behaviour)
2 Something the pupil wants and enjoys
3 Provided as soon as possible after the pupil chooses to behave appropriately (if you see the pupil working, *immediately* tell him you like it)
4 Provided as often as possible
5 Planned out before being utilised

Here are some examples:

- Praise notes or telephone calls to the pupil's parents.

- Awards (class certificates, which you or pupils can design).
- Special privileges
    games
    puzzles
    choosing group activity
    teaching younger children
    choosing friend to do activity with
    special projects
    monitor jobs
    time on computer
    time with equipment which is on restricted access
    work on hobby
    privileges agreed with parents

Remember that rewards are not always of intrinsic value: recently a trainee teacher used silver and gold pens to tick pupils' work and was able to reform a rebellious class by this means. How was she able to achieve this? It worked because she was able to communicate to them that she respected them and wanted good work. She also worked out rules for good behaviour and sensible punishments, and gave clear feedback about their work.

Successful rewards

Note down your own examples of successful rewards, continuing to develop your existing collection in your Professional Development Portfolio.

207

Listening for answers

There are many ways of helping pupils to resolve their learning and behaviour difficulties, and yet we are sometimes overcome by a feeling of hopelessness, doubting our own ability to make the difference. One of the reasons for this is that we find it difficult to balance the needs of the individual and the needs of the class. Many of the solutions which have been offered so far, have concentrated on the individual within the whole class for obvious reasons. There may be issues which remain unresolved for that pupil in spite of the fact that you, the teacher, may have managed a successful resolution to conflict within the lesson. You may not be able to work out what the problem is, and it would be valuable to consider the following ideas. Initially you may wish to have a senior colleague present. Under the Children Act you need to consider confidentiality issues and familiarise yourself with the school's policy on disclosures by pupils to staff. It is valuable to enlist the support of a colleague as co-worker – someone to bounce ideas off. An initial meeting with a pupil might lead to a weekly meeting for twenty minutes: you can achieve a lot even in a five minute meeting if you adopt the strategies described here.

With increased pressures on teachers over the last few years the time available for listening to what pupils have to say has gradually been eroded.

Consequently, the listening skills which all good teachers already possess may have been under-used. Research shows that two thirds of talk in the average classroom is teacher talk (Flanders, 1970) which leaves little opportunity for pupils to express themselves about their concerns.

But why should we revive our listening skills? In allowing pupils to talk we give them the opportunity to voice concerns over their work and to express emotional problems affecting their learning. If we encourage them to talk fully and openly we can gain greater insight into their problems and as a result make it easier to help them to talk their own way towards a solution.

Active listening

Active listening is one way in which we might encourage the child to express his/her feelings. It involves concentrating fully on the child, forgetting one's own experiences and opinions and giving him/her time to speak. In doing this we should acknowledge what the child is saying and try to reflect this back in order to check for meaning. There are many different levels of control when discussing a problem with a child, and active listening is the least intrusive and most child-centred approach.

Different degrees of support

The child's viewpoint

A	**Active listening:** teacher hopes to help child to be open.
C	**Mirroring:** teacher repeats back to child what the teacher thinks has been said a) to check meaning, b) to help child to reflect.
O	**Questioning:** teacher asks questions to find out more about
N	the problem.
T	**Joint problem solving:** teacher and pupil use information shared, as above, for seeking a realistic solution.
I	**Deciding what the problem is:** teacher may describe the problem.
N	**Looking at choices:** teacher offers different solutions.
U	**Recommending:** teacher makes one solution more 'right' than the others.
U	**Telling:** teacher tells pupil what to do.
M	**Teacher solves the problem:** by taking action on the pupil's behalf.

The teacher's viewpoint

If active listening techniques prove ineffective with a particular child, 'solution focused brief therapy' may offer another way forward. This method was developed by family therapist Steve De Shazer (1988) in the USA and basically involves listening to the 'client', finding out what it is that the 'client' wants and working with the 'client' towards achieving it. During the process issues may need to be covered which seem wholly unrelated to work and several meetings may be necessary. A realistic and achievable goal needs to be set at an early stage and the child must be helped to decide how to achieve the goal and predict what it might feel like to be there. 'Exception finding' (for example finding occasions when pupils who never do any work *do* achieve something and praising them for this) is part of the process. Discussion of the problem is minimised and solution-focused talk is employed with the teacher expressing a genuine belief that the child will change, measuring progression towards achieving the goal and giving useful positive feedback.

Unlike non-directive counselling, brief therapy is based upon the need for the adult to be quite dominant in highlighting events which are good for the child. A sequence of constructive problem-solving techniques will include the following four major areas:

- identifying the goal which is appropriate and achievable
- identifying exceptions to the usual pattern of problems
- measuring the child's progress towards achieving the goal
- giving useful and positive feedback.

1 Problem-free talk needs to be used at the start, to give the child a positive focus (perhaps a hobby).

2 Small steps of change can be traced – 'What have you done that is good for you since last time?'

3 Scaling can be used. 'On a scale of 0 (worst) to 10 (best)' – a stepladder image can be used for primary children – 'where do you think you are in terms of your schoolwork (behaviour) friendships, etc?' Most children are surprisingly realistic. If a child places himself on '4', discussion can focus on what he will need to do to reach '5' or even '4.5'! Small realistic steps of progress are powerful agents for change. De Shazer reverses the scale values – 10 (worst) to 0 (best) – 'to create a rolling down rather than a climbing up-hill feeling' (George *et al*, 1990).

4 The miracle question can be used: 'In the night a miracle takes place; you don't know that it has happened. When you wake up, what is the first thing that will happen which will tell you that everything is better again?' This can be upsetting for both child and teacher if the child describes an event which the teacher knows to be impossible – for instance father, who has left home, is miraculously there again at breakfast. Nevertheless, it can be used if we remember that children are better able to slip in and out of unreality than adults are. This example could be discussed and then replaced with a more realistic hope.

5 Near the end of a session a list of compliments emphasising strengths and successes (which has been compiled during discussion) can be read out to the child. This may seem artificial, but it represents a sincere and powerful device for making failing children feel better about themselves, and for emphasising the good changes which are already taking place.

The sequence of a session would characteristically follow this pattern:

- problem-free talk
- problem definition
- exception finding
- goal setting

- small steps of change
- short breaks for teacher to think
- compliments – which should in fact be used throughout the session
- the intervention: set the child a task which seems appropriate, realistic and likely to make things better.

Noisy Nora

Alison describes how she was asked to see a 15 year-old girl called Lucy, considered to be very bright and also considered by staff to be insolent and confrontational.

208

Lucy walked in to see me feeling stroppy. She wouldn't even look at me. She was so good at playing her role that I could feel myself bristling and going into teacherly 'I can get stroppy too' mode; just like the people in Goffman's 'The Presentation of Self in Everyday Life'. There was not going to be any problem free talk on this, our first, session.

So I told her, in broad terms, what I knew about her. She is the middle of three girls. Her older sister is anorexic. Her younger sister has a chronic and painful skin complaint. I commented that she, Lucy, looked fit and strong. She managed to agree, grudgingly, that this was true and I mused out loud about how odd it might be, to be the healthy middle one, and wondered what people's expectations of me might be. She managed to look at me now and I commented that her situation reminded me of Noisy Nora, a children's story in which Nora is the naughty middle one of three young mice. Lucy told me that Noisy Nora was in fact her favourite book! By now she had decided that she could talk to me and we found some exceptions to her bad behaviour: she spoke animatedly of certain staff whom she admired, and described herself as a model pupil in their lessons. We moved on to do some scaling of her behaviour in lessons which proved difficult for her. As so often with scaling, she was realistic, placing herself often at 2 or 3 out of 10. We then discussed, for each of three teachers, how she might move up to the next number – she knew the answers to her own problems, as Carl Rogers would have predicted.

| 0 | 1 | 2 | 3 | 4 | 5 | 6 | 7 | 8 | 9 | 10 |

In one case she needed to move away from a friend, in another case she needed to do the homework set between lessons and in the third she needed to accept that she must take the examination and should therefore focus properly, stop baiting the teacher and consider the lesson from his point of view as well as hers. These became her goals.

We met again the next week and Lucy had the scaling diagram with her, in her pocket. She was able to tell me of some improvements, but also confessed that she is completely unaffected by school punishment. Praise from me seemed well received, but she also spoke of other tensions such as going 'clubbing' with older pupils (she wanted to be with them but found it boring and sometimes frightening). I had to make the decision to bring her back into the realm of schoolwork and over the weeks she improved noticeably but not as much as I would have liked: it was frustrating to know that she was often not using her intelligence for educational purposes, rather that she enjoyed using her intellect for the Tom and Jerry game of teacher baiting. Moreover, Lucy's home problems were major and beyond other people's control.

Creative visualisation might have been helpful: creative visualisation is the conscious use of your creative imagination for active use in daily life: goal setting, problem solving and improving your quality of life. It can be used with any age group. In Lucy's case it might have been useful for helping her to change her belligerent attitude towards some teachers: she could perhaps visualise herself as the Incredible Hulk and try to control the impulse which turned her into the Hulk during lessons.

SUMMARY

In conclusion, it is clear that careful courage is needed if you wish to develop such techniques. It can complement approaches which are more appropriate for managing the whole class – and by listening carefully to one pupil you may also sometimes have insights which can be of benefit to the learning of the whole group. It is unusual to make a major breakthrough. Alison was lucky with Noisy Nora. Listening and making a little time are often good enough.

Useful references

Canter, L. and Canter, M. C. (1977) **Assertive Discipline.** London: Lee Canter Associates (0171 499 7789).

Davie, R. and Galloway, D. (ed.) (1996) **Listening to Children in Education.** London: David Fulton Publishers.

Day, J. (1994) **Creative Visualization with Children.** Shaftesbury, Dorset: Element.

De Shazer, S. (1988) **Clues: Investigating Solutions in Brief Therapy.** New York: Norton.

Goffman, I. (1959) **The Presentation of Self in Everyday Life.** London: Penguin.

Nelson-Jones, R. (1988) **Practical Counselling and Helping Skills.** London: Cassell.

Robertson, J. (1996) **Effective Classroom Control.** London: Hodder and Stoughton.

Scott-Baumann, A. (1996) 'Listen to the Child' in Jones, K. and Charlton, T. **Overcoming Learning and Behaviour Difficulties.** London: Routledge.

Shakti, G. (1978) **Creative Visualization.** Milton Keynes: New World Library. A workbook is also available.

Smith, C. J. and Laslett, R. (1993) **Effective Classroom Management: A Teacher's Guide.** London: Routledge.

Wells, G. (1976) **Noisy Nora.** London: William Collins.

Wheldall, K. and Merrett, F. (1989) **Effective Classroom Behaviour Management.** London: Paul Chapman Publishing.

Different Teaching and Learning Styles

If you expect me to teach the National Curriculum and differentiate then I can't do it. I'll teach to the middle, the rest will have to hang on. There's just no time to do it any differently. (Christine)

My worst lessons are those where I don't make time to differentiate. If I make time beforehand to work out who is going to do what at which point in the lesson then my stress levels go right down and there are more of them on task too. At the end of that lesson there's no twenty minute recrimination and I can actually concentrate on doing a bit more work because I'm happy. (Peter)

LEARNING OUTCOMES

This chapter will enable you to review and develop your knowledge and application of differentiation and assessment techniques, looking particularly at the following: differentiation by response, different ways in which pupils can present work and various kinds of active learning (with an activity for you!). You will also have looked at some of the issues surrounding classroom support and, finally, have had the opportunity to carry out a departmental audit of learning and teaching resources, and a review of learning support within your school.

Introduction

Tharp and Gallimore (1988) believe that teaching is fundamentally a problem solving activity involving constant hypothesis building and testing which is geared to establishing the learner's level. Being a good teacher involves assessing the child's current level of learning (Vygotsky and Wood), planning meaningful work (Donaldson), instructing and explaining the task thoroughly (Donaldson, Elliott, Wood, Bruner), asking appropriate questions (Wood), checking and scaffolding when required (Vygotsky), using alternative approaches to tap into creativity and hidden strengths (Gardner) and finally assessing again to make sure the task has been understood (Piaget).

Vygotsky's ideas are still inspirational yet can be impractical, because one-to-one teaching is the best way of providing the scaffolding which is an integral part of the zone or proximal development. A neo-Vygotskian trend has developed among researchers such as Tharp and Gallimore. They re-work Vygotsky's influential beliefs about the intrinsically social nature of learning, the ZPD and the value of language in developing thought. Often the practicalities of whole class teaching are taken into account in this more recent work. Reformulation of Vygotsky's ideas can lead to many useful outcomes in terms of different teaching and learning styles. Adey and Shayer (1994) developed an effective combination of Piaget and Vygotsky when planning and implementing a thinking skills programme based on Feuerstein's Instrumental Enrichment. Feuerstein's material is Piagetian in content: Adey and Shayer used Vygotskian types of collaborative discussion and whole class problem solving in order to teach this material. For detailed analyses of the changing ways in which Piaget and Vygotsky are interpreted, see Smith, Dockrell and Tomlinson (1997).

Sara Meadows (1993) looks at possible combinations of different teaching and learning styles in order to provide pupils with ways of scaffolding their own learning. She believes, for example, that traditional forms of rote learning do not merit the degree of criticism that Tharp and Gallimore (1988) bring to bear on them.

What is interesting here is the relationship between different ways of learning. Might it possibly be the case, for example, that an early history of good scaffolding so to speak, 'sets up' learners to become their own scaffolders, so that they can both take their rote learning and mechanical information processing 'beyond the information given', and act in a Piagetian mode as never ceasing equilibrators, continually seeking a deeper and broader and more flexible understanding of their worlds? (Meadows, 1993)

Beliefs about differentiation

209

Use the above text as a prompt to try the following activity.

This activity invites you to consider which types of teaching you believe to be most effective. In a group of three or four proceed as follows:

1 Rank these ten different teaching styles below according to how effective and valuable you believe them to be. Cluster them in groups (tie-ranking) if you wish, in other words you may consider two or three styles to be equally effective and valuable.

2 This process should be agreed as a group – you may discover some interesting differences in the ways in which you and your colleagues prioritise these items.

Alternatively, you can do the activity alone. Whether working as a group or alone, you will want to involve your mentor. You will find wide variation among teachers in their beliefs about different types of differentiation, and you may feel, for example, that Gardner's seven intelligence types can be applied in a wide variety of teaching contexts.

1 All children work at their own individual level on different assignments within a given topic (differentiation by task)

2 Teach to the middle; give the same materials (books, worksheets, assignments, questions) to all pupils

3 Divide the class into ability groups; set different work (within the same topic area) to each ability group

4 Teach to the middle as in (2) but give extension work to the most able. This could include use of Gardner's seven intelligence channels

5 Grade questions and assignments so that only the more able pupils get to the more demanding aspects of the topic

6 Set the same, very open assignments to all children which can be interpreted at different levels; differentiation by outcome rather than by task or process

7 Tasks selected by pupils themselves from a given range

8 Same assignment for all pupils, but in groups pupils help each other (taking account of Vygotsky's ZPD when grouping them)

9 Give the same book or set of worksheets to all pupils, but they work through them at different rates (differentiation by work rate)

10 Core and options. All pupils attempt some aspects of the topic unit and then have a range of differentiated choices (or guided choices): the 'must, should, could' sequence

Differentiation by response

The Vygotskian idea that thought is culturally determined is itself culturally determined and may not be more valid than any other idea regarding the sources of thought. How can we explain the existence of original thought and creativity if all thoughts are culturally determined? We must accept that all children are different and not all flourish as social constructivists (Turiel, 1989). This is particularly important when considering the ways in which we make a personal response – which we do constantly – to pupils' learning needs.

Teaching and learning styles can be varied by looking at the ways in which you develop differentiation by response: you respond constantly and often unconsciously to individual pupils' work – by a smile, a comment, a piece of advice. You are not always available to offer this support and assessment through teaching. Therefore we can look at aspects of differentiation by response which you can build into your planning.

Planning for assessment

210

The following seven strategies indicate how it is possible to make assessment an integral part of planning. Make notes over a half term period on the following areas:

1 **making course objectives accessible:** for example discussing with pupils the National Curriculum levels, the content of the Programmes of Study and the connection between these two. Another technique is to develop a departmental resource of study guides. These can contain student targets which make explicit the learning objectives of the topic, the way in which the work will be assessed, the resources required, the actual tasks to be undertaken and any hints about how to work through the material. It may be possible to involve the pupils retrospectively in producing study guides for other classes. This, in itself, is a valuable learning approach.

2 **making assessment criteria explicit:** for example inviting pupils to decide which National Curriculum levels they believe they have achieved. This is difficult even for teachers and they need to understand that there may not be an identical pathway through the levels.

3 **creating a system of response partners:** for example setting up a climate of trust in which pupils can discuss their work with each other

because they have the objectives and the assessment criteria made available to them. Articulating their beliefs to a peer often helps a pupil to move on to a higher learning level.

4 **providing learning logs:** for example developing habits in a class which will lead them to keep an informal diary of progress towards the end of each lesson. Such material can also help the teacher to plan future directions.

5 **small group tutoring:** for example lesson management structures which enable you to concentrate five or ten minutes of uninterrupted tutoring time on each small group in rotation. Self-discipline is required on the part of the teacher and the pupils because individual performance when measured against assessment criteria can lead to very detailed comparisons. You will need to evolve shortcuts which nevertheless allow you to give some detailed support to each group member. This could be done at half termly intervals and they could be instructed to bring their planning notes with them. (Look at the section later in the chapter on Use of Learning Support.)

6 **Individual Education Plans:** for example those recommended within the structure of the Code of Practice. From Stage Two onwards the IEP should involve the pupil and periodically the parents in active participation. Deciding upon a focus, monitoring and reviewing progress are difficult and time-consuming, yet this is a valuable way of making it possible for the child to be actively involved. (See Chapter 27 on the Code of Practice.)

7 **ensuring that response reflects what the pupil has achieved:** in this context it is important to have an accurate understanding of the pupil's actual past achievement, rather than measuring the pupil's attainments against your ideal piece of work. The ideal can be discussed, but always within the context of actual performance at present. Pupils have a high regard for teachers who are able to make time to provide individual appropriate feedback.

Presentation of work

Teaching and learning styles should be very flexible and take account of the fact that there may be major discrepancies between the way pupils think about your teaching and the way they record the work. You may have pupils who are able to do the work yet cannot write it to the high level of their understanding. Therefore presentation of pupils' work is a major issue.

Approaches to presentation

Pupils can present the results of their work in a variety of ways to show their own achievements. Among these can be the following. Develop your own proforma to help you to keep a record of different approaches you have used with pupils. Add your own.

● oral explanation to the teacher – discussion
● a taped oral presentation

- making use of IT, using W/P and DTP
- using flow diagrams
- making posters
- using a scribe where a pupil is unable to write
- producing leaflets or news sheets
- basic written presentation
- use of role play/simulation
- production of an artefact
- using IT to produce graphs and diagrams

Active Learning

Active Learning is a way of teaching pupils to take control of their own learning. You can develop their understanding of ideas, concepts, phenomena and processes (including rote learning, which can be very valuable!) by varying the ways in which they interact with the learning material: they may be reading, writing, listening and talking. They may also be working with different types of equipment and materials, for instance painting, computing or making collections of artefacts.

Latin fun

Consider Dr Virginia Webb's approach to enlivening a so-called 'dead language'. Look for examples of various types of presentations of pupil participation.

212

First of all choose a User Friendly Course e.g. the Cambridge Latin Course which uses the Direct Method theory, prevalent in the 1960s, and adds in various degrees of Theory and Grammar as desired by the teacher.

This excellent course also contains charmingly titled ParaLinguistic Material, in other words non-linguistic material which is background information on the Roman world and way of life. This is tied in with the theme of each stage, and can be used as the source for extra activities like posters, cartoons, empathetic writing, or plain old-fashioned knowledge.

Teaching the Use of the Dative *– this is introduced in the Stage which features Quintus, the son of the family who live in Pompeii, going to the baths on his birthday. Of course the Dative, which is introduced in its simplest form, the indirect object i.e. giving **to** someone, is easy to **demonstrate**. Volunteers or a volunteer called for, pretend Roman coins all ready – old English pennies will do perfectly – and a Role Play can be used, with **Quintus** handing his money **to** the slave to gain entry to the baths. Then get class, in pairs, to do the same, and to identify **who** is going to be in the **dative**.*

Teaching the use of the Accusative. *Initially use simple **English** sentences, on the theme of 'I fed my **hamster**' 'I hit my **sister**' then change to 'My sister hit **me**'. Even better 'My brother kicked **me**' 'I kicked **him**'. Now look at the range of simple sentences on this pattern in the Stage, and write a whole series of examples on the board. Explain the significance of the **-um**, **-am** and **-em** endings. Class copy them out and translate. Then tell them to **reverse** them e.g. Caecilius Metellam salutat. Change this to **Metella Caecilium salutat**.*

(Watch out for the mistake of giving them sentences which don't reverse!)

Active Learning methods

Look at the following list of examples of active learning methods. Make your own proforma and modify the list in the light of your own experiences. If possible then select 3 to 5 of them and describe to a colleague in the same subject specialism how you would use them and how you would assess them.

Active Learning methods

People centred

- Teacher demonstration
- Pupil demonstration
- Formal presentations to peers
- Drama
- Role play
- Interviewing
- Games
- Group problem solving
- Case studies
- Fieldwork
- Debating
- Experimentation
- Small group discussion
- Surveys
- Visits
- DARTs (Directed Activities Related to Texts)

IT centred

- CD ROM
- Developing multimedia presentations
  e.g. using an authoring programme like Hyperstudio
- Computer Assisted Learning (CAL)

Individual centred

- Individual problem solving
- Creative writing
- Case studies
- Experimentation
- Writing reports
- Learning logs
- Diaries

List adapted from Capel, Leask and Turner (1995)

The term 'Active Learning' can also refer to an approach to teaching/learning which actively involves the students in creating a physical model of a concept or idea as well as creating the abstract thought. This strategy is useful in reinforcing an idea already tenuously held, but invaluable when trying to superimpose a more accurate model where a less accurate one has already been accepted. Students are encouraged to 'show' their own model and test it against the new model which is created in the lesson.

Making electricity simple

214

Peter provides an example of active learning which exemplifies good practice. To obtain maximum benefit this should be tried first with a group of friends and other trainees.

The following example lends itself particularly well to providing an alternative framework for teaching of the following twin concepts (see Driver in Chapter 26 page 230).

1) that electricity is a flow of charged particles (electrons) and 2) energy is never 'used up' but always *transferred*

and addresses a number of misconceptions in this area across both Key Stages 3 and 4.

The classic approach for teaching flow of electricity and transfer of energy usually involves a simple schematic of an electric circuit, as shown below.

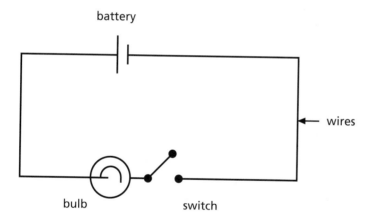

The pupils are then invited to construct the circuit, and observe the changing strength of the light from the lamp as the voltage is changed. Teachers then propose that the electricity is 'a flow of charged particles, electrons'. As we move through the key stage we produce different circuits and once again ask the pupils to observe the phenomenon and investigate the factors which affect the strength of this phenomenon.

We nearly always assume that the basic model that they have in their mind is similar to the one the teacher has and, more importantly, accurate enough to act as a foundation for further additions and complications encountered through the key stages.

This in my experience is a dangerous assumption to make; if the foundation model is inaccurate further modification will be difficult for the pupil. In many cases the pupil will actively resist having to 'alter' the existing model or, heaven forbid, change it completely.

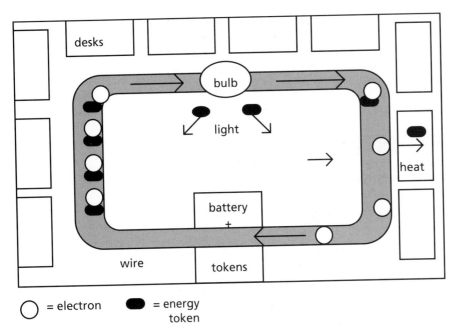

One way of ensuring that a single model is considered in this instance, is to create a class size model using the pupils as active working 'parts' and observers.

The class room furniture is rearranged as shown above so that there is an area marked battery, an area marked bulb and the shaded area represents a pathway (wire) about 1 metre wide along which the pupils (representing the movement of electrons) can flow.

Place a number of pupils (about 12) at the start – in the battery area. Each pupil is told that they represent an electron and that they must pretend that they are tiny, about the size of a wasp. All pupils face the same way in a clockwise direction representing 'free' electrons in the wire. All the other pupils act as spectators and umpires to see fair play, and may have their turn in another round.

As the battery 'pushes' each electron into the circuit, it provides them with 'energy' (this can be represented by a paper token with the word energy written on it). If these tiny electrons meet a 'resistance' (like having to go through a thin wire in the bulb) they may have to pass on a lot or all of their energy to the resistance as they squeeze through.

In this circuit these electrons always have enough energy to get back to the battery, pick up more energy and have another go.

One pupil stands in the circuit to act as a bulb (a resistor). The light bulb is a resistance and collects the tokens and gets very hot and excited. The bulb can only hold so much excitement and as more tokens arrive it screws up all the tokens (turning them into light particles). If these tokens are white paper the pupil representing the bulb who is hurling them all around the room will be throwing out 'white' light, thus transferring energy.

In all the excitement the bulb may not collect all the tokens and some electrons pass by still carrying all their energy but have to give up their energy as heat as they move along the wire. They all have sufficient energy in this example to return to the battery to be given more energy and enough push to complete another circuit.

If one starts with 12 students as electrons and 100 tokens as available energy it is easy to show:

i) that none of the electrons (pupils) disappear
ii) that even though all the tokens may be gone from the battery (it is now flat) *all* the energy has been transferred to heat and light and still exists even though its usefulness has gone.

At the other end of the scale for Key Stage 4 this 'circuit' activity can be adjusted to show other effects of electricity flowing, as in induction and transformer theory. Whatever the level, such an active lesson would benefit from additional adult support. This would improve differentiation.

Organising support for learning

We usually don't analyse the learning context: it's hard to capture because it is constantly changing, multifaceted and impossible to see in its totality. Development of lesson-support workers has evolved and been hailed as a 'good thing' but the team work aspect has not been looked at. As Thomas (1992) states: 'Good teams are more than the sum of their parts, but most teams are unfortunately not good'.

Thomas believes that there has been little planning over the last fifteen years for the increasing numbers of adults in classrooms. They include: educational assistants who may be supporting pupils with statements of special educational needs; peripatetic teachers who may be supporting pupils in class and seek to guide the teacher too; parents who may be giving free help in many different ways. Teachers often develop a close and deeply personal relationship with their classes and these visitors may seem intrusive and difficult to communicate with, in terms of joint planning. Indeed, many class teachers in this situation may deny that they are part of a team and distance themselves from their possible role as a team member (as in Goffman's 'Role Distancing', 1961).

After years of research in this area Thomas asserts that we must develop team thinking in order to provide a cohesive and effective education for our children. His research shows that we attribute roles in terms of either status or definition. Definitional roles are more workable than status roles – a teacher's 'status' may not be the key to making the lesson work at a highly differentiated level. It is the teacher's 'defined role' which is more relevant. In other words the job which is carried out in the lesson is the most important factor for the team, although status may help along the way. For example, the class teacher could negotiate with the support teacher to reverse roles – the support teacher takes the class and the class teacher circulates and/or works with small groups. Even if the support teacher is 'tied' to a statemented pupil, this approach is viable and ethical at least once a half term. Do not forget that the statemented pupil's needs are not always best met by one-to-one support.

Support as differentiation

215

Now analyse the advisory role of the 'Learning Manager' in the following case studies. They have been produced by Irene Hunt. There are two parts to this task:

1 They will form a valuable resource upon which to base discussion with your SENCO. Use these case studies to compare and contrast the provision made for these three pupils, with provision made in your school. N.B. Each school makes different use of its limited resources for SEN. For this work refer back to Irene's school case study in Chapter 1 and look at Chapter 27 on the Code of Practice.

2 Use these two case studies to consider how you could use some of the teaching and learning techniques outlined in this chapter, to support these two pupils.

Please remember that you need to document your thought processes and your findings in order to derive maximum benefit from these tasks.

Stage 1 Code of Practice

Emily is a Y7 pupil. When she transferred to Secondary school there were no indications that she would have any difficulties. She had enjoyed Primary school and coped reasonably well, although she had not been a high achiever. Her standard reading quotient was 90 (NFER 6 12) maths 87 (NFER) and non-verbal quotient 89 (NFER, DH) (100 is considered to be 'average').

Within a few weeks of facing a secondary curriculum she became withdrawn in some lessons and rather boisterous in others. Classwork was poorly presented and homework rarely completed. Subject specialists in Science, Maths, History and Geography added Emily's name to their SEN register at Stage One.

At the first progress check, Emily's tutor reported an uneven range of comments in practical and creative subjects Emily was improving, whereas subjects demanding high levels of reading and writing skills told a different story.

The Learning Manager for Y7 discussed Emily's progress with her. In Science she had more or less given up. In history there were some positive signs because a support assistant was available, to work primarily with another pupil, but Emily had benefited from some additional teaching.

Details for the second progress check (after nearly a term at the Secondary school) were discussed with parents. A decision to move to Stage 2 of the register was suggested, following assessment of Emily's needs by the SENCO.

It was obvious that Emily was struggling with higher order reading skills even though she had a good sight vocabulary and was conversant with phonics and wordbuilding. No support was directly targeted on Emily, but support staff were alerted to watch out for difficulties if they were in her lessons. At this time, no definitive programme has been arranged, but the skill areas Emily needs will be addressed through the Y7 Tutor programme next term. More formal involvement of the SEN team will be decided after the next progress check. Emily is likely to be a pupil with a transitory need rather than long-term special educational needs.

Stage 3 Code of Practice

Aarti is a Y9 pupil. In the primary school she had a statement because her language development was slow and overall progress fell within the slow-learner category. The Annual Review in Y6 indicated significant progress in basic skills and the LEA ceased to maintain the statement. Following LEA guidelines, the school put Aarti on the SEN regis-ter at Stage 3 in order to monitor her progress and regularly review provision. In Y7 Aarti worked in a small withdrawal group in English. The SEN teacher modified pro-grammes of study to allow learning from a Key Stage 2 programme in terms of literacy and language awareness. At the end of Year 7 Aarti had made some progress, but her reading age remained three years below her chronological age. Aarti continued with her modified English curriculum during Year 8, expanded to include a greater emphasis on reading for pleasure and to access the wider curriculum rather than on basic skills. Now at the start of Year 9 she has a reading age of about 10 years.

There is no extraction from other curriculum areas but Aarti received extra support in Science, Design and Technology, Maths, French and Humanities. Although written work remained at a low level, Aarti was able to access a full curriculum through this support. Her IEP in Year 9 concentrated on reading development with a target to improve spelling and handwriting by the end of Key Stage 3. Her tutor is of importance in moni-toring this plan and takes advice from the SENCO on each step needed. There have also been problems of poor behaviour, especially abusive language and aggression towards others. The EBD support worker sees Aarti individually for some counselling and report-ing back each day. She is 'on report' so that behaviour is monitored. Her reward is a let-ter home if she meets her targets for good behaviour. The Year Learning Manager works closely with the EBD worker to ensure consistency. It is likely that Aarti will be allowed a reader for her KS3 SATs, but it is hoped that by then her skills will make her more independent so that she will be able to benefit from KS4 study and achieve some qualifications.

Departmental audit

Use the following 2 forms on pages 358 and 359 for developing your own proforma to look at differentiation resources within a department.

216

School review

Using the key points from Ray's paper on learning support in Chapter 1 and Gary Thomas' list of recommendations on page 359, evaluate the effectiveness of provision in a particular school. You will need to develop five questions for a semi-structured interview of the SENCO and/or a Head of Faculty. You may wish to develop a questionnaire (brief! no more than ten questions) for pupils. Remember to use Chapter 31 and its reference list to guide you.

217

Different teaching and learning styles: Self Evaluation Sheet
PARENT SCHOOL

School _____ Dept _____ Evaluation Topic Differentiation

HOD _____ SM _____ Aims of Evaluation To review the use and availability of resources which support different teaching and learning styles

Evaluation Questions	Information Sources to be considered	Collection Methods for 'Learning School' assignment	Findings: with details
Is there a range of printed resource material for a variety of reading ages. Is there non-print material?	Resource base stores LS Department HOD SM	Stock check Reading age analysis	
Is IT easily accessible? e.g. how many machines? Are pupils allowed on them? etc.	Teachers in IT Department	Interviews Questionnaires	
Is a range of useful software available? e.g.	Resource base Teachers	Stock check Interviews	
Is there a range of subject specific software for all pupils? If yes, what	Resource bases	Stock check Classroom observation	
Are there enough subject specific texts for all pupils?	Resource base	Stock check Interviews	
Is there sufficient subject specific equipment for all classes?	Technician	Interviews Questionnaires	
Are different teaching techniques discussed with the department?	Colleagues	Learning log, kept by trainee	
Are different learning techniques discussed with the department?	Colleagues	Learning log, kept by trainee	
Identify gaps in resourcing	HOD Teachers	Interviews Questionnaires	
Identify problems of accessibility	HOD Teachers	Interviews	
Others e.g. marking and assessment criteria			

Different teaching and learning styles: Self Evaluation Sheet
TWIN SCHOOL

School _____   Dept _____   Evaluation Topic   Differentiation

HOD _____   SM _____   Aims of Evaluation   The use of support

Project   materials and personnel
in the department

Evaluation Questions	Information Sources	Collection Methods	Findings
Where does the department need more help from the support teachers?	HOD Staff	Interview Questionnaire	
Where does the department receive help from support teachers?	HOD Timetables Staff	Interview Document search	
Is a member of the department responsible for differentiation?	HOD Staff Resource base	Interviews	
Are support materials available to supplement basic texts and work sheets?	HOD Staff Resource base	Observation Stock check	
Have extension materials been prepared? Is Inset needed to support teachers?	HOD Staff HOD Staff	Document search Interviews Observation Interview	

Gary Thomas' recommendations

1 The shared classroom should be seen in the context of developments which are worthwhile and worthy of promotion by the school. The formulation of whole-school policies on parental involvement, community participation and special educational needs will be beneficial, if the whole-school community, including ancillaries, visiting teachers and parents, is genuinely involved in the process of developing such policies.

2 Opportunity should exist from the outset for discussion about the pedagogic, professional and affective concerns and expectations of team members. Tension that arises out of a mismatch between participants' concerns and expectations appears to be at the root of *team defences* which inhibit teams' effective working.

3 Teamwork stresses are likely to be handled more successfully through clear task and role definition than through strenuous attempts to resolve mismatches through improved communication among participants. Strategies directing attention to the task are more likely to meet with success than those directing attention to the participants.

4 Planning for teaming will ideally be a joint exercise involving all classroom participants. People need to be able to discuss the roles they will be fulfilling and whether they would feel comfortable undertaking a particular set of tasks. The opportunity of exchanging and interchanging roles needs to be discussed.

5 Individuals' strengths and weaknesses need to be identified during planning.

6 Clear definition of classroom tasks and activities needs to be made during planning.

7 The composition of the team needs to be considered carefully. On the basis of this research there are grounds for believing that heterogeneous teams will experience fewer stresses than homogeneous teams.

8 The team needs to meet regularly to discuss and evaluate the way that they have been working. The openness of a 'quality circle' (see Chapter 2 in Thomas, 1992) has to be the hallmark of such meetings; the atmosphere should be informal with individuals encouraged to suggest ideas.

SUMMARY

We have looked here at different teaching and learning styles, for developing pupils' strengths and meeting their needs. Meadows (1993) questions whether schools can ever be successful, if neo-Vygotskian 'scaffolding' is indeed the best way to learn – it is such a labour-intensive form of teaching and learning that it seems often to be incompatible with whole-class teaching. Yet many schools are very successful, as she also points out. Some provision can be made for individuals with whole-class teaching, and learning support through judicious use of the approaches discussed here, and others which you will develop yourself. These different ways of learning may, to an extent, be internalised as a way of solving learning problems, enabling the learner to become independent at least some of the time. Moreover, all pupils have special educational needs and provision should be accessible to all by differentiation within your lessons, your department and your school.

Useful references

Film Education, 41–42 Berners Street, London, W1P 3AA (0171 637 9932/9935).

Goffman, I. (1961) **Asylums.** Harmondsworth: Penguin.

Meadows, S. (1993) **The Child as Thinker.** London: Routledge.

Smith, L., Dockrell, J. and Tomlinson, P. (eds) (1997) **Piaget, Vygotsky and Beyond.** London: Routledge.

Tharp, R. G. and Gallimore, R. (1988) **Rousing Minds to Life: Teaching, Learning and Schooling in Social Context.** Cambridge: Cambridge University Press.

Thomas, G. (1992) **Effective Classroom Teamwork.** London: Routledge.

Turiel, E. (1989) 'Social Constructionism as a Social Construction?' in Damon, W. (ed.) **Child Development Today and Tomorrow.** London: Jossey Bass.

Evaluation and Reflection (3)

And my mind observed to me,
Or I to it, how ordinary
Extraordinary things are or

How extraordinary ordinary
Things are, like the nature of the mind
And the process of observing.   ('An Ordinary Day' by Norman MacCaig)

LEARNING OUTCOMES

By the end of this chapter you should be aware of how you can recognise and develop your existing skills and strengths as a teacher and continue to work on areas where you feel less secure. You should feel confident of your ability to take charge of your classroom or teaching area, however you will be aware of the need to set challenges for yourself in consultation with your mentor. You should have thought about how you will use the support available to you as a newly qualified teacher. You will have begun to work on setting targets for yourself as you prepare to start your first job as a fully qualified teacher.

Challenge for the trainee and the mentor

Towards the end of any school-based course there is a danger of 'plateauing' – of the trainee performing competently enough but not extending their teaching into new areas of challenge. There can be a comparable difficulty for the mentor in relaxing with the feeling that the task of mentoring is complete with the achievement of passing competence.

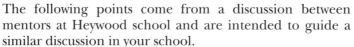

Providing challenge

The following points come from a discussion between mentors at Heywood school and are intended to guide a similar discussion in your school.

218

- It is recognised nationally that there is a risk that training is good at supporting trainees, partially successful at providing them with vision, but not as successful at challenging them and moving them on beyond the plateau of competence they reach in the last part of the year.

- Sometimes we tend to provide trainees with high levels of support whilst only offering low level challenge, with the result that we may just turn out 'safe' teachers – Mr and Ms Average. We should be taking trainees into the area of high challenge and high support which can then lead to real growth in the student.

- The trainee should always be involved in their process of challenge. We should facilitate a situation in which trainees set their own targets in agreement with their mentor.

- Challenge might be present within the school culture itself e.g. certain pupils/groupings provide the challenge. However, challenge should not just be seen as 'more of the same'. It is important that the trainee experiences success, that this is witnessed by the trainers, and also that pupils get something out of the process.

- We should be explicit in setting challenges for the trainee, and ensure that trainees are aware at the planning stage that this is one of the aims. The trainee must feel secure and have the confidence to try different methods, styles and strategies. When they become NQTs it is hoped that they will take this culture of challenge to their new school.

- If the mentor and the trainee are able to teach parallel groups using similar resources and approaches, much can be gained by comparing experiences. This is as valuable at the end of a course as it can be earlier on.

- The mentor can allow the trainee to be more adventurous by taking on the role of a helper/technician and thereby freeing the trainee to concentrate on more advanced teaching techniques or learning strategies.

- Returning to team teaching used at the start of the PGCE year, both the mentor and the trainee can identify areas in which the teaching and learning process can be moved to a higher level.

At the end of this discussion John Matthews, a training manager, suggests that he will provide a list of 'challenges' and the subject mentors can add to this list for the next meeting.

Later that year the school mentors talked to the course leader about their role. It was clear that the notion of challenge had become an essential part of their dealings with the trainees. What was interesting was they recognised that the same need to go beyond competence applied to their own work as well. In taking on a wider responsibility by being mentors they had developed competences themselves. This was recognised by the management of the school who used the mentors' observation skills in the interviewing process for new appointments.

REFLECTION

219

During your training year you have been encouraged to evaluate your teaching and to use evaluation as a tool to develop your skills, setting yourself specific targets as you move on in your course. At the end of your training you should be able to identify the positive aspects of your skills as a teacher, while setting targets that you wish to achieve during your first year as a teacher. You will probably have documentation available to assist you in this process, but you may find that the work suggested in this section is of practical assistance to you in building up a clear profile.

Before reading any further, think about what qualities you would rate as your major strengths as a teacher. These may be aspects of your personality or skills, or approaches to work in the classroom where you feel confident of your own ability. **Jot down two or three aspects of your teaching where you feel you have achieved some success and satisfaction.**

Do you think these are the same qualities that you would have identified at the start of the course?

Now try to identify an area in your teaching where you still wish to improve your skills. Which ways of improvement will be available to you as a newly qualified teacher? If you are not sure, by the end of this section you should have some ideas about how you can continue to be a reflective practitioner, with the assistance of fellow professionals.

Mark

220

Mark is in his final school placement towards the end of his training year. He is asked by his subject mentor to complete a self-appraisal form as preparation for a discussion that aims to evaluate his progress over the year. Mark's mentor agrees with Mark that he should feel confident about his ability to teach the normal range of games and sports. Mark is satisfied about his approach to gymnastics but has limited expertise in this area. His mentor feels he is coping with his gaps in knowledge, but that he should now extend significantly his teaching of gymnastics. In short Mark needs to be challenged and to set himself challenges. The mentor suggests that Mark should observe two or three gymnastics lessons before jointly planning a scheme of work. In this area of his teaching Mark needs to re-focus on what is important, to begin the process of learning to teach by observing, co-planning and co-evaluating. In other words, in order to reach a higher level Mark has to begin again, using learning approaches from the beginning of his course.

As you complete a year in training, you will find that challenge can be welcomed rather than feared. The discussion between Mark and his mentor above indicates that individual targets provide the opportunity to extend and broaden your skills. This process will happen at an accelerated pace during the next academic year when you will be an NQT.

Personal development

221

1 Explore your areas of success and satisfaction, identified at an earlier stage in reading this chapter, in more detail. Try a spider chart or 'mind map' to assist you in this.

Take your notes to a discussion with your subject mentor, perhaps when you are working together on the production of a career entry document, which outlines your competences and strengths as you complete your training and begin teaching.

2 Now look at the area (or areas) where you are aware of a need to continue to develop. Plan how you might go about this and discuss the plans with your subject mentor to ensure high level of support and high level of challenge. Produce a planning document that you can use to help you carry out this procedure in the future as you become aware of other areas that need further development.

Provision of NQT Support

222

Sylvia Odell's case study which follows, indicates the ways in which one school has responded to the need for provision of NQT support. As you work through this material you will be invited to apply it to your own professional development.

Starting any new job is one of life's major causes of stress. Newly qualified teachers need help in adjusting to their new professional role and the organisation of their school. Without a careful induction process the NQT can easily become disillusioned when the reality of the immense range of tasks involved in being a teacher becomes far greater than their expectations.

The success of a school is dependent to a large extent on the quality of the teaching and learning process experienced by pupils. A school needs high quality teachers who are both committed and well motivated. Teachers are a school's most important and most expensive resource, if they are good then so is the school. Schools are committed to induction, they have a vested interest in the development of NQTs not only as new entrants to the profession but also in ensuring that their pupils have access to the best education available. Induction is an initiation process into both the culture of the school and the culture of the profession.

The effective induction of NQTs should:

● Explain the expectations of the school for the NQT
● Maintain motivation and commitment
● Foster good work habits
● Improve understanding of the school ethos
● Develop in the NQT a sense of value, this is important if they are to perform well in the classroom
● Reduce performance difficulties

An effective induction programme may be subdivided into lists of information and skills which the NQT must, should and could know or have. What information will you as an NQT need, before taking up the appointment, in the first three months? What information do you need to share with the school? What support will you seek? Who will you need support from?

The first post

223

With a partner or in a small group make lists of the information you will need when taking up your first teaching post, for example staff handbook, job description, schemes of work.

The induction practices found in most schools have many common features. Overall responsibility for the induction of all new teaching staff, not just NQTs, is given to the school's staff development tutor who is normally a member of the senior management team of the school. In addition an NQT is also likely to have a mentor assigned to them. This mentor will probably be either the head or an experienced teacher from the NQTs main teaching area. Many schools also consider the encouragement of a teaching colleague, often with one or two years experience, to act as a 'buddy' to the NQT. The majority of schools have an induction policy for new staff in which a timetable for the induction process is detailed along with an indication of responsibility for the various aspects of the process. However, the existence of an induction policy does not guarantee that it is effectively implemented or carefully managed.

Teachers are also human beings and as such often feel the need to talk about their experiences with others. This can be of great value not only in alleviating anxiety or stress but also can promote ideas for easing difficulties. During your first year of teaching you will need to unload issues in this way but who would make a good listener? Which listeners would be the easiest to talk to, which would be the most objective, who could provide the best support?

REFLECTION

Consider the advantages and disadvantages of each of the following people as listeners:

224

Person	Advantages	Disadvantages
teacher colleague		
'buddy'		
staff development tutor		
a member of SMT		
mentor		
friend outside school		

The school will have expectations of their teaching staff. What will they expect from you, as an NQT? What, do you think, will be their areas of concern?

The complex demands on teachers inevitably means that an Initial Teacher Training course is only the first stage in preparing teachers fully for the range of demands they are likely to encounter. Inevitably many skills have to be developed during the first years of teaching. Induction is the first stage of this process of continuing professional development. (Ofsted, 1988)

Staff induction

225

Finally, you need to consider the staff induction timetable which is presented opposite.

Inservice induction		For	By
Term 1	Tutor group procedures	Tutors	HOY
Term 1	Record keeping/faculty policies	Teachers	HOF
Term 1	Rewarding pupil effort and achievement	All staff	HOS/SDT
Term 1	Discipline procedures	All staff	HOS/SDT
Term 1	Management skills (effective meetings, delegating, communicating)	Managers	SMT
Term 1	SEN provision	Teachers	SEN Coord
Term 1	IT provision	Teachers	IT Coord
Term 1	Familiarisation with other personnel within school	All staff	Staff Dev Tutor
Term 1	School policies	All staff	Staff Dev Tutor
Term 1	Profile/Report writing	Teachers	HOF
Term 2	Tutoring skills	Tutors	HOY
Term 2	Leadership skills (counselling, motivating, target setting)	Managers	SMT
Term 2	Handling difficult pupils	All staff	HOS/HT
Term 2	Communicating with parents	All staff	HOS
Term 2	Familiarisation with other areas within school	All staff	Staff Dev Tutor
Term 2	Pupil/teacher/task pursuit	All staff	Staff Dev Tutor
Term 1 and 2	In-post observations with feedback	NQT	HOF/SMT
Term 3	Role of outside agencies (EWO, Social services, medical)	NQT	HOS/HOY
Term 3	Role of outside agencies (Educ Psychologist)	NQT	SEN Coord
Term 3	Appraisal system	All staff	Tutor
Term 3	Familiarisation with primary and FE links	Teachers	HOS
Term 3	Review of year	All staff	Staff Dev Tutor

Some of these may take the form of individualised help, discussions over lunch or informal sessions with a named member of staff, appointed to be your mentor/tutor. Do you think such a programme would work for you? How would you ensure that you receive the support you need and want? Keep a list and add to it during the last few weeks of your training, in preparation for the new school year.

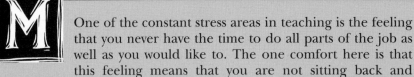

SUMMARY

One of the constant stress areas in teaching is the feeling that you never have the time to do all parts of the job as well as you would like to. The one comfort here is that this feeling means that you are not sitting back and forgetting about evaluation. With the support of a head of faculty or department, or other mentor appointed to you in your new post, you should be developing into a reflective practitioner and building on the experiences of your training, which are likely to be acknowledged on your Career Entry Profile document.

- Keep listing the positive achievements; remember the effectiveness of success as a motivator.
- Take seriously those who do offer you praise – accept it and enjoy it.
- Don't be afraid to ask pupils to evaluate your work. Their comments are rarely all negative.

As an NQT you will be entitled to professional support in your first post. The school should inform you of the induction process available in the school and it is sensible to make good use of this system, even if it seems to infringe on your time, so precious and so limited.

As you go on you will be entitled to an appraisal of your work as a teacher. The school should have a system set up that fits in with the government legislation on teacher appraisal. This must include observation of your teaching, the collection of information about your work from colleagues nominated by you and an appraisal interview with your appraiser. This leads to the production of an appraisal statement, which summarises the findings of the interview and other aspects of the appraisal and includes your targets for future development. Your appraiser should be able to assist you with the implementation and monitoring of these targets.

Useful references

Calderhead, J. and Lambert, J. (1992) **Induction of newly appointed teachers.** London: General Teaching Council Initiative for England and Wales.

DES (1992) **Induction and probation of new teachers 1988–1991.**

DES (1988) **The New Teacher in School.** London: HMSO.

DFE (1992) **Induction of newly qualified teachers** (administrative memorandum 2/92).

Earley, P. and Kinder, K. (1995) **Initiation Rights: Effective Induction Practices for New Teachers.** NFER.

Ofsted (1993) **The New Teacher in School.** London: HMSO.

Tickle, L. (1994) **The Induction of New Teachers.** London: Cassell.

APPENDIX

APPENDIX

This section explains the procedures used within the Gloucestershire Partnership for the assessment of the postgraduates.

Key terms below are explained and exemplified on the following pages:

- **The Career Entry Profile (CEP)**
- **The Professional Development Portfolio (PDP)**
- **The School Placement Summary Sheet**

What is the Professional Development Profile (PDP)?

The PDP is based upon the Career Entry Profile piloted by the Teacher Training Agency during 1996. All new entrants to the profession are required to have completed a CEP, the precise format of which has yet to be established. There are four areas of competence:

1 Subject knowledge and understanding
2 Planning, teaching and class management
3 Monitoring, assessment, recording, reporting and accountability
4 Other professional requirements

Although these four general Standards are still not finalised, they are unlikely to change radically. There are plans for subject-specific competences within Mathematics, English and Science to be part of the National Curriculum for Initial Teacher Training.

There is no intention to impose a methodology for the assessment of these Standards. An example of how this might be done is provided by the Gloucestershire Partnership arrangements.

The purposes of the PDP are:

1 To set out what trainee teachers have shown they know, understand and can do at various stages of their training, in relation to the Standards. (See below.)
2 To help trainee teachers take responsibility for identifying their own professional achievements and development needs, and to get targets for improvement.
3 To help all those involved in the Initial Teacher Training Programme to support the trainee teacher in achieving the Standards and, wherever possible, achieving strength in the identified target areas.

Discussion about the Standards will be on-going in weekly Subject Mentor and Training Manager sessions with the postgraduate.

The PDP is a dossier of information which provides evidence that the trainee teacher fulfils the criteria contained in the Standards. It is a core requirement for the successful completion of the course and the award of Qualified Teacher Status. Each trainee is responsible for collecting the evidence for the portfolio.

What should the PDP contain?

Nature of evidence in PDP

Evidence of meeting the Standards can be obtained from various sources:

1 **Lesson Plans** – only a selected range of lesson plans should be included showing evidence of planning, preparation and evaluation. (See page 372 – Lesson Planning Proforma.)
2 **Classroom Observation Sheets** – only samples showing strengths and needs should be included. (See page 211 – Observation Proforma.)
3 **Agreed Target Sheets** – all to be included. (See page 373.)
4 **Written Assignments** – all to be included.
5 **Portfolio Record Sheet** provides evidence not covered by the above, for example extra-curricular activities, wider professional skills, personal contributions and expertise. (See completed PDP Record Sheets on pages 374–6.)
6 Subject Pathway Sessions can also provide evidence to be included within the PDP, written up onto PDP Record Sheets on pages 374–5.
7 Self-evaluation proforma (page 375).
8 School placement summary sheet (page 376).

What is the school placement summary sheet?

At the end of each school placement a summary sheet will be completed describing performance within each area of competence. This summary sheet is in two parts – one will identify positive aspects and the other will identify areas needing development, written in the form of targets for the next placement. The summary sheets will be completed by negotiation between the postgraduate and the Training Manager. (See page 376 for an example of one completed School Placement Summary sheet.)

The grade for each school placement will be based on the Professional Development Portfolio (which provides evidence that the postgraduate fulfils the criteria described in the Standards) and the grade criteria for the school placement.

At the end of the course all of the above elements will be used to aid completion of the Career Entry Profile which each newly qualified teacher will take to the first teaching post.

Lesson plan: **Rachel**

Activity Transpiration   **Lesson No** 5   **Class** 10Y3
Learning outcomes The four factors affecting transpiration rate. Adaptation of plants to different climates. Group work.
Materials/resources needed Worksheets. A4 lined paper. Pictures of plants. Two plant adaptation sheets.

Timing/phase	Pupil activity	Organisation	Teaching points	Comments: Teaching style Assessment Differentiation Special needs
11.25 Registration		Hand out files rather than call register		
11.30 Homework discussion			Virtually all got the stomata sheet correct – those who didn't I've corrected it	Design a plant Some didn't do it Detention if incomplete homework again Also some very good ideas to be discussed later
11.32 Transpiration stream activity	Group activity	Four groups, one for each factor	Four factors: temperature, light, humidity, air movement Must cover Temp: heat and cold Evaporation cools leaf down Humidity: diffusion of water vapour from one area high to another low Air movements: moves humid air pockets away Light intensity: photosynthesis Stomata open for CO_2 in and O_2 out	
11.40 Presentation and discussions	Groups present ideas	Listen when not your turn to speak Speak clearly		
11.55 Worksheets	Reading and writing	10 minutes		Extension questions on board
12.05 Go through answers	Question and answer session	Table by table		
12.10 Adaptation group work	Group work	5 minutes to think, then group by group	How has your plant adapted? 1. Water lily 2. Cactus 3. Succulents 4. Deciduous 5. Ivy 6. Fir and Pine 7. Palm Plant adaptation all the above	1. Sides stop flooding 2. Spines/hairs stop air movement 3. Big fleshy leaves 4. 5. Evergreen 6. Evergreen 7. If time ask two pupils to describe their plant design
12.20 Hand out sheets for next lesson				

Biology   Yr10:3   Lab 4   Tues P3   Rachel

TEACHER/OBSERVER AGREED TARGETS SHEET

● What went well:

The amount they knew when you recapped and their group of scientific terms/vocabulary was impressive for this set.
You disciplined effectively over plant homework.
Good relationships and pupil management.
Well presented resources.
Good consolidation exercise/task and progression to opportunities to apply theory to plant adaptation. This was an impressive lesson because this group is not an easy one. It was a good learning opportunity for them. Well done!

● Future Targets:

1 Explore opportunities to use wrong answers as opportunities for learning, celebrate stuckness – e.g. osmosis, photosynthesis. Get them to work this through with you providing structure/scaffolding.

2 Look again at the 30 minutes of teacher explanation. Consider breaking this into smaller sections to allow for assimilation and internalisation. Ask yourself if you could have created opportunities for higher order learning and engagement by using well structured group work with clear criteria and learning outcomes. You also need to ask yourself if you are giving opportunities for Multi Intelligence development and acknowledging M.I. preferences. Remember Visual, Auditory, Kinaesthetic as well as cognitive – Linguistic and Numerical. Also remember interpersonal intelligence.

3 Now look at learning outcomes for each phase of the lesson and ask yourself if the way you are managing learning in each phase is the most effective in terms of SACK or if you could really develop SACK by demystifying and setting really clear criteria that have high expectations.

Teacher signature: R.O.

Observer signature: S.G.

Date:

Gloucestershire Initial Teacher Education Partnership
Professional Development Portfolio Record Sheet

Name Adrian   **School**

Training Manager Trevor   **Mentor** Jo

Main Subject Mathematics

Subject Co-ordinator Alan

Write down any points you want to include in your PDP

I know no LOGO, so when discussing an article from a maths journal for GS007, I deliberately chose one on LOGO. I have also been involved in the teaching of angles to a Year 8 Group with my mentor. We planned a series of 12 lessons, 4 of which involve LOGO. During these 4 I have acted in a supporting role so that I can learn LOGO (and how to teach with it) from my mentor along with the class. So far I have learned only basic functions, but we should be using more advanced ones in the remaining lessons.

Subject Co-ordinator's Note

In fact this trainee learned a lot more in the college session the next week as well. By the end of a one and a half hour session he had written a procedure for drawing Pythagorean Spirals using recursion, conditional statements and colour! This task arose because another trainee wanted to teach spirals to a Y8 group and both decided to work on this LOGO challenge.

Signature of postgraduate ....   Date ....

Signature of colleague ....   Role ....

Copies to be placed in PDP and given to Training Manager/Subject Mentor/Subject Co-ordinator.

Self-Evaluation Sheet

This is an example of a self-evaluation sheet, devised by a trainee. You will want to devise your own to reflect your needs, but this provides a useful model.

Context: Art. Designing a seed packet picture

The pupils' task, in the first lesson of the sequence, involved producing a flower image on a computer which reflected Georges Seurat's painting style pointillisme (the use of small dots of pure colour side by side mixed by the viewer's eye). The pupils had to apply their newly acquired knowledge and understanding of the technique whilst using the computer to investigate its graphic qualities. They worked from their colour observational flower studies produced in a prior lesson. In this sequence of three lessons I reflected upon the two Attainment Targets 'Investigating and Making', 'Knowledge and Understanding' and planned learning activities that would develop pupils' competence within these areas.

I developed this self evaluation sheet. Tom (my mentor) made comments and I wrote down a brief summary of these for future action. (Sarah, trainee.)

Judged on: Very Good
              Good
              Satisfactory
              Poor

1 **Were the learning outcomes achieved?**
   Very Good – All pupils achieved the aim/task to the specified level – they understood the concepts. Some pupils achieved a higher level of appreciation knowledge through the task – all achieved the minimum.

2 **Were students participating?**
   Good – All on task, some were particularly enthusiastic once they had tried the technique and had seen the visual impact/result of placing complementary colour side by side.

3 **Were pupils on task during the lesson?**
   Very Good – All on task. All knew what they had to do and all wanted to achieve a good final result in the following lesson.

4 **Were the concepts communicated effectively to pupils?**
   Very Good – The concept was simple and clear and most importantly visually suported/reinforced. All pupils understood the use of contemporary colour and furthermore the value of this reflecting upon their task.

5 **Did the atmosphere in the class inspire meaningful learning?**
   Very Good – All pupils very interested in the progress of their work – not one pupils questioned the activity in a negative way.

6 **Did the lesson use resources effectively?**
   Good – Prints displayed on the board and books available to look through. A resource corner using contemporary examples of complementary colour use would have fully reinforced and balanced conceptual learning.

7 **Were all learning abilities served/considered?**
   Good – There was plenty of work for the higher ability students to do, experimentation of the technique through an extension of the task allowed them to continue stretching their skills and enhancing knowledge. Lower abilities coped well – understood the aim and task of the lesson – worked comfortably at their own pace.

8 **Were all pupils motivated?**
   Satisfactory – If more resources had been available to handle, stimulation in that respect would have been increased.

9 **Was the lesson well prepared?**
   Good – Resources were set up and materials distributed to avoid time loss and excessive pupil movement. Books available to access and prints on blackboard visible to all pupils.

10 **Was the time managed effectively?**
    Very Good – Students produced a good amount and standard of practical work. There was also time to reflect upon the use of complementary colour and evaluate the qualities of the different media used.

11 **What could be developed?**
    More reflection upon the seed packet qualities of their drawings:
    Look at trends and styles of packets.
    A trip to Gloucester docks packaging museum would have been an excellent means of making pupils appreciate Art in everyday life.

Assessment Summary Sheet

Martin

GS301 – The first school placement
Subject Knowledge and Understanding

Please give a descriptive assessment of individual performance with reference to evidence as necessary:

i) Has a secure knowledge of metal, plastics, electronics extending beyond A level.

ii) Has a sound understanding of formal drawing and design process, including Auto CAD. Degree in Mech. Eng. ensures good knowledge link to maths and science.

iii) Has been encouraged to look at journals and books on current thinking and to incorporate ideas into teaching.

iv) Has provided support to department through metal-working knowledge, areas of design process and aspects of electronics and electricity.

v) Has been involved in KS3 work, design and practical at Y7, Y8 and Y9 levels.

vi) Has made use of word processors and some investigation of CD ROM.

Please give a descriptive assessment of individual needs with reference to evidence if necessary.

i) Needs to review basic techniques and processes as assumptions tend to be made and key points have been forgotten.

ii) Has significant weakness in areas of woodworking and graphical presentation, which must be addressed urgently as they impinge on all areas of the subject. Has spent time on woodwork lathe.

iii) Wishes to develop aspects of control technology.

iv) Needs to develop awareness of the core subject areas of food and textiles in which he has, as yet, had very little experience.

v) Should further study 'design process' as applied in school situation.

vi) Needs to study further the requirements of – and needs lots of experience of – teaching subject applications of KS3 and how they have followed on from KS2.

vii) Should further investigate uses of IT, including spreadsheets, databases and CD ROM to further develop IT skills.

Examples

Key Stage 1: Checklist for Class Teacher

All responses should be affirmative. If they are not, further investigation or action by the teacher may be required. Action can range from the setting of a review date to ensure progress is monitored, through to the development of a clear action plan with parents.

Pupil's name:

Pupil's age on completion of stage (in years and months):

Academic skills

All reported at Key Stage 1

English

- AT1 Speaking & Listening
- AT2 Reading
- AT3 Writing

Mathematics

- AT1 Using & applying mathematics
- AT2 Number
- AT3 Shape, space & measures

Science

- AT1 Experimental and investigative Science
- AT2 Life processes and living things
- AT3 Materials and their properties
- AT4 Physical processes

Study and attention skills

- responds to class directions, for example *pack up, line up . . .*
- follow routine sequence of instructions to class, for example *When you've finished your maths put the book on my desk and get on with your topic*
- listens and responds contextually, staying to the point, for 5–10 minutes
- can recount an experience in sequence
- can get out and put away equipment independently
- asks for help when needed
- has the confidence to make mistakes
- has the confidence to make an initial attempt at something new after explanation, without adult support
- completes a task well within competence, during time given, without nagging
- given time in a 2nd lesson, for example after break, can pick up and finish work after reminder about task and content
- after an introduction to familiar work, knows what to do and can make a start
- can complete a short task, for example construction, with two others

Social and personal control

- has a friend or a group to play with
- can take part in a group activity sharing equipment
- can accept some give and take in play
- approaches adult to ask for help, e.g. *they've bullied me*
- can admit when they have done something wrong and accept the consequences
- can generally behave acceptably and safely in the playground
- can move around school acceptably and safely
- can generally conform to rules of the class
- able to occasionally lose in a game without having a tantrum

Independence

- can see to personal needs – eating, dressing, toileting and personal hygiene
- usually arrives at school with 'things' for the day, e.g. book-bag, dinner money
- can convey a written message between home and school
- looks after belongings and looks for them if they get mislaid
- knows the routines of the class and school

Self-confidence

- has the confidence to express an opinion in a group
- can assert themselves at times in a small group
- has the confidence to go somewhere new with a friend
- feels they are good at something in school and can tell you a little about why they feel this
- can identify something they would like to improve at and feel about to work on
- talks positively about themselves at times, e.g. I'm good at swimming/I look nice in my new dress/Jo and Les like me

Physical/medical

- has no damaging habits
- hearing good
- near and distant vision good or wears glasses if needed
- no new medical problems identified other than those already recorded
- no new medication other than already noted in records
- speech clear and audible, structure and vocabulary commensurate with peers

Key Stage 2: Checklist for Class Teacher

All responses should be affirmative. If they are not, further investigation or action by the teacher may be required. Action can range from the setting of a review date to ensure progress is monitored, through to the development of a clear action plan with parents.

Pupil's name:

Pupil's age on completion of stage (in years and months):

Academic skills

All reported at Key Stage 2

English

- AT1   Speaking & Listening
- AT2   Reading
- AT3   Writing

Mathematics

- AT1   Using & applying mathematics
- AT2   Number
- AT3   Shape, space & measures
- AT4   Handling data

Science

- AT1   Experimental and investigative Science
- AT2   Life processes and living things
- AT3   Materials and their properties
- AT4   Physical processes

Study and attention skills

- listens quietly to information given to class for 20–25 minutes
- follows sequence of instructions given in previous lesson
- can make a note of at least two key points from oral presentation
- arrives at lessons with right equipment
- listens and responds contextually for 30 minutes
- can say what potential risks are associated with using equipment, e.g. scissors and compasses

- can use equipment safely
- can work for at least 30 minutes with independence and confidence, and complete task assigned within the time
- can seek help when needed
- gets on with work while waiting for help

Social and personal control

- can operate within class rules
- can assert themselves acceptably with adults
- knows who else they can approach if they have difficulties in communicating with an adult
- is aware of, and can accommodate, someone else's needs
- is accepted by peers
- can form a friendship
- can deal assertively with common levels of conflict with other children
- knows when a situation is potentially beyond them and can seek help
- can behave generally acceptably and safely in and around school
- queues without disruption while waiting for adult/dinner
- can listen to others' opinions
- can respond appropriately (for example politely) to peers and adults

Independence

- has established routines to ensure they arrive at school on time and with packed bag
- can convey an oral message between home and school
- can ensure written communications are received and noted by parent and teacher
- can follow a timetable
- can look after belongings and, if they are mislaid, looks for them at appropriate times
- can find their way around school site unsupervised
- tidies up after themselves
- can find appropriate resources for task in hand after instruction has been given

Self-confidence

- can express an opinion at times in a group
- can volunteer themselves in class for an activity when they want to
- can identify something in school they are good at and say why
- can identify something they would like to work on and be able to give one way they will try to improve
- can talk positively about themselves
- will discuss an issue of concern to them with a chosen adult

Physical/medical

- has no damaging habits
- hearing good
- near and distant vision good or wears glasses if needed
- no new medical problems identified other than those already recorded
- no new medication other than already noted in records
- speech clear and audible, structure and vocabulary commensurate with peers

Mentors and progress
by Christine Counsell

The following document contains suggestions for how subject mentors can help the trainee to relate the development of subject knowledge and subject application to the profile of competences. It also gives examples of how a trainee might identify and articulate aspects of their progress using PDP entries and provide a method of auditing subject knowledge.

GITEP HISTORY MENTORING

USING THE COMPETENCES IN YOUR TRAINING AND MONITORING

1) MOVING THE HISTORY POSTGRADUATES FORWARD THROUGH LESSON EVALUATION

These sheets give you examples of how you can keep a focus on the key history issues so as to develop and monitor *subject knowledge* and *subject application* as prescribed in the competences.

Use them to give you and your colleagues fresh ideas for post-observation feedback and to support the postgraduates in producing their own high quality lesson evaluations.

Remember: even *class management* issues will usually have a *subject application* dimension.

Help the history postgraduate to:

● **Use the Key Elements in Planning (SKU)**
● **Relate these to the selection of precise learning objectives (PTCM)**

What aspect of Key Element 2c are you trying to focus upon in that sequence of lessons?

What type of causation is this? It isn't enough just to mention Key Element 2b. Which earlier topics can you draw upon to help pupils see that this is the *same kind* of historical problem?

If you help pupils to classify the issues into economic factors and technological factors, what problems will they face? How can you redesign the table so that pupils see the problem of overlap? How will this move them on from the kind of Key Element 5 work they did last term with me/their usual teacher?

● **Explore the role of historical knowledge in developing historical understanding (SKU/PTCM)**
● **Relate this to the development of enthusiasm and retention of interest in all pupils (SKU/PTCM)**

How much do they need to hold in their heads to make sense of the question/activity you have set them? Was there any evidence (from the pupils) that you needed to reinforce the key facts a little more? How might you have done this, whilst securing their attention and interest?

Their answers were disappointing because they were generalised, confused and full of anachronism. What does that tell you about what you needed to do prior to the task to ensure that answers were more historically grounded?

● **Pay attention to progression at all times (SKU/PTCM)**

In which topics have pupils encountered this type of source before? As you plan these two lessons how will you ensure that (a) they revisit the key issues surrounding the use of photographs as evidence and (b) they move forward in their ability to use photographs critically?

They already know something about parliament from the previous unit, but will have forgotten the detail. How can you tap their memories and ensure that they use prior knowledge to make sense of new knowledge?

● **Differentiate teaching imaginatively and achieve high standards of learning for all pupils through a range of tasks (balancing differentiation and entitlement) (PTCM)**

In what ways did that additional sheet for lower attainers help those pupils to understand the *core issue* at the heart of the lesson?

Do you think that by the end of the lesson this group of pupils were able to get beyond hunting for detail and able to see the big issue about the characteristics of 'total war' which you wanted them to see?

How clear were these pupils about how their new understandings *helped* them to answer your big historical question (How civilised were the Romans?) which is governing these three lessons? *At what point* did you need additional differentiation (extra prompts? sheet with headings? extra reinforcement?) so that *this* group of pupils had access to the fundamental point of the lesson?

● **Evaluate lessons perceptively so as to inform future practice (SKU)**
● **Demonstrate active engagement with problems in the subject (SKU)**
● **Relate both of these to choice of learning objectives (PTCM)**

You talk about research skills here. What do you really mean? Can you describe more precisely exactly what moves you expected this bright Year 8 pupil to make? Was she really using her time in the library effectively? What additional prompts about the characteristics of Tudor monarchy might you have fed in to ensure that she was hunting purposefully? Were her difficulties in separating out the characteristics of a monarch's power similar to (or different from) those of other pupils?

You say that these pupils clearly enjoyed their boardgame on the abolition of the slave trade. How did their knowledge of abolition issues increase? Why was this? In what ways might you break up the components of attitudes towards abolition to ease their understanding of abstract issues? What insights do you gain from this about how to adapt your introduction when you do this with the lower attaining group?

How do you think that *this* lesson will help pupils in *future* lessons to become more skilled and confident in framing their own historical questions (Key Element 4b)?

2) HELPING THE POSTGRADUATE TO IDENTIFY AND ARTICULATE ASPECTS OF THEIR PROGRESS USING **PDP** ENTRIES

These sheets give you examples of how the postgraduate might identify their own developing competence with particular reference to **subject knowledge** and **subject application**.

Remember, a good PDP entry will show how the postgraduate is integrating their learning from the various parts of the course, thus making the training bigger than the sum of its parts.

Sample entries

Sample entry for a PDP Record sheet (1) (use self-carbonised copies). Support with evidence from learning log, teaching file, as appropriate.

Developing understanding and improved practice in my use of historical sources (subject knowledge and subject application)

1) During Session 1 of Module GS026 (Developing History Teaching) we examined different ways in which teachers use sources in history lessons. I realised the importance of being extremely clear about learning outcomes. For example, to use a source for stimulus or information is very different from using it as evidence to be evaluated in terms of its historicity.

2) Further reading, notably Sean Lang's <u>What is Bias?</u> (Teaching History etc . . .) and practical guidance in the NCC manual showed the dangers of encouraging pupils to hunt for bias so much that they develop a distorted view of the concept of reliability. All sources are reliable for something. We have to help them to establish what they are reliable for.

3) I have successfully used sources on public health with the Sixth Form. I now need to consider ways of pushing these students to higher levels in their evaluation of evidence. I can now see that I pitched it too low. My work on the crusades with Year 8, also utilised sources. My lesson evaluations and my learning log indicate how the above insights could have improved my use of sources with these pupils, by being clearer about learning objectives in evidential work.

Sample entry for a PDP Record sheet (2) (use self-carbonised copies). Support with evidence from learning log, teaching file, as appropriate.

Planning and teaching for continuity and progression in history (subject application and assessment)

1) Discussion with my mentor concerning a recent lesson sequence with Year 8 on the French Revolution led me to conclude that I have treated each lesson too much as an isolated unit. Introductions are critical: they motivate, pick up prior knowledge and address pupil misconceptions. Also I had failed to take into account the importance of laying foundations for future lessons which will draw upon the knowledge of social structure gained in this early lesson sequence.

2) During Session 2 of Module GS026 (Developing History Teaching) we examined varied techniques for building upon prior knowledge and understanding from earlier lessons. Other postgrads had more varied examples than my own and the Subject Co-ordinator gave us ideas for 'warming-up' learning which had taken place earlier, in motivating and rigorous ways.

3) A sequence of lessons on the Industrial Revolution in Year 9 helped me to develop this competence explicitly. I built heavily upon (and thereby reinforced and assessed) work which the usual class teacher had done earlier on 18th century villages. I also devised strategies for maximising progression in the short term by ensuring that each lesson was enriched by previous content. These lessons formed part of the overall targets in Key Element 4b which the history dep't set this group in this term of Year 9.

signed by any two relevant colleagues from Mentor, Subject Co-ordinator, Training Manager

---

TRIAL AUDIT OF SUBJECT KNOWLEDGE

AREA OF SUBJECT KNOWLEDGE AND UNDERSTANDING	Inadequate	Adequate, but requires significant improvement	Good, with no significant weaknesses	Very good, and capable of making a distinctive contribution to a history department team
List specific areas within each unit as appropriate	I have never covered this at A level or degree level. **OR** past coverage was too superficial/too long ago to be helpful to me now. I would not be able to construct lesson plans and lesson sequences without a great deal of assistance. I am not confident about subject related questions which-pupils may raise	I can select a key lesson focus/aim and translate it into valid and challenging learning outcomes. I can relate some of the details to larger historical themes and issues, but I have still not got the detail of my fingertips. I need more understanding of the latest scholarship if I am not confident to handle questions of evidence and interpretation.	I am confident in my subject knowledge and understanding for this level. I can choose appropriate historical issues and questions which this content area will illuminate. For example I can identify opportunities for consideration of causation, change, continuity, evidence or interpretation which the Key Elements prescribe.	I have expert knowledge in this area and would be an asset to any department wanting specialist input. I am capable of translating this knowledge into a programme of learning which will foster progression, in pupils of all abilities. I can support colleagues in finding opportunities for enthusing and challenging pupils in difficult areas.
SU1 Medieval Realms				
SU2 Making of the United Kingdom				
SU3 1750–1900				
SU4 Twentieth-century world				
GCSE Aspects of syllabus in parent school				

APPENDIX 4

Part One

Actions and Case Studies: possible listings under the Standards

Subject Knowledge and Understanding (SKU)

A10	Infant and juniors	A45	Wood's five levels
A28	Apostrophes	A47	Lesson structure
A29	Task analysis	A48	Subject specific
A31	Subject specific issues	A51	Subject specific
CS32	Human sense	A56	Subject specific
CS35	Mass media	A80	National Curriculum
A36	Human sense	A81	Abbreviations
CS40	Iconic representation	CS82	National Curriculum and Adrian
A41	Iconic representation	A83	Subject orders
A42	Bruner's three stages	A87	Subject specific

Planning, Teaching and Class Management (PCTM)

A9	Classroom organisation	CS37	Appropriate support
A11	Spoken language	A38	Going independent
A20	Bullying project	A39	Group work
A21	School rules	CS43	Collecting stages
A22	Pupil talk	A54	Motivating staff and pupils
A24	Code of practice	CS59	Vicky
A30	Positive rules		

Other Professional Requirements (OPR)

A1	Observation schedules	A99	Support
A3	Talking to teachers	CS62	Jack (1)
A4	Learning support	A63	Behaviour
A5	Learning support	CS65	ADHD
A6	Headlands learning support	A78	Differentiation
A13	Key Stage 1 checklist	A79	Differentiation
A14	Mathematics	A84	Behaviour
A15	Number	A85	Lesson management
A16	Science	A86	Rules, rewards and punishments
A17	Writing	A87	Lesson planning
A18	Spelling	A89	Planning your lesson
A19	Reading	A91	Lesson phases
A23	Key Stage 2 checklist	A93	Using signals
A25	Primary and secondary	A98	Self appraisal
A26	Secondary transfer liaison	CS101	Early problems
A34	Wason	A102	Evaluating lessons
A70	Implementation		

Monitoring, Assessment, Recording, Reporting and Accountability (MARRA)

Part Two

Planning, Teaching and Class Management (PTCM)

Monitoring, Assessment, Recording, Reporting and Accountability (MARRA)

Other Professional Requirements (OPR)

Part Three

Subject Knowledge and Understanding (SKU)

CS160	Jack	**A196**	Making a Contribution
A175	Class Management	**CS201**	Peter: an NQT
A181	Subject Specific 16–19	**A209**	Differentiation beliefs
A193	Spiritual Development	**CS212**	Latin fun
A194	Your Subject and SMSC	**A213**	Active learning
CS195	Peter: the big ideas	**CS214**	Electricity

Monitoring, Assessment, Recording, Reporting and Accountability (MARRA)

CS184	Absence Notes	**A216**	Departmental audit
CS186	Tutors' Reports	**A217**	School review
A206	Stage 2 IEP	**CS220**	Mark
A210	Plans for Assessment		

Other Professional Requirements (OPR)

CS162	Interview Preparation	**CS182**	Choice at 16+
CS163	Documentation	**A185**	Exchanging Information
A166	New Groups	**A190**	Changing Expectations
A167	Being a Newcomer	**A191**	PSE
CS168	The Department	**CS192**	Jo
A169	Meetings	**A197**	Documentary Evidence
CS172	Jack	**CS215**	Support as differentiation
A173	Suggested Approaches	**A221**	Personal Development
A174	Counteracting Bullying	**CS222**	NQT support
A176	'No Blame'	**A223**	The first post
CS177	Bullying	**A225**	Staff induction

Planning, Teaching and Class Management (PTCM)

A179	Pupils into Students	**A205**	Behaviour Plans
A180	Conflicting needs	**A207**	Rewards
CS199	Lesson planning	**CS208**	Noisy Nora
A202	Using approaches	**A211**	Presentation
CS203	Sophie	**CS218**	Challenge
A204	Writing a Script		

Index